"I Choose Life"

New Directions in Native American Studies
Colin G. Calloway and K. Tsianina Lomawaima, General Editors

"I Choose Life"

Contemporary Medical and Religious Practices in the Navajo World

Maureen Trudelle Schwarz

University of Oklahoma Press : Norman

Also by Maureen Trudelle Schwarz

Molded in the Image of Changing Woman: Navajo Views on the Human Body and Personhood (Tucson, 1997)
Navajo Lifeways: Contemporary Issues, Ancient Knowledge (Norman, 2001)
Blood and Voice: Navajo Women Ceremonial Practitioners (Tucson, 2003)

Library of Congress Cataloging-in-Publication Data

Schwarz, Maureen Trudelle, 1952–
    I choose life : contemporary medical and religious practices in the Navajo world / Maureen Trudelle Schwarz.
        p.   cm. — (New directions in Native American studies ; v. 2)
    Includes bibliographical references and index.
    ISBN 978-0-8061-3941-8 (hardcover : alk. paper) — ISBN 978-0-8061-3961-6 (pbk. : alk. paper) 1. Navajo Indians—Medicine. 2. Navajo Indians—Religion. 3. Surgery. 4. Traditional medicine—Southwest, New. 5. Christianity and other religions—Shamanism. I. Title.
    E99.N3S3577 2008
    610.89'9726—dc22

                                                        2008002278

"I Choose Life": Contemporary Medical and Religious Practices in the Navajo World is Volume 2 in the New Directions in Native American Studies series.

The paper in this book meets the guidelines for permanence and durability of the Committee on Production Guidelines for Book Longevity of the Council on Library Resources, Inc. ∞

Copyright © 2008 by the University of Oklahoma Press, Norman, Publishing Division of the University. Manufactured in the U.S.A.

1 2 3 4 5 6 7 8 9 10

There is an [Anglo] doctor . . . while he was examining his [Navajo] patient . . . he said, "I don't know why I have this ache. I had a body ache every day. I try to go to the doctor and get some medicine, but it seems like it doesn't work, so I don't know what is wrong with me." Then all of a sudden the patient brightens up and looks at him and he says, "I know. Why don't you come to my house, come and visit me and I will take you to a medicine man. Where I live there are a lot of medicine men around. I'll take you to one and I'm sure they'll cure you." So the doctor stood there for awhile, a few minutes, then he says, "OK. So, I'll come and see you." "Yeah[,] do that, I live just not far from here." All of a sudden he remembered what his patient told him. So he decided to go drive down there where his patient lived. Instead of stopping at the patient's house, he just made a beeline down the road. He said to himself, "I'll probably find a medicine man on my own, so I don't think I need him." He went down and sure enough, the first hooghan [traditional Navajo earthen-floor home] with a corral he came to, he found a man putting his sheep away and so he ask him, "I am looking for a medicine man to perform a ceremony on me." The man looked up and he said, "I know one, so just wait a minute. I'll put my sheep away and I will come to the hooghan, go wait in the hooghan, I'll be in there." So the doctor went in and sure enough the hooghan was nice and clean. The Navajo man came in, put the sheepskin down with a pillow for the doctor and then one for himself. Then he left. So the doctor sat down there and he was facing east. He quietly waited. Soon the Navajo man returned. He told the doctor, "Put your feet out like this, the way the medicine man usually do." Then, he wash his hand and then he look around and was thinking to himself, "What should I do? What kind of ceremony should I do?" He was thinking that and then all of a sudden in came the cat, a black cat came in, and he went across the front of the patient that the man was to perform on, and he went by and then he came back and then the man grabbed the cat by its legs and arms. The cat was making a loud noise; the noise is errrrrrrr. It is making all that noise with the fur standing up and the man started massaging the patient with it! Then so, the doctor really sit there quietly and the man really massaged him with the black cat. So about five minutes later he let the cat out and he turn around to the patient and says, "Now how do you feel?" And then the doctor says, "Oh, I feel fine. Just fine. And I don't feel no pain. Thank you." "OK!" So that doctor turned around to the person and says, "How much do I owe you?" And then the man stands there for a minute or two and then he says, "$100 for a walk-in and $400 for a cat scan." So the doctor said, "OK, all right," and he pulled out his wallet and he paid the man and he walked out and so the man, the man that he paid wasn't even near any kind of medicine man. He was just a sheepherder that ripped him off. So that is the cat scan joke. Whoever hears it, enjoy it.

AMELDA SANDOVAL SHAY, LUKACHUKAI, ARIZONA
July 2005

Contents

Preface

This project resulted from a personal interest in medical and religious forms of identity coupled with a long-standing personal advocacy for Native people and their rights. My first and foremost goals as a scholar are to foreground Native voices whenever possible and to present Native views with respect. This position of advocacy skews my choice of topics for study toward issues of direct concern to Native Americans. Accordingly, this project was selected because the Navajo people have a growing problem with diabetes. As a result of diabetes-caused complications, the Navajo have the highest lower extremity amputation rates of any group of people in the world. End Stage Renal Disease is also rampant among their population; kidney transplantation is the optimal treatment therapy. These are critical health causes for the Navajo Nation.

This project focuses on the ways Navajo people accommodate biomedical technologies such as blood transfusion, transplant, cardiopulmonary resuscitation (CPR), and surgeries like amputation within the context of medical and religious pluralism. Most specifically, I look at how Navajo individuals use notions about the body to reinforce collective identity and resist colonization. As a whole, the research and analysis involved in this work build upon my previous work. My first book considered Navajo cultural constructions of personhood, with special emphasis on manipulations of the body in ceremonial contexts; my second major fieldwork-based project focused on the life courses of Navajo women who are ceremonial practitioners.

Field research for this project was conducted during 2004 and 2005. As with my previous research, prior to starting an interview I asked every person with whom I consulted to complete, sign, and date a consent form specifically developed to comply with Navajo Nation Historic Preservation Department requirements. Among other things, these documents ask consultants to indicate whether they want their names used in any future publications. Most of the people with whom I consulted indicated that they wanted to be given credit for their contributions and asked that their names be used in future publications. In accordance with their wishes, the actual name of every consultant who chose this option is used throughout the text. Those who chose not to have their names cited were asked to select a fictitious name by which they are referred to in the text. There is one notable exception to this policy. In my discussion of organ donation I substituted "anonymous elder" for the name of a consultant to prevent undue embarrassment.

Research for this project was supported by the Appleby-Mosher Fund at Syracuse University, a National Endowment for the Humanities Summer Stipend #FT-53166-05, and funds from the Maxwell School of Citizenship and Public Affairs at Syracuse University. Throughout the time I have been a guest among the Navajo, my research has been aided in countless ways by dozens of Navajo people. While not everyone can be named here, I want to thank them all for their generosity to me and my family. Special thanks to Mae Ann Bekis of Tó'tsoh, Arizona, and Amelda Sandoval Shay of Lukachukai, Arizona, for their consistent support and encouragement; also to Dr. Wesley Thomas of Dine College, Tsaile, Arizona, for friendship, unconditional support, and help with translations. Thanks to Ellen Rothman, a physician at the Kayenta Indian Health Service Clinic, who, after taking an interest in this project, generously arranged for me to interview her associates in that community. Thanks to the College of Arts and Sciences Dean's Office at Syracuse University for leave time during the 2005–2006 academic year, which afforded me the time to analyze material and draft the manuscript. I also thank the series editors at the University of Oklahoma Press, as well as the anonymous readers who gave painstaking attention to the manuscript draft. The book was greatly strengthened through the incorporation of your many detailed recommendations for corrections and revisions. Lastly, thanks to my spouse and children—Greg, Ragen, Adam, Ryan, and Kim. *Ahéhee' shiyázhí* to each of you for your continued unconditional love and support.

"I Choose Life"

CHAPTER ONE

Groundings

DD: The only thing that normally happens after part of the body had been removed is to seek a medicine man to have a ceremony done to correct some of those imbalances and to help them [surgical patients] mentally so that they can better accept whatever may have been done with them and also to . . . pray to the Holy People, pray to the gods or the divinities to help them heal. . . .

MS: So, are you saying that having, like, your uterus or a limb removed creates an imbalance?

DD: Yes, it does. . . . [I]n Navajo belief, any time that a foreigner cuts a body it needs to be corrected. And so Navajo, we believe that we should not be cut, or any kind of lacerations or operations or any kind of surgical procedures done to a Navajo body—

MS: Any kind?

DD: Any kind. . . . That would be considered a contamination with a foreigner.

MS: What if it was a Navajo surgeon that did the surgery?

DD: Navajo surgeon that would have done the surgery, that would be different.

MS: Oh?

DD: They would not follow up with an Enemy Way ceremony.

> MS: OK, so let's start with this then. . . . This is great, see, 'cuz I
> have no knowledge of this, so let's go back to the beginning.
> DD: OK. . . .
> MS: I don't know where the beginning is. You're going to have to
> tell me where the beginning is. (Denetdeal, July 11, 2004)

This conversation with Donald Denetdeal, a professor of Navajo History who is originally from Klagetoh, Arizona (see the appendix for more information on Professor Denetdeal and each subsequent consultant), reveals that in spite of more than a decade of experience conducting research on Navajo issues, from a Navajo perspective I had not begun my research on the appropriate topic when setting out to understand how Navajo people accommodate "new" biomedical technologies within their religiously and medically pluralistic lived-world. My initial focus for the project was amputations and transplantations because these procedures are frequently needed by those with secondary complications of diabetes mellitus—a major health concern of the Navajo.[1] Previous research on Navajo views of the body and personhood made me aware that detached body parts are considered to retain lifelong effects and that many Navajo still hold to traditional taboos against any contact with the dead, with a deceased person's uncleansed personal belongings, and with the place at which a death occurred or human remains are present (Schwarz 1997). Collectively, these beliefs left me with a profound interest in how Navajo people grapple with the biomedical technology of organ transplantation. Would a Navajo consider herself connected to the person from whom she received an organ? Would a Navajo accept a heart that was harvested from a dead person? Could a Navajo live with the organ of an enemy inside him or herself?

To answer these questions, I began my investigation by conducting directed interviews with Navajo consultants who, like Professor Denetdeal, pointed out that organ transplantation was not the appropriate place to begin the analysis. Rather, I would have to start with Navajo understandings of surgery and contamination. In fact, the scope of my project progressively broadened when consultants mentioned "old" biomedical technologies such as transfusions and cardiopulmonary resuscitation (CPR). After noteworthy conversations such as the one with Denetdeal at the start of this chapter, it became clear that each of these procedures must be explored in turn within the broader frame of traditional cultural tenets, Navajo views on health and illness, the historical circumstances of colonization, Navajo understandings of relatedness, the nuanced web of contemporary religious and medical pluralism, Navajo notions of collective identity, and oppositional politics to more fully understand how *Nihookáá Dine'é*, or "Earth Surface People," fit globally available medical technologies into their world.

The way people label or define illness, for example, offers indications regarding their personal sense of connectedness and identity. Additionally, medicine and medical practices are aspects of the cultural positioning by which contemporary Nihookáá Dine'é define both themselves and the colonizing other. Careful attention to what people say reveals how, at different levels of understanding, what are perceived to be recently introduced diseases such as diabetes, cancer, and heart ailments stand for social change, loss of tradition, and conflict with Anglos, or Euro-Americans. This is the polar opposite of Navajo narratives portraying health as living according to Navajo traditions. For many contemporary Navajo people, a contrast noted between Navajo and non-Navajo people explains why certain types of blood, organs, pharmaceutical drugs, and curing strategies are not deemed effective for Navajo patients while others are. Retaining the differences between Navajo and non-Navajo bodies is a means by which Nihookáá Dine'é still engage with the powerful global forces that are impoverishing them and redrawing their political, cultural, and national horizons.

Countless Navajo people take advantage of biomedical technologies made available through the Indian Health Service or private medical care without adjusting their fundamental beliefs about health, illness, or curing. Simultaneously, thousands of Navajo people today celebrate spirituality through membership in introduced religions, such as the various sects of Christianity or the Native American Church currently flourishing throughout the reservation. Moreover, individuals are often affiliated simultaneously with more than one religion. Thus, many Navajo people have adopted Euro-American understandings of health, illness, and the body. This is the context in which decisions are made about CPR, amputations, other surgeries, and preferences regarding donation of blood or organs.

Health, illness, and healing are not neutral in the Navajo world. The source to which people attribute each of these elements offers important clues into how they see the contemporary moral and political landscape.

Cultural memories of the first encounters between Navajo and Europeans have established paradigms for representations of the contact, colonization, and relationships with descendants of the colonizers or enemies. This is evident in Navajo narratives about illness and biomedical technologies. Physiological differences in Navajo bodies are intentionally recognized, marked, and retained in the contemporary medical context as a means to reaffirm Navajo collective identity and non-Navajo difference. Because many Navajo view their oral tradition as a philosophical wellspring that offers insights into understandings of illness, notions of identity, as well as medical and religious plurality as practiced on the reservation today, we must look to the old to understand the new.

INTRODUCTION TO NAVAJO ORAL HISTORY

Prior to European colonization, Navajo people employed multiple life-sustaining paradigms. They included (1) continuing the charter left by *Asdzą́ą́ Nádleehé*, or "Changing Woman," and the other deities to maintain life within the sacred mountains; (2) seeking curing power from new sources; (3) telling stories about the Hero Twins, who became ill after fighting their enemies; and (4) adhering to prophecies, especially the one that cautioned them to be alert for the return of the descendants of a deity known as the Gambler—for contact with one's enemies risks contamination. These cultural teachings created stress in early Navajo encounters with those they considered the Gambler's descendants. The prophecy concerning the Gambler made them very cautious in their dealings with his progeny, while the second of the prophecies made them willing to experiment to attain new forms of healing power. As evidenced in the narratives of those with whom I consulted, this tension continues today.

While consultants frequently mention twelve underworlds, most written accounts have three or four underworlds with a color sequence of black, blue, yellow, and white (Yazzie 1971:9). Each underworld is portrayed in a state of chaos and disorder, resulting in the need to travel to the next world.[2] In the last underworld, the first male and female beings with human-like form lived as man and wife, as did their offspring. First Man, First Woman, and their progeny flourished for a time until lust led to adultery. The adultery led to a conflict between First Man and First Woman, which resulted in the separation of men and women. During the separation, both genders' libidinous desires became ever stronger. To appease their sexual passions, the women are said to have masturbated with various objects—cacti, deer tendons, or rocks—while the men tried to relieve their longing with mud or the flesh of recently slain game animals (Haile 1981:25; O'Bryan 1956:8; Stephen 1930:99; Yazzie 1971:30; Zolbrod 1984:63). Eventually, realizing that each gender could survive without the other but that they could never flourish, the men and women agreed to rejoin and live as one group.

Shortly after the reunion, a flood necessitated escape through a great female reed (Fishler 1953:4; Goddard 1933:130–31; O'Bryan 1956:8–10; Yazzie 1971:15). The journey upward culminated in arrival on this, the earth's surface, at the *hajiináí,* or "place of emergence." At this location First Man and First Woman built a sweathouse in which they thought and sang the world, as the Navajo know it, into existence (Witherspoon 1977:16–17). To strengthen the earth and demarcate Navajo sacred geography, the Holy People placed a mountain at each of the four cardinal points (Wyman 1970:16). Next, they created plants and animals with which to populate the world and dressed each mountain with a particular precious stone or shell and various cosmic elements. Thus, each of the sacred mountains, colors, qualities, holy personages, and *ntł'iz,* "hard goods," that make up the fundamental components of Navajo cosmology became associated with a season of the year, a time of day, and a phase of life.

The newly created world was said to be in a state of "natural order" in which all living things were in their prescribed places and their proper relationships with all other living things. But this orderliness did not endure. It was disrupted as a result of the sexual aberrations and excesses of the last underworld, when the women who had masturbated with quills, cacti, antlers, stones, and bones gave birth to twelve misshapen creatures that grew to be huge and began preying on the healthy children. Their births pushed the Navajo ancestors to the brink of extinction (Haile 1981:25–27; O'Bryan 1956:8; Stephen 1930:99; Yazzie 1971:30; Zolbrod 1984:63).

To resolve this dilemma, the Holy People arranged for Changing Woman to be found on Gobernador Knob—one of the central mountains of Navajo sacred geography. When sent to investigate, Talking God found a baby girl lying under a rainbow while it was raining. She was raised by First Man and First Woman, who fed her multiple forms of pollen and flower dew. As a result of this special care, she matured at an accelerated rate: within two days she was walking, in four days she was talking, and in twelve days she began to menstruate.

As a symbol of the restoration of healthy reproduction on the earth, her menstruation was cause for great rejoicing. The first Blessing Way ceremony, the *Kinaaldá*, "puberty ceremony," was celebrated in honor of the event. Shortly afterward, Changing Woman mated sequentially with Sun and Water, subsequently giving birth to twin sons, Monster Slayer and Born-for-the-Water. As adolescents, they went on a quest to find their father. When they found him, he made them endure several trials to prove their parentage. They persevered, and finally Sun supplied them with a particular weapon he kept over his north door. It looked like a bow and arrow but was really lightning (O'Bryan 1956:81; Yazzie 1971:46). Armed with this weapon, the Hero Twins slew the monsters (Fishler 1953:51–56).

The first monster to be slain was *Yé'iitsoh,* "Big Monster," who lived on top of Mount Taylor (Yazzie 1971:31). Monster Slayer and Born-for-the-Water "swooned" after this monster was slain. They were treated ceremonially and soon recovered (Haile 1938:22). This cure was not to last, however; instead, the Twins sickened with each subsequent slaying and their overall condition gradually worsened. As the dominant twin, Monster Slayer was more affected than his brother by the slaughtering. Thus, a very specific ceremony was developed and performed to cure Monster Slayer (Yazzie 1971:72).

Once the monsters had been slain and Monster Slayer's health had been restored, Asdzáá Nádleehé grew lonely for companionship. Changing Woman "wished to have a people that she could call her grandchildren. They would carry on the lore that she would teach them. They would respect and hold holy the prayers and chants that she would give them" (O'Bryan 1956:166). To fulfill her need, she created the Nihookáá Dine'é by rubbing skin wastes from her own body and mixing them with ground white shell, turquoise, abalone, jet, and corn of all colors. She molded these materials into cylindrical forms that she ritually transformed into human beings.

Significantly, these first Earth Surface People were not made to live as individuals; rather, they were immediately matched and paired to found the

Navajo social order. It is generally agreed that Changing Woman selected men and women from among these people to live as husband and wife and thus established the four original clans of the Navajo and the practice of clan exogamy (Aronilth 1985:83; Matthews 1994 [1897]:148; O'Bryan 1956:167; Reichard 1950:28; Wyman 1970:458, 634; Yazzie 1971:74). After their creation, Asdzáá Nádleehé and the other *Diyin Dine'é*, or "Holy People" (Navajo supernatural beings), decided to turn the world over to the Nihookáá Dine'é, entrusting them with stewardship over the geographic area demarcated by their sacred mountains, known today as *Diné Bikéyah*, "Navajoland."

At this juncture, Asdzáá Nádleehé taught them crucial bodies of knowledge—songs, prayers, and ceremonies—with which to sustain themselves in their special form of life and to restore proper relations whenever disruptions occurred. In combination, these *diné bike'ji*, or "Navajo ways," formed a charter between the Navajo and the Holy People which guaranteed that if the Nihookáá Dine'é carefully followed the teachings of the Holy People, the natural order of the Navajo world would be preserved and their special way of life would flourish. Reciprocity is one of the dominant characteristics of Navajo social ethics. As a morally binding relationship, it links the supernatural realm to the realm of humans. This is demonstrated by the acquisition of new ceremonial knowledge.

Importantly, the body of knowledge Changing Woman gave the Nihookáá Dine'é at the time of the Holy People's departure did not include cures for all illnesses. In fact, the plot of the origin story for most Navajo ceremonies (the Red Ant Way and Moth Way are exceptions) centers on a single hero or heroine or, at most, a few getting into a series of predicaments from which they must be liberated by supernatural aid. Examples include the Stricken Twins of the Night Way (Matthews 1902) and the Sunlight Boy of the Water Way (Haile 1979). The process of extrication usually involves an extensive journey to visit various Holy People to acquire ritual knowledge useful to healing. Notably, in each case the hero or heroine is exposed to uncertainty, must demonstrate effort and perseverance, undergoes tests, and overcomes difficulties but emerges from his or her tribulations to endow other Navajo with the power of a new healing ceremony before taking his or her place as a member of the Holy People (Reichard 1950:150; Wyman 1965:65). A critial element of this knowledge is identification of the correct *'ayeel*, or "offering," that must be made to the Holy People *to compel them to assist in the requested healing* (Aberle 1967:17). *Based on this core component of ceremonial origin stories, I contend that the quest for curing power is a basic philosophic tenet that has resulted in a cultural pattern for action by Navajo people.* With these stories as models, Navajo people can be seen as culturally preconditioned to seek and adopt new sources of healing power as they become available.

To maintain good fortune and avert catastrophe, prayers and offerings such as *tádídíín* ("pollen"), ntł'iz, and, as will be shown, other specific items must be made to the Holy People. Some of these oblations must be made at specific sites within Navajo sacred geography. Once this knowledge had been transferred, the Diyin Dine'é departed to take their places as inner forms residing within each feature of Navajo sacred geography (Wyman 1965:91). Their adoption of residence within these forms established imманent supernatural power throughout Diné Bikéyah.

Given their origin—made in part from Changing Woman's skin wastes and that deity's current role as the inner form of the earth—the Nihookáá Dine'é can be said to be *literally constructed from Mother Earth.* In a very real sense, then, their identity is inextricable from their sacred geography on multiple levels.

RELATEDNESS

Navajo beliefs about the lifelong influence of detached body parts raise questions about connections between donors and recipients: What is the nature of these bonds? Do they fall under the rubric of "kinship," a topic that was unquestionably at "the very heart of anthropology for nearly a century" (Carsten 2000:2)? Kinship analysis reigned supreme from the mid- to late 1800s until the early 1970s when theories and debates within the discipline resulted in its "dethronement" (Peletz 1995:344–45). In his groundbreaking monograph on American kinship, David Schneider (1968) differentiated between the symbols and meanings of relatedness through blood (in biogenetic terms, shared substance) as opposed to both those formed through marriage (relatedness in terms of law, the code for conduct) and the more encompassing conceptual domains of nature and law or culture. In *A Critique of the Study of Kinship* (1984), Schneider launched a full-scale assault against the way anthropologists since Lewis Henry Morgan have applied Euro-American notions of human procreation to the study of how people understand their connections to others in societies around the globe. He held that previous anthropological studies were based on the unwarranted assumption that people everywhere devise kinship systems on the basis of the "natural" facts—read, biomedical—of procreation (Stone 2001:1). Demonstrating convincingly that not all societies have something comparable to what we call "kinship," Schneider proposed the wholesale rejection of the category from anthropological analysis (1984).

Janet Carsten has suggested that we ask how the people we study define and construct their conceptions of relatedness and what values and meanings they give to these notions rather than superimpose our own views upon them (2000). Sally Falk Moore has noted that "in any society there are types of social and emotional feelings of connectedness, of which biological relationships are only one part. The category of 'relatedness' is obviously more capacious than the category 'kinship,' hence, it enlarges the analytical territory. By requiring that kinship be placed in a wider frame of social connections, 'relatedness' opens the door to a broad social contextualization of kinship" (Moore 2004:745). Following Carsten, the term "relatedness" is used herein to convey a move away from the "pre-given analytic opposition between the biological and social on which much anthropological study of kinship has rested" (Carsten 2000:4).

Among many peoples around the world, relatedness is derived from acts of procreation as well as from living, eating, and loving together. This point was poignantly demonstrated to me by Kenneth Black, Jr., a self-proclaimed traditionalist from Monument Valley, Utah. While discussing the long-term influence marriage to a non-Navajo can have on a surviving Navajo spouse, he said, "Let's say I am married to a white woman[,] then we are sharing things. We are living together, we are having kids. Well . . . when we live together, [if] something happened to her . . . it will still affect me because my body makeup has still the blood; it still is one" (Black June 16, 2005). Black's statement reveals that some Navajo believe that in the case of intermarriage, intimate relations result in a commingling of substances that alters the nature of one's blood, leaving the surviving Navajo spouse with contaminated blood.

Black's example clearly indicates why practices that involve the exchange of substances cannot be easily differentiated into biological versus social activities (Carsten 1995:236). Furthermore, it begs the questions asked by Kath Weston: "If kinship can ideologically entail shared substance, can transfers of bodily substance create—or threaten to create—kinship? Can they create—or threaten to create—other forms of social responsibility? What investment do people have in depicting the transfer of blood, organs, and sperm as sharing, giving, or donation" (Weston 2001:153)?

When meeting a Navajo stranger, Navajo individuals communicate their social identity by stating their clan affiliations rather than providing personal or given names. First and foremost, an individual is considered to have been born into his or her mother's clan. This is appropriate given that the strongest bond of relatedness in the Navajo world is that of mother-child, a bond based on reproduction and the sustenance of life (Witherspoon 1975:21).

Accordingly, as noted by Gary Witherspoon, Navajo people refer to those with whom they share *k'é*, or "intense, diffuse, and enduring solidarity," as *shik'éí*, "my relatives by descent" (1975:37). K'é is anchored in birth because it is through the act of birth that a child becomes affiliated with relatives on his or her mother's and father's sides. Using the terminology of his mentor David Schneider, Witherspoon wrote:

> The primary bond in the Navajo kinship system is the mother-child bond, and it is in this bond that the nature and meaning of kinship become clear. In Navajo culture, kinship means *intense, diffuse, and enduring solidarity,* and this solidarity is realized in actions and behaviors befitting the cultural definitions of kinship solidarity.
>
> Just as the mother is [the] one who gives life to her children through birth, and sustains their life by providing them with loving care, assistance, protection, and sustenance, kinsmen [and women] are those who sustain each other's life by helping one another, protecting one another, and by giving or sharing food and other items of subsistence. Where this kind of solidarity exists, kinship exists; where it does not exist, there is no kinship. (Witherspoon 1975:21–22, emphasis added)

Navajo people consider themselves to be "born to" their mother's clan and "born for" their father's clan. Those who are born for one's own clan or who are members of the father's clan are cross-cousins, referred to as *bizeedí*. As Louise Lamphere clarifies: "First, every Navajo is born of a woman (coming up and out of her womb). Birth affiliates a child with her or his mother and the mother's relatives or clan. These would include the mother's mother, the mother's sisters, and the women of the same clan and children of any women in the same clan. Other important relatives would be males of the same clan, including mother's brothers, sister's sons, and mother's mother's brothers. It is birth from women linked directly to the births of other women that is central to identifying one's clan" (Lamphere 2001:38).

On the other side of the relatedness equation, the major form of non-kinship solidarity among the Navajo is affinity. The primary affinal bond exists between husband and wife. Genealogical ties other than mother to child and affinal ties other than husband to wife are secondary and more distant because they are linked by one or more intermediary persons or categories. Witherspoon noted that along with the husband-wife and mother-child relationships, there are father-child and sibling-sibling relationships in the Navajo social system. The latter two relationships are traced through, and linked by, the all-important category of mother. The line initiated by the father into the mother's womb, which continues out of her to the children, involves both a strong kinship bond and a weak affinal bond (Witherspoon 1975:35).

Witherspoon observed that throughout his lifetime, every Navajo man is virtually thrust between two women, and through them he acquires his status and achieves his societal role. As he has pointed out: "His relationship to these two women involves two kinds of relationships to a womb. One is a kind of extrusion; the other is a kind of intrusion. One is symbolized by birth; the other, by sexual intercourse. One is described as the utmost in security; the other is considered to hold latent danger. *One involves sharing; the other, exchange*" (Witherspoon 1975:27, emphasis added). In *Navajo Kinship and Marriage* (1975), Witherspoon explores the possibility that the Navajo father-child relationship might best be characterized by affinity, but he concludes that Navajo fathers are linked to their children by both kinship and affinity. The intensity of this relationship is proportionate to that of the mother's relationship to the father. When the parents' relationship dissolves, the father-child relationship also dissolves; indeed, children often refer to their fathers as in-laws (Aberle 1961:152). Further, the distance of this relationship is evidenced by the fact that some Navajo reportedly say it is good to marry into one's father's clan (Reichard 1928:62–63, 65; Witherspoon 1975:31).

The degree to which the concept of exchange permeates a husband's relationship with his wife and children was clearly demonstrated to me through this therapeutic narrative shared by Julia Mathis. She feels a profound sense of affection for and gratitude to her father, who died a short time before our interview. Over and beyond the gratitude any daughter feels toward a good father, Mathis's indebtedness to her father derives from an experience they shared when she was very young. It is a tender story her father reminded her of numerous times as his health declined and his need for assistance increased:

> JM: I am the only one in the family—when I was an infant—that had a blood transfusion. And my dad, until the day he passed away, *he wouldn't let me forget, "My blood is what saved your life.* I walked with you and I carried you from here all the way to Chinle and caught a ride from Chinle to Fort Defiance" [over seventy miles away]. . . . I guess I had double pneumonia and something else so . . . I was very thankful to my dad. That he had the courage to walk and that I had the strength to hang on to life until I was given a transfusion. And I got to where I needed to be. So, *when he started getting sick, and he started going down, he used to tell me, "I am going down. And my blood is your blood and I don't mean to be boring you with it but that is what kept you going[,] and I hope you stay strong for me* and for many more years to come."
>
> MS: And you have.
>
> JM: And I have. (Mathis, June 11, 2005)

Julia Mathis's father's reminders clearly indicate that he expected direct reciprocal compensation in the form of dutiful care during his old age and ill health in return for the blood she received as a child. This marks the exchange as affinal, a form typically expressed through economic reciprocity and mutual cooperation, as opposed to genealogical relationships expressed through sharing and solidarity.

Navajo individuals are defined only secondarily by their paternal relationships, as evidenced by self-identifications expressed during greetings. All children with fathers who are members of the Salt Clan, for example, are put into a category called "those born for the Salt Clan"; all people in this category are each others' brothers and sisters. Importantly, this category excludes the father, so the Navajo people as a whole cannot be said to be patrilineal. They also reckon genealogy through their mother's father's and their father's father's matrilineal clans because they consider these men's matrilineal relatives to be important. Navajo people practice clan exogamy. Clan membership is also significant in establishing and maintaining reciprocity, prohibiting incest, providing a system for passing on ceremonial knowledge, establishing and fostering a relationship to place, and passing on customary use rights to grazing and agricultural lands. The latter two functions have much to do with every Navajo's connection to Mother Earth. A lifelong connection therefore exists between every Navajo and the four major clans from which she or he claims ancestry.

The second major relationship deriving from the union of husband and wife is that between siblings, with the mother's womb again providing the connective link. Sibling bonds are second in strength only to those between mother and child. This uterine-based bond between siblings is expressed in the term 'bił hajííjééhigii', or "those with whom one came up out of the same womb" (Witherspoon 1975:35). As a collective, the Navajo people are linked to those who arose from the womb of Mother Earth at the place of emergence, where First Man and First Woman thought and sang the world, as the Navajo know it, into existence. It was within this sacred geography that they were made by Changing Woman, as part of her own flesh. It is she who gave them a set of diné bike'ji as a charter for life.

Navajo people use body parts and substances to reaffirm or strengthen relatedness to Mother Earth—by means of the placement of the placenta and the umbilical cord or disposal of ceremonial shampoo and bathwater. As will be demonstrated, in the context of biomedical technologies they also use body parts to reaffirm connections to relatives by exchanging organs and blood with them. These are some of the practices that distinguish them from non-Navajo people.

Anthropological analyses have tended to privilege positive and harmonious aspects of relatedness, yet genealogical and affinal relatedness is also about "disconnection and disjunction" (Carsten 2000:24). Among the Navajo, for example, not all enduring social bonds are positive; rather, an underside of relatedness exists. Exclusionary aspects are demonstrated in the Navajo case by how the blood and body parts of enemies are scorned, as well as in rules prohibiting incest and in incest taboos more specifically. In regard to foreignness and organ transplantation, a vital element of concern surrounds whether a donor is a *"native of the land"* (Goldtooth, July 18, 2005). On this basis, the distinction between Navajo and non-Navajo has been conscientiously maintained to the present day. Collectively, these insights shed light on Navajo notions of relatedness in general and on contemporary Navajo perspectives on the age-old issues of contamination and oppositional politics. Navajo consultants frequently stated preferences regarding the source of donated bodily organs and fluids. Navajo understandings of relatedness, therefore, hold significance for making sense of their donor choices within the broader societal context—a context based on a sense of themselves as members of four foundational clans, with a multifaceted integral connection between Nihookáá Dine'é and their sacred geography. This context was disrupted by interactions with Europeans and European-Americans.

THE LONG WALK AND NAVAJO COLLECTIVE IDENTITY

Francesca Polletta and James Jasper define collective identity as an individual's "cognitive, moral and emotional connection with a broader community. . . . It is a perception of a shared status or relation, which may be imagined rather than experienced directly, and it is distinct from personal identities, although it may form part of a personal identity" (Polletta and Jasper 2001:285). Alternatively, collective identity can be seen as "the processes of identification by which people sort their environment into like and unlike, self and other" (Andrews and Sutphen 2003:1). It is identity in this sense that has generated much recent scholarly attention from historians, sociologists, and anthropologists (Alexander et al., 2004; Andrews and Sutphen 2003; Polletta and Jasper 2001) and with which this study is mainly concerned.

A causal link exists among tragedy, collective identity, and cultural trauma. Jeffrey Alexander has noted that "cultural trauma occurs when members of a collectivity feel they have been subjected to a horrendous event that leaves indelible marks upon their group consciousness, marking their memories forever and changing their future identity in fundamental and irrevocable ways" (2004:1). Yet even trauma is a socially mediated attribution (Alexander 2004:8). As Ron Eyerman has pointed out, for example, in the case of slavery in the United States:

> Resolving cultural trauma can involve the articulation of collective identity and collective memory, as individual stories meld into collective history through forms and processes of collective representation. Collective identity refers to a process of "we" formation, a process both historically rooted and rooted in history. While this common history may have its origins in direct experience, its memory is mediated through narratives that are modified with the passage of time and filtered through cultural artifacts and other materializations that represent the past in the present. Whether or not they directly experienced slavery or even had ancestors who did, blacks in the United States were identified with and came to identify themselves with slavery. The historical memory of the Civil War was reconstructed in the decades that followed, and blackness came to be associated with slavery and subordination. A common history was thus ascribed and inscribed as memory, as well as indigenously passed on. In this sense, slavery is traumatic for those who share a common fate and not necessarily a common experience. (Eyerman 2004:74)

For the Nihookáá Dine'é, who consider themselves a chosen people living in a world designed especially for them, the pivotal event responsible for initiating a process of "we" formation in this world was their being brutally rounded up and forced to march 300 to 400 miles, depending on their point of departure, under guard to *Hwéeldi*, or "the place of suffering." That place is commonly known as Fort Sumner, a reservation 165 miles south of Santa Fe, New Mexico, where approximately 8,000–9,000 Navajo were held in captivity during the years 1863–68; half of that number died while there or en route to or from the location (Bailey 1988[1964]; Correll

1979; Johnson 1973). Although not all Navajo were forced to go to Fort Sumner, most were affected by the tactics of Colonel Kit Carson who, under the direction of General James Carleton, the U.S. Army commander in New Mexico, was charged in the early 1860s with rounding up New Mexico's Native peoples and herding them onto the Bosque Redondo reservation. An experienced and efficient campaigner, Carson had soon forced the Mescalero Apache into full retreat, and he sent 400 of them north to Fort Sumner from their homelands in the Sacramento and Guadalupe mountains. Carson next turned his attention to the Navajo, against whom he launched a scorched-earth campaign. This policy dictated that Navajo hooghan (traditional Navajo earthen-floor homes) be burned, cornfields destroyed, water holes poisoned, sheep and other livestock killed, and peach trees and other food supplies destroyed. Perhaps most lethal was the fact that the U.S. military armed Ute, Hopi, and Zuni warriors as well as other residents of New Mexico, then granted them full license to raid the Navajo and capture women and children, whom they were allowed to sell to anyone they wished (Iverson 2002:45–65; Johnson 1973; Roessel 1980:11). The buying and selling of captives was nothing new, however, for as historian James Brooks has written, "In New Mexico, Spanish and Indian men found that even more than horses, guns, or hides, their counterparts valued women and children, and they established a nominal agreement that these would serve as objects and agents of intersocietal exchange" (Brooks 1997:113). Indeed, captured women and children were the "most precious and contestable 'resource' of borderland societies" (Brooks 1999:24), and Navajo captives were no exception. According to some estimates, by Carelton's time there were 5,000 Navajo slaves in New Mexico, with 500 in Santa Fe alone (Brugge 1985; McNitt 1972).

From the beginning, Navajo people knew their ancestors had been created by Changing Woman (the inner form of the earth), that they had entered this world through the hajiináí—which they considered the womb of Mother Earth—and that they had been chosen to live within their sacred geography. Any sense of collective identity as a body politic, however, was limited to clan affiliations, extended family, or the geographic area within which an extended family rotated residences throughout the year. Prior to Hwéeldi, during the Spanish and Mexican periods, subsistence patterns were changing as new forms of plants and livestock were introduced. Pueblo refugees frequently sought sanctuary among the Nihookáá Dine'é. Women from these and various other native groups married into the Nihookáá Dine'é and founded as many as twenty of the sixty Navajo clans. These new members brought innovative ideas regarding every aspect of life. It was only when 8,000–9,000 Navajo people were rounded up from isolated areas and removed from their sacred landscape in which their deities dwelled that a collective identity as a body politic began to form.

Although the event was unquestionably tragic for every individual involved, if we apply Alexander's logic regarding how slavery became a cultural trauma for African Americans to the Navajo situation, what has come to be known as the Long Walk and the circumstances surrounding it cannot be said to have been culturally traumatic for the Navajo as a people until vivid narratives about their years of internment and early reservation life were created and circulated over a period of generations. Against these vocalized images, their captivity and loss could be retroactively cast as an assault on them as a group and could become a true cultural trauma. That is, the Long Walk and the Navajo internment at Hwéeldi were focal points against which collective identity could be forged because of the way those events came to be remembered and reproduced.

For this transformation to occur, individuals, often referred to as "carrier groups"—a phrase coined by Max Weber in *Economy and Society* (1968:468–517)—must serve as collective agents of the trauma process; that is, they negotiate the gap between event and representation (Alexander 2004:11). While the Navajo were at Hwéeldi, this role was filled by head men such as Barboncito and Manuelito. They were the ones who negotiated with the soldiers for their people's deliverance from incarceration, thereby framing the event as a collective tragedy.

After their release and return to a portion of their homeland, all of the survivors became carrier group members. Those who returned from Fort Sumner narrated accounts about the horrors they had experienced at the hands of the U.S. military and Native raiders to Navajo families who had remained hidden in remote parts of the numerous canyons that distinguish their homeland, on top of Black Mesa, north of the San Juan River, or in equally out-of-the-way locations within the area demarcated by the four sacred mountains.

A new master narrative was created as the Navajo who had not experienced Hwéeldi firsthand began to internalize the suffering of those who had to such a point that they, too, became traumatized by the events. This happened gradually as narratives were related about what had happened, who was affected by the events, and who was responsible for them (Alexander 2004:15). The Navajo had been removed from their sacred geography, held in captivity, starved, raped, murdered, brutalized, and subsequently allowed to return to only a portion of their homeland. The cold reality quickly set in that their freedom was forever gone and that this portion of their beloved homeland was now a reservation to which they were restricted. Regarding responsibility, the Euro-American colonizers were clearly culpable for much of what had occurred, but interestingly—according to many documented accounts—the Navajo also deemed themselves partially responsible (Frisbie and McAllester 1978:14, 17; Johnson 1973). Moreover, unlike slavery, which is something from the past for contemporary African Americans, colonization is an ongoing process for all Native Americans—including the Navajo people.

Thus, what began as a tragedy for individuals and families became the decisive cultural trauma for the Navajo. Accounts told by those who survived Kit Carson's onslaught and the years of internment at Hwéeldi, as well as the countless narratives passed down for generations—which include information about the men, women, and children who hid in remote canyons of Diné Bikéyah as well as those who walked to and from Hwéeldi or who perished at some point during the episode—over time have expanded to become narratives about the loss and disenfranchisement brought on by colonization: loss of language, loss of culture, loss of control, loss of tradition, loss of subsistence. These vivid recountings turned this tragedy into a cultural trauma, against which backdrop a collective identity of the Navajo people was forged.

In the first half of the twentieth century, Clyde Kluckhohn and Dorothea Leighton stated:

> Fort Sumner was a major calamity to The People; its full effects upon their imagination can hardly be conveyed to white readers. Even today it seems impossible for any Navaho of the older generation to talk for more than a few minutes on any subject without speaking of Fort Sumner. Those who were not there themselves heard so many poignant tales from their parents that they speak as if they themselves had experienced all the horror of the "Long Walk," the illness, the

hunger, the homesickness, the final return to their desolated land. One can no more understand Navaho attitudes—particularly toward white people—without knowing of Fort Sumner than he can comprehend Southern attitudes without knowing of the Civil War. (Kluckhohn and Leighton 1974[1946]:41)

Indeed, stories of the Long Walk, many of which have been captured in *Navajo Stories of the Long Walk Period* (Johnson 1973), are still "told around kitchen tables and sheep camp fires across the reservation" (Linthicum 2005). The importance this event retains today is evidenced by the solemnity that accompanied the dedication of the more than 6,000-square-foot Fort Sumner State Monument at the site on June 4, 2005. Because the stories of this cultural trauma have remained alive within the society, a general distrust pervades attitudes toward Euro-Americans, most of whom are still considered enemy outsiders.

HEALTH CARE CHOICES AND FORMS OF CONTAMINATION

The Navajo have long been recognized for their propensity to adapt introduced technology to their own design for living, yet the process by which this is accomplished with any specific type or form of technology has yet to be clarified. Following the work of Evon Vogt (1961) and John Farella (1984), I argue that the Navajo label the new as old and that, in an attempt to stay traditional, they incorporate very selectively what they want to adapt from available biomedical technologies; moreover, as will be demonstrated, they mold these borrowed technologies to fit their age-old philosophy. Although no systematic study exists of exactly how Navajo people accommodate biomedical technologies, snippets of information appear in the plethora of literature on the Nihookáá Dine'é.

Of direct relevance here, as one example, is an observation by Paul Mico, a member of a University of California School of Public Health team that undertook a project based out of the Public Health Service Hospital (PHSH) in Tuba City, Arizona, from 1959–1962, designed to ascertain Navajo perceptions of Euro-American health and medicine. Mico stated that "[t]he

Navajo have a fear of surgery, perceiving the process as similar to the 'butchering of sheep.' In cases of elective surgery, wherein the patient has the option of deciding to have surgery at an early or a later date, the surgery is usually put off until it becomes a serious or an emergency case. This usually results in a more complicated task for the surgeon" (Mico 1962:16). In the 1960s, Dr. John Porvaznik, who also worked at the Tuba City PHSH, noted that Navajo patients were pursuing modern medicine practices in medical and surgical specialties, yet "virtually all Navajos still have a ceremonial sing in some form before or after hospital treatment" (Porvaznik 1967:182). Porvaznik offered no specific information or explanation regarding the religious rites engaged in before and after biomedical care, but such practices were confirmed by those I consulted. In contrast, the vital points raised by Denetdeal do not support Mico's claims, as Denetdeal made no correlation between surgery and the butchering of sheep; rather, his comments were focused on issues of contamination.

One form of contamination—that derived from contact with the dead, a deceased person's personal belongings, the place at which death occurred, or human remains—plays an extremely important role in the areas of organ transplantation, CPR, and blood transfusion. Navajo concerns over contact with the dead have been widely covered in the scholarly literature (Brugge 1978:323; Franciscan Fathers 1910:453–54; Frisbie 1978:303; Kluckhohn and Leighton 1974[1946]:202; Reichard 1928:141–43; Shufeldt 1891:305) and were therefore anticipated before this project was undertaken. I was also aware of a second form of potential contamination, alluded to by Denetdeal and derived in part from the curse of a Navajo deity known as the Gambler— contact with non-Navajo. As Leroy Nelson—a Blessing Way singer from Iron Water Springs, Arizona, who is a counselor with the Behavioral Health Division of the Navajo Nation—explained:

> LN: Way over there there was a deity, a brother to Coyote. . . . I guess
> they knew witchcraft. They knew skin walking. They knew all of
> these unhealthy things. . . . This deity . . . did a lot of unhealthy
> things, to where there is a lot of mysterious things that happened,
> that arose. . . . There were followers to this individual, there were
> helpers. This individual . . . had the color of skin that was white. . . .
> Like an albino. . . . [He] was born for the sun. It was Sun's second

oldest. . . . So he had white skin, blue eyes, and white hair. This deity, he knew the fullest detail of . . . traditional stories, ways, ceremonies, dos and don'ts, he knew it all. . . . Coyote, Born-for-Water-Child, and the Monster Slayer—all of a sudden they were challenging one another in games, and different things, and their supernatural powers, too. These two deities came across this [white-skinned] deity and then they challenged themselves to a game. This is what we say *Nááhwíiłbįįhí,* "it would draw you in." . . . The story goes that they started in a game and within this game started collecting, winning at the casino. It is like a gambling thing.

MS: Is he referred to as the Gambler?

LN: Yes. He knows that evil to where he could look at you and speak some words and go into your mind and get your mind. It could be about sex or different things. It will just get you like this in an instant second. Just one look, one word, one touch. It will make you not think. It will make you not speak. It will make you feel good and you go into that person and be whatever thing that, he is the controller. . . . So there are things, songs and different things they did. They won; Born-for-Water-Child and the Monster Slayer won. Now at that point in time what they said is, "Well, you [the Gambler] are not appreciated here. You don't belong here. . . . You will go on the other side of the world. That is where you are going to go. If you go over there to [the] other side of the world, whatever you do it is your thing. Over here you are not welcome. You shouldn't be here because there is a lot of negativity that arose. There [are] a lot of unhealthy things that arose because of you." So he was put on the other side of the world, we were told. But when he went he said, "One day I will come back! My children, they are gonna come back! I am sure of it! I will destroy you! One day it is going to happen." So that is what happened. (Nelson, July 20, 2005)

Navajo views on contamination from contact with non-Navajo *without death as an element of the context*—such as through the intimate contact involved in surgery—were completely unknown to me prior to my conversation with Professor Denetdeal and my subsequent conversations with

Leroy Nelson and others. Prior to these discussions, I had simply accepted the understandings outlined by Father Berard Haile in his canonical work *Origin Legends of the Navaho Enemy Way,* wherein he notes:

> The sight of a foreigner's blood, or of his violent death, or that of his beast, may affect the pregnant woman, the child in her womb, or even her husband. Such incidents, as the sight of, or contact with, a corpse of a slain or deceased enemy, the sight of a scalp, contact with bones in a ruin or cemetery, or even the sight of the blood of a stranger accidentally hurt, are no cause for alarm in themselves. But when such incidents cause swooning, indisposition, or troubled sleep, they are attributable to Enemy Way, which alone can remove the cause. *The rite always has reference to the dead foreigner,* specifically to his disembodied spirit, which implies that sights, contact, or sexual relations become operative *only after the death of the foreigner.* (Haile 1938:25, emphasis added)

In looking back through the literature after my initial conversations with Denetdeal and Nelson, I found only two passing references to potential danger of contamination by non-Navajo through the intimate contact of surgery; they occur in passages Gladys Reichard wrote about illness. In the first she states: "T's wife became ill with what the white doctor diagnosed as cancer of the breast. After both breasts had been removed, she improved. The Flint (Knife) Chant was sung to free her *from the obvious evil of the surgeon's scalpel.* I saw her nearly two years after the operation; she was again very ill. . . . The diagnostician . . . prescribed the Female Shooting Chant to be followed by the War Ceremony. . . . After the War Ceremony she was said to be 'all right'" (Reichard 1950:95, emphasis added). The treatment schedule outlined in this isolated passage—a Flint Way followed by a War ceremony (commonly known as an Enemy Way)— closely parallels those recalled by most of the Navajo people I consulted about surgery, with Shooting Way (commonly known as a Lightning Way) called for in cases involving cancer. This clearly indicates that some Navajo people believed that being cut by a non-Navajo required ritual intervention (although the extent of the belief cannot be determined) at the time Reichard did her fieldwork and that procedures for rectifying it were similar to those used today. Reichard's rationale for the purpose of the Flint Way—to free the patient from the evil of the surgeon's scalpel—coincides precisely with explanations for the ceremony given by Navajo consultants with whom I spoke.

Elsewhere, Reichard discusses the case of a child, wherein such a connection is made again. She notes:

> A girl was to have the Big Star Chant sung for her, but on the night it was to start she was taken to the hospital, where her disease was diagnosed as endemic, non-contagious meningitis. After five weeks, she was dismissed as cured. . . . Although from the time she left the hospital she had seemed perfectly well, not until after the Big Star Chant, and several months later, the War Ceremony had been performed for her, did the Navaho consider her out of danger. Her disease was so severe and strange that it was ascribed to indefinite causes—effect of the dead, possible witchcraft, or even witch-objects shot by the dead—and to make certain of including other indeterminable causes, *possible evil due to strangers, including white people who treated her at the hospital*, the War Ceremony was performed for her. (Reichard 1950:83, emphasis added)

While Reichard mentioned this form of contamination more than half a century ago, to the best of my knowledge it has not been pursued as an area of scholarly interest by other researchers who study the Navajo and medicine or any other topic. It is of particular interest, however, because analysis of Navajo oral history and contemporary narratives reveals it to be a linchpin in understanding medical discourse as an idiom through which Navajo people simultaneously express resistance to colonization as well as convictions about collective identity and oppositional politics. As Edward Said noted in *Orientalism*, to some degree all societies derive a sense of identity by contrast, most often simply establishing a familiar space as "ours" and designating everything beyond that space as "theirs," without animosity (Said 1978:54). When strangers enter one's world intending to conquer it, however, a group is forced to make such a differentiation. By these means, people everywhere essentialize "others"—that is, they dimish an entire society to a mass of soulless, unfeeling enemies. In the Navajo case, contact with their others came to be considered dangerous because of possible contamination.

NEGOTIATING PLURALISMS

Members of local groups do not passively accept what comes to them through global flows; rather, indigenous people have and exert agency. Thus, as Lenore Manderson and Linda Whiteford learned through their analysis of numerous cross-cultural health care situations, acceptance works in different ways in each case, depending on the given power relations and other local circumstances: "In health, the local circumstances are environmental, eco-logical, and epidemiological as well as political, social, and ideological, and for this reason single solutions are rarely appropriate. . . . [P]ublic health planners continually struggle with the intersection of global agendas and local settings, and communities struggle to understand the kinds of programs that they are being offered and in which they are expected to participate" (Manderson and Whiteford 2000:7).

The inextricably linked local circumstances, which are critical in the Navajo case, are the by-products and present-day ramifications of ongoing colonialization and what noted anthropologist Charlotte Frisbie has described as "the eclecticism of the People, and, in the area of religion, their pragmatic interest in multiple affiliations and syncretic combinations, anything that may yield a wider range of options and offer solutions, explanations, or at least relief from personal, tribal, and cultural problems" (1987:197).

The significance to this study of the Navajo people's so-called eclecticism cannot be overstated, for this long-recognized propensity for simultaneously practicing multiple health or religious forms, most frequently termed "plu-ralism," extends to medical as well as religious issues in the Navajo world. Peter Berger has defined this concept as "the breakdown of taken for granted traditions and the opening up of multiple options for beliefs, values, and lifestyles" (2002:16). A preamble is in order before the term is applied in the Navajo case. While the term itself is appropriate, as has been shown based on the leitmotiv for the origin stories of individual ceremonials (Haile 1979; Matthews 1902; Reichard 1950:150; Wyman 1965:65) and as will be shown based on ethnohistorical sources that document Navajo adoption of new forms of curing throughout the colonial period (Faris 1990:17; Haile 1950: Part 2, 297; Stewart and Aberle 1957:35; Trennert 1998:33), the Navajo can be said to be inherently inclined to seek out new forms of healing or avenues to supernatural power. Thus, no "breakdown of taken for granted traditions" or "opening up" occurred, so the widely held definition of the term is not appropriate to the Navajo case. *It is more accurate to say that their cultural heritage preconditioned the Navajo to practice medical and religious pluralism.*

Insights into analyzing such a pluralistic system are available from work conducted across time and space in a variety of colonized societies, by medical anthropologists as well as scholars interested in religious phenomena. I looked to both areas of scholarship for illumination because in the Navajo world, what scholars term alternatively as religion and medicine are inseparably linked. The Navajo epistemology of life focuses on the maintenance of harmonious relationships between humans and other entities within their environment as well as with the Diyin Dine'é. Navajo ceremonials, which have been extensively described in the anthropological and medical literature, are focused primarily on healing (see Coulehan 1980; Kluckhohn and Wyman 1940; Porvaznik 1967; Reichard 1950). Understandably, the introduced religions that have most interested Navajo people are those with a curing component (Pavlik 1997).

Medical pluralism refers to the social organization of healing practitioners, who often occupy different religious, ideological, ethnic, and class positions in their communities. It also refers to the coexisting and competing discourses of affliction and healing with which these practitioners legitimate their therapeutic power. Plural healing systems have long been of interest to medical anthropologists (see Leslie 1978; Rubel 1979). Research in communities around the world has explored the complex operation of plural healing systems and their internal variations while taking into consideration articulations with colonialism and capitalism.[3] The study of medical pluralism further addresses what anthropologists have classically termed "health-seeking behaviors"—that is, the process of defining a symptom, seeking a healer, and evaluating treatment options. Medical pluralism also includes exploration of the underlying logic that guides people's choices (Brodwin 1996:14; see also Chrisman 1977; Young and Garro 1981).

These are the dialectics of healing power in the Navajo world represented in the remaining chapters of this book. The multiple healing practices in the Navajo world are interwoven with other domains of social life, especially local and introduced forms of religious worship and affiliation. My analysis attempts to demonstrate how, by negotiating among competing medical discourses and practices, Navajo people creatively respond simultaneously to an immediate crisis of illness or accident, specific contradictions within their family and community, and the ongoing fragmentation of traditional society. Care will be taken to consider whether each healing system has both a moral component and explanatory power. In the Navajo case, this translates into whether a healing system treats both symptoms and cause or only one of these. As will be shown, this distinction is vital. Additionally, following Paul Brodwin (1996:16), do the Navajo couch their responses in an idiom that is at once moral, religious, and therapeutic?

Wherever Europeans met so-called primitive peoples globally, the combined crusade of Christianity and biomedicine was irrepressible, and medicine quickly became "the cutting edge of civilization" (Comaroff and Comaroff 1997:332). As a result, contemporary medical pluralism everywhere involves hierarchical relations among medical subsystems. In the United States, these relations tend to mirror the political, economic, and social relationships and divisions of the greater U.S. society (Baer 1995:501). The Navajo case documents a shift from a situation of intense competition between the local and the global. When the Navajo were first colonized and incorporated into the U.S. hierarchical medical system, attempts were made to exert dominance over subordinated systems and replace them with the preeminent systems—the aim was for allopathic medicine and Christianity to dominate and replace the indigenous systems.

Today, the Indian Health Service seeks to develop collaborative relationships between biomedicine and traditional Navajo health care choices. In terms of the lived experience of contemporary Navajo people, a noncompetitive model currently exists among biomedicine, traditional Navajo curing techniques, the Native American Church, and most Christian forms of healing. Competition does exist, however, between the previously mentioned curing systems and some Christian sects, which are exclusionary on the basis of their internal doctrines.

This analysis of how the local is negotiated in interaction with the global is accomplished through an analysis of Navajo narratives about how blood transfusions, CPR, amputations, transplants, and other biomedical procedures are made possible or about why the procedures are deemed unacceptable. Through these accounts, I quickly learned that there is more to coexistence than meets the eye.

While a small percentage of the contemporary Navajo people with whom I consulted consider themselves to be living only according to the diné bike'ji established by Changing Woman, the Diyin Diné who created them here on the earth's surface, most do not. Those closest to making this claim are individuals who rely on traditional Navajo diagnosis and ceremonies, who have been baptized Catholic, and who make use of the biomedical care provided by the Indian Health Service. Overall, though, there is a comparatively high frequency of change in religious affiliation throughout life spans and a tendency for religious practitioners to be affiliated simultaneously with different religious forms.

None of the people with whom I consulted limit themselves to the use of one health system such as traditional Navajo diagnosticians, herbalists, or ceremonial practitioners, the Native American Church road men and women, Christian pastors and congregations, or the Indian Health Service hospitals and clinics. The vast majority of those consulted mix health beliefs and behaviors from two or more of those available to treat a single ailment. For example, those who readily mix beliefs and practices draw on parallel and seemingly distinct structures, causing the health-seeking decision-making process to become quite complex and compelling at times. These cases vary from an individual stricken with diabetes-related complications who has chosen to use traditional diagnosis and ceremonies, Native American Church meetings, and biomedicine to someone who relies on Pentecostal prayer and biomedicine to cope with health problems related to high blood pressure.

Fundamentally, religion provides a framework within which to make sense of illness. As Thomas Csordas has pointed out, the "therapeutic principle of Christian healing is conversional with healing typically predicated on adopting Christian values and a Christian way of life" (1999:10). That was the case for Irene Gorman of Nazlini, Arizona, whose narrative was told to me by her husband, Eugene Bahe, when she was detained en route to our scheduled interview. He described her conversion to Christianity after her family had done all it could for her through traditional means when she was taken ill as a child.

> EB: Well, it all started when she was about ten years old [and] going to school at the boarding school here in Nazlini. . . . One day she woke up just like routine, gets out of a bunk bed . . . took the sheet off, and she tried to get down from her bed, and she just fell down. She couldn't feel her legs and one of the dorm ladies pick her up. . . . They took her up to the hospital and found out she has polio. They sent her on into Albuquerque and they did a surgery on her. When she usually get home . . . her family, they would get her a medicine man and do all kinds of rituals on her and ceremonies and the singings and all that. And so, she had a lot of, several livestock and they started selling them to pay the medicine men. And finally the funding just went out. And so, from that time on, she never trusted the medicine men . . . or any traditional ceremonies, she said, "It never worked on me." She never got healed after all of the things that they did on her. She never trusted it anymore from that time on. I guess one day she was in the hospital trying to recuperate from that surgery. There was this one lady that would usually come in to talk to her and she was Catholic I think, a sister that used to talk to patients. And she kept praying for her, and finally one day she said, "God can heal you. You can walk again." And so from that time on she prayed with her all the time, and pretty soon she started having that feeling back in her legs, and one day she got home and she had her cast on from the waist down, all the way down to her ankle. So one day she said a prayer to God, "I know you can heal me and so I'm just putting my trust in you." Then she just took that first step, and from that time on she started walking again. So that's how her belief is, everything is, her trust is in God, she never had ceremonies done for her from that time on. . . .

MS: Does your wife believe it was Jesus Christ who healed her?

EB: Yes. She trusts in that all the time, and that is all she talks about. All her prayers and everything is always Jesus Christ, she puts her whole trust in him. (Bahe, July 22, 2004)

This account of Mrs. Bahe's miraculous recovery through prayer serves as a vivid example of a contemporary genre of inspirational curing narratives centered on the power of prayer. Moreover, as her account makes clear, Navajo oral tradition is no longer the only ancient story or text Navajo people look to for guidance. As a child, Irene Gorman Bahe found moral force and validity in Jesus Christ, yet she remained a member of a family that believed in the Holy People and followed traditional practices. Her story coupled with that of her daughter Eugenia, a liver transplant recipient, offers insight into how medical pluralism is negotiated within multiple generations of a Navajo family. Irene subsequently met and married Eugene, another Christian. The Bible thus contains the origin story to which the Bahe family—now devout Pentecostals—looks for guidance. It is the text to which thousands of other Christian Navajo also turn for counsel, while thousands of other Navajo look to the origin story of peyote's healing powers.

Ursula Knoki-Wilson of Ganado, Arizona, told me that her mother took the family to the Catholic Church. Her father was a Blessing Way singer as well as a Native American Church road man, "so we went to those ceremonies too." Much of this was placed into context as she explained how her family deals with a medical crisis.

UKW: Well, if it is an emergency, we don't hesitate to go to the ER. But while the person is over in the health facility, then you would find someone to do a Protection Prayer or else if you found someone like a Native American Church [NAC] person or something was set up and . . . we would call an emergency NAC prayer meeting to pray after that person that went to the hospital. And then depending on the ceremony, they might recommend certain herbs that we have to take to follow that person if they were real sick, flown to an ulterior for intensive care somewhere else. . . . We might follow them down there and take herbs that they recommended or do some kind of a bedside blessing while they were in the hospital. Or if the medicine person is available we might take them along and let them do a bedside blessing or something like that. But if not, then upon the person's return from the hospital they would have a follow-up ceremony with . . . the NAC or else maybe the family would decide, "OK, let's find out what caused them to get sick to begin with. And let's go through a [traditional] diagnostician and then find out what we are supposed to do." And so then they might do that and come up with a [traditional] ceremony that they would recommend based on the findings of the diagnostician. And then usually follow-up treatment with either herbs, or if they had surgery or something like that they would do a Life Way, gather some Life Way herbs and do that Life Way chant. And then after about a month or two they would follow up with a Blessing Way ceremony, which is to put them back into balance with everyday life, and that would be what they would do. (Knoki-Wilson, July 5, 2005)

As this account reveals, health-seeking behavior is a family affair in the Navajo world. For the most part, therefore, medical and religious pluralism does not occur on an individual basis; rather, it takes place as a series of negotiations within a family followed by collective actions on the family's part.

Typically, when someone falls ill, he or she returns to the matrilineal home and allows relatives to take control of the situation. Unless it is an emergency, such as that described by Ursula Knoki-Wilson, family members most often seek a diagnosis before deciding on a course of action. Such decisions are complicated when religious affiliations are divided within families, as described by Knoki-Wilson.

ZOOMING IN

The nature of this project allowed me to address a related area of concern previously identified as needing attention; that is, whether Navajo diversity in religious practice has resulted in changes in Navajo "health beliefs and behaviors" (Kunitz 1983:122–23). Since Stephen Kunitz first voiced this interest, work by other scholars had shed light on the matter (Begay and Maryboy 2000; Csordas 2000; Garrity 2000; Lewton and Bydone 2000; Milne and Howard 2000; Storck, Csordas, and Strauss 2000; Tom-Orme 1988).

When I began this project, however, questions remained regarding whether the Native American Church or any of the various sects of Christianity that have gained followers within the Navajo Nation provide specific doctrines about the body, health, and curing. I focused on these issues to nuance the degree to which these religious beliefs have influenced understandings about health and well-being as well as choices in regard to medical care for oneself and one's family members. I also attempted to address additional questions raised by Kunitz regarding whether the Native American Church and the various sects of Christianity currently present on the reservation have formulated their own distinct notions about disease causation and classification (Kunitz 1983:130). This effort was particularly successful when I conducted interviews with members of families within which religious pluralism exists. I attribute this to the fact that rather than passively living their religious or medical beliefs and practices, these individuals are being challenged on these important topics and have therefore thought them through very carefully.

Consider, for example, Eloise and Harrison Watchman, of Fort Defiance, Arizona. The Watchmans have been married for over thirty-five years, and they shared a remarkable story about respect for each others' religious beliefs during times of family illness. In discussing his personal choices in life, Mr. Watchman revealed a refreshingly forthright pragmatism. Harrison told me that his grandfather, a traditional ceremonial practitioner, tried to teach him that ceremony, but "I never picked up any of his singing ways or any of his teachings. . . . I have no Navajo culture." He explained further:

> HW: We came from a very, very, very poor family. Well, I came from a very poor family. My mom was a rug weaver and she used to do rugs. . . . My father did different odd jobs, he was mostly in El Paso doing labor during the 50s and 60s. . . . Sometimes we didn't have nothing to eat. Sometimes we'd find some crusty bread, and then my mom would bring back some bacon from somewhere and she would fry it in the pan, and then me and my little sister, we used to dip our bread right into the grease there [makes a gobbling motion with his hands and mouth]. . . . But that's what drove me

to stay in school there. . . . Everything that I was taught, everything that has guided my life came from boarding school. (H.
Watchman, June 21, 2005)

When Eloise introduced herself and her husband, she quickly said,
"Harrison is a born-again Christian, but I am traditional" (June 21, 2005).
She excused herself shortly after our interview was under way, at which
point Harrison mentioned that he was "raised Christian Reformed" while
"Eloise is a Catholic" (June 21, 2005). When Eloise rejoined the interview, she offered this explanation of how family members respect their
differences in religious preference.

> EW: We asked for [Christian] prayer requests [when Harrison was
> ill] and because [of] the way Harrison was brought up he chose—I
> guess it is just an understanding between us . . . that he didn't want
> to practice any type of Navajo religion or have any kind of cere-
> mony performed on him, and so I respected his wishes. . . . But
> [we wanted] to try to strengthen . . . ourselves with the help of
> God. I think that was probably the best decision we went through.
> Along with some of Harrison's illnesses, there were times when I
> actually think that God presented himself to Harrison. He's got
> some real nice, some real neat stories about some of the times that
> he felt that. I think that God was close. I guess you hear about
> dreams or predictions or things that he saw through his illnesses,
> and we just knew that God was there for him. So because of that,
> we just didn't go through any type of Navajo religious ceremony
> for him. (E. Watchman, June 21, 2005)

Their agreement to allow each other to pursue personal religious
choices without interference from the other was tested, however, with the
onset of parental responsibilities. As Eloise explained, a critical childhood
illness caused them to rethink this agreement and come to terms with
which medical and religious options should be sought in times of need.

> EW: Like I said, we met thirty-five years ago, and my family is very tra-
> ditional. We practiced [the] Navajo tradition and we had ceremonies

done and Harrison respects that. . . . So I guess the understanding was always that . . . if one of the kids got sick, I always told him that I would just use every resource that I could to find help if they ever got sick. And the first encounter that we had was when my daughter, the oldest one, was two years old or a year old and she got really sick, and she cried like a whole week and couldn't eat, had diarrhea. So we had prayers done on her—

HW: We took her to a doctor and the doctor couldn't do anything.

EW: There was really nothing that we could do for her, so finally I told him I have to resort to the Navajo way, to my tradition. So we went to see a crystal gazer. When we went there they took a piece of glass out of her stomach, and then after that she got well and there was nothing wrong—all the sickness that she had just left her. So I guess in a way it made him kind of like a believer. But he never really said "I really believe that" or anything. But . . . from that day I think he has understood . . . "If you have to practice the Navajo way, then do it and I won't stand in your way." And he's pretty good about it. (E. Watchman, June 21, 2005)

This type of situation is not unusual. Other consultants discussed the ongoing commitment required to negotiate between divergent religions within one family. In doing so, key differences are nuanced. In what follows, for example, Asdzaan Taachiini from Vanderwagen, New Mexico, distinguishes between what outside researchers tend to refer to as "Navajo religion" and the "Navajo way of life." Most Navajo insist that these are artificial categories used to describe what is fundamentally a way of life rather than a religion. Taachiini followed this pattern of Navajo logic by choosing to refer to involvement with Christianity from a young age as "the Christian way of life" rather than involvement with a "Christian religion." As she pointed out:

AT: Ever since I was a little child, I was raised as a Christian. My maternal grandmother was Christian and so when I was growing up, I was exposed to the Christian way of life, and so we've been taken to church and we participated in Sunday Schools and Bible studies sessions. My grandmother took us to these Christian churches and

I've been involved with Christianity. . . . When I met my husband, it was a little difficult in that my husband is a traditional Navajo. . . . Today I still have some difficulty in trying to connect with traditional values or traditional ways of believing, and ceremonialism is kind of hard for me. However, I just continue to believe in Christianity and my children are all Christian, and we attend church and we continue to do so. But for my husband's side of the family, they are traditional practitioners and so we just kind of work around that. But for myself, I'm still Christian and I don't [plan to] change to any other's [religion] at this point. (Taachiini, June 2, 2005)

Leeanne Johnson of Vanderwagen, New Mexico's description of the delicate negotiations that must continually occur between multiple generations of a large Navajo family is particularly telling.

LJ: I grew up in a Christian home. My parents were very, very diligent. . . . They made us go to church every Sunday. And every Wednesday night there [were] prayer meetings and so my whole family was required to be there—whether we liked it or not. . . . But I think through that you make good choices in life. And we had a set of missionaries that came from Kansas City that was running the church. I really appreciate them because they were like my mentor parents because my parents, both of them, had very little or limited education. But my missionary, that really, really motivated me to stay in school. How easy life would be if I went beyond high school. . . . And things I learned from them I practice still today. . . . I went to college in the Mormon environment. . . . That just supported even more of my purpose in life. And I am really happy that I went the way that I did. . . . My parents talked to us about the traditional way of life, that there is that existence. There is a Native American Church, they talked to us about that. . . . These were choices that we could take, but basically our foundation was already kind of like bottled in a really secure place in our minds. At least for me it was. It was like I knew what my foundation was. And I knew how we were raised. I knew the importance of prayer. And I knew the importance of family. . . . When I'd come home here, my parents were practicing a little bit of [the] traditional [ways]. They would do the Beauty Way [*Hoozhónee*] singing and it just correlates nicely with their philosophy—with the Mormon Church and the philosophy of the Christian church. So my parents are saying, "Every day you should be in the mentality. You just don't think that today is Sunday and today you are somewhere. You know, it is every day, you just don't forget about it. It should be a part of your everyday routine." . . . And right now we practice a lot of the traditional ways. We go to Beauty Way singing. We partake of our families who are having different types of ceremony. We go there. My sister sometimes is into Native American Church services. We go there, we will help them with the celebration or whatever is going down there. But we don't really separate. I tell [them] there is no separation. All of this is just a strand—if people have faith in something, you will have respect for that. Because they are your relatives, she is your aunt, she is your sister, he is your brother. So she is not different with her religion. I try to be an example too, to be a part of everything that my family partakes of. And not say "we don't believe that" or "if you don't believe in our way don't come" or "you are not invited" or anything like that. I try to be neutral about everything. . . . But all of our experiences have been good. It has not disrupted our family life and values. It has not disrupted that. (Johnson, July 3, 2005)

Furthermore, as the next two stories exemplify, within a context of such religious complexity, labels such as Christian, born-again Christian, Native American Church, traditionalist, and Catholic can be misleading and confusing. Harrison Watchman described what it means to him to be a born-again Christian:

HW: A lot of people have different versions of born-again. The way the Pentecostal people talk about born-again Christians is, you go to church and in the Bible it says "I am the way and the life" and "nobody comes to my father except through me." So that is one way of saying that you are gonna be a Christian and then forgive all of your sins and then give your soul or your heart back to the

Lord. In the Pentecostal Way they said that you pray hard . . . and you ask the Lord for forgiveness and you receive what they call the Holy Ghost or the Holy Spirit, and you have probably heard of people speaking in tongues and shaking and dancing. But I never went that far, and they say that when you do that you're a born-again Christian. But with my belief I think a born-again Christian is when you give yourself to the Lord and you—I guess you feel comfortable, there's a heaven and hell, right? So they say you always want to go to heaven, so you prepare yourself for that. You always try to give yourself to God and live by God's word, but not everybody can do that. I myself can't live every day by God's rules. I make a mistake every once in a while, but I think born-again Christian is when you believe in the Lord and try to live by his word. And that is my interpretation. Some people say you have to receive the Holy Ghost and start shaking and start speaking in tongues, which I don't believe in. That's just my version and I've been around Pentecostal ever since, shoot, ever since I was nine years old. So that's my interpretation. (H. Watchman, June 21, 2005)

In like fashion, Julia Mathis, a devout Catholic from Chinle, Arizona, who also uses traditional herbal remedies for personal health problems, described how she differentiates between Christian and Catholic—a distinction I would not have anticipated before beginning this project.

JM: I don't consider myself a Christian, but I feel that I am a strong Catholic because not only do I pray in the church, but I pray here at home. Not just through the Lord God, but when I am here I use my corn pollen [tádídíín] . . . and then I go to church as well. So I pray with different things in mind—the Lord, Jesus, and then all the Holy People. I've asked for prayers from the church, and they help me. Just like, I went through a real bad depression. I hit bottom, you know. And I was almost over the edge. And I sought help not only from the Catholic Church but [also from] the Baptist Church, the different churches that offers prayers. . . .

MS: You said you don't consider yourself a Christian, but you do consider yourself a Catholic. How are those different?

JM: See, people say they're Christian, like the ones that go to other churches, they say "I am a Christian" just because they go to church. Every Sunday they go to church. Any time there are services, they are in church. So they feel that to be in church and to be praying all the time, you're a Christian. But for me, I am a Catholic. I am a strong believer in the Lord and in Jesus, but I don't like to say that I am a Christian because being a Christian, you have to be sinless, you have to be free of sin.

MS: Oh, I see.

JM: You have to just give everything up. You've got to be out there to witness to the people. You've got to give the first commandment. . . . Where for me, I am not gonna say that I am not gonna sin. I fall, I pick myself up. (Mathis, June 11, 2005)

I therefore make no attempt in the body of this text to categorize the Navajo individuals with whom I consulted in terms of religious affiliation. Instead, I report the self-identifiers they used to describe either themselves or others.

The multiple narratives captured in subsequent chapters argue against a static view of health seeking among the Navajo. I have therefore come to conceive of my analytic objective as threefold. First, I wish to gain an understanding of how Navajo people inscribe and reinscribe differences onto their bodies so they can reiterate their collective identity within the medical context and distinguish it from non-Navajoness—however that distinction is personally understood. Second, I wish to nuance the ways traditional Navajo ceremonial practitioners, peyote road men, and Pentecostal and Baptist pastors each stake their claims in religious terms while drawing on several discourses—including those of traditional Navajo religion, the Native American Church, and Christianity—regarding the moral value of the Holy People, the Creator, and God. A major concern of this project is thus to learn how each type of healer justifies his or her moral worth and legitimizes his or her therapeutic power and, by extension, how each patient legitimizes the moral worth of his or her chosen therapy. Third, I wish to elucidate the health-seeking behaviors through which

Navajo families negotiate the services available to them by treaty with the federal government within a context of multiple medical and religious options, with special emphasis on how they have found a place for biomedicine within their world.

ZOOMING OUT

The primary focus of this study is not transplantation or any other specific type of biomedical technology per se. As research in numerous cross-cultural settings has shown, the globalization of biomedicine and its frequently invasive technologies allows these forms of health care to transcend geopolitical boundaries and to be carried out within the nexus between global forces and socially constructed local identities (Manderson and Whiteford 2000:1–2). The connection between the global and the local cannot be overstated at this point in time. This is evident when in the midst of a single conversation Julia Mathis describes the ancient beliefs about blood her grandmother passed on to her that are relevant to transfusions as well as what she learned about them on "the news" (Mathis June 11, 2005).

An analysis of the ways the local—in this case, the Navajo traditional religious-medical system in combination with the Native American Church and its values—is negotiated within two powerful global forces—Christianity and allopathic medicine—initially introduced to the Navajo as a means by which to further colonization offers the potential for greater insight into the interaction between the local and the global.[4]

In the broadest sense, this project is about globalization versus localization; that is, how components of biomedical health services—transfusion, CPR, amputation, surgery, and organ transplantation—are situated within the context of local understandings of illness, spirituality, health, curing, identity, oppositional politics, and death. Through its selection of ethnographic area—the Navajo Nation, currently more than 290,000 people, the majority of whom occupy a 13 million acre reservation that spans parts of Arizona, New Mexico, and Utah—and topic, the project merges two of the various subjects that have come to define medical anthropology since the mid-1970s: indigenous systems of medical practice and new biomedical technologies (Cambrosio, Young, and Lock 2000:3).

This study also revisits a long-standing interest of cultural anthropology—medical and religious pluralism—to explore the dialectics of healing power within the context of articulations among local experience, shifting religious affiliations, colonization, collective identity, historical trauma, and global processes. The past—including the cultural traumas of battles, forced marches, internment at Fort Sumner, and other indignities—is recalled through language. It is also recalled through association with bodily differences in the medical context, wherein it is conjoined with the capacity to make difference visible. Information drawn from participant observation and consultations with traditional practitioners, amputees, diagnosticians, Native American Church road men, organ recipients, Navajo Christians, grandparents, fathers, mothers, sons, and daughters reveals that medicine is a key aspect of the cultural positioning by which contemporary Navajo people define both themselves and the colonizing Other. At the broadest level, such demarcations between Navajo and non-Navajo bodies serve as signs to call up collective memories that remind Navajo people of traumas their ancestors endured at the hands of the colonizers. When recognized, these prompts reaffirm individual and familial commitments to Navajo cultural ways, family values, and the teachings of the Holy People.

CHAPTER TWO

Christianity, Biomedicine, and the Native American Church

*The gambler who was finally overcome by Sun's child was so
angry at his defeat that he hurled maledictions at the people:
"I will kill you all with lightning! I will send war and disease
among you! May fire burn you! May the waters drown you!"*

(Reichard 1950:275)

*The Gambler is called the "Nááhwíiłbįįhí." It is very bad, you
know. It happened . . . somewhere in Chaco Canyon, in Chaco
ruins at some point in time. . . . I guess there were gods that
were able to overpower people and make them their slaves. . . .
There is some game activity that took place, where he [the
Gambler] was winning. He was sent off, shot off into the moon
somewhere. And the moon god over there made him, his own
people move on, way to the east, and there is speculation that
the people . . . that were made for him again out there were the
white people, were the Spaniards, the Europeans. And some
day it is all coming back. "I will come back. I will get back. I*

will get even with you. I will be back. And you will see what I am about in the future!"

(Kenneth Black, Jr., June 16, 2005)

By the fifteenth century, when Europeans began taking control of what was later known as the Americas, colonization was explicitly associated with conquest (Tinker 1993:119). Thus, although Navajo interactions with Spaniards varied over time depending on the objectives of those in charge at any given moment, military engagements and other forms of hostility prevailed. This resulted in part from the fact that the Spanish had just completed seven centuries of conflict with North Africans that left them resolved to conquer, rather than negotiate with, peoples other than themselves (Iverson 2002:21–30). An additional factor was the Spanish preference to have Navajo women and children as slaves, a situation that fostered cultural and economic exchanges and ultimately resulted in an "enmeshment of borderland interests" (Brooks 1999:31).

At the time of initial European contact, the Navajo relied on hunting-and-gathering–based subsistence supplemented by some agriculture (Brugge 1983). Extended family units, generally centered on matrilocal residence and the strength of the clan system, lived in widely dispersed settlements. Spanish Franciscans first attempted to convert Navajo people when they built a mission along the Rio Grande in 1627; it was soon abandoned (Hodge, Hammond, and Rey 1945:85–89). Although their oral history preconditioned Navajo people to seek new forms of curing when faced with critical illness, subsequent Franciscan efforts over the next two centuries met with little success until 1749, when a mission was again established. Approximately five hundred–six hundred Navajo settled near this facility close to the Pueblos of Laguna and Acoma, where they were offered food and protection from marauding Utes. The Navajo only stayed until the food ran out, however (Pavlik 1997:43–44). A significant commitment to improve American Indian health care did not exist during the colonial era (Trennert 1998:15).

When livestock was introduced into the region, a pastoral economy developed based on sheep and goats. In Navajo oral tradition, these and other forms of herding and farmyard animals are attributed directly to descendants of the Gambler. Frank Goldtooth of Tuba City, Arizona, provided this account to Stanley Fishler in 1950:

> There was once a man who was a great gambler. He was very lucky at
> winning many things. He was called Earth Winner or nixilbi hi. After a
> time of being very lucky, he began to lose everything he had won. He
> talked too much about what he had and whom he had gotten it from.
> All of the people decided it was not fair for someone to talk like that
> so they took a black bow and put it on his tongue and cut it out. The
> people put his tongue on backwards, and the man began to mutter a
> new language. They put him on an arrow and shot him to heaven, and
> he kept mumbling all of the time. When he was shot into the air, he said,
> "I will be back someday to settle with you." (Fishler 1953:105)

Navajo people turn to the stories that constitute Navajo oral histories,
such as this account about the Gambler, as important sources of information
about their world because the stories contain ancestral knowledge, understood as part of the Navajo charter for life. These narratives do more than
simply tell where the Navajo came from and where they have been; they
constitute a philosophical system that underlies the cultural construction of
every aspect of the Navajo world. Navajo people like Frank Goldtooth, Leroy
Nelson, and Kenneth Black, Jr., seek guidance on matters of current concern
from the oral history because it is a wellspring for explaining the nature of
life, the world, and all living things—including livestock and Europeans.
Ancestral knowledge is considered a fundamental element of present reality
rather than a "distanced, inert position of wisdom or truth"; for the Navajo,
history is "the process of what is constantly in the making" (Pinxten and
Farrer 1990:249).

According to Goldtooth, when the Gambler got to the middle heavens he
encountered deities known as "Bego Black," "Bego Blue," "Bego Yellow,"
"Bego White," and "Bego Silver." When he asked these deities to recreate
some of the monstrous beings who had once devoured Earth Surface
People, they instead fashioned cows, hogs, chickens, wagons, and mules.
After these things were made, "This man and his things were sent away.
They all started off and came down in the land to the east, and that is where
they live (Europe). The descendants of this man are thought to be Spanish.
The Pueblos and some Navaho believe they got the sheep and horses from
these Spaniards. The Navaho had sheep over here which had long curly black,
brown and white wool. They also had goats of all kinds and horses and small

mules. The big mules, sheep with rough heavy wool and the chickens came from overseas" (Fishler 1953:105–106). The Navajo population and area of settlement gradually expanded as new crops, animals, and technological innovations continued to be added to their subsistence base during the Spanish and American periods.

HWÉELDI

On February 2, 1848, the United States defeated Mexico in the Mexican War and, through the Treaty of Guadalupe Hidalgo, assumed political jurisdiction over most of what is known today as the American Southwest, including the Navajo homelands. Members of an 1849 U.S. military expedition into Navajo country were impressed by the size of the Navajo sheep and goat herds, as well as tribal members' well-nourished and healthy condition.

Westward expansion resulted in frequent clashes between Navajo and outsiders, leading ultimately to American military intervention. The Navajo endured many hardships at the hands of the Gambler's descendants, the European and Euro-Americans conquerors. The general good health noted in the 1840s was undermined by Kit Carson's scorched-earth tactics and the forced march to and interment at Fort Sumner from 1863 to 1868 (see Chapter 1; Bailey 1988[1964]; Correll 1979; Johnson 1973). Those compelled to go on this journey were apprehensive, for they understood that leaving the area demarcated by their sacred mountains was potentially dangerous because it violated Navajo stewardship and reciprocity with the Diyin Dine'é. According to the dictates of Changing Woman, to maintain good fortune and avert catastrophe, prayers and offerings were to be made regularly at specific sites within Navajo sacred geography (Aberle 1993:161, 169; Kelley and Francis 1994:33–35; Wood and Vannette 1979:24). A Catholic Church was established at Bosque Redondo, although few Navajo used it (Pavlik 1997:44). Also, as was the case with many other colonized people around the globe, it was while interned that the Navajo were first introduced to allopathic medicine.

At Fort Sumner the Navajo suffered from difficult living conditions, some of which hastened or exacerbated the spread of disease. Medical reports from the overcrowded camps document that pneumonia, typhoid, dysentery, pleurisy, and various skin problems and fevers were rampant. Epidemics of cholera, measles, and smallpox spread repeatedly throughout the reservation. In addition, unfamiliar foods and alkaline water led to gastric upset and other problems (Johnson 1973:32, 149, 152, 214, 226; Trennert 1998:24, 33).

For the most part, while at Hwéeldi the Navajo continued to rely on their own traditional healers. These practitioners were limited because they were dislocated from their sacred geography. They were also hampered by not having access to a full range of pharmacopoeia—over a hundred roots, seeds, leaves, and other natural products used historically by tribal members for both internal and external purposes—as laxatives, purges, diuretics, poultices, and pain relievers (Wyman and Harris 1941).

They carried on the best they could throughout the Navajo internment, using sweat lodges wherein heated stones sprinkled with water engulfed the patient in steam and performing ceremonies on a regular basis (Trennert 1998:32–33). Oral narratives passed down through the generations from the time of internment document performances of the Night Way, Fire Dance, and Enemy Way (Johnson 1973:264). Notably, traditional practitioners are said to have conducted Evil Way and Enemy Way ceremonies at Bosque Redondo "*to purify individuals contaminated by contact with disease-carrying outsiders*" (Trennert 1998:33, emphasis added). Oral accounts detail that the Enemy Way ceremony had to be modified while the Navajo were in captivity so it could be performed without horses (Johnson 1973:119, 215). Descendants of those who survived Fort Sumner recall with great pride performances of the *Mạ'ii' bizéé'nat'ą́*, or "Put Bead in Coyote's Mouth," ceremony. In the Navajo view, this rite enabled them to successfully negotiate the treaty that resulted in their release and the establishment of their reservation (Johnson 1973:136, 178, 212). In addition, survivors' accounts document that Navajo apprentices learned the Sucking Way and the Chiricahua Apache Wind Way from other Native healers at Fort Sumner (see Frisbie 1992:463 for more on this diffusion of ceremonial knowledge while at Fort Sumner).

The global forces of Christianity and allopathic medicine to which the Navajo have been systematically subjected from the time of Hwéeldi to the present are not "a-cultural" or "supracultural";[1] rather, then as now, they are "historical artifacts that derive from Western domination: they reflect

Western values of rationality, competition, and progress, in which context there is an implicit assumption that with modernization, local 'traditional' institutions and structures will be replaced by Western systems and patterns" (Manderson and Whiteford 2000:3). As John and Jean Comaroff have demonstrated through their extensive work among the Tswana in South Africa, Christians felt mandated to both heal and convert by specific biblical texts, specifically the Gospel of Matthew and Luke 9.1–2—wherein the apostles were called together and given the power and authority "to cure diseases" and were then immediately sent "out to preach the kingdom of God and to heal" (Comaroff and Comaroff 1997:332). Within such contexts, colonizers make concerted efforts to undermine the authority of traditional healing specialists.

A plethora of correspondence between doctors and military personnel at Fort Sumner demonstrates both groups' opposition to traditional Navajo medical activities. George Gwyther, the camp physician at Fort Sumner from 1862 to 1865, attributed the captives' poor health directly to "the influence of their medicine-men," who he believed encouraged them to avoid allopathic providers (Gwyther quoted in Trennert 1998:33). In reference to the custom of compensating Navajo singers for their services, post commander General Crocker wrote, "These Indian doctors are the worst class of humbugs[,] frequently leaving a whole family destitute of clothing for a few days attendance on a sick member of it" (Crocker quoted in Trennert 1998:33).

Navajo people would not have taken denigration of their ceremonial practitioners lightly, for healers occupy a high place within the society. While a fundamental purpose of Navajo religious ceremonies is to heal, the rituals and those who perform them hold far greater significance within the society. These men and women know best and pass on the diné bike'ji taught to the Navajo ancestors by Changing Woman; as Peter Iverson has pointed out, therefore, they are the individuals who unite "theology, law, and medicine" (1981:42).

The Navajo tendency to use multiple health care treatments is evident even at this early date. Medical records from Bosque Redondo indicate that despite initial caution regarding the new forms of treatment offered by allopathic practitioners, Navajo internees were willing to try some aspects of the newly introduced medical care. They accepted smallpox vaccinations administered by puncturing the skin, as well as pills and pain relievers, but they objected to extended stays in the camp hospital (Trennert 1998:33).[2]

The Bosque Redondo experiment ultimately proved a failure. On June 1, 1868, a treaty was signed that established a reservation on a portion of the Navajo homelands to which the captives were allowed to return.[3] The treaty required that Navajo people refrain from further military action against Euro-Americans and send their children to American schools (Correll 1979; Roessel 1980).

POST–FORT SUMNER

After the captives' return, the Navajo economy and population gradually recovered (see Bailey and Bailey 1986 for more on the reservation years). Trading posts slowly began to appear on the reservation after the transcontinental railroad was completed in the 1880s, and a barter economy developed wherein male lambs and items of Navajo manufacture were traded for coffee, flour, lard, canned goods, and other food staples (see Adams 1963; Gillmor and Wetherill 1953[1934]; Hegemann 1963; McNitt 1962; Moon 1992; Powers 2001 on traders and trading posts). The influence on diet was gradual, however, for Navajo consultants who grew up in the 1910–1920 period reported a diet composed of many wild vegetables and seeds as well as game animals such as deer, antelope, and rabbits. In addition, families consumed apricots, corn, squash, goat milk, and mutton (Wolfe 1994:437).

Systematic allopathic medicine arrived at the same time as Christianity, shortly after newly elected President Ulysses S. Grant initiated the now famous Indian Peace Policy in 1869. This policy was intended as a benevolent effort to provide for humane treatment of the Native population. Its intent was to develop reservations, create an atmosphere conducive to acculturation, place Christian men and women in charge of agency affairs, and eliminate fraud and counterproductive politics from the Indian Service. To improve the quality of reservation life and make Native Americans more receptive to the civilizing agenda, advocates of the Peace Policy recognized the need to provide Indians with federally funded medical care. "As a result, religiously oriented agency physicians became a common, if not always dependable, part of reservation life during the 1870s" (Trennert 1998:39).

The Indian Peace Policy opened the door for Christianity on the Navajo reservation, which was allocated to the Presbyterians in 1869 (Pavlik 1997:45). The first agency physician to arrive on the reservation was John Menaul. Although he did not have a medical degree, he took his post at Fort Defiance in 1871. His lack of training was not unusual, however, because no specific qualifications for agency doctors were in place at the time (Trennert 1998:44–45).

Christian missionaries are broadly understood to have "served as the vanguard of colonialism" across the globe (Comaroff 1985:1). As such, men such as Menaul are commonly implicated in imperialist expansion. While missionaries did not always work as agents of colonialism, for the most part in the Americas they were an integral part of the colonizing effort (Tinker 1993:120).[4] This is so because, as Robert Berkhofer has pointed out, the dual goals of civilizing and Christianizing Native peoples were inextricably combined in the minds of American missionaries working in the pre–Civil War period (1965:1–15).

Importantly, Menaul envisioned himself as someone "who could use medicine as a tool in the lofty goal of converting the Navajo to Christianity" (Trennert 1998:45). By way of example, non-Navajo working in clinics and schools taught that modern practices and foods were superior and that traditional Navajo ways were "old-fashioned" or "otherwise inferior," thereby undermining confidence in traditional wisdom (Kopp 1986:3). Such rhetoric was successful, for the Navajo slowly abandoned many nutritious and culturally convenient practices such as breast feeding and replaced many traditional foods with foods with less nutritional value (Kopp 1986:2–3). The latter is best exemplified by the use of white flour in the now ubiquitous fry bread.

The early years of the twentieth century were riddled with cultural and economic hardships on the Navajo reservation caused by sustained drought (Frisbie 1992:466), loss of livestock as a result of poor forage and a series of severe winters (Bailey and Bailey 1982:210), and an estimated 10 to 15 percent reservation-wide mortality rate sustained during the Spanish influenza pandemic of 1918–19 (Russell 1985:381). Lack of moisture and overgrazing, coupled with fluctuations in livestock and wool prices, resulted in a shift toward dependence on wage labor and the production of woven goods and silverwork for the off-reservation market (see Amsden 1974[1934],

Kent 1985, and Wheat 2003 on weaving; Cirillo 1992 and Lincoln 1982 on silver; and Parezo 1991[1983] on dry paintings on boards). To accommodate developing resource extraction–based industries, including coal and uranium, a federally designed centralized government—the Navajo Nation Council—was installed on the Navajo reservation in the 1920s. Since its inception, Navajo leaders have adapted and molded this system into an effective means by which to control and dispense much-needed goods and services (see Iverson 1981, 2002 on the development of the Navajo Nation).

In the opening decades of the twentieth century, many wild plants used for food became scarce and household gardening became difficult as a result of drought and land erosion (Wolfe 1994:438). Navajo people became dependent on trading posts for staples such as flour, potatoes, sugar, coffee, lard, and salt (Steggerda and Eckhardt 1941). Federally mandated stock reductions diminished family herds in the 1930s. This constituted a major loss, since the typical Navajo diet consisted of mutton, coffee, wheat flour, and potatoes, with occasional canned fruit or fresh fruits and vegetables (Kopp 1986:6). The stock reduction, coupled with sequential droughts, resulted in increased dependence on wage labor on and off the reservation, as well as increased acceptance of non-Navajo religious beliefs and practices such as Catholicism, Protestantism, Mormonism, and the Native American Church (Aberle 1982b). These were also decades of intense prophetic activity (Schwarz 2001:70–110).

Mission schools were essentially the only facilities serving the growing Navajo population on the reservation until the 1930s, when Superintendent of Indian Affairs John Collier helped develop a network of community day schools. Prior to that, Navajo children were sent to off-reservation boarding schools. Day schools were followed by public schools in the 1950s. Increased exposure to the non-Navajo world through military service and employment in war-related industries during World War II led to the adoption of non-native foods (Kopp 1986:9) and lifestyles and thus to increased use of government-run health care and educational facilities (Adair, Deuschle, and Barnett 1988:15–45; Emerson 1983). One thing remained constant from the time of the compulsory school attendance provision in the 1868 peace treaty until the 1960s: the general Euro-American sentiment to "remove their natal culture and language" (Niezen 2003:87) and see Native American people assimilate into mainstream America (Adams 1995; Emerson 1983).

Christianization played a major part in this process. Consultants' narratives are replete with stories of the role of religion in their first boarding school experiences. Harrison Watchman recalled how Christianity "found him" at boarding school:

> HW: They lined us up and said 1, 2, 3, 1, 2, and 3 going down the line. "All you 'ones' step forward, all you 'twos' step back." So they divided us that way. . . . And when they did this, "You're gonna be LDS [the Church of Jesus Christ of Latter-Day Saints]," and "you're gonna be Christian Reformed," and "you are going to be Catholic." . . . So that's how my religion was selected. I became a Christian Reformed. I went to [the] Christian Reformed [Church] all the time and that's how I was raised. And then during summer school and during summer vacation we would have Bible classes, and Christian Reformed would have Bible classes. She's a Catholic [referring to his wife, Eloise] and I'm Christian Reformed, but this is the way I was raised. . . . When I was going to school I said I wish I was a LDS because Christmas parties, man, they were making all kinds of noise, they were making all kinds of games, and people were looking over the fence and LDS is having more fun. The Christian Reformed Church, they would give us just a pen for Christmas and that was it, but that's how my religion was selected. (H. Watchman, June 21, 2005)

While Harrison Watchman used humor to assuage his discomfort over the inequity of toy and gift distribution between religious groups, Thomas Deschene, Jr., a Native American Church road man from Kayenta, Arizona, learned from other students how to manipulate the system to his benefit. He chuckled while telling this story:

> TD: When I came up to Kayenta boarding school, we went to have church on Sunday, then I noticed some kids had—around Christmas? . . . They had a whole bunch of toys. And candy, and bags, small bags. And I asked how they did it, "How'd you guys get a lot of toys?" Then they told me, "Go to all different kinds of church[es]. Go to different churches here and there and then during

Christmas time they will send you lots of toys" (Laughs). Then I
started doing that, going to Assembly of God, Catholic, Bible
Church, and different ones. (Deschene, June 15, 2005)

Like Harrison Watchman, Kenneth Black, Jr., recalled in this account
that when he attended boarding school in the 1960s, students were given
numbers by which they were assigned religious affiliations. He used humor
to couch unsettling childhood memories of unexplained depersonalization.

KB: My first encounter with any religion was Christianity. . . . I was
in boarding school and we were given numbers. "You have number
'five,' you go to this wing over here. You have the Catholics, over
there" or "the Seventh-Day Adventist is over here." Every Sunday
we would go there as part, I guess, of the curriculum. And then
there would be the Mormons and there would the Protestants. They
would give you numbers. I don't know about Christianity. . . . You
had to participate. . . . We didn't actually go to a church, it was
more like a boarding school that has these dorm wings and that is
where all the sessions take place. I believe my first church that I
went to was Catholic. . . . But over time I got baptized in a lot of
Christian churches. I got baptized in Mormon, I got baptized in
Seventh-Day Adventist, I got baptized in Pentecostal. I don't know
what it all meant. Just so I go somewhere and get into the water,
get baptized. (Black, June 16, 2005)

Thomas Deschene, Jr., once again applied humor to good effect while
recalling his first encounters with Christian training: "They had a church
teaching . . . every Wednesday from about 3:00 until 4:00, and they would
provide candy for us to learn a certain verse in the Bible. If you learn the
verse, the following week then we can just eat candy" (chuckles) (Deschene,
June 15, 2005). With time, however, Deschene became savvy about the
politics of religious studies. His next comments make clear that over the
years he has come to realize what was lost when he was vying for candies
or toys: "But . . . people say now that we should learn about our traditional
culture. And they should have done that way back, if what church we
belonged to, if they could have put traditional [teachings as an option]

back then, there are a lot of things about the traditional that we should have learned, and some of the Navajo traditional [culture] would have been saved. We think that way now" (Deschene, June 15, 2005).

Thomas Deschene, Jr., is using a childhood tale about encounters with Christianity to make a statement about colonialism; that is, the colonizers have gradually replaced Navajo traditional culture. Whether through Bible School psalm or nursery school rhyme, whether through American history lessons learned in English, *Sesame Street,* or MTV, Navajo oral history and traditions have been replaced year after year by the dominant culture's narratives. As Mae Ann Bekis, a Blessing Way singer from Tó'tsoh, Arizona, who is also an herbalist, noted, at one time children "were brought up with a lot of help by their mother and father, and there is a lot of don't do this and don't do that, which we don't have any more because of TV now. And the kids are more interested in TV. They don't ask questions no more. Like to their grandparents. They never say, 'Grandfather or grandmother, tell me the story of certain things.' And they don't ask us no more of those questions, but they just take on the TV any more, which is very, very unlike Navajo" (Bekis, August 5, 1992).

Collectively, these personal testimonies fit well with received wisdom on Native American Christianity, which has tended to focus on missionaries and their intentions. Michael McNally has pointed out, however, that this stance fails to equip us with the ability to appreciate the complexity and variety of ways of being both Native and Christian. Such a focus keeps our attention on Christianity as an indicator of acculturation while blinding us to its possibilities as a potential resource in Native struggles to act as agents in a history otherwise conditioned by domination. In other words, we need to think about "what native peoples made of the Christian tradition" (McNally 2000:834–36). McNally suggests, "The signs and practices of the Christian tradition, variously presented by various Euro-American Christians to various native communities under various material and social circumstances, are better understood as part of the process of culture change rather than as a product of that change. This is because those signs and practices—especially the practices—became a medium through which many native people exercised their own agency within the tight confines of history and through which some articulated resistance as well as accommodation" (McNally 2000:841). McNally calls for analysis on the basis of practice rather than belief, and, as will be demonstrated, the Navajo case offers opportunities for doing so. Missions did not only provide education and spiritual guidance, they also provided early health care to the Navajo.

After decades of requests for hospitals from missionaries and Indian agents, followed by rejections of allocations of funds, the Good Shepard Hospital, established by the Protestant Episcopal Church, opened its doors in Fort Defiance in 1897. The Methodists, the Protestant Episcopal Church, and the Christian Reformed Church of America had missions in place on the Navajo reservation by the turn of the twentieth century—at Fort Defiance in 1890, Fort Defiance in 1897, and Fort Defiance and Tohatchi in 1900, respectively (Pavlik 1997:45). Catholics reentered the Navajo world when Father Anselm Weber arrived in 1898 to build St. Michaels Mission. This was followed by a boarding school at St. Michaels in 1902, as well as churches at Chinle in 1905 and at Luckachukai in 1910.

Despite intense need, no further hospitals were built until 1911. In that year a congressional appropriation for Indian Health Services resulted in funds for small school hospitals at Leupp and Tuba City, which opened in 1912. A larger forty-bed school hospital in Fort Defiance, for which construction began prior to 1911, also opened in 1912 (Trennert 1998:110). The Navajo Agency Sanatorium opened in late 1915 to care for Navajo tuberculosis victims (Trennert 1998:111). These facilities, however, were chronically underfunded and understaffed.

In the days before antibiotics, Navajo justifiably considered hospitals places for the dead, places to be avoided at all costs unless one was ready to die (Adair, Deuschle, and Barnett 1988:22; Kunitz 1983:131; Reichard 1950:84). Buella Allen, the first Navajo woman physician who currently heads the Tsaile Health Clinic, provided this explanatory account:

> BA: When I was a child, and even at the present time, there are people that come into the hospital who will not get onto the gurneys because the gurneys are called "carriers of dead people," and a lot of times the ambulances are thought of that way. The term for them is "carriers of dead people." The expression is *hoł ndaabąąsígíí*. So it's like a *ch'įįdii* (ghost) is a spirit . . . or it's something that has been dead and the contamination is still there. And if they're carrying that and you get on it, that's liable to affect you too. So a family came in

to Fort Defiance one time and they came into the hallway, and there was a gurney that was up against the door . . . just inside of the entrance, and one of the young men jumped up on it and sat on it and one of the elders told him, "You are sitting on one of those hoł ndaabąąsígíí" and he jumped off like that [snaps her fingers] and moved quickly. . . . Back in the day when hospitals were established out here, that's what happened with people is they died in the hospital. We had a lot of tuberculosis and people when they got tuberculosis died off by droves, whole families wiped out. So the idea of someone coming into the hospital is like, you go there to die, you do not go there to be cured. That idea has changed with time because people have realized that [allopathic] medical care is valuable and it improves things. (B. Allen, June 10, 2005)

The principal legislation authorizing federal funds for health services to Native American tribes is Public Law 67-85, the Snyder Act of 1921. In ratifying the Snyder Act, the federal government intended to provide appropriations "for the benefit, care, and assistance of the Indians throughout the United States . . . [and] for relief of distress and conservation of health" (Public Law 67-85, November 2, 1921). Navajo utilization of biomedical facilities and procedures has fluctuated historically in direct response to changes in available services and the diseases most prevalent at the time (Trennert 1998). By the mid-1950s, however, when responsibility for Natives' health care was transferred from the Bureau of Indian Affairs to the Public Health Service, Navajo people became increasingly avid consumers of biomedicine. This trend continued during the 1960s (Porvaznik 1967). By some accounts, over time Navajo people decided that certain types of illnesses are better treated by allopathic doctors and other types of illnesses are better treated by traditional practitioners. I asked Dr. Buella Allen if she thought this was accurate. She replied in the affirmative, and I inquired further:

MS: So what types of illnesses do you think they think are better treated by biomedical doctors and which ones do you think they feel are better treated by traditional doctors?
BA: Infections, gastronomies, fevers, strep throats, gallbladder infections, those kinds of things [are better treated by allopathic doctors].

I have had patients coming in saying, "I went to the medicine man for this and he told me to come to the hospital." He said . . . "You've got this problem, I think that's what it is and they can treat it better. So I will treat you for this over here and make sure that you are OK, and then you go to the hospital and get their medicine."

MS: So the ceremonial practitioners send patients to the hospital for infections?

BA: Yeah, there's cross-referral on a lot of those things. That's the value of the shots. People have learned that if they have fevers or if they have infections that shots are helpful, and that goes back a long way. (B. Allen, June 10, 2005)

On the face of it, none of this should be surprising, for, as has been demonstrated on numerous occasions throughout the lengthy period in which Navajo people have been studied, the Navajo are well recognized for their willingness to accept foreign technology such as agricultural methods from Pueblo groups or sheep herding methods from the Spanish. In the mid-1940s, Clyde Kluckhohn and Dorothea Leighton noted:

The really astonishing thing is the degree to which The People have taken over parts of white technology with so little alteration in the distinctive flavor of their own way of life. Most Indian groups which have accepted so many European material objects have tended to abandon their own customs and become a rather degraded sort of "poor white." The Navahos show, on the one hand, a general lack of emotional resistance to learning new techniques and using foreign tools, and on the other, a capacity for making alien techniques *fit in with their preexistent design for living*. (1974[1946]:67, emphasis added)

The point made by Kluckhohn and Leighton, and repeated elsewhere, is that the Navajo tend to make introduced technology fit their own design for living (1974[1946]:67). While this tendency is now an accepted fact in Navajo studies, the process by which it is accomplished has yet to be made completely transparent.

Evon Vogt (1961) maintained that the Navajo have followed what has been termed an "incorporative" pattern of integrating introduced or borrowed cultural materials into what he terms their "core." This has been evident since their initial contact with other Native peoples, through the Spanish and Mexican periods, and on to the present day. Edward Spicer has noted that the defining aspect of incorporative integration is that elements are adopted from one society into another in such a way that they seamlessly "conform to the meaningful and functional relations within the latter" (1961:530). In Vogt's view, attempts by non-Navajo to influence core elements of the Navajo lifeway have most often been met with resistance. When adjustments are made, they follow a process whereby "elements from other cultures are incorporated into Navaho culture in such as way that the structural framework of the institutional core . . . is maintained, and the borrowed elements are fitted into place and elaborated in terms of the pre-existing patterns" (Vogt 1961:328). On the economic front, for example, this pattern of incorporation is demonstrated by the fact that Pueblo-derived agriculture, Spanish-derived sheep husbandry, Mexican-derived silver smithing, and American-derived wage labor have all been adopted while the fundamental Navajo dispersed residence pattern and accommodation of transhumance have not been altered (Wagner 1975:175–76).

In *The Main Stalk* (1984), John Farella nuances the mechanism by which the Navajo make the incorporation of outside technologies appear seamless. Criticizing what he terms previous "acculturation studies" for their overemphasis on "things," he calls instead for a consideration of philosophy of knowledge: "[T]hese technological changes are, in fact, an attempt to maintain a traditional epistemology. . . . [T]he specific epistemological strategy employed is paradoxical—a labeling of the new as old and of change as an attempt to stay the same. Thus I am arguing that the Navajos are not change oriented but rather, that they are changing in order to remain 'traditional.' Specifically, they are altering their technology to maintain their epistemology" (Farella 1984:189–90). Farella's insight that a distinction must be drawn between technology and epistemology in the Navajo case has much merit.

While I agree with Farella's point about the significance of philosophy to an understanding of Navajo strategies regarding change, I am not ready to throw out the proverbial baby with the bathwater. I also find merit in Vogt's incorporative model of integration, particularly as applied by Wagner (1975) to illuminate Navajo adoption of the Native American Church.

NATIVE AMERICAN CHURCH

Peyote is a cactus (*L. williamsii*) containing psychoactive alkaloids, including mescaline. The modern peyote religion, known as the Native American Church (NAC), became formalized in western Oklahoma sometime around 1880 (Stewart 1987:xiii). Indigenous people living in the area of peyote growth, along the lower Rio Grande and south into present-day Mexico as far as Queretaro, were familiar with the cactus and its properties at the time of European contact. Peyote, however, had been used for millennia in a much wider area—from as far south as Oaxaca, throughout central Mexico, and as far north as Santa Fe—as a medicine to be taken internally or applied to sores as a poultice, to foretell future events, to locate lost objects, as a stimulant before warfare or other strenuous activity, and in group religious practices (Stewart 1987:17). While some elements of this religion carried over into the North American version of the peyote religion—use of a gourd rattle, the ritual number four, cleansing in fire, an all-night ceremony, smoke and incense, cigarette smoking, and belief in the peyote plant's supernatural power—the differences are also significant. Those differences led Omer Stewart to conclude that the peyote religion in the United States is not a direct diffusion of an entire complex (1987:41–42).

Ethnographic, historical, and ethnomusicological evidence indicates that it was the Carrizo who originated the North American version of the peyote ritual and taught the religion to the Lipan and the Comanche of the southern plains during the second half of the nineteenth century (Stewart 1987:49–50). The religion blossomed as a result of the confluence of peoples—including several familiar with peyote and its uses—cultures, and conflicts created by the U.S. government in the establishment of Indian Territory (Stewart 1987:53). From Oklahoma it spread to the prairies and the Rocky Mountain West.

In its current form, NAC is a pan-Indian, semi-Christian, nativistic, redemptive religion focused on the ritual ingestion of peyote. David Aberle has noted that a special relationship exists between "God and the Indian, and specifically between God, peyote, and the peyotist" (Aberle 1982b:180). As part of this relationship, peyote and the peyote way are understood as having been "given to the Indians as their path to God," and it is through peyote that Native Americans are able to communicate with God (Aberle 1982b:180). In

NAC, an individual must confess all his or her sins since childhood during the initial peyote meeting (Aberle 1982b:167).

The ceremony is syncretic, embracing several central tenets of Christianity within what is best labeled a pan-Indian ritual framework. Attenuated Christianity, visible through such features as reading from the Bible, using a crucifix, and giving a biblical interpretation to nearly every phase of the ceremony, was part of the cult in the United States by 1890 (Stewart and Aberle 1984:37). The prayers and songs used in each ceremony are rendered in the language of the community in which the ceremony is performed. Two road men from the Kiowa-Comanche reservations—the Comanche chief Quanah Parker and a Caddo-Delaware medicine man named John Wilson—had a lasting influence on the developing peyote religion in the 1880s.

Parker's and Wilson's influence is reflected in two major styles of peyote meetings used to the present day. The theologies of both ceremonies are similar. Peyote comes from God, it is good, it teaches one to think good thoughts and to know good from evil, and it can cure anything as long as one is sincere and full of devotion.

In what is known as the Cross Fire ceremony, associated with John Wilson, an altar shaped like a horseshoe, rather than a crescent or half-moon, is used. In addition, a mound representing the sun is built opposite the tepee door to the east of a heart-shaped mound of ashes and a cross. A line—referred to as the "Peyote Road"—is drawn from the center of the doorway through the "sun" and on to the center of the altar, where the Chief Peyote (or exemplar button) is placed, sometimes surmounted by a crucifix. This ceremony incorporates Jesus, the crucifix, and the Bible into the meeting more often than the alternative ceremony does.

The Half Moon ceremony, which is associated with Parker and most commonly used among Navajo peyotists, is characterized by a smaller half-moon–shaped altar. This ceremony features placement of an exemplar peyote button at the center of the altar mound, prayers to the Great Spirit and Mother Earth, emphasis on Native American oral histories and prayers, the use of tobacco, and placement of sagebrush all around the outer edge of the tepee, where participants sit. Joseph Calabrese finds ideological parallels between this altar style and two fundamental Navajo beliefs. In his view, because the arc depicted in the moon is always identified as being "in the direction the sun travels" and one of the rules of every NAC meeting is that participants and ceremonial objects move around the tepee in that same clockwise (sun-wise) direction (Calabrese 1994:520), the altar's arc symbolizes Navajo views on life; second, it reinforces the structural homology of sun-wise directionality.

In the crescent moon symbol, life is depicted as a parabolic curve— increasing in potency from birth until it reaches its peak and then decreasing as it approaches death. Moreover, the officiant is referred to as a road man because the road of life is marked along the altar's crest. In the words of a road man who advised Calabrese:

> You stay on this road. If you go this way, you're gonna fall into the fire, you're gonna hurt yourself. If you go this way, you're gonna fall off the cliff. So if you stay on this road and live a good life, then you'll reach old age down on the other side. And that's the ultimate goal—that's what that represents. [And in the middle of the road they put the Father peyote?] Yeah. They say somewhere along the way you're gonna need help and you're gonna come up on that Peyote. And it's gonna help you out to continue on in life. That Peyote is there always to help you with your hardships. (Dan Goodman [fictitious name] quoted in Calabrese 1994:513)

The Navajo first became familiar with the Native American Church through the Ute and other sources at Towaoc, Colorado, as early as 1914, but they did not accept the new religion on a large scale for approximately twenty years (Stewart and Aberle 1957:25). Early Navajo peyotists are documented as having learned the Half Moon ceremony from John P. Heart, a Cheyenne from Oklahoma who brought it to the Ute sometime around 1918 (Stewart 1987:294).

Peyote meetings were initially observed on the northeastern edge of the reservation in 1935. According to David Aberle, the 1936 initiation of the now infamous livestock reduction programs on the reservation under the John Collier administration was the catalyst for the new religion's rapid acceptance and spread (Aberle 1982b). An additional motivation was the fact that members of NAC are believed to have immortal souls (niłchi'i) that return to God (Aberle 1982b:154), so the Navajo may have also sought out the religion as a cure for witchcraft.

In seeking to reconstruct a precise chronology of the development of the peyote cult among the Navajo, Omer Stewart unearthed information documenting a series of at least four peyote meetings in Lukachukai, Arizona, perhaps beginning as early as 1934 or 1935 and known to have run until 1938 (Stewart and Aberle 1957:58–59, 63, 77–78). Because she was born circa 1930, Vivian Yadeesbah of Lukachukai's memories of her father's work as a tribal police officer are especially relevant here. When I asked her about her first recollections of the Native American Church in her area of the reservation, she told me:

> VY: We were just kids. That's when my dad, my father, was a Navajo police [officer] and he had a horse. He was on horseback. . . . Every day is a problem that people report to Chinle. That's where the police station was, in Chinle. . . . They would contact him. . . . He would go there and talk to the people. I think it was mostly counseling that he probably did. But in the rare cases where it was really bad, a person would go to jail or something. . . . They [NAC members] had their first meeting. . . . And my dad was told by the police department in Chinle to be there in case things got out of hand. . . . And he would bring the peyote home. And there was a tree out in front of the hooghan and he had it hanging there. But he told us, "Never, never take that stuff as long as you live," because he said "it's a drug," but he really didn't say that it was a drug or something, he said, "it's no good for you. Don't take that, don't ever take it." And I remember it now, and I tell my kids that. (Yadeesbah, July 5, 2005)

In 1938 a second nexus of diffusion arose south of this area in the communities of Tohatchi, Fort Defiance, and Window Rock. Struggles over the religion began on the reservation when two road men were arrested that year. In 1940 the Navajo Tribal Council held hearings to determine if the NAC was a threat to the traditional ceremonial system, resulting in a ban that held until 1967 (Bailey and Bailey 1986:226; see also Wagner 1975).

Even for Dr. Buella Allen, who is more than a decade younger than Mrs. Yadeesbah, impressions of the Native American Church derived from her childhood are skewed by the fact that they come from a time of suppression. She explained: "At that time the Native American Church was very secretive and it was not an open religion like it is today. . . . The practitioners were often prosecuted for that, and there were all kinds of rumors about that religion and what it did to people and so forth. So it was not something that I was familiar with except as a kind of a secretive organization" (B. Allen, June 10, 2005).

Healing is the primary reason Navajo people give for joining the Native American Church (Aberle 1982b). It has gained wide acceptance among the Navajo, with NAC membership estimates ranging from 40 to 50 percent of the Navajo population by the 1980s (Quintero 1995:78; Wood 1982). Throughout its history within the Navajo Nation, the majority of Navajo peyotists have claimed membership in the Native American Church of Navajoland, the Native American Church of the Four Corners, or the Northern Navajoland Native American Association (see Stewart 1987).

As pointed out by Ursula Knoki-Wilson in the next account, part of NAC's appeal to contemporary Navajo people lay in its shorter ceremonies and lower costs compared with traditional services, which fit more easily into the hectic schedules of families adapting to the modern wage-work economy. In addition, while the NAC supports education and wage earning, it does not oppose the Navajo language, traditional values, or history (Frisbie 1987:198).

From the road man's perspective they would probably tell you that that ceremony is sort of an all-purpose ceremony. . . . It is for whatever purpose that the patient brings to the altar. It is how they run their ceremony. So if I wanted help with my asthma, I would go to [the] Native American Church and say, "I am having difficulty breathing; this is my problem." So I want healing for that. The ceremony will focus on my—everybody will pray and sing and everything for my asthma. And that is how you get healed. But if I went to a traditional practitioner and said "I need help with my asthma," the diagnostician might say, "Well, you need to go see a Wind Way chanter. The Wind Way chanter has to do x, y, and z to you." I go to Wind Way chanter [and] I say, "I need x, y, and z done." The Wind

Way chanter says, "I only know x and y. I don't know z. So you have to go to find another chanter to do the z part." So then I can either have him do the x and y and then later find a chanter to do the z part. . . . But with [the] Native American Church you can have x, y, and z taken care of in one night. At least that is their philosophy. So that is how come the road man will tell you that it is kind of an all-purpose ceremony. (Knoki-Wilson, July 5, 2005)

Within a decade of its acceptance in the mid-1930s, a broad spectrum of syncretic experiments began to occur between the NAC and traditional Navajo religion in areas across the reservation; they continue today.[5] As Rosalind Shaw and Charles Stewart have pointed out, however, "simply identifying a ritual or tradition as 'syncretic' tells us very little and gets us practically nowhere, since all religions have composite origins and are continually reconstructed through ongoing processes of synthesis and erasure" (1994:7). It is more useful, therefore, to focus on processes of religious synthesis and discourses of syncretism. These necessarily involve attending to the workings of power and agency (Shaw and Stewart 1994:7). The syncretism evident between the NAC and traditional Navajo religion ranges from parallels in ideology to incorporation of isolated elements into each ritual format to extensive recombination of ritual units (Wagner 1975:163).

In the summer of 1968, Roland Wagner witnessed what was then termed a "double-meeting" because it involved a regular NAC ceremony plus a dry painting and traditional ceremonial elements, or units. The purpose of the witnessed ceremony was to exorcise witchcraft, which was to be attracted inside the hooghan where its power would be trapped in a quartz crystal. This ceremony was known as *Saa*, or, in contemporary orthography *Sǫ́*, meaning "star," because the altar involved a large central five-point black star constructed on a bed of white sand, approximately three feet in diameter. Analysis of Mary Wheelright's description of the Big Star Evil Way (Wheelright and McAllester 1956) led Wagner to conclude that key elements of this ritual were condensed into a single night's version and incorporated into the double-meeting (1975:168).

The first portion of the evening followed the standard Half Moon meeting format (see Aberle 1982b:125–56). At midnight an abrupt transition signaled the start of the actual exorcism of witchcraft. During this hour-long portion

of the meeting, the lights were turned off; the road man sang a passage from
Evil Way and recited a litany the sponsor repeated after him. Once completed, the lights were turned on again and the standard Half Moon Native
American Church meeting resumed, interrupted briefly so family members
could go outside to offer corn pollen at dawn (Wagner 1975:167–68).

Based on Vogt's incorporative model for Navajo integration of introduced
ideas and materials (1961), Wagner has provided an insightful analysis of
forms of syncretism between the NAC and traditional Navajo religion
(1975). He noted that the Navajo ceremonial system is "a complex body of
ritual that no one knows in its entirety" (Wagner 1975:170). Each chant
consists of its own set of "song groups" that recount a specific portion of
Navajo oral history crucial to that particular ceremony. Within each of these
groups are "stem songs," which must be sung in a fixed order in alignment
with ritual procedures, as well as "branch songs," which can be inserted into
the ritual with great freedom of choice and relative order of occurrence.
This gives each Navajo ceremony an inherent flexibility of structure. Thus it
"usually has two-, five-, and nine-night versions that are built up by the simple
addition of these branch songs onto an underlying skeleton of stem songs
selected from each song group" (Wagner 1975:174–75). For further clarification of this structural process, Wagner cites a passage in Kluckhohn and
Wyman's *An Introduction to Navaho Chant Practice,* where they note:

> A Navaho chant is a framework into which are fitted more or less
> discrete units ("ceremonies" and "acts and procedures") either as
> dictated by fixed associations or in accord with the practice of indi-
> vidual singers, the wishes of the patient or the patient's family, the
> precise nature of the "illness," or various other circumstances. The
> same unites are used over and over again in different chants, some-
> times with slight modifications. Single unites (ceremonies) may be
> given independently or, more often, two or three may be combined
> in a rite lasting only a portion of a day or night. (1940:13)

Wagner cautions, however, that while the organization of a Navajo chant is
highly flexible, the structure of the discrete elements that make it up is not.
If mistakes are made, "[T]he power conjured up through the ceremony

may have injurious effects rather than the desired curative effects" (Wagner 1975:171).

John Garrity, another scholar of the Navajo NAC, found substantial syncretism while in the field between 1993 and 1997. As he points out:

> Some road men began as Traditional practitioners, and we have found that, on the whole, Navajo road men increasingly are creatively integrating more Traditional diagnostic techniques, treatments, and explanatory models into their therapeutic repertoire. These include diagnostic practices such as "listening" and "stargazing." Road men are also beginning to conduct peyote meetings that expressly correspond to Traditional ceremonies such as Blessingway (Hózhǫ́ǫ́jí) and Lightningway or Shootingway (Na'at'oyee'jí), as well as Evilway (Hóchxǫ́x'íji) and Windway (Niłch'ijí). One road man even referred to plans to learn and integrate traditional sandpaintings into his NAC prayer meetings. (Garrity 2000:527)

While it is clear from this description that road men are incorporating elements of Navajo ceremonies into NAC rituals, it remains unknown whether these elements are synthesized within the meeting or set apart, as in the double-meeting discussed by Wagner (1975). This distinction is significant because it offers insight into what source is granted moral authority and legitimacy at each specific point in the ritual, and this is the faction that equals power.

Johnson Dennison, a Wind Way practitioner from Round Rock, Arizona, who is also a Native American Church road man, described how he calls upon his knowledge of traditional healing practices while conducting NAC healing meetings. As he carefully pointed out, however, he does not incorporate the traditional ceremony en masse into the peyote meeting; nor, as the road men who consulted with Garrity prefer, does he attempt to have the meeting correspond to a traditional Navajo ceremony. Rather, as he explained:

> JD: Another patient who couldn't walk who lived in San Francisco came back for the weekend for me to run the ceremony for him. . . . After midnight he got up and walk[ed] and ran. He ran so fast people

had to catch up with him [and] told him to come back to the ceremony. And then through that ceremony we come to realize what
kind of illness it is. So we do medicine according to the illness.
Like for him it was Snake Way ceremony. So in that way, then, it
doesn't have to be provided in that ceremony again [meaning the
Snake Way medicine would not have to be provided for the patient
in a separate Snake Way ceremony], and then we do this ceremony.
If you are skillful enough to understand that Navajo ceremony, then
you can do that. But most of the road men . . . are not to become
medicine man; they was a road man. So then they had the limited
knowledge of traditional medicine. Very few of us are both medicine man over here and then road man over here—a few of us.

MS: So were you meaning to say that you recognized that the man
couldn't walk because of Snake Way? So you were able to do the
short version of the Snake Way?

JD: No, I don't even have to do that. . . . It was just the medicine.
Yeah.

MS: You did the medicine?

JD: I used medicine to treat the Snake Way.

MS: To treat the Snake Way during the peyote meeting?

JD: During the ceremony. (J. Dennison, June 22, 2005)

Some, such as Harry Walters of Cove, Arizona, a professor of history at
Diné College in Tsaile, Arizona, take the melding of the two belief systems
a step further. Rather than simply being comfortable with inserting traditional knowledge into Native American Church healing meetings, Navajo
individuals such as Walters consider those meetings an integral part of the
traditional Navajo religion. He elucidated his views on the interchange-
ability of NAC meetings with the Blessing Way:

HW: The Native American Church is a Blessing Way ceremony. The
Blessing Way ceremony is in a class by itself. . . . All Navajo ceremonies are organized by Blessing Way. I mean, there is a little bit
of Blessing Way in all ceremonies. Even ceremonies that deal with
the Evil Way or the Enemy Way, it still has Blessing Way in it. . . .
Native American Church is that way. It is a Blessing Way ceremony,

and it also works the same way as Blessing Way. So nowadays instead of having the traditional Blessing Way, they would have a Native American Church meeting. (Walters, August 18, 1992)

Labeling a Native American Church meeting a Blessing Way—the core ceremony of the Navajo religious system—is extremely powerful syncretic discourse. Doing so legitimizes NAC meetings within the traditional system, thus empowering them with the moral authority of the Holy People.

Although he refers to it as the Peyote Way rather than the Blessing Way, a Chiricahua Wind Way practitioner interviewed by John Garrity considers the NAC meeting the most recent chant given to the Navajo by their Holy People. As the singer explained to Garrity:

A long time ago when the peyote was placed on earth, and they were going on down the line naming everything that was created . . . the peyote ceremony was forgotten . . . and the peyote spoke up for himself . . . and said, "To this day and sometime in the future, there will come a time when the people will come short of some ceremonies. Then I will come about. . . . This peyote is placed in a far away place. . . . When you finally reach the peyote, you will be relieved, and starting from there he will give you hope, and you will start back with hope in you. You will come home." This is what they said about the peyote. (unidentified Chiricahua Wind Way singer quoted in Garrity 2000:531)

Additionally, researchers such as Joseph Calabrese have found direct parallels between the ideology proffered by road men with whom they consulted and traditional Navajo philosophical tenets. In regard to the purpose of the peyote meeting, for example, Calabrese was told: "What you're trying to do is to get in harmony with everything. Everything is there—you're part of it. As I said, you're part of the four elements of life, that's why you gotta respect it. You're part of nature; you're part of anything that lives" (Dan Goodman [fictitious name] quoted in Calabrese 1994:512). This road man was referring to the Navajo tenet dictating that all entities in the Navajo world consist of the primary elements—moisture, air, substance, and heat—that are permeated by vibration. As Harry Walters explained:

HW: The element . . . is in everything. It is holy. When you put it together in a certain composition, it is human. And [when] it is put together in a certain composition, it is a tree. And [in] another certain composition, it is an insect. . . . And then . . . when those die and go back, and then we drink the same water, we breathe the same air, and we eat the food from the earth. And then all of these things, the elements, come together, and where they are put together there is life again. The elements are the seeds, the plants, so that is the cycle right there. See? It is a cycle. (Walters, August 12, 1993)

In addition to sharing substance, all made forms in the Navajo world share several structural features, including sun-wise directionality. This feature is evidenced by the "swirls" at the back of the top of the head and on the fingers and toes, as well as by the wrapping of hair in the traditional bun. The swirls identify Nihookáá Dine'é as living entities functioning within the natural order of the Navajo world. Structural homology with other persons in the Navajo universe also includes attention to the trajectory of growth from the ground upward, which is carefully attended to in all ceremonial contexts; a pathway, or "way out," enabling factors to move from inside to outside; and a binary division of the person that distinguishes left (male) from right (female) (Schwarz 1997).

This division reflects another fundamental principle of Navajo philosophy and cosmology—complementarity, which delineates and informs all aspects of the Navajo world including human relationships and the human body. Harry Walters elucidated the matter this way: "Everything is in terms of male and female in the Navajo. This is the duality. There is a male part and then the female counterpart in everything, even us. I am a man, but my left side is my male side, my right side is my female [side]" (Walters, August 20, 1992). As Walters pointed out, this complementary pairing establishes a base paradigm found throughout Navajo cosmology, in which male and female are paired in myriad homologues. On the cosmic plane, the universe consists of Mother Earth and Father Sky. Since the last underworld, men and women have been considered necessary counterparts. Being complete, a couple represents a stronger entity than a single person does. Therefore, on the social level no man or woman is considered complete or whole without a counterpart of the complementary gender

(Dooley, August 19, 1992).[6] On an individual level, every person is regarded as a whole that has both male and female aspects or qualities, a pairing demonstrated in the actual composition of the human body.

The concept of complementarity is central to the therapeutic strategy for helping couples experiencing marital problems that a NAC road man from near Ganado, Arizona, shared with Gilbert Quintero. This case demonstrates why we must remain vigilant in looking for evidence that supports or refutes Farella's claim that Navajo people "are changing in order to remain 'traditional'" (1984:190). According to Quintero, "During the course of a prayer service . . . [the road man] prepared a mixture of Peyote medicine for the two patients. He placed rolled medicine in his male (left) hand and gave it to the woman. He placed rolled medicine in his female (right) hand and gave it to the man. His aim was to help each person gain insight into what it was like to be the other. They would thereby gain understanding of each other and renew hopes to resolve their present difficulties" (1995:80). The incorporation of such foundational philosophical tenets—the sharing of the fundamental elements of life and structural homology, including complementarity, which includes a physiological blending of femaleness with maleness—into NAC ideology lends moral authority to traditional Navajo religion.

The most important aspect of the contemporary Navajo religious experience is the tendency toward multiple affiliations. Most Navajo practice one or two religions in addition to what might be considered their primary religion. According to Steve Pavlik, "It seems clear that Christianity in itself, while increasing somewhat in popularity, has not emerged as a major spiritual force. Only when combined with some form of Native religion, in particular the NAC, has Christianity proven to be attractive to a significant number of Navajo people" (1997:54).

Many Christian converts freely participate in traditional Navajo religious ceremonies or Native American Church meetings. These options are not available, however, to members of all evangelical Christian sects, many of which discourage or forbid members from utilizing the two non-Christian healing traditions. The use of alternative religious or healing treatments varies from family to family, from community to community, and within a family or a community over time. As circumstances change, though, Navajo individuals may draw on all three traditions at different points in their lives.

CHRISTIANITY

PDH: The home that I grew up in was not so much traditional. My father and my mother were educated. My father went to war and came back and started the logging business. I think stating that they were in the logging business tells you that they had a higher level of knowledge of the business world. And we really did not have the Navajo language spoken in the home. . . . [M]y maternal grandfather was educated . . . and my maternal grandmother had very limited education and she worked with the BIA [Bureau of Indian Affairs] as a cook until she retired. And my maternal grandfather was a missionary and then went into farm work in the Ganado area.

MS: Do you know what church he was a missionary in?

PDH: With the Presbyterian. . . . He finished school at Christian Training School in Phoenix a long, long time ago, the early 1900s. And on my paternal side, my paternal grandfather was half Navajo. My paternal grandmother never received an education and she was the traditionalist in that home. . . . My [paternal] great-grandfather came from Maine. . . . He came out with the cavalry and met my great-grandmother and they had a family of, I think it was nine boys and one girl. . . .

MS: [I]t sounds like a really interesting family background. What religion or religions have you practiced in your lifetime? I mean, you had a maternal grandfather who was a Presbyterian missionary, and I didn't really get a clear idea of what your paternal grandfather's religious background was, but your paternal grandmother—

PDH: He was Episcopalian.

MS: Oh. Your paternal grandmother was traditional. So . . . thinking back on your childhood, when there was a medical crisis in the family, what resources would your family draw on to seek help with healing?

PDH: My mother tried to go the traditional way, but . . . I think her father just told her that was not the way to go, and with my father, they had the Enemy Way ceremony for him when he came back from the service. But in [the] way of medical problems, I'm not aware of him having traditional doings. I am aware that my paternal grandmother did have Native ceremonies or Navajo ceremonies, but I am also aware that my paternal grandfather did not participate in them. (Henderson, July 14, 2005)

The Presbyterians, who were established at Fort Defiance in 1869, were joined on the reservation before the turn of the century by Methodists, Episcopalians, Christian Reformed missionaries, and the Church of Jesus Christ of Latter-Day Saints (see Dolaghan and Scates 1978; Warner 1970, 1973). The men and women associated with these religions set out to convert the Navajo people. Through conversion, one is said to be saved from "the guilt of sin"; that is, to be forgiven for the sins committed to that point in his or her life. This is to be followed by a second conversion to open the way for the gifts of the Spirit—speaking in tongues and healing. Because the term "save" in Navajo carries none of the Christian connotations of personal guilt, the circumstances under which a Navajo might feel a need to undergo this process would presumably vary considerably from those that might compel a Euro-American to do so (Rapoport 1954:52).

Catholic missionaries have a reputation for greater success in conversion on the Navajo reservation than their Protestant counterparts, in part because they have historically been more responsive to Navajo material needs. In addition, the Franciscans have typically demonstrated greater respect for Navajo people than Protestant missionaries have. As Pavlik has noted, "At a time when traditionalism flourished, the Franciscans found it easier to work with, rather than against, existing beliefs and practices. Indeed, the friars of St. Michaels were pioneers in the fields of Navajo linguistics and anthropological studies. . . . In contrast, the Protestant missionary effort was characterized by an attempt to discredit, condemn, and often outright suppress existing traditional culture, especially religion" (Pavlik 1997:46).

The twentieth century brought expanded missionization, new denominations, increased proselytizing, and some Navajo pastors (Frisbie 1987:196). Since the 1930s the three most active groups among the Navajo have been the Native American Church, the LDS, and Evangelical Protestants (Aberle 1982a:219).

Evangelical Protestants generally believe the Bible is the literal word of God, that people may be forgiven for their sins if they are born again in Jesus and follow the injunction in the Gospel of Matthew to spread the faith. The standard mission church was run by non-Indians; thus it was separate from Navajo community life. During the mid-twentieth century, traveling evangelists held camp meetings that drew large numbers of Navajo with the promise of healing. In 1950 there were 36 organized Evangelical congregations with pastors, two of whom were Navajo. The so-called camp church quickly gained popularity because it has Navajo preachers who maintain their place within kin networks. Also during those decades, independent Pentecostal churches headed by Navajo ministers began to spread throughout the reservation and are plentiful today. In 1978 there were 343 congregations, 203 of which had Navajo preachers. The fastest-growing denominations have been the Nazarenes, Baptists, and Pentecostals (Dolaghan and Scates 1978; Frisbie 1992:467). The majority of these churches exist in remote areas, attended and supported solely by local, rural Navajo people (Lewton and Bydone 2000:488).

Of the more than 300 new congregations that sprang up across the Navajo reservation between 1950 and 1977, 100 were Pentecostal (Dolaghan and Scates 1978). Pentecostalism is a form of perfectionism insofar as it assumes that humans are corrupt and unable to help themselves morally or spiritually. Salvation must come from outside themselves. Divine forgiveness of one's sins stems only from repentance. Expressions of possession by the Holy Ghost such as prophecy, healing, and speaking in tongues are symptomatic of the attainment of perfection (Hodge 1969:74). Rejection of the world and its unsaved inhabitants becomes a moral requirement.

The Pentecostal morality code forbids smoking, drinking, dancing, swearing, watching commercial movies, wearing makeup, jewelry, or cologne, dressing provocatively, and having premarital or extramarital sex (see Anderson 1979; Dayton 1987). These restrictions emerge from a specific theological doctrine. In the Pentecostal view, church members must reenact in their own lives the biblical drama of humankind's creation, fall, and redemption (Dayton 1987:23). As Elizabeth Lewton and Victoria Bydone have explained, "Illustrative of this idea is the fact that a Navajo who converts to Pentecostal Christianity must dispose of any paraphernalia used in or symbolic of Traditional Navajo religion or the Native American Church" (Lewton and Bydone 2000:488).

Church services, which are often held once or twice on Sunday, take place in a variety of locations, ranging from small churches to private homes or tents. The service frequently opens with singing and music, and congregants are free to join together at the altar for the singing. This is followed by the pastor, a guest, or a series of members of the congregation reading from the Bible and offering their testimonies. Once this portion of the service has been completed, congregants may approach the altar for individual prayer.

Josephine Whitegoat of Lukachukai, Arizona, is an elderly widow who was raised traditionally but turned to Christianity in 1962. Whitegoat was born in 1927 above Lukachukai in a place referred to as "where the stones line up." Her family had over three hundred sheep and goats, so, she recalled, "I grew up herding." At a young age she entered into an arranged marriage and had eight children. Her spouse, who worked off-reservation in the Colorado mines, returned to Lukachukai in ill health. He died within two days, leaving her to raise the children alone. She did so primarily by raising sheep and weaving. Although she was raised in the traditional ceremonial belief system, as a widow she chose a different path for herself and the children. As she explained:

> JW: [It was] 1962 and from there I led the children into the church. We sought help from them. We spent our days doing that since then. To this day, we continue. All the children today are all still there. No Navajo ceremonies are conducted on them. They do not know how a Navajo ceremony can be conducted on them. They are prayed for in church. Our belief is based in the church. The past I do not know about. I am involved in the church and nowhere else. Some of the children are now the foundation of the church. . . . We are still on that route. (Whitegoat, July 17, 2005, translated by Amelda Sandoval Shay and Wesley Thomas)

Whitegoat told us how prayer is dispensed to her congregation: "He [the pastor] himself does pray for us. He prays for us all the time. He tells us to come to the front one by one, and he prays for us. At the end, each person in need has been prayed for" (Whitegoat, July 17, 2005). I noted that she did not identify her church, so with the assistance of Amelda Sandoval Shay, a respected grandmother from Lukachukai, Arizona, who helped me with on-the-spot translations, I pursued information regarding her church's denomination. Her reply is very revealing:

MS: Ask her if she can tell us more about the church that she goes
to. What type of church is it?

AS: What kind of church do you go to?

JW: The Believers. I do not know what the English name is.

AS: What is the name of the church? . . .

JW: I do not know the church name, but the preacher's name is Sam.
He is "white." He tells us the word of the Lord. (Whitegoat, translated by Amelda Sandoval Shay and Wesley Thomas, July 17, 2005)

The fact that she refers to her congregation as *Oodlání*, or "the Believers,"
and does not care what denomination it is is significant. Oodlání is the word
Navajo generally use when referring to Christians, rather than the name of a
particular sect such as Baptist or Assemblies of God. Based on what Whitegoat said, the critical factor is that the preacher shares the word of the Lord
with those assembled. As John Garrity has noted, this collective identity
as Oodlání rather than as members of particular sects demonstrates that
Navajo Christians are establishing more independence from the mainstream church headquarters outside Navajoland. Moreover, while Garrity
predicts the future development of a Navajo indigenous Christian church
similar to the NAC of Navajoland (2000:528), given the existence of independent congregations and networks of congregations, including what he
terms proto-denominations—all of which are headed by Navajo pastors—
Thomas Csordas considers that the emergence of a distinct Navajo form
of Christianity is already under way (1999:11). Regardless of whether one
sees these phenomena as emerging now or as yet to be, what is happening
on the Navajo reservation is an excellent example of the type of cultural
occurrence McNally refers to in describing how Native Americans are
adapting to the Christian tradition (2000:834–36).

In addition to Sunday church services, Wednesday evening prayer
meetings are frequently held. These services follow a pattern similar to the
Sunday service. Church members also gather on an impromptu basis to
offer support to those in need. Additionally, camp meetings are held out-
doors in the summer months with the intent of proselytizing. These lively
events are important social occasions that allow congregants opportunities
to visit with one another.

Navajo Pentecostals may use *discernment* to determine an individual's problem, heal by means of *laying on of hands,* read from the Bible, or anoint another person with oil. Patients report falling or collapsing, dancing or singing, having visions, being able to speak in tongues, and experiencing feelings of warmth, lightness, and tingling. Pastor George S. Davis of Lukachukai, Arizona, described an example of the latter form of healing, with the help of Lawson Nakai:

> GD: There was a lady that came here and she couldn't move her right arm. . . . That lady came up here and sat down and was talking to us. She told me that she couldn't open her right arm at the elbow. And she was saying it was numb up to her fingertips and me and him [Lawson Nakai] we prayed for her right here, and she felt that tingling actually beginning and it moved up her arm. I think that following week, she came back and told me . . . that that tingling feeling wasn't there any more. That elbow was actually flexible when she came back. (G. Davis, July 18, 2005, translated by Lawson Nakai)

William Hodge noted that he doubts that any of the people he met were serious converts to Pentecostalism. Instead, he believes they used elements that could be fit into a traditional conceptual framework, in which case "two widely varying ceremonial systems can have grossly different types of practitioners supported by irreconcilable beliefs or doctrines and yet each can have the same meaning to those who have experienced both forms" (Hodge 1969:89). He found that the role of *hataałii,* or "singer," was equated with the role of gospel preacher, and Pentecostalism was reinterpreted so it took on the meaning of traditional ceremonial practice.

When Robert Rapoport did a comparative study of Galilean and Mormon missions in a Navajo community during 1949 and 1950, he concluded that

> The principal focus of Navaho religious orientation is that of curing. Whenever Navahos have taken traits of alien culture and molded them into the genius of their own religion, the curing emphasis has been raised to primacy. The fact that Christianity has an important

supernatural curing theme was taken up and emphasized by the Navahos. Jesus' miraculous cures and the power and interest in curing manifested by the Lord were certainly important correspondences in promoting communication, though for some Christian churches this Navaho emphasis would constitute a radical distortion. (Rapoport 1954:52)

In a similar vein, Pavlik has maintained that a primary reason most recent Navajo converts to Christianity have been drawn to the LDS, Evangelical Protestant sects, or the NAC is because all three emphasize healing—while the other Christian denominations on the Navajo reservation talk about the power of God, these three demonstrate that power through healing acts (1997:53).[7] Further insight is thus gained into what Navajo people make of the Christian tradition (McNally 2000:834–36).

This thinking echoes the reasons Navajo people gave earlier in the twentieth century as to why they joined the Native American Church (Aberle 1982b). It also resonates with the actions of Navajo people who accepted vaccinations, pills, and pain relievers from their captors at Fort Sumner (Trennert 1998:33). It explains why Navajo apprentices learned the Sucking Way and the Chiricahua Apache Wind Way from Native healers who had originated with other tribes but married Navajo women at Fort Sumner (Haile 1950:297). In addition, it offers insight into why some Navajo patients seek out Ute, Hopi, Laguna, and other Rio Grande Pueblo practitioners of the "sucking cure" to remove foreign objects shot into them through witchcraft (Stewart and Aberle 1957:35). This action in itself does not appear to have been new, for some Navajo historians maintain that the Night Way ceremony was acquired from the Ancestral Pueblo (formerly known as Anasazi) people around A.D. 1000 (Faris 1990:17). I suggest, however, that Navajo willingness to seek cures for bodily ills from such diverse sources does offer insight into a deeper underlying cultural archetype.

In his study of religious pluralism in Zambia, Thomas Kirsch (2004) found that a group's former relationship with the supernatural establishes a paradigm that continues after exposure to global forms of power such as Christianity. The Gwembe Tonga people, for example, were not always confident that "the spiritual powers that had infused particular instances of religious practices with power would do so on every future occasion," which meant they had to be ready to shift religious affiliation whenever needed. This included shifts to Christianity once it became available (2004:700).

Based on what consultants told me, this shifting is not unlike the contemporary Navajo situation. Since the changing of religious affiliation is not new, it begs the question of what the Navajo people's primordial relationship to the supernatural entailed. For the answer, I looked to the stories that constitute Navajo oral history as the most important source of information about the Navajo world, for they contain the ancestral knowledge many Navajo view as a charter for life.

A critical juncture in every apprentice's mastery of a ceremony is learning the origin story of that particular chant. This process, which can take weeks or months, can only occur in the winter months, after the first frost and before the first thunder. Regardless of its specific purpose, careful attention to the origin story of most Navajo ceremonies reveals that each one focuses on the travails of a single hero or heroine—or at most a few—who has gotten into a series of predicaments from which he or she can be liberated only with supernatural assistance. Extrication involves visiting a variety of Holy People to acquire ritual knowledge. In each case the hero or heroine is exposed to uncertainty and overcomes obstacles but ultimately emerges from his or her tribulations to endow other Navajo with the power of a new healing ceremony (Reichard 1950:150; Wyman 1965:65). I contend, then, that questing for curing power is a basic philosophic tenet that has resulted in a cultural pattern for action by Navajo people.

With these stories as models, Navajo people can be seen as culturally preconditioned to seek and adopt new sources of healing power as they become available; moreover, like the Gwembe Tonga people of Zambia, they do not expect their pleas to the supernatural to result in healing every single time. As Kenneth Black, Jr., explained from his personal experience with a particular problem, "Well, you have to have a big ceremony. Sometimes it will work, sometimes it wouldn't" (Black, June 16, 2005). And as Johnson Dennison counseled, in some cases the illness might be so severe that the cure "may or may not be successful" (Dennison, June 22, 2005).

This propensity would seem to work nicely for those Navajo who adopt the NAC, for religious relativism is a primary tenet of that religion (Aberle

1982b:181). It is open to debate, however, whether this paradigm is applicable to Navajo individuals who make use of allopathic medicine. Some researchers maintain that over time, Navajo patients and practitioners have adopted the perspective that the traditional healing systems and biomedical systems perform very different functions, with biomedical physicians treating the symptoms of an illness rather than the underlying etiology—that is, the causes or origins—of disease, which is best addressed by traditional practitioners (Adair, Deuschle, and Barnett 1988:170). This point is further clarified by Stephen Kunitz, who has noted that "Navajos in the past have often equated [allopathic] physicians with herbalists from whom they seek symptomatic relief" rather than a "cure" for the underlying cause (1983:119).

Paul Mico has noted that the traditional Navajo seeks "'White Man's Medicine' not to be cured but to obtain relief from painful symptoms. Curing is obtainable only by the elaborate ritual performed by the medicine man. . . . Symptomatic relief of pain or discomfort, pending the ceremonial cure, may be obtained from Anglo medical practitioners, Navajo herbalists, and/or Hopi Indian medicine men: all are perceived as having [an] equal role and function, that of providing relief from painful symptoms" (Mico 1962:11).

While this may have been a universal truth at the time these researchers were working among the Navajo, it cannot be assumed to remain so today. Navajo exegeses throughout the remainder of this book will shed light on the issue of whether contemporary Navajo people from the various religious faiths represented on the reservation seek allopathic medicine for cures or whether they rely on it only for relief of symptoms. Care must be taken not to confuse expectation with result, insofar as we may presume that in at least some cases the Navajo individuals in question *sought cures* from each of the various sources from which aid was negotiated but that they ultimately may have only obtained relief of symptoms from allopathic medicine and had to look elsewhere to alleviate the underlying cause.

Regardless of whether they were sought out for relief of symptoms or for cures, dramatic changes in facilities and services occurred after responsibility for the Natives' health care was transferred from the Bureau of Indian Affairs to the Public Health Service in 1955. The number of hospitalizations decreased steadily from 1940 through 1955, nearly doubled between 1955 and 1960 (during the tuberculosis epidemic), increased again during the 1960s, and reached a plateau during the 1970s (Kunitz 1983:154–55).

In 1970 the Indian Health Service (IHS) replaced the Division of Health and further decentralized health care administration, fostering improved communication between the IHS and tribes through local area offices. Following passage of the 1921 Snyder Act, Congress created a process for transferring BIA and IHS health programs to tribal governments through Public Law 93-638, the Indian Self-Determination and Education Assistance Act of 1975. In doing so, Congress noted the past inadequacies of Native American health care and reaffirmed its intention to involve tribes in health care programs through tribal self-governance.

In many cases these health care facilities and programs within them are currently run on a contract basis with, rather than by, the IHS. This is possible because Public Law 93-638 was passed with the goal of moving many programs away from the BIA while maintaining U.S. legal and moral support for the services. The law allows tribes to take much of the responsibility for and control of tribal health services away from the IHS, giving them more freedom to design and administer tribal programs.

INSTITUTIONALIZED COEXISTENCE

Previous scholars have shown concern for how the indigenous curing system might coexist with biomedicine on the Navajo reservation (Adair, Deuschle, and Barnett 1988). Their interest was focused on whether the Navajo traditional system might cause patients to delay seeking medical care or neglect a treatment regime prescribed by a physician (Adair, Deuschle, and Barnett 1988:161). They also wondered whether the biomedical system had begun to displace the traditional healing system. Tracking one hundred patients who had been seen at the Many Farms clinic in 1961 for acute, chronic, or semi-chronic conditions, this team found that eighty-two of those patients had undergone a traditional curing ceremony for the same complaint before or after their clinic visit (Adair, Deuschle, and Barnett 1988:168). From this they concluded that these two systems were able to coexist in a noncompetitive relationship, with no individual or institutional conflict. This does not mean, however, that the systems are coequal in terms of power and dominance, for the notion that local practice might in itself be seen as regulatory and as a point of departure from which to build policy has not gained widespread support in any cross-cultural setting (Craig 2000:107).

In a more recent study of three hundred Navajo patients interviewed at an IHS facility, 62 percent had seen Native healers and 39 percent reported using Native healers on a regular basis. Users were not distinguishable from nonusers by age, education level, income, fluency in English, identification of primary provider, or compliance. Pentecostal patients, however, used Native healers less frequently than patients of other faiths (Kim and Kwok 1998). What this study does not tell us is how Evangelical Protestantism, Mormanism, Pentecostalism, NAC, or various other religions available to contemporary Navajo people influence perspectives on health, illness, and healing. The Navajo narratives on transfusions, amputations, organ transplantations, and associated issues that are highlighted throughout this text do provide insight on this important topic.

Outside observers have predicted that forced assimilation coupled with increased exposure to the non-Navajo world, Euro-American education, and the increased demands of a wage-work economy will become "the nemesis of the traditional healing system" (Kunitz 1983:120). Despite such predictions, signs of the contrary outcome exist. As examples, the Rough Rock Mental Health Training Program for Medicine Men and Women was founded in 1968 (Frisbie 1987:259–68). In 1979 the Navajo Medicine Men's Association was formed (Kunitz 1983:120). In 1996 the Navajo Nation was granted funds by the Department of Veterans Affairs to begin reimbursing Navajo veterans for traditional healing services. And under certain circumstances, the Internal Revenue Service now allows deductions for expenses incurred in engaging in Navajo healing ceremonies.

In the closing decades of the twentieth century, the Indian Health Service made major efforts to incorporate Navajo opinions into its operations and to make facilities more accessible to Navajo practitioners (Chew 2000; Cobin 1998). In 1985 the Continuing Education Department at Diné College began offering a two-and-a-half-day immersion program in "cultural orientation" to teach non-Navajo medical workers about Navajo beliefs and outlooks on healing. Toward the end of the session, program staff discussed methods for integrating traditional and biomedical practices (Davies 2001:188). This was used as a pilot for similar programs at other hospitals within the Navajo service area.

Other evidence that the IHS health care program grew more receptive to the traditional concerns of its Navajo patients is the fact that hooghan were built on hospital grounds for healers and patients to use as they chose. The IHS hired Jones Benally, a Navajo medicine man, as a permanent staff member at the Winslow, Arizona, facility in 1996 to offer traditional services to patients in a hooghan erected on the hospital grounds (Davies 2001:187). Efforts were made to have the doors of new hospitals face east and to feature Navajo artwork and signage incorporating symbols accessible to monolingual Navajo visitors. New precedents were established with the completion of the Chinle Hospital in Chinle, Arizona, and its interior healing sciences room, complete with a ventilating system to accommodate ceremonial smoke and a long pipe to connect the facility with the earth below (Davies 2001:171). In addition, Johnson Dennison was hired as founding director of the Office of Navajo Healing at Chinle Hospital, which was initiated to build a bridge between biomedicine and traditional Navajo medicine. Members of his staff offer patients traditional counseling and care while in the hospital. They arrange with hospital staff to allow traditional herbalists, ceremonial practitioners, and Native American Church road men to perform necessary procedures on hospital grounds.

On a related note, the New Mexico Cancer Center opened in July 2007 in Gallup, New Mexico. As the first radiation treatment center to serve Gallup and the nearby Navajo Nation, it will greatly assist Navajo cancer patients and their families because of its proximity to their homes. With a commitment to the integration of traditional healing practices in the treatment of cancer, New Mexico Oncology and Hematology Consultants designed and built the center with their Navajo patients' desires and concerns in mind. The complex includes a traditional hooghan to be used by Navajo patients to blend traditional ceremonies, herbal remedies, NAC procedures, and allopathic treatments.

With this historical context in mind, I will attempt to develop an understanding of the Navajo notions of relatedness, perceptions of collective identity, and tendency for multiple religious and medical affiliations by considering the "incorporative pattern" noted by Spicer (1961), Vogt (1961), and Wagner (1975), Navajo epistemological tenets as suggested by Farella (1984), and the outcomes of the Navajo propensity to seek new cures for medical problems derived from oral traditions associated with ceremonials.

In any particular instance, the pattern, tenet, or propensity considered will be one specifically identified by consultants as intersecting with blood transfusions, CPR, amputations, surgery, and organ transplants. But first, we must examine contemporary Navajo views on health and illness.

CHAPTER THREE

The Politics and Language of Well-Being

MS: What causes illness?

JD: In Navajo culture, Navajo medicine there is no such thing as diabetes or heart disease. We don't have that.

MS: What about cancer?

JD: There is no cancer. But if you cross the line you come over here (indicating left with his hand on the table in front of him), in the Western medicine you have cancers, diabetes, breast cancer, everything is over here. That is on this side (indicating left again). There is no diagnostician who would say "you have cancer." There is no diagnostician that says "you have diabetes." So that is the problem. So we have the *bilagáana* [European-American] illness over here (indicating left) and then Navajo illness over here (indicating right with his hand on the table). . . .

MS: This is really interesting.

JD: Do you want me to explain it first, or do you have another question?

MS: No, I am just amazed. I am sorry. I didn't mean to interrupt.

JD: OK, over here we feel lousy of whatever illness we have. And we get diagnosed with diabetes over here (indicating left). Then we come home and they say "hey, this is a bilagáana illness," and

we turn around and go to the diagnostician who says "you have to
have a Lightning Way ceremony. . . . The lightning strike caused the
illness. So it comes from the nature." So then we do the Lightning
Way ceremony. Then we find that we have breast cancer or colon
cancer, then the Navajo diagnostician would not say "you have
cancer." He won't say that. . . . But then he says "this is a snake-
caused illness. You are off balance with an animal or a bird or whatever; it is causing the illness and the disease." Even the common cold
is caused by the wind or by the dirt or the season. . . . There is no
diabetes in Navajo illness. So medicine man has a lot of problems
in finding diabetes. So [if] you go to medicine man or diagnostician for ceremonies if you have been told you have diabetes . . .
they won't say "you want to have this ceremony?" There is no one
answer to this. . . . Again over here (chopping his left hand on the
table to indicate bilagáana), in the lab or whatever, nobody is going
to say "you have a Lightning Way illness." It is out of this world if
you do that. So over here (chopping his right hand on the table to
indicate Navajo), it is the same way; it is out of this world to have
breast cancer or anything like that. This is a different medicine.
MS: That is extremely enlightening.

(J. Dennison, June 22, 2005)

Johnson Dennison is a gifted educator. He was a school principal for
twenty years and a dean of instruction at Diné College for seven years; he
is a Native American Church road man, has been performing the Wind
Way ceremony for more than three decades, and heads the Office of
Navajo Healing at Chinle Hospital. I gained unique insight into the differences between allopathic and traditional disease and illness from the perspective of a Navajo who practices religious and medical pluralism when
we had the conversation just presented.

"TAKE CARE OF YOURSELF"

LT: Well, my grandpa used to say that if you are going to be living a
healthy life . . . you get up early, then you offer prayer, then you be

jogging or running, and then after you come back from running you don't go back to sleep, you stay up and maybe go look for the horses or maybe chop wood to have the fire going for breakfast. . . . And at noon the same thing and at evening the same thing. You don't eat too much and you be working all the time, herding sheep, maybe herding cattle. Then walking a lot and in springtime . . . you have to go out in the field and get ready for planting corn. So there is a lot of jobs to be done. So you will be on foot mostly all day to live a healthy life. (Todachinee, June 28, 2005)

Understandings of health, illness, and healing are not neutral in the Navajo world. The sources to which people attribute the cause of disease and the power of cures offer important clues about their notions of relatedness, about how they comprehend the contemporary moral and political landscape, as well as about their personal and collective identity affiliations. Larry Todachinee's reply to my question regarding what he considered necessary to live a healthy life is fairly typical. The age-old teachings other consultants mentioned in response to this query included rising early (Amelia Benally, July 13, 2004; Black, June 16, 2005; Goldtooth, July 18, 2005), running (Amelia Benally, July 13, 2004; Black, June 16, 2005; Goldtooth, July 18, 2005; Knoki-Wilson, July 5, 2005; Nelson, July 20, 2004), and praying (Black, June 16, 2005; Goldtooth, July 18, 2005; Knoki-Wilson, July 5, 2005). In regard to morning runs, Leroy Nelson remembers being told: "All these deities, they will be watching, looking, observing at certain moments in the morning. . . . If you are running there and they see you, then they can get a chance to know you. And then you are rewarded with blessings, and there is goodness in life in terms of growth—mentally, emotionally, socially, and spiritually. . . . The teaching behind that was some day we are not going to be here for you, you need to learn. . . . There is going to be life, there is going to be death. You are going to face these" (Nelson, July 20, 2004).

Special emphasis is also placed on values such as industriousness (Black, June 16, 2005; Nelson, July 20, 2004; Todachinee, June 28, 2005). Ursula Knoki-Wilson explained how these principles were taught in her natal home.

UKW: They always said that there was a time and a place for every-thing and you had to do things in moderation, and it is always *"t'ą́ą́ bee bóholnííh,"* which means "it is up to you." . . . The kind of choices that you are going to make in life are the ones that are going to carry you forward into old age. . . . There was a lot of emphasis on not being lazy or not lying around. You were supposed to be industrious, and a person that was just lying around a lot or being lazy or whatever was thought to be inviting the people of poverty to come into your life or to upset your balance. And my grandmother used to describe it in terms that I used to imagine that they were little people. . . . Because she would call them people of poverty. Or she would say, "The people who bring thoughts of poverty to your mind." (Knoki-Wilson, July 5, 2005)

Kenneth Black, Jr., generously offered enlightenment on how traditional values such as rising early and staying industrious, in combination with exercise, contribute to preventive care in addition to helping keep the body fit. He recollected hearing this advice from a medicine man "a long time ago":

KB: There is a purpose why we have holes in our nose and our mouth and different holes in our body. They are like plumbing. They have all these different veins and thruways, and if you don't exercise enough, if you don't cleanse yourself, if you don't sweat yourself off, if you don't treat yourself like in the holistic approach, things will get clogged up. . . . If you run, get up early like the philosophy says, you get up early in the morning and greet the sun. If you live by those examples, you will live long. You take care of your body and treat it like it is holy, you will live long. If you watch what you eat, you will live long. And if you pray, if you have a belief, you will overcome a lot of things. (Black, June 16, 2005)

Along similar lines, Tso Allen fondly recalled her parents' and grandparents' protective natures and how her father in particular shielded her from certain types of knowledge and experiences that he called "unhealthy" during her formative years:

TA: My parents always stressed, even my grandparents, my grandmother always stressed that you had to "take care of yourself."

That you had to avoid certain unhealthy situations. . . . My father did not take us to Enemy Way ceremonies, to the healing ceremonies, like the Mountain Way, Mountain Top Way. . . . He said "because those are healing ceremonies, and you don't go there," so he never took us. So I had never been to a *Yé'ii Bicheii* [Night Way ceremony involving the Grandfathers of the Holy People] until I got out of college . . . because their belief was that it affected you in some way by attending. (T. Allen, July 15, 2005)

In addition to her parents' and grandparents' proactive behavior, Tso Allen thought back to the preventive herbal mixtures referred to as *'azee'*, or "medicine," brought by her grandmother on an annual basis; these herbs protected her and her siblings from seasonal ills: "My grandmother would come and she would bring a bundle of herbs in a big bag. . . . I don't know what they were, but they were herbs called life herbs. They were to keep you well. My grandmother would bring it and she would say they were life herbs, and she would instruct my mother how to chop that and how to boil it and how to give it to us, so beginning about October we drank that herbal tea every morning before we ate anything else. We were never affected by colds and illnesses during the winter, and the big bundle of herbs lasted until about March" (Allen, July 15, 2005).

Sheila Goldtooth, a Blessing Way singer from Round Rock, Arizona, deepens our understanding of traditional Navajo notions of preventive health care with information about prophylactic ceremonies meant to shield Navajo people from seasonal illnesses. She explained:

SG: In our philosophy we are supposed to have certain ceremonies done at certain times, protection blessings. And I think a lot of people just tend to forget that, and I think they just don't think it is necessary or they are working or financial may be the reason why they don't have it. And so I think in a lot of ways that causes stress and it causes illnesses later on when they have so much stress. And they don't do the things they are supposed to do for themselves— prayers and certain ceremonies. . . . The way our ancestors' lives were was that every spring they would have maybe a protection prayer for the whole family. . . . And it was something that was

ongoing where the whole family participated in these prayers or in
the blessings. . . . They did offerings to the Earth or they did offerings
at certain times like in the spring and in the summertime. And
what they'd ask for was protection from certain illnesses. Like
epidemics, like flus that would come around, and . . . they would
ask for protection from these things that are in the air or things that
might be coming about. . . . I don't think many people do it no
more. But every household was supposed to do that. (Goldtooth,
July 18, 2005)

On the subject of protective or preventive care, Dr. Buella Allen added
a note regarding behavioral requirements after any type of ceremony,
whether done as a prophylactic or for healing purposes. As she pointed
out, these precautions are necessary for a healthy life:

BA: If a person has a ceremony, then there are four days after which any
kind of injury is not to be done. So a person has to behave so that
they don't cut themselves or that there is no digging or wounding
of Mother Earth, they're not allowing their blood to flow. They
can't have any vena punctures, or they can't have anything that
is going to cause their blood to leak out in any way. They have to
be careful about foods under certain circumstances. Some of the
ceremonies require food restrictions, and they are generally told
to stay by themselves and to leave those four days for just caring
for themselves and reflecting on the ceremony, making sure that
they understand that this has been done for them. It's a time when
the ceremony is reemphasized in their minds. . . . [T]hey're supposed to be reserved, they're supposed to "take care of themselves,"
not go about acting foolish and doing things that might harm themselves. (B. Allen, June 10, 2005)

While acknowledging these teachings, Sheila Goldtooth also pointed
out a marked decline in the number of Navajo people adhering to them.
Noting the diversity of people who make up the present-day Navajo population, she commented:

SG: Well, you look at [Navajo] society today, and they are just spoiled. It seems like there are still those that believe traditional and then there are those that are really modern. So you kind of wonder, what is what to whom? I think it is kind of difficult to really answer. . . . I would say that a healthy life for Navajo is just having respect for themselves and having respect for others, having respect for the environment. And I know we used to get up early in the morning and we would run and we would pray at dawn, and that was in itself living a healthy lifestyle, but now it seems like less and less people do that. And the only thing that some of us still do is pray at dawn and meditate and that type of stuff. . . . So I think it takes a strong belief and a strong respect for yourself and everything else. (Goldtooth, July 18, 2005)

Close attention to what these and other Navajo people elsewhere in this text have to say about illness reveals how, at different levels of understanding, what are perceived to be recently introduced diseases such as diabetes, cancer, and heart ailments actually stand for social change, loss of tradition, and conflict with their colonizers. This form of historical trauma is self-consciously the polar opposite of the portrayal of health as living according to traditions.

HISTORICAL TRAUMA AND LOSS

Various forms of historical psychological distress among Native Americans have been recognized and explored for several decades (Duran and Duran 1995; Jilek 1981; Townsley and Goldstein 1977). In a groundbreaking series of essays, Maria Brave Heart coined the phrase "historical trauma" to refer to the collective distress Native Americans have experienced since colonization. Brave Heart links Native American genocide, ethnic cleansing, and policies of forced assimilation to the Holocaust experience and correlates patterns of symptoms experienced by Native Americans to those experienced by Holocaust victims and their families (Brave Heart 1998, 1999; Brave Heart and DeBruyn 1998; Brave Heart–Jordan and DeBruyn 1995).

As is the case with Native Americans across what has come to be known as North America, complex changes have occurred in Navajo society since the initial experiences with Spaniards, Mexicans, and Americans—including economic shifts in subsistence from hunting and gathering supplemented by agriculture to herding and agriculture, which was gradually replaced by a dependence on wage work. Most specifically, since their capture and internment at Hwéeldi in the 1860s, the Navajo have been constantly dominated and controlled by the greater U.S. society.

Ever since the Navajo release from Fort Sumner and the subsequent establishment of a reservation on a portion of their homelands, colonial assault has been repeatedly demonstrated at different times through repression of Native language and traditions, enforcement of boarding school attendance, threats to Navajo land and resources by stock reduction in the 1930s and 1940s, land disputes, resource depletion through timber harvesting and coal and uranium mining, and impediments to religions freedom—including unsuccessful attempts by the Navajo to preserve their sacred sites. While the last several decades have witnessed movement toward political self-determination and cultural renewal, many Navajo kin groups have been shattered as a result of complex economic, social, and health problems. These concerns have included economic underdevelopment, chronic unemployment (reservation unemployment rates far exceed national norms), the concomitant need to work off-reservation, the high rate of diabetes, illnesses and deaths from improperly regulated mining and radioactive waste spills, problems associated with alcohol, and continuing poverty for many (Frisbie 1987:197; Iverson 2002; Kunitz and Levy 1994; Levy and Kunitz 1974; Levy and Kunitz, with Gabriel et al. 2000). It is within this context of rapid cultural change and fragmentation that Navajo people have searched out new sources of curing, including those available from Christianity, the Native American Church, and biomedical technologies.

Of critical importance when considering the notion of historical trauma is the fact that Native American people did not face a single catastrophic period; rather, such cataclysmic events are ongoing and present in their lives. Moreover,

> [E]thnic cleansing did not end with military defeat and occupation of territory. Rather, it persisted for generations. This means that American

Indian people are faced with daily reminders of loss: reservation living, encroachment of Europeans on even their reservation lands, loss of language, loss and confusion regarding traditional religious practices, loss of traditional family systems, and loss of traditional healing practices. . . . The losses are not "historical" in the sense that they are in the past and a new life has begun in a new land. Rather, the losses are ever present, represented by the economic conditions of reservation life, discrimination, and a sense of cultural loss. (Whitbeck et al. 2004:121)

In the next account, Leroy Nelson expresses the direct connection between illness and the complex challenges incurred by being required to live according to foreign ideology, morality, and philosophy within the contemporary Navajo community:

LN: The changing lifestyle that is here with us has come in from another world. . . . The United States government came into our grounds, into our homelands. . . . The law is in place. We have to abide by that. . . . We have to live by somebody's rules, somebody else's ways, somebody else's way of life. If we don't do so, then we are incarcerated. . . . There is a lot of challenges here today. You have to be educated and learn how to read and write to be able to be civil. . . . A lot of people within our past time, our forefathers and grandfathers, they went through the changes of having the United States government taking our language and our culture away from us. . . . It took a toll on us. There was a lot of abuse that took place. . . . Within that would be another way of looking at the sickness. (Nelson, July 20, 2005)

When I discussed notions of *as'ah na'adá*, or "living a healthy life," with Donald Denetdeal, he noted, "In the Navajo thinking, there are four basic areas to make one healthy. And that's a healthy mind, a healthy physical body, and a healthy spiritual being, believing, being spiritual. And the fourth one is observance of the ecosystem because we are nature in it. So we're working with a scale of four: mind, spirit, body, and environment" (Denetdeal, July 11, 2004). If any one of the four areas is off balance, health can be affected.

Denetdeal stressed that "[t]he key to wellness in the Navajo thinking is to have a very strong balanced mind" (Denetdeal, July 11, 2004). In concordance with this perspective, Denetdeal considers the mental strain of living according to the requirements of a foreign worldview a contributing factor to current Navajo health concerns (Denetdeal, July 11, 2004). He opined that "[n]ot having a healthy mind is created by all these challenges of the white race that we're being subjected to by the outside force. Keeping up with the bills, having a job, operating on time, go there, go here, do this, do that, hurry, hurry, hurry, hustle and bustle, that is not good for the mind. And so those challenges are cutting into the balance of the mind. So that's one of the reasons that Navajo are becoming very unhealthy, because they don't have time to think and have a strong mind; every moment is just surviving because of the way life is today" (Denetdeal, July 11, 2004).

The views of Leroy Nelson and Donald Denetdeal are not unique among colonized peoples (see Trawick 1992), nor are they aberrant among Native Americans. Rather, they echo the Dakota voices captured in Gretchen Lang's essay "'Making Sense' about Diabetes: Dakota Narratives of Illness" in which this affliction is understood to have developed among the Dakota because their entire lifestyle is out of balance and people are not adhering to tradition. In the Dakota community, diabetes is also seen as the most recent instance of white man's destruction of Indian society and culture (Lang 1989:319). These Navajo voices also parallel the Native exegeses captured in *Disciplined Hearts* (1996), wherein Theresa O'Nell recounts how Flathead notions of cultural loss have become embodied in depression. Stress and strain can result from simply visiting the local Indian Health Service hospital or clinic because Navajo people experience cancer and certain other diseases within the entanglement of power dynamics inherent to the colonial context.

In Ursula Knoki-Wilson's view, Navajo people are losing sight of what is sacred and of their ancestral spirituality because traditional values are not being taught with as much consistency as they were in the past: "And I think probably [there has also been] a loss of some of the emphasis on keeping your traditional values the way they were taught traditionally. . . . There was a lot of emphasis on the spirituality. . . . Honoring the times of the day, like at dawn and at noontime and at twilight; making offerings at those specific times. . . . Spiritual teachings were integrated into activities as daily living" (Knoki-Wilson, July 5, 2005).

With the loss of traditional values has come a loss of respect for what is sacred. Donald Denetdeal believes that in terms of spirituality "we have lost focus, we are really losing ground on that. . . . We're very weak in [the] spiritual and so that invites disease, that opens us up to sickness, that opens up a whole can of worms where Navajo people are, our imbalance is great. And so that's the challenge" (Denetdeal, July 11, 2004). "Coming from a traditional view," Sheila Goldtooth noted, "I think it is that the respect for life itself is just not there anymore. And I think people don't really have respect for what was sacred. And I think they just go on and on doing as they please and not really respecting what was supposed to be respected. Do[ing] what was supposed to be done at certain times" (Goldtooth, July 18, 2005).

Kenneth Black, Jr., agreed with this assessment, tying the breakdown in spirituality to the fact that ancient values and teachings are no longer taught to the youngest members of the Navajo Nation:

> KB: [N]owadays a lot of families, young or old, they seem to have disconnected themselves from the Navajo tradition—the way of life and the teachings. . . . A lot of these good teachings are not really taught in their homes. And I think some of those [disconnections] cause a lot of social dysfunctions. . . . Like the story goes, like what the woman represents. Our society . . . is a matrilineal society. . . . So therefore, the story goes back and ties back into the Changing Woman, the White Shell Woman, a lot of the great deities. So therefore, our society is supposed to be treating the women with great reverence and respect. And there is a lot of teaching that goes with that. I don't think those [things] are being taught anymore. . . . And I think a lot of those different stories are lost and are not taught to small kids. (Black, June 16, 2005)

Leeanne Johnson of Vanderwagen, New Mexico, who combines Christianity with traditional ceremonialism, offered insight into how the dramatic economic shifts in subsistence—from hunting and gathering supplemented by agriculture to herding and agriculture, which has been largely replaced by a dependence on wage work—she has witnessed during her life have resulted in an enormous reduction in physical activity. This lack of activity is recognized as having had major consequences for Navajo health and well-being.

LJ: Lifestyles have changed dramatically. . . . I was born and raised in a place where I had responsibility with lifestyle, cornfield, house, we had to walk. I mean, we did everything walking. . . . Now children don't do that. They don't get up at dawn anymore. I mean, you go out here at 5:00 or 6:00 A.M., get in your car; you drive from here to Gallup[, New Mexico,] you are not going to see a single soul; Navajo people walking around, even just around their homes. You won't even see smoke coming out of their hooghan. Totally we have gone, we have just changed our lifestyle. When I was growing up at 5:00 A.M. we had food cooking on the stove. We were out with the sheep, we were out raking in our front room area, and we were going over to our relatives. . . . And people were moving around at dawn and that took place all the way until evening. Now, today you are not going to see that. You are going to see people in cars. . . . People have changed their lifestyle totally. We have as Navajo people. (Johnson, July 3, 2005)

These views echo those noted by Kathleen Huttlinger and her associates (1992) in their study of diabetes mellitus among Navajo people. Most of those with whom they consulted stated that diabetes was a "white man's" disease. Many of those stricken with it see diabetes as a metaphor for assimilation into mainstream American society. These individuals consider themselves embroiled in a battle against a white man's disease (Huttlinger et al. 1992:710).

THE POWER OF LANGUAGE

[O]ur grandparents, they never talk about illness. They say that if you talk about illness, then it is going to come to you. So our grandparents never talk about illness.

(Larry Todachinee, June 28, 2005)

As Larry Todachinee, a crystal gazer from just north of Jeddito, Arizona, makes clear, it is inherently inappropriate to even ask a Navajo person what causes illness because of the power language has to call things into being in their world. Not wishing anyone ill, I began interviews with introductions and routinely asked Navajo people to tell me what they considered to be the Navajo view on as'ah na'adá and what they believed caused illness. As will be demonstrated, regarding health, consultants repeatedly spoke of core values they were taught in childhood, which many see as being lost. To alleviate some of the discomfort created by bringing up the subject of illness, when possible I tried to focus our conversation around the consultant's own illness narratives; that is, his or her commentaries on disease progression, curative action, and related events (Early 1982). This strategy worked, and people were generally willing to discuss their views on both illness and health in the contemporary Navajo world.

In an effort to be explicit and direct in discussing negative information with their patients, allopathic providers unintentionally conflict with age-old Navajo values and ways of thinking, thereby generating tension between themselves and many of their patients. Informed consent requires disclosing the risks of biomedical treatment or treatment refusal. Truth telling requires disclosure of "bad news," or the truth of a patient's condition (Carrese and Rhodes 1995:826). Language choices played a significant role in Amelda Sandoval Shay's daughter's brief battle with cancer and in the family's continuing struggle to cope with the disease. Indeed, Mrs. Shay noted that to this day she cannot forget her daughter's haunting screams after hearing the carefully chosen words used by a biomedical oncologist who was dutifully following his profession's standards for care.

> ASS: My daughter, her name was Carmella. She died October 23, 1983. . . . We knew my daughter was going to die. We know about it because they told us that she has cancer in her uterus and she started having problems sometime in February, so we keep going to that hospital with her. So they were testing her and testing her until sometime around this time in June we found this out, she had a cancer in her uterus. It kill us all and we didn't know what to do, what to say, how to accept it. And when the doctor told my daughter, she screamed. She screamed, she cried, and she grabbed the doctor and said, "I can't die of cancer." I sometimes—when I lay in bed, I could still hear her, what she said that particular afternoon. I can't get that out of my head. . . . She was only eighteen. (Shay, June 15, 2005)

Awkward and inappropriate language choices continue today. This was demonstrated when Mae Ann Bekis was hospitalized while I was conducting research for this project. Despite the fact that the sign in the hall clearly stated that visiting hours ended at 8:00 P.M. and that no more than three visitors were allowed per room, two of Bekis's sisters, three daughters, and five grandchildren were in her room as we entered at 8:25 P.M. Mrs. Shay and I shook hands with all present. Bekis's younger sister was in the middle of a story. When she finished everyone laughed and another story began. This time Bekis herself was the teller, and the story was about her day at the hospital. She used humor to deflect the indignation brought on by the detached clinical language of providers at the Indian Health Service Hospital in Chinle, Arizona. She said, "Well, they needed to run some tests, so they drew blood. And the nurse asked me, '*Ashįį łikán nish ninil*' 'Are you sugar?' I said, 'No, I am not. I am a human being'" (Bekis 8/5/05). The group of visitors dissolved into pools of laughter.

I was shocked to learn that this was how nurses were asking such a simple question. Curious to know what terminology has been used over time to ask patients if they are diabetic, I reviewed previous studies to ascertain this information. Paul Mico lists two phrases under diabetes: (1) '*Ashiih łikán dil biihazlįį* (sugar became present in the blood) and (2) '*Ashhįį łikán 'ínilyí* (sugar killing [one]) (1962:44). Interestingly, the first phrase is said to be commonly used in the community, while "the second is the term *being introduced by the Navajo health education personnel* into the communication processes" (Mico 1962:46, emphasis added). Navajo proscriptions on death make the introduction of such a question to a Navajo population suspect; when coupled with Navajo views on the power of language, however, it appears not only ignorant but, at the very least, counterproductive.

The constitutive power performativity theory grants to language closely parallels Navajo views on the power of language and voice. In his seminal analysis, John Langshaw Austin distinguishes between constatives and performatives. The former are statements that describe some state of affairs; the latter are utterances that accomplish, in their very enunciation, an action that generates effects (reported in Parker and Sedgwick 1995:3). By some accounts, "[T]he Navajo world was actually created or organized by means of language. The form of the world was first conceived in thought, and then this form was projected onto primordial unordered substance through the compulsive power of speech and song" (Witherspoon 1977:47). These special abilities continue on with the language given to the Earth Surface People. As Kenneth Black, Jr., told me, "[T]hey say that at the tip of our tongue it is really holy" (June 16, 2005). Moreover, as Sunny Dooley of Vanderwagen, New Mexico, detailed, "In Navajo, when you say it it will happen. That's why they tell you, you shouldn't talk nonsense, you shouldn't just blah blah blah. . . . You can't be saying things any old way, meaning negatively. . . . We believe that when we say it, when it comes out of our mouths, it is like little bubbles that put into motion all kinds of events" (Dooley, August 21, 1992). As Dooley indicated, this attribute of language has direct applicability in day-to-day conversation.

When I asked Mae Ann Bekis about the various phrases I found referring to diabetes, she warned me not to use 'Ashı̨́ı̨h łikán 'ínilyı̨́: "What happens, they talk in terms that they are going to be dying right off. You don't want to be saying that" (Bekis, March 9, 2006). To use Austin's terminology, saying 'Ashı̨́ı̨h łikán 'ínilyı̨́ is a performative speech act, or "the act of enunciation that brings into being the object it names" (reported in Morris 1995:572).

Likewise, when I asked Mrs. Bekis about the terms for cancer previously identified as in common usage (Csordas 1989:464), she recognized them immediately but cautioned me not to use naałdzid, saying, "It is nicer to say lood doo naałdzidi" (the sore that does not heal). While she acknowledged that naałdzid does mean cancer, she continued, "We only use that other word after a person has been diagnosed by doctors at the clinic" (Bekis, April 4, 2006). This falls into line with practices done daily to accommodate the special force of the Navajo language. In other words, using the term "the sore that does not heal" is like saying "those animals who are waddling on the mountains, the black ones" rather than "bears" (Kee, August 3, 1992) or substituting "the crawlers" for "the snakes," "the lizards, or "the black widow spider" while any of these striking beings are in hibernation (Bekis, July 23, 1998). Lood doo naałdzidi, then, is a circumlocution used to avoid talking about cancer because to do so risks calling it into being.

Bekis told me, "Lood doo naałdzidi, that is the proper word to use in regular conversation rather than the other word because using that other one is 'making it known to your people,' wishing it against people. The

doctors say it, and the people get scared because they're calling death"
(April 4, 2006). It cannot be overlooked that in this case, the instigating
power is granted to the biomedical provider. Moreover, at its core, Bekis's
statement means it is inappropriate to say a word in Navajo unless a biomedical physician has first said something in English; this is a powerful
political statement whereby—at least in the case of cancer—linguistic
dominance over life and death is granted to the colonizer's language.

While no harm is intended and new protocols for verbal exchanges in
clinical settings are being developed (Carrese and Rhodes 2001), American
oncologists generally maintain what is termed a "discourse of hope,"
whereby they attempt to keep the patient's outlook optimistic and to high-
light every bit of good news along the way. A certain degree of disclosure
about a patient's disease and treatment is deemed necessary, however, to
build partnerships with patients, to ensure that patients accept toxic therapies
such as chemotherapy and radiation, and to make patients responsible for
eating well, taking their medications, and keeping appointments (Good,
Good, and Schaffer 1990:75).

Despite these new protocols, words and language play a meaningful part
in interactions between allopathic physicians—especially oncologists—and
patients. This was the case at the University of New Mexico's Cancer Center
in Albuquerque, New Mexico, where Beverlianna Hale was sent for treatment
after her mastectomy. Her account offers particularly thoughtful and vivid
insights into this new form of discourse. First, rather than unabashedly proffer
a prognosis as the biomedical practitioner did in Carmella Shay's case, in
current procedure the oncologist speaks around the issue until the patient
asks questions about death, as Hale does in this narrative. Second, the biomedical oncologist engages Hale in a discourse of hope—although some
would term the encouragement lukewarm—when she replies to Hale's query
regarding the purpose of the treatment.

> BH: July 17th [2002] was my first trip to the Cancer Center [in
> Albuquerque, New Mexico] not knowing what I was headed for,
> not knowing what was in store, not knowing what was going to
> happen to me, what was going to go on. Nobody really explains
> those things to you. They tell you, "OK, you got cancer, and you
> are going to die; but yet you are going to go over to the Cancer

Center and get treatment." That is all they tell you. And when you get there, you've never seen these people, and the doctor is always telling you about your prognosis, and you say "OK." I walked in and the doctor told me: "There [are] five stages in breast cancer. And we stage you by your disease. One is good because it is curable. Five is no turning back. You don't have that much time left." I says, "So where do I stand?" She goes, "You are at stage three; you are right in the middle. You can either go this way or you can go the other direction." So I said, "Great, so in other words, I am going to die?" And she says, "It is a possibility." So I said, "So why am I doing treatment? What is the treatment for?" And she says, "Well we are going to try to kill the cancer cells in your body. We will see what happens." (Hale, June 13, 2005)

Discourse of hope or not, such statements by biomedical providers regarding prognosis are especially inappropriate when speaking to Navajo patients because of the power attributed to language in the Navajo world. As a performative speech act, saying naałdzid calls the disease of cancer into being.

Bekis noted that patients become "scared" when physicians use the unspeakable term for cancer, and that is precisely how Navajo consultants such as Beverlianna Hale (June 13, 2005) and Julia Mathis (June 11, 2005), a mother and wife who is a lifelong resident of Chinle, Arizona, described their initial response to providers' assessments. As Mathis notes in the next excerpt, she made a concerted effort to avert negative thoughts about her illness derived from listening to biomedical providers. This concurs with the findings of Joseph Carrese and Lorna Rhodes (1995:828), who observed: "Informants commented often that it was important to 'think and speak in a positive way.' . . . Given the Navajo view regarding the power of thought and language to shape reality and control events, and the related idea that health is maintained and restored through positive ritual language, the prominence of this theme is logical." Mathis did this by focusing on "beating" the cancer.[1]

JM: When I was diagnosed with cancer, I had to really train my way of thinking. All the negative thinking, I had to push it aside. Although it does, it scares you, and the first thing that comes to your mind is your kids. You know, what are my kids going to do? But then you start thinking, well, this is me, I am talking about me. . . . I am gonna beat this cancer. I am going to defeat it and I am going to be a walking example. And I am going to have other people see how you can fight the cancer. So . . . I did a lot of praying. In fact, I think my belief got stronger. I went to church, they helped me with prayers, plus my own traditions, like the prayers that they provided for me, all of that. (Mathis, June 11, 2005)

This image of beating the cancer was reiterated by Beverlianna Hale (June 13, 2005): "They tell me I have a very aggressive breast cancer. It is very aggressive but I keep thinking it can't be that aggressive, I am more aggressive. I am going to beat this thing. I don't care what they tell me, I am going to beat this thing. I've gotta be here for my kids." Each woman presents herself as capable of beating a fatal adversary called into being by the words of biomedical providers. Importantly, it does not mean they have fully accepted this ideology; it only means they recognize the danger of the providers' speech and accept the challenge to fight it.

HEALTH IDIOMS

A term I often heard while listening to Navajo consultants talk about their views on health and illness is balance. Like loss and harmony, it is one of several terms repeated over and over in testimonials about illness and health. These turns of phrase are valuable clues, for as Linda Whiteford has pointed out, "Whereas health may be commodified by global economic and political forces, transformed through international health policies and programs and interpreted by history and proximity, it is internalized in local idioms and identities" (2000:59).

As previously mentioned, the Navajo origin story details the construction of this world and the creation of the Earth Surface People. The fact that a charter was given to the ancestral Nihookáá Dine'é indicating how they must live to keep the world in harmony, along with songs, prayers, and ceremonies to restore its natural order when disharmony occurred, indicates that imbalanced states were anticipated and even prophesied (O'Bryan 1956:111; Reichard 1950:275; Schwarz 2001:152–80).

Insofar as illness is a prime indicator that disharmony exists, Navajo religious ritual can be considered health-oriented. What, then, is the traditional Navajo health idiom? Received wisdom maintains that Navajo traditional healing considers that afflictions result from a loss of harmony or balance caused by etiologies such as spiritual violations and unfortunate events or encounters (see Coulehan 1980; Porvaznik 1967; Reichard 1950; Wyman and Kluckhohn 1938).

A fundamental Navajo cultural idiom is thus *hózhǫ́ naashá*, or "to walk in beauty," which is synonymous with "to live in harmony or balance," meaning within their sacred geography according to the guidelines established by Changing Woman and the other Diyin Dine'é before the world was turned over to the Earth Surface People. As Johnson Dennison alluded in his discussion of nature, animals, and birds, Navajo epistemology focuses on maintaining harmonious relationships between humans and other entities within their environment as well as with the Diyin Dine'é.

The notion of having true respect for every living thing in one's environment, especially the intimate relationship between Navajo individuals and animals, insects, and reptiles—including snakes—was brought home by Frank C. Young, a seventy-seven-year-old ceremonial practitioner from Chilchinbito, Arizona, who performed a multitude of ceremonies including the Ant Way, Snake Way, and *Hóchxǫ́'jí*, or "Evil Way," among others, when in his prime. His daughter Nora Young recalled a pertinent incident that occurred while he was staying with her:

> NY: Snakes were gathering around the house. . . . We were like . . . "Why are these snakes coming over?" And in his dream it came to him. When he was young he was working at a construction site, building roads . . . and he was asked to chop up all of the snakes to destroy them. So that was his job and that was what he had done. And in his dream it came to him, bits and pieces of snake parts. . . . The ones that were crawling around and he could actually see them like that as he looked out the window. When one was passing through it was turning into little pieces. And so he had that ceremony [the Snake Way] done, too. And he was like paralyzed all the way from the neck down. And right after that ceremony was done for him . . . he got flown in [to a hospital outside reservation

boundaries] and that is where they found out that a chipped bone
was pressing against his spinal cord, and he recovered immediately
from it. (N. Young, June 14, 2005)

The primordial logic underlying Navajo relations with animals, reptiles,
and insects—as well as the seemingly countless guidelines governing their
everyday interactions with those creatures, including rules against chopping
up snakes—was further elucidated by interviews with other consultants.
For example, my knowledge of Native American Church (NAC) understandings of illness was immeasurably advanced by a conversation with
Thomas Deschene, Jr., who shared this account, which he credits to Navajo
oral history. His inclusion of the Creator entity and reference to sacrifice,
however, reflect Christian influences emblematic of NAC syncretism.

> TD: A lot of these illnesses and a lot of these stories, it goes back to
> the beginning of time when the earth was made, the fire, the water,
> the universe. The Creator made a lot of Holy People too and made
> a lot of different plants for our food and herbs. And there were a
> lot of different insects. During the time that the Creator decided
> to make a human being, he made a young man. And the Creator
> told them, every living creature—I guess the insects were people
> back then—he told them, "Take care of this person." And he went
> somewhere with the Holy People to build all these animals and
> things. And the human was curious and started doing things he
> was not supposed to and he started picking on the Lightning, that
> Man-with-the-Lightning. And Lightning was really mean; he didn't
> want to be bothered by no one. But he [the human] kept picking on
> him and he got him really pissed off, and the Lighting Man turned
> around and struck him. And that young man that got hit by the
> Lightning was splattered all over the ground, all of his parts every-
> where. And the people, the animals, and all these creatures, they
> got into an argument, "How are we going to do this? How are we
> going to fix this?" . . . Certain groups, like the ants, they want to
> put this person back together, they were having an argument when
> the Creator came back. He asked them, "What happened?" They
> said, "That Lighting Man struck him because he was picking on

it." "That's where you guys were supposed to be taking care of this person." . . . The Holy People were sent back to the holy place, and he got after all these Earth [Surface] People and insects and reptiles and he told them, "This young man, its body, its parts are way beyond repair. You can't fix it." And they were asked to sacrifice themselves to be used as human parts. "If you don't want to sacrifice yourself, then you are going to vanish from this earth. You have a language now, you will take your language with you and you will only communicate with others that have that one language—with the different insects or different animals." . . . So they sacrificed themselves to put that person back together, and the insects that were chosen to put this person back together were those little ants, sugar ants, the ones like crystal, like glass ants? . . . They are the ones that were chosen for that person. And sure enough a lot of parts were really damaged. And that is where a lot of those insects and reptiles became part of that person's body. When they [had] put that person back together, that person was still dead, wasn't moving, so they made an offering to the Lighting Man and Lightning Man put life back into that person to bring it back to life. And from that day on all the insects, reptiles, and birds that volunteered to sacrifice their lives to help this person, that's where a lot of our traditional ceremonies came in to where if for no reason at all you can't kill a spider, if for no reason at all you do that, you are going to have certain kinds of health problems. . . . For instance . . . the insides were so damaged, the snake was put in there as part of our intestines, and that is what it is. . . .

MS: And how about the spider? You mentioned the spider.

TD: A spider was also used.

MS: A spider was used to remake the man?

TD: Probably most of the insects, and that's how we live with them up until this day. And if you do something to them, they will get back at you, a certain part of your body will start having health problems. . . .

MS: I have never heard that story before, and that is really, really helpful to me.

TD: The snake is just part of the story. There are a lot of other stories. Each insect has their own story about how they volunteered to help the human, and that is how we live with them. (Deschene, June 15, 2005)

In the view of Navajo traditionalists, Earth Surface People do not stand apart from nature; rather, what is made apparent in this account are the intimate interconnections Navajo individuals have as integral components of nature. In addition to providing information about the elemental relationships humans share with animals, reptiles, and insects, this version of what is commonly referred to as the "restoration episode" has much to tell us about contemporary Navajo notions of health and illness (Spencer 1957:100–102).[2] First and foremost, as Katherine Spencer pointed out half a century ago, the fact that the hero can be restored after being completely shattered and having his body parts scattered indicates that *there is no conception of an ailment beyond the bounds of treatment in traditional Navajo medical philosophy* (Spencer 1957:32).

While offering such insights, Deschene's account is differentiated by a coherent logic dictating that if you harm an insect, reptile, or animal, "a certain part of your body will start having health problems" (Deschene, June 15, 2005). Moreover, Deschene presents this story as if the insects and reptiles were given only one option by which to redeem themselves— to sacrifice themselves as parts to be used in restoration of the hero. Is this how the story appears in Navajo oral history, or is it a revisionist account made to conform to an alternative religious doctrine or doctrines? To answer these questions, I reviewed three previously documented accounts of the restoration episode, in which a hero is shattered by a hailstorm, thunder, and lightning, respectively, and is subsequently brought back to life. These accounts are the Flint Way told to Berard Haile by Slim Curly of Crystal, New Mexico, during the winter of 1930–31 (Haile 1943); a version of Hail Way told to Mary Wheelwright by Hastiin Tlah of Newcomb, New Mexico, prior to 1937 (Wheelwright 1946); and an account of Hail Way told to Gladys Reichard by Hastiin Tlah in the winter of 1938 (Reichard 1944). While insects do play vital roles in each of these versions in terms of finding body parts and reassembling the hero, in each case the focus is on restoration of the account's hero rather than redemption of those in whose care he was left. Presumably, these various ants, bees, and other entities helped on the basis of generalized reciprocity, for none of these accounts mentions that those beings needed to help with the respective hero's restoration to ensure their own redemption.

The plot outlined by Deschene fits well, however, with Christian ideas of *redemptive suffering*—the sacrifice of Jesus for mankind (Porterfield 2005:131). Like Jesus, the beings in this narrative are told by the transcendent Christian God—referred to here as Creator who, unlike Changing Woman, is incidentally gender masculine—that they *must* sacrifice themselves for the good of others. This simultaneously demonstrates how Christian doctrine has been introduced through the NAC and reveals Thomas Deschene, Jr.'s, account of the restoration episode to be an example of syncretism. If we follow Shaw and Stewart's suggestion and look for evidence of power and agency in examples of syncretism (1994:7), this alteration of the account can be seen to give moral authority and validity to both traditional views about Navajo interdependence with all other living beings in their world—including the Holy People to whom an appropriate prestation is made in exchange for Lighting Man reinstating life to the reassembled hero—and to the Christian God, thereby further empowering Deschene as a Native American Church road man.

Not all Navajo consultants professed syncretic views. Tso Allen is a self-proclaimed traditionalist from Hunter's Point, Arizona, who, after years of experience as a public health nurse, is dedicating her expertise to the Navajo Nation Special Diabetes Program. When asked what causes illness, she used the traditional cultural imperative that all movement occurs in a sun-wise, or clockwise, direction to illustrate how not obeying the rules established by Changing Woman and the other Diyin Dine'é will bring illness upon oneself: "It is breaking the belief system, breaking the natural laws or the laws that are given to the Navajo people, the common laws that are given to the people. . . . They say when you are taught to do something, you are supposed to do it that way. So when you go counterclockwise, when you go against and [do] not do those things, they say that is when you cause disharmony within yourself. Therefore, you bring about illness upon yourself, is how they explained it" (T. Allen, July 15, 2005).

As consultant accounts such as those of Nora Young (June 14, 2005), Tso Allen (July 15, 2005), Johnson Dennison (June 22, 2005), and others reveal, breaches of the diné bike'ji or other circumstances may result in

disharmony or imbalance in the form of illness—which was prophesied in
the oral histories.

> MS: What do you think—and answer this from any perspective you
> want—what do you think causes illness?
>
> NY: We believe in balance. It's a spiritual balance, and . . . once one of
> the strands kind of unravels, it creates that illness or that imbalance.
> There's this belief that as we're growing up we're taught based on
> the four sacred mountains and . . . the significance of each one.
> Like for the east mountain, there's so many things that it's like a
> whole set of doctrines that we regard when we think of the sacred
> mountains. An example is that it [the eastern mountain] deals with
> our mental state—it controls our mental state. And then the south
> mountain, the turquoise mountain, it deals with a physical strength;
> and then the west, our social strength; and the north, our spiritual
> being. So all of that is like an inter-rolled part of well-being. So
> when we think of illness, we think that something is wrong in one
> of these four states that we have. And we try to figure out which
> one it is, and that's how ceremonies are set up. So when I think of
> illness, I think uh-oh, we did something, we didn't revere some-
> thing the right way or we did something wrong. That normally
> comes to mind. (N. Young, June 14, 2005)

These chronicles capture what for decades has been the accepted understanding of Navajo views on illness. Doctors Alexander and Dorothea
Leighton provided this summary in *The Navaho Door* (1944).

> The Navaho theory of illness is not that illness is caused by germs,
> wrong food, or improper functioning of the body, as we believe, but
> rather that by some means the patient fell out of harmony with the
> forces of nature, and this discord makes him susceptible to catching a
> sickness from another person, breaking his leg, or developing any of
> the symptoms that can plague a human being. The natural consequence
> of this belief is that, when a person falls ill, the most important thing is
> to restore through ritual the harmony which has been disrupted so the
> body can heal itself. (Leighton and Leighton 1944:55)

Much has changed in the Navajo world since the Leightons wrote this statement. While many consultants pointed to loss of harmony and several consider stress to be a cause of illness (Black, June 16, 2005; Goldtooth, July 18, 2005; Mathis, June 11, 2005), like those who spoke with the Leightons, no one with whom I spoke pointed to germs as a source of illness. Other people with whom I consulted attributed illness to contact with the dead, monsters, original sin, the prophecy of the Gambler's return, the devil, lightning, changes in lifestyle, improper functioning of the body, the need for confession, problems with foods, and pollutants. All of these topics were either not mentioned or outright denied by the Leightons. When asked about the causes of current diseases plaguing Navajo people, those interviewed found insights in ancient stories and texts with characters as diverse as Adam and Eve, human-devouring monsters, the devil, and the Gambler.

The Bible—both New and Old Testaments—is frequently drawn upon by Christian Navajo (Lewton and Bydone 2000:491; Rapoport 1954). Based on his research among Navajo members of the Galilean and Mormon congregations in 1949–50 at a Navajo community that he called Rimrock, New Mexico, Robert Rapoport reported that in the view of *at least* these congregants, the Bible can be said to be the Christian origin story. As such, "Changing Woman, who created the earth people, is taken to be God. Monster Slayer, the son of Changing Woman (God), is then identified with Jesus. The identification is enhanced by Monster Slayer's activities on earth. Like Jesus, he came onto the earth to 'save' the people by ridding the earth of the dangerous monsters that occupied it before mankind's emergence" (Rapoport 1954:52).

In fact, several of my consultants alluded to or actually incorporated this text directly into an interview. The latter is the case with Pastor George S. Davis, recaptured here, when I visited him on the grounds of his church in Lukachukai, Arizona:

MS: What causes illness? What makes people ill? Makes them sick?
GD: It's an evil spirit itself. I'll show you. We believe the Holy Bible is the word. The word is Jesus. Jesus is the word. So, sting, sting, red ants, using these, uh—
MS: Sting?
GD: Sting. How do you spell that?

MS: S-T-I-N-G. . . . But I asked you about illness and you said it is
an evil spirit. Does someone have to do something to have the
evil spirit come into them? Does it come into them?

GD: No, it's himself. You can't see. You can't see the evil spirit. . . .
There is a way, the evil way, when the evil gets on someone with
his power and with his—

MS: But what makes the evil get on someone?

GD: See, the sting of death is sin and the strength of sin is the law. If
the evil gives someone power, if the evil has power, the sin is the
law and the evil spirit is—this is the way he went. He gives his
power to this person to steal, he is going to . . . kill that person
that he is—that he was, and his strength is, you can't get away
from it. You got to do the same way. Right here.

LN: 1st Corinthians, chapter 15, verses 55 and 56, I believe it is.

GD: Right, and then you read it from here to here (pushing the Bible
into my hands and indicating a passage)—

MS: Out loud?

GD: So we can hear.

MS: "The sting of death is sin and the strength of sin is the law, but
thanks be to God who gives us the victory through our Lord Jesus
Christ. Therefore, my beloved brethren, be steadfast and movable
always abounding in the work of the Lord, knowing that your
labor is in vain to the Lord." So, the evil spirits just take over
someone and that makes the person ill? Is that what you are saying?

GD: Yeah. See, if you have a headache, who is doing it? Yourself?

MS: That is what I am asking you.

GD: Or your grandpa or your *nálí* (his or her paternal grandparent)
or your *shimá* (my mother) or your sister, brother, are they the
ones giving you a headache? . . .

MS: I don't know. That is why I am asking you.

GD: See, that is the reason I ask you. You don't know this. You don't
see it. It is from the evil spirit. The devil, he is the one that gives
you pain, illness, cancer, all this. . . . He is the one doing it. So we
have to cast them out.

MS: How do you cast them out?

> GD: In the name of Jesus. He is the only one. He says, I am the way, the truth, and the life. . . . This is a Holy Bible. There is a lot of sin, a lot of evilness, sickness [of] all kinds. Bad things right in front of you, but if you believe Christ and you have this . . . this is holy. The word is holy. God's son, Jesus, the word is Jesus. If you really believe it and [are] born again, then you will have this, if there is a lot of sickness in front of you, you just pass by it in Jesus's name. (George Davis and Lawson Nakai, July 18, 2005)

George S. Davis says the devil brings pain and illness to people and that these must be cast out by Christians. His claim that a believer's devotion, or will to believe, is essential to the agency through which healing occurs fits precisely with the modern concept of faith healing (Porterfield 2005:116). This enables him to proclaim that the power of the word of Jesus enables born-again Christians to walk past illness and other evils with impunity.

An important element binding these multiple texts is that in each case illness was expected or prophesied. For example, Hastiin Lonewolf of Del Muerto, Arizona, stated enthusiastically, "I've been Presbyterian ever since I was born. I grew up as a Presbyterian and my family, having, being religious, Presbyterian, going to church and all that, believing in the Lord, I served to that all my life" (Lonewolf, June 10, 2005). When asked what causes illness, such as that which led to him having a heart transplant, he replied, "Well, what they preach, what they teach is that there's sickness in the world, that it's not just because the person was doing wrong, but *there is always sickness in the world that was caused from the beginning of time*" (Lonewolf, June 10, 2005). Also referring to the nascence of the world in his account, Harrison Watchman, a devout member of the Christian Reformed Church who currently attends the Assemblies of God Church, denoted illness as a form of punishment for wrongful acts: "I would say that, I don't want to use the words Adam and Eve, but when they made a mistake back in the creation of time, the Lord says, 'You've made a mistake, now you're gonna have to pay for it. Now you have to work hard and then there's going to be illness.' And that's where it comes from, I think, the Lord's payment. 'I gave you good earth and you messed it up, now you have to suffer the consequences.' And I think it's where illness comes from" (H. Watchman, June 21, 2005).[3] Not unlike traditional Navajo views on the origin of certain powerful sources of danger in the contemporary world, Watchman portrays illness as the predestined outcome of ancestral impropriety.

Analysis of the particular idioms used by adherents of the Native American Church or the various sects of Christianity practiced on the reservation offers insight into the philosophical tenets guiding their decisions regarding health and healing, just as the idiom "living in harmony" provides insight into the views of those practicing traditional Navajo religion. Such idioms therefore serve as windows into different perceptions of curing and health.

• • •

Beliefs regarding health, illness, and healing are not neutral in the Navajo world. The sources to which people attribute the causes of disease and the power of cures offer important clues about their notions of relatedness, how they understand their contemporary moral and political landscape, and how they comprehend personal and collective identity affiliations.

According to consultants, ancient teachings deem rising early, running, and praying to be necessary for a healthy Navajo life. Traditional Navajo notions of preventive health care include information about prophylactic herbal mixtures as well as ceremonies done to shield Navajo people from seasonal illnesses. Importantly, historical trauma has taken its toll, and contemporary Navajo consider the mental strain of living according to the requirements of a foreign worldview a contributing factor to their current health concerns.

Allopathic providers unintentionally conflict with age-old Navajo values and ways of thinking in efforts to be explicit and direct in discussing negative information with their patients. Such discourse generates undue tension between them and many of their patients because of the power of Navajo language to call things into being. Careful attention to discourse also reveals prominent idioms such as loss and balance or harmony, redemptive suffering, and predetermination in consultants' testimonies about illness and curing.

CHAPTER FOUR

Sources of Pathosis

We are all encountering all these different kinds of situations where illness comes throughout our body and our mind and in one instance, people go to funerals the way the Anglos do. We're not supposed to do that. Only certain designated people are supposed to take that body out to the graveside and take care of it. There is supposed to be quarantine; you build a shelter and stay there for four days, and after that the family members wash themselves with certain herbs and then they come home. But now Navajo people go to the funeral. The whole family, people, relatives, they go there and they kind of indulge—some of them even touch the body. This is an unbalanced area and so when they come home, sometime after that they get [an] illness or bad dreams or emotional problems, things like that. So, that is one way. Another form of illness comes from nature, like in the form of lightning, being killed by that or being near the area where lightning struck. This causes an unbalance in the body. So, that is where that occurs. And also the hurricanes or tornadoes, things like that.

(F. Laughter, June 16, 2005)

In this narrative, eighty-five-year-old Fred Laughter's response to my query regarding the causes of illness in the Navajo world is framed within the traditional belief system. While he does not dismiss the types of illness that derive from inappropriate contact with elements of nature such as lightning, hurricanes, and tornadoes, Laughter chose to emphasize instead illnesses incurred as a result of contamination by contact with death. When queried on the topic of sources of illness, other consultants pointed to the monsters of old or environmental pollutants and contaminants. Death is not the only source of contamination; a second major source is contact with outsiders—that is, enemies, alive or dead. Contamination from living enemy-outsiders plays out in many important areas of Navajo life including intermarriage, warfare, and, most relevant to our purposes, surgery. Contamination specifically caused by contact with the dead—whether Navajo or non-Navajo—plays an extremely important role in the arenas of organ transplantation and blood transfusions.

DEATH—DANGEROUS AND OTHERWISE

Death and everything connected with it are horrible to The People. Even to look upon the bodies of dead animals, except those killed for food, is a peril. . . . This intense and morbid avoidance of the dead and of everything connected with them rests upon the fear of ghosts. Most of the dead may return as ghosts to plague the living. *Only those who die of old age, the stillborn, and infants who do not live long enough to utter a cry or sound do not produce ghosts, and for them the four days of mourning after burial need not be observed, since they will not be injurious to the living.* Otherwise, any dead person, no matter how friendly or affectionate his attitude while he was living, is a potential danger.

A ghost is the malignant part of the dead person. It returns to avenge some neglect or offense. (Kluckhohn and Leighton 1974[1946]:184–85, emphasis added)

One of the conundrums of Navajo ethnography is the near constant mention in the published literature of the Navajo so-called fear of the dead and taboos surrounding death, concomitant with the recognized but heretofore underanalyzed fact pointed out by Clyde Kluckhohn and Dorothea Leighton in the previous quotation—and noted by numerous other scholars over the years—that in the Navajo world, *not all forms of death are deemed dangerous* (Franciscan Fathers 1910:508; Kluckhohn and Leighton 1974[1946]:184–85; Kunitz 1983:123; McNeley 1981:57; Wyman, Hill, and Osanai 1942:16–17). Navajo traditional views regarding which forms of death are dangerous can be nuanced by considering the two noted exceptions—stillbirths and the deaths of elders.

While opinions have always varied among Navajo people regarding exactly what it is that is lost to the body when life ends, general consensus exists among those holding to traditional beliefs that a ch'įįdii, or "ghost," separates from the corpse and that it maintains "individuality" (Brugge 1978:312) or a "personal identity" (Shepardson 1978:384) for a variable period of time. Gladys Reichard claims that when a Navajo dies, "that which is good in him becomes amalgamated with the great concept of universal harmony," while "that which was bad, earthly, fleshly is his 'dead part,' his 'ghost'" (1949:69). She continues, "Nothing anyone can do in this life can change this maleficent part of man. Inevitable, it must be avoided" (Reichard 1949:69).

Ch'įįdii are believed capable of returning to the earth to avenge wrongs done to the person of whom they were a part during life (Brugge 1978:324) or offenses such as improper burial, the holding back of their belongings, failure to kill a horse or sheep, or disturbance or removal of grave goods or their body parts after interment (Wyman, Hill, and Osanai 1942:11). They are also deemed capable of causing "illness, misfortune, and premature or unnatural death" (Frisbie 1978:304). Illness through contact with the dead may result from a variety of circumstances, including combat situations (B. Allen, June 10, 2005; Nelson, July 19, 2004; Shepard, June 3, 2005), automobile accidents (Goldtooth, July 18, 2005; F. Laughter, June 16, 2005; Nelson, July 20, 2004), and contact with human remains in archaeological ruins, in burials, or, as Fred Laughter mentioned, at funerals (B. Allen, June 10, 2005; F. Laughter, June 16, 2005; Long, July 13, 2005; Nelson, July 20, 2004). Because of these possibilities, Navajo death rites are "oriented towards the prevention of such return rather than towards the loss situation" (Wyman, Hill, and Osanai 1942:23).

Navajo people are cautioned from earliest childhood to avoid contact with the dead, both Navajo and non-Navajo, whenever possible to prevent encounters with this maleficent component of the inner form, which is made up of intertwined winds.[1] According to Navajo individuals with whom I consulted, the inner form enters the body shortly *after* birth as the first gulps of air taken by a newborn, which is not considered to be alive until it breathes and cries (Bekis, July 28, 1993; Denny, October 8, 1993; Walters, August 18, 1992). This corresponds with information documented by the Franciscan Fathers in 1910 (451).

In seeming contrast, the Navajo consultants with whom James McNeley conferred indicated that two winds enter the fetus *at the moment of conception,* an additional wind enters the newborn at birth, and other winds sequentially enter the individual one at a time for the remainder of his or her life (McNeley 1981:49). Careful attention to the Navajo accounts documented in McNeley's *Holy Wind in Navajo Philosophy,* however, reveals that the pair of winds that enters the fetus at conception is derived from the parental fluids involved in conception (McNeley 1981:49). Because the first pair of winds McNeley discusses does not technically "enter" the completed fetus but is part of the fluids constituting it, I find no inherent disagreement between the model of conception described by McNeley and the one offered by those with whom I spoke. With the exception of the terms used to label the bodily substances involved, this description of Navajo understandings of human conception corresponds directly with that from my consultants, which also relies on male and female fluids (McNeley 1981:33–34; Schwarz 1997:69). Furthermore, the important additional wind believed to enter the child at birth in the model explained by McNeley's consultants parallels the inner form believed to enter the child at birth in the model proposed by Navajo people with whom I consulted. In both instances, additional single winds capable of influencing individuals enter sequentially, one at a time, throughout their lives.

A newborn's death is considered to pose no threat to others because he or she has yet to think, speak, acquire knowledge, or do evil (Davies 2001:7; Wyman, Hill, and Osanai 1942:17; see also Kunitz 1983:123). Because of Navajo beliefs about varying degrees of dangers assoiciated with death at different stages of life, there was little risk to Julia Mathis's father in offering blood to his infant daughter (Mathis, June 11, 2005); for, as noted, a newborn's death is considered no threat to others.

Importantly, a child's first laugh indicates that the intertwined winds, which enter the body soon after birth, *have become fully attached to the body*; prior to this point, an infant can easily die. The person who makes the baby laugh for the first time is obligated to sponsor an *'Awéé' ch'ídaadlóóhgó bá na'a'néé'*, or "First Laugh Ceremony," in honor of the event (T. Begay, July 26, 1991; Bekis, August 5, 1992; Tso, July 14, 1991).

This rite celebrates the child's initial expression of emotion. Relatives use the occasion as an opportunity to ensconce the child firmly within his or her social landscape through initiation into the complex system of communication and reciprocity operating within kin networks. A child's first laugh initiates his or her lifelong involvement in the daily interchange expressed through humor and reciprocity. Thus, children are anchored firmly within the network of reciprocal relations vital to communication and cooperation in Navajo life simultaneous with the firm anchoring of their inner forms as individuals.

Those who die in the prime of their lives, while their inner forms are well attached, are considered the most potent etiologic agents because their ch'įįdii can cause "ghost sickness" in others, leading to death if not treated by the proper ceremonies (Davies 2001:7; Kunitz 1983:123; Wyman, Hill, and Osanai 1942:30–32). According to McNeley, small winds from the cardinal points are believed to assist individual Navajo by strengthening their inner forms, shielding them from harmful winds, and warning of dangers inherent in any course of action (1981:46). The inner form also monitors personal behavior and, if need be, provides guidance for returning to the correct path. Support and guidance are withdrawn if the individual fails to comply, at which point the person becomes weak (McNeley 1981:47). When the inner form is taken from the body by the Holy People, death occurs (McNeley 1981:47, 57). McNeley further clarifies the particulars: "If despite the advice and warnings given by Winds sent by the Holy Ones and the availability of their help through prayers and offerings, a person disregards the succorance and persists in a wrong way of life, his Wind may be taken from him, an indication that it is no longer leading him along the good way. It appears to be for this reason that the departed Winds of those who do not live to an old age are to be feared. Their faults, their harmful characteristics, are taken for granted" (1981:49). McNeley's consultants indicated that what is to be feared at death is the accumulation of all missteps—intended or not—bad deeds, and evil acts committed by the individual to that point in his or her life, which collectively taint the corpse and are embodied in what he terms "harmful Winds which have departed from the bodies of the deceased and which rotate sunward" (McNeley 1981:49). The latter are what most scholars simply refer to as ghosts.

While burial customs have been changing across the vast Navajo reservation over the past several decades in response to various influences (Griffen 1978; Shepardson 1978),[2] until recently inhumation practices have reflected profound concern over contact with "what is feared at death." Conventional Navajo mortuary practices include strict avoidance of contact with the deceased to prevent illness or unnatural death, as well as strict burial procedures and rules, and they do not involve public events or celebrations (Frisbie 1978:303); moreover, rules regarding cultural displays govern when and where Navajo people can demonstrate their loss after a loved one's death.

In such cases, as Donald Denetdeal noted, interment is a private or "family" matter, and only the minimum number of people needed to perform the requisite procedures (Franciscan Fathers 1910:453; Frisbie 1978:303) and willing to expose themselves to the potentially dangerous effects of death are involved in the process (Reichard 1928:141): "The immediate family shows a lot of respect. . . . [O]nly two people are selected to clean up and dispose of the body. That is the way it was traditionally. . . . It was not meant for all the extended relatives and family. . . . It was not meant for a whole community because death is between the Maker and that person— and it should be private and it should be respected, people should stay away" (Denetdeal, July 11, 2004).

Strict regulations govern the verbal and nonverbal behavior of participants, as well as their attire and sustenance. Accordingly, tradition dictates that all members of the burial party strip to breechcloths or skirts, untie their hair and leave it flowing so that not even a hair tie is unnecessarily exposed, wash and dress the deceased in his or her finest clothing and jewelry, and select the items that will accompany the body as grave goods (Franciscan Fathers 1910:453; Frisbie 1978:303; Reichard 1928:142).

Once a site for interment has been selected, the burial party transports the corpse and grave goods to that location. Family members pay close attention to ill relatives, and care is taken to remove the dying from the hooghan before death occurs. If someone does die in a hooghan, "[T]he east side, or doorway, is closed, and an opening is made in the north side through which the corpse is carried out for burial. The hogan is then burnt and leveled to the ground, while the earthen pots used in cleaning the corpse, or cooking utensils, are broken there and then" (Franciscan Fathers 1910:456).

On the way to the place selected for internment, the burial party is forbidden to spit or indulge in unnecessary conversation, and unsuspecting travelers are motioned away from their path. After carefully arranging and burying the body and grave goods in the chosen place, breaking or otherwise mutilating shovels and other burial implements, and often killing the deceased's favorite horse, the members of the burial party erase their tracks and return home, in a "skip and hop fashion," by an alternate route. After purifying themselves by various means, members of the burial party rejoin the deceased's family, who then ends the fast begun at the time of the death. All those involved abstain from travel, labor, and unnecessary conversation during the four-day mourning period, which is most often spent in a shelter built south of the family home, between it and the gravesite (Franciscan Fathers 1910:454–55; Frisbie 1978:303; Reichard 1928:142–43).

Within the confines of this system of practices, keening and weeping are allowed only in the presence of relatives and close friends. The bodily aspects of emotional expression partially explain mourning rules that limit people's contact with grieving individuals. To make cultural sense, these various concerns must be contextualized within the wider framework of the principle of synecdoche—one of the Navajo tenets governing personhood. This principle dictates that every part is equivalent to the whole, so anything done to or by means of a part influences or has the effect of the whole. The part therefore stands for the whole. As Marcel Mauss explained, "Teeth, saliva, sweat, nails, hair represent a total person, in such a way that through these parts one can act directly on the individual concerned, either to bewitch or enchant him. Separation in no way disturbs the contiguity; a whole person can even be reconstituted or resuscitated with the aid of one of these parts: *totum ex parte*" (1972[1902]:64).

Put another way, "[T]he personality of a being is indivisible, residing as a whole in each one of the parts" (Mauss 1972[1902]:64). The connection remains in force even after separation. Therefore, the influence continues after physical contact has ended, and it may be permanent. Moreover, it holds that people, objects, and other entities that have contact with one another may influence each other through the transfer of some or all of their properties. People therefore avoid such contact because they know the mourners' tears will convey their emotional state and cause all those present during their expulsion to experience the same emotions.

At funerals and during periods of mourning, family members cry openly up until the time the body is buried.[3] On the fourth day after the interment, when it is believed the deceased has safely made his or her journey to the afterworld (Wyman, Hill, and Osanai 1942:38), the mourning period closes with a ritual purification of all involved, a brief period of wailing (Franciscan Fathers 1910:455; Frisbie 1978:303; Reichard 1928:143), and a communal meal that marks the reincorporation of the bereaved into social life (Shepardson 1978:387). Close kin are advised to stop crying altogether (Reichard 1928:143; Shepardson 1978:387–88); otherwise, they will be anticipating another purpose—that is, another death. Elders of the family advise all those assembled to forget the dead and turn toward life and the living (Shepardson 1978:387–88). Don Mose, Jr., a self-proclaimed traditionalist from Piñon, Arizona, shared his personal experience regarding what happens when one does not follow this advice.

Mose first became aware of the consequences of not limiting one's mourning to the proscribed time after the loss of his father. He recalled, "When my dad died I had a nightmare with him [in it]. He fell out of his casket and he was falling on me and I screamed bloody murder, and they had to take me back to my grandfather to do 'Hóchx̨ǫ́'jí.' They had to do the Blackening Way for me. I got over it; I never had a dream about him again. There is this special body, but it doesn't really belong to us; it belongs to the Holy People" (Mose, June 13, 2005). This lesson was reinforced years later when his brother passed away. Mose willingly revisited these painful memories to teach the lesson at hand: overly long mourning causes one's loved ones to linger.

> DM: He had pancreas cancer and he died. . . . We were very close and we did everything together. . . . But my uncle who is a medicine

man came to me and said, "Don't cry; cry if you want, but don't overdo it. It will have an effect on you again." He said, "If you cry too much it stays, it hurts even more. You have got to release it. . . . You don't want to let your crying go too far because that is dangerous. He is in a better place. . . . He is gone now. But he still is here with you as well." And I honestly believe that now, what he was trying to tell me. After he had these good comforting words for me, it always [came] back. I go to the school and I go into his classroom and I had that sad feeling again. It kept going like that for about two months. And one night I went in my bedroom. I closed the door with the windows open and I fell asleep. . . . I thought I heard the door open to my bedroom. . . . I saw an image standing there. All I could see is the glasses, my brother wore glasses. I saw the glasses and then I wasn't scared. . . . I just lay still and I was probably more amazed than anything else. He had the same height, but I couldn't see his face, all I can see is black, the whole image is dark. When he finally spoke he said, "Is it OK if I stay here for the night? These people are always asking me to do things and I am getting tired. I want to rest." And I said, "Yes, there is a place here for you if you want." So he walked right here and he lay down and that is when I woke up. I visualized everything but there was nobody there, but I saw out the window, the drape was pushed in. Ever since then, I got over the death of my brother. What my uncle was telling me [was], "There's a fine line between the living and the dead. They are still here with us." . . . Now that is why he told me, "Don't be crying and bawling because all you are doing is hindering him. You are bringing him back. You are not letting go of him. That is why he keeps coming back." (Mose, June 13, 2005)

Relevant to the notion of bringing or calling the deceased back is the fact that in some areas of the reservation the Navajo system governing mourning also requires that family members refrain from mentioning the deceased's given name, in Navajo or in English, for a year or longer after his or her death (Brugge 1978:323; Kluckhohn and Leighton 1974[1946]:202; Shufeldt 1891:305).

As with newborns, the deaths of elders are not considered dangerous (Davies 2001:7; see also Kluckhohn and Leighton 1974[1946]:184; Kunitz 1983:123; McNeley 1981:57). During the aging process, the attachment of the inner form lessens, and it is believed to completely leave the body during the final stage of an illness. Death at such a time is considered natural. Wyman and colleagues explained, "A very aged person who has been respected, 'who has lived out his life,' and dies a natural death does not release a malignant influence" (Wyman, Hill, and Osanai 1942:17).

In direct opposition to the situation noted for young children, a direct correlation exists among the degree of detachment of the inner form, degree of reduced involvement in reciprocal relations, and danger attributed to a deceased elder's corpse and ghost. This is tied in with notions of autonomy and cooperation, which are demonstrated through consideration of individuals from whom Navajo seek aid when a ceremony is needed. In her analysis of ceremonial events in *To Run after Them*, Louise Lamphere found six cooperative activities characteristic of five-day sings: constructing or repairing a hooghan; hauling wood and water; contributing mutton, flour, coffee, sugar, shortening, potatoes, and other vegetables; butchering livestock; preparing food; and assisting with the ritual—such as constructing a dry painting or gathering needed materials (1977:150). These responsibilities are done by members of the patient's residence group and other select relatives, depending on the age of the patient.

When a child requires a ceremony, his or her parents take the lead in making all requests for assistance with relatives and neighbors, as well as arrangements with the ceremonial practitioner. If the person requiring ceremonial assistance is middle-aged, his or her siblings and those of the spouse assume the most critical responsibilities: offering aid and providing needed assistance (Lamphere 1977:151). This is so because sibling bonds, expressed in the term 'bił hajííjééhigii' (those with whom one came up out of the same womb) are second in strength only to the bonds between mother and child (Witherspoon 1975:35). In the case of an elderly patient, his or her children and grandchildren make requests for assistance and supervise the proceedings to make sure everything is done properly. In this case, the spouses and spouses' relatives play a supportive role (Lamphere 1977:151).

This summary reveals that at no time are grandparents considered primary suppliers of ceremonial care. Rather, at least in this area of reciprocal relations—one of the most demanding in Navajo life—individuals' responsibilities are most taxing during their early adult years and midlife, while they are parents of dependent children or siblings of adults who need ceremonial aid. Such responsibilities attenuate as individuals age until they are essentially nonexistent. As a result, a Navajo person's reciprocal obligations increase and attenuate parallel to the attachment of the inner form, discussed previously. This means an elder approaching what is culturally determined to be the ideal age will have fewer and fewer obligations simultaneous with the inner form's attachment becoming weaker and weaker just before death.

In contrast to other dead people, those who reached this point in life attained great prestige. Thus, rather than avoid them, individuals intentionally seek personal contact with deceased elders as a form of blessing. As Donald Denetdeal explained:

> DD: Navajo believe that the age 102 is the magic number. That is Navajo destiny. Every Navajo who believes in traditional ways, in traditional life, is to reach that ultimate golden age of 102. In Navajo they call it "old age kills at 102 and beyond that." . . . And so our destiny is to ultimately reach that goal. To reach that goal, you've got to have a good mind, a good physical body, a good sense of spirituality, and a good relationship with nature. As long as you have those four skills and are on the right course and balance, you may have the lucky ticket to that age. When one reaches that age, in Navajo thinking you are special. . . . So one becomes a saint or the equivalent of what we would use in the Christian school of thought—this person in Navajo, reaching 102 and beyond is a saint, special, they're very, very holy and equivalent to a saint. And that is how we all want to be—saints. . . . So when a person dies at 102, Navajo people, they used to bless themselves with it. Touch the body, say "I want to reach this too." (Denetdeal, July 11, 2004)

Like the elders who pass away after living to the ideal age, *haa'eeł*, or "stillborns," as well as *t'áadoo ha'cha da*, or "ones who do not cry" (that is, live births who die before crying or making any other sounds), are not considered dangerous to handle and do not require the same care in burial procedures as Navajo children who breathe and cry. As the Franciscan

Fathers noted long ago, stillborns are not to be cared for with the mortuary practices considered appropriate for Navajo children and adults up to age 102. Rather, a stillborn's remains are to be "quickly deposited in the branches of a tree pointing northward and left there" (Franciscan Fathers 1910:451). This was confirmed by Kenneth Black, Jr., and Ursula Knoki-Wilson, who collectively informed me that stillborns are granted two forms of special status. Black pointed out that those who are "stillborn are still Holy People. Most holy of the holiest; *they are pure*. Therefore, they are the ones that you put back up into this certain type of tree and then bundle them up and put them back up there, and that is the proper burial for them versus into the ground" (Black, June 16, 2005). When I asked Knoki-Wilson why stillborns are cared for differently than children who live long enough to breathe and cry, she told me it has to do with their special relationship with a certain group of Holy People—the Wind People. She explicated:

> UKW: You dedicate them to the Wind People because the wind is how we get our breath. And the Wind People said, "These children are the essence of my being and because they didn't breathe, they belong to me."
>
> MS: Because they didn't breathe, they belong to the Wind People?
>
> UKW: Yes. Because when we breathe it is a gift from the Wind People, and the Wind People didn't give it as a gift so it is still theirs.
>
> MS: They [Navajo families] give back the children that didn't breathe because they still belong to the Wind People?
>
> UKW: Right. See, if I have this (holds up a cup), it is mine unless I give it to you. If I didn't give it to you, then it is still mine.
>
> MS: So all fetuses in the womb belong to the Wind People?
>
> UKW: Yes.
>
> MS: Until they are given a gift of breath?
>
> UKW: Yes.
>
> MS: OK, then it belongs to the mother, the family?
>
> UKW: Right. (Knoki-Wilson, July 5, 2005)

In the next excerpt, Mae Ann Bekis details that separate procedures are deemed appropriate in such cases because the described placements of these frail human bodies are considered *offerings* rather than burials.

MAB: In [the] Navajo way, you are not supposed to have a funeral for a fetus like that. And when K.C.'s daughter, she had a miscarriage. It was a full body, a full-grown baby. Because she did some cleaning in her house before she went to the doctor, she said she could move some things around and they were heavy, and that night she got home and had cramps and she went in and the baby came and didn't cry. It was stillborn.

MS: Awwh.

MAB: And K.C. went down there and they wanted the baby for an autopsy, and K.C. said "no." . . . [And they said,] "What are you going to do with it," and he said, "I am going to take it home." So he brought it home, and then his son-in-law put the baby somewhere way out there where generally there is nobody walking, and they just put it up on the tree. They wrapped it up with a sheepskin like that (motions with her hands as if swaddling an infant). It may look horrible, but *that is an offering to Mother Earth, Father Sky, and all these other Holy People* they are offering to. That is how it is done. And they say, if you had a funeral for a fetus like that, you are no longer going to be receiving jewelry and sheep, horses, and all these things that are good to have, and you are alienating yourself from all that. That is the way he put it. . . . And then, there is no four days to keep holy on it because the baby was already dead when it was born, but [K.C.] said, "The offering is already done." (Bekis, July 15, 2004)

As Bekis noted, having a European-American–style funeral for a stillborn or following any other culturally inappropriate mortuary practices for such a child is believed to cut the individuals concerned off from future material wealth. This demonstrates that it is obligatory to offer stillborns to the Wind People and that not doing so is a breach of an age-old reciprocal relationship in which Nihookáá Dine'é provide human offerings in exchange for the breath of life, healthy children, and material wealth such as sheep, horses, and jewelry. Yet Knoki-Wilson pointed out that when stillbirths occur in reservation hospitals, increasing numbers of Navajo families are doing just that—calling professional morticians to care for these children as they do for other deceased relatives (Knoki-Wilson, July 5,

2005). In regard to this breach—having a mortician handle the burial preparations for a stillborn—Bekis believes "it is the Christian people that do it" (July 15, 2004).

The similarities between stillborns and elders continue in this area insofar as there are also special considerations for how the aged are cared for after death. According to Donald Denetdeal, the accoutrements of European-American–style funerals—especially the use of embalming and air-tight, hard-sided coffins—are controversial in regard to the burial of Navajo adults and children alike. As Bekis noted for stillborns, it seems human corpses have an intended purpose after burial. Recalling the words of an elderly woman dear to him, Denetdeal provided this explanation:

> DD: "Death, think about it this way," she said. . . . "In the old days we used sheep as money in the bank, as basically our lifeline. And . . . when we want meat or when we are hungry for mutton, we go and slaughter a sheep because that is our livelihood, that is our lifeline. The same concept that Mother Earth and Father Sky has, we as mankind—the five-fingered people—we are their livestock, we are their sheep. . . . Mother Earth and Father Sky are the sheepherders. When Mother Earth wants meat or Father Sky wants meat . . . they will select one of their flock, and that is why we have to bury our dead so that Mother Earth can partake of the flesh, the meat."
>
> That is how it is, so we are basically only sheep and livestock to our Creator, and we should respect them since we don't know when our time is coming. Therefore, Navajo in their burial practices traditionally, they never had caskets, they never had any kind of embalming of the body because when a person dies they are supposed to be eaten—in Navajo terms, eaten means decomposed. . . . That was the rule. And so they just wash the body, then wrap it in a rug and dispose of it quickly. . . . So Navajo elders today, some of them say, "It is because we are prohibiting, we are holding back Mother Earth's partaking of the body by putting the body in caskets or locking [it in] vaults—today's burial practices—that more and more people are dying because we are not feeding Mother Earth. We're just prohibiting her from eating and so now she wants more.

And that is why the death rate is high." It is what some of the elders argue, and that makes one think.

MS: Do you think that is why so many young people die in auto accidents [and from similar causes]?

DD: That's what the elders claim, yes. We are dying from auto, we're dying from food, we're dying from diabetes, we're dying from all these foreign diseases, foreign plagues that we have never heard of like hantavirus, HIV, all these cancers, all that is man-induced so that more death would occur because we are not feeding the Earth like we are supposed to. How would you act if you were a human being? You are hungry for a certain thing, and if somebody puts that in a can and you can't get it, you will get more cans and see which one will open sooner. That is basically what is happening, is what some of the elders say.

MS: That is interesting. . . .

DD: That is why when elders have some sense that they are not going to be around [much longer] they say, "Don't put me in a locking vault, don't put me in a locking casket. Just get something that will decompose quickly because that is my purpose." (Denetdeal, July 11, 2004)

In the view of Navajo traditionalists, ignoring the rules governing correct care of stillborns or the proper burial of other Navajo people is of no small consequence, since these reciprocal obligations form part of the charter between themselves and the Holy People. That charter guaranteed that if the Nihookáá Dine'é carefully followed the teachings of the Holy People, the natural order of the Navajo world would be preserved and their special way of life would flourish.

ENEMIES AND FOREIGNNESS

TL: To me it all relates to [the] Anasazi [Ancestral Pueblo people who occupied the area prior to approximately A.D. 1200]. . . . Well, as far as I remember, [it was] near my home back somewhere in the late 60s. We were working out there with different houses or homes, and we were digging for waterlines, so there was a place where I was digging and I didn't know that there was a burial of the Anasazi. As I recall, there was a skull that came out and then it rolled out and it split open. But I didn't really pay too much attention at that time because we were working. . . . So through a hand trembling diagnostician, that is what he told me, "I think you dig out something from an Anasazi." . . . In our custom that is really a no-no. But accidentally, if it happens like that, you can't help it. But "it will catch up with you," they say. So to me that is where it all started. What happened at that time, that I removed that skull from the ground.

MS: So the hand trembler thinks that is when all your health problems started?

TL: That is the way I believe, that it is all linked together. (Long, July 13, 2005, translated by Hanson Ashley)

Contact with Ancestral Pueblo remains has long been recognized as problematic to the health and welfare of Navajo people. It is the cause to which Tsosie Long, Sr., a retired welder from Kaibito, Arizona, attributes his long-term health problems. As an organ recipient who has suffered from diabetes, a stroke, and ruptured blood vessels in the eye, Long uses Native American Church and traditional Navajo religious ceremonies in combination with biomedical care to combat illness. While agreeing with Long that the Ancestral Pueblo are enemies of the Navajo and, as such, a potential danger to Navajo health, Dr. Buella Allen delineated several other enemies recognized in the Navajo world.

BA: White people have been considered the enemy ever since we were at war with white people and Mexican people; the Spanish are also the enemies. So *anyone that has made war with the Navajo—those are all the enemies.* In the old days there were some difficulties and some fights with the Pueblos. So, for example, the Anasazi areas are considered to be enemy territories, and if you walk on those areas then that can contaminate you. Now that young people are going off to war, that also is a problem. So if you have to go under the care of

a non-Navajo or a traditionally thought of enemy, then certainly you
are going to want to have protection. (B. Allen, June 10, 2005)

Allen concurs with Denetdeal's statement about the relationship between
Navajo people and non-Navajo surgeons when she points out that Navajo
individuals must protect themselves and dependent members of their families
from biomedical caregivers descended from groups traditionally thought
of as enemies. This statement contains two main points. First, it alerts us
to the fact that in marked contrast to situations involving the deaths of
Navajo people—where contact is not dangerous in all instances—*contact
with non-Navajo people is dangerous whether they are dead or alive.* Second,
it raises the issue of who exactly is considered an enemy in the Navajo world
and how such a categorization is made.

Allen named several ethnic groups that are considered enemies—white
people, Mexicans, Spaniards, Ancestral Pueblo and other Pueblos, and any
other group with whom Navajo military personnel are currently engaged.
Worthy of note, she stated that each of these bodies politic is now or was
once at war with the Navajo. Are all enemies therefore defined by combat, as
implied by her itemization?

In response to my queries, consultants drew upon two specific episodes in
the oral tradition—the accounts in which monsters were slain by the Hero
Twins, which have much to do with warriorhood and conflict, and the stories
of the Gambler, which have less to do with combat. Leroy Nelson turned to
the Gambler narrative to delineate precisely which groups of people are
enemies of the Navajo. He described the means by which even some of those
who were formerly Diné became alien by the cutting of their tongues. Nelson
stated that after the Gambler was shot off into outer space, the fate of his
followers was left to be determined. After some deliberation, the Hero Twins

LN: cut their tongues to where they were mute, and they left toward
the east direction, south direction, west direction, and the north
direction. . . . They became different tribes. They became eastern
tribes, southern tribes, western tribes, and northern tribes. The
one[s] that went to the north, they didn't cut their tongues. . . .
Now they have our language over there, *Dine' hólǫ́nii* ["the Navajo
who live out there"], way over there in Canada. . . . They didn't

cut their tongues like Mescalero Apaches to the east. To the west would be White Mountain Apaches and then to the north is the Dine' hólǫ́nįį. Certain ones they didn't cut their tongues; they still have our language. . . .

MS: Do the Navajo fear contact with any other ethnic groups?

LN: Yes, thereafter the ones that cut their tongues. They are enemies. Likewise, if you have the Navajo blood, if you have the traditional language and then the clan; that is where the clan came [from].

MS: So if your tongue wasn't cut, you are not an enemy. If your tongue was cut or you're descended from the Gambler, you are an enemy?

LN: Yes. (Nelson, July 20, 2005)

Leroy Nelson clarifies that the Mescalero and White Mountain Apache groups, as well as the Athabaskan-speaking groups in Canada and northern California, are considered relatives. All other Native peoples who do not speak languages related to Navajo are considered aliens and, as such, enemies because they are descendants of those who had their tongues cut.

As descendants of the Gambler, all people with light-colored skin are also deemed enemy outsiders. Nelson added that this distinction was not made at the whim of contemporary Navajo people. Instead, "It is within stories and history; it is like, this is the way it is going to be. . . . We don't want to say this, but it is a curse on us. The true meaning of sickness is . . . a diagnosis happens, and all of a sudden this is what it is. And then there are ceremonies and if that ceremony happens, people get well. So it is a curse on us. We didn't make the rule. So we don't like to use the term 'enemy.' . . . If you are foreign, then you are an enemy" (Nelson, July 20, 2005). Among these enemies, primary concern focuses on contact with European-Americans, where the fundamental issue centers on the Gambler's legendary ability as "the controller" (Nelson, July 20, 2005). Contact is to be avoided with him or his seemingly countless descendants because of their ability to "get you in an instant second" with "just one look, one word, or one touch"; that is, their power "to win you over" (Nelson, July 20, 2005).

Another feature that distinguishes these narrative cycles is that while the Gambler is clearly an outsider, the monsters are not. Monsters are enemies as a result of their combative nature, but they are technically not complete outsiders because they are related to those they stalk. As is documented in

Navajo oral history, twelve monsters were born to the young women who abused themselves with objects such as petrified wood, fuzzy elk horn, feather quills, deer sinew, and whittled sour cactus in the last underworld (Haile 1981:25–27; O'Bryan 1956:8; Stephen 1930:99; Yazzie 1971:30; Zolbrod 1984:63). The child-eating monsters were therefore born to women related by birth or marriage to the mothers of the children upon whom they were preying; that is, they were consuming their own relatives. Thus, contamination associated with the demise of any of these monsters is complicated by relatedness and therefore comes in part from death rather than solely from contact with an outsider.

Sheila Goldtooth explained what she was taught about the defining elements that determine enemy from non-enemy. In the case of the monsters slain by the Hero Twins, contamination is derived from death, whereas in the case of contact with Anglos, contamination stems from their inherent foreignness—that is, their being "not native of the land." Unlike the account proffered by Leroy Nelson, in the scenario she recounts, this foreignness does not extend to the Hopi, Utes, and other Native groups in the area because they have lived in proximity to the Navajo for generations.

SG: In our stories when we came into being, we were not the only group that [was] there. There were other groups, Utes, Apaches, Hopis, but when the Anglos came across, they [the Anglos] were foreign to the Navajos so it was something that was unknown to us. Something that was foreign and because of that, the contact, is why they [Navajo ancestors] felt a ceremony needs to be done because they [Anglos] are foreign people. Whereas with our other races like the Hopis, we kind of live with them because they lived around there and so we had contact with them. But with the foreign people, they came from somewhere else.

MS: Now earlier . . . you said that it [the origin of the contamination associated with foreignness] went back to the time when the twins slew the monsters.

SG: Uh huh.

MS: And it was definitely related to death. But now you are talking about it and there is no mention of death, so it is not an issue of the Anglo doctors dying?

SG: Well, *there are two different issues.* That with the contact with
monsters and other things and the killing that did cause that as well.
But with contact inside the body or with the Anglo doing surgery
with the person, then that [relates] to how they are foreign. *They are
not native of the land,* and that is why they have that thing [associa-
tion] with the enemy. . . . That goes the same way with some of the
diseases that we have now like diabetes, cancers. They are foreign to
us. That is why we don't have cures. (Goldtooth, July 18, 2005)

Given the sacred nature of Navajo geography as delineated by specific
mountains, Goldtooth has raised a pertinent point. According to Navajo
oral history, the Navajo people as a collective are linked to those who *arose
from the womb of Mother Earth* at the place of emergence; with this statement, she indicates that foreignness marks those who are not so linked.

In addition to marking people as non-native, such geographic areas are
potentially dangerous because Navajo people can be contaminated by contact
with a foreign environment, which is why they are said to need ceremonial
intervention after being away from Diné Bikéyah for an extended period.
Larry Todachinee pointed out, "If someone goes over that mountain, outside
of these mountains, outside of [the] Navajo reservation, then if you live there
for a long time . . . their mind is kind of affected. So when they come back
into [the] Navajo reservation that is when they have these traditional [ceremo-
nial rites] so their mind will be OK and everything will be OK for themselves,
that is what they do for [them]" (June 28, 2005).

Navajo have long-standing traditions of cleansing tribal members of
unwanted contamination acquired through contact with outsiders. Albert
Tinhorn, a Native American Church member from Kayenta, Arizona, noted:

AT: You have to remember that in the old ways, when a person went
away from his community he had to be cleansed before he got back
to the village, and there are certain ceremonies that they would do
where they would put different corn pollens and different things
like that [on the ground] and he would have to step on those. And
they were going to the hooghan and they would have a place for that
person to sit, and nobody could touch him or talk to him or have any
interactions with this person because he's been contaminated by

something foreign. And a ceremony would have to take place and this person would have to take off all their clothes and be washed, cleansed. And only then when the ceremony was done could you approach that person. (Tinhorn, June 14, 2005)

Tinhorn is describing an age-old ritual. Oral accounts documenting this cleansing ritual have been passed down for generations within families. The next account was told to Chahadineli Benally by his grandmother, who was taken captive by Mexicans in the early 1860s. Benally was an eighty-five-year-old medicine man from Valley Store, Arizona, at the time he narrated the story. After many hardships, his grandmother escaped and made her way back to Navajo country. Shortly thereafter, she found her family's homestead. As Tinhorn noted in the previous account, when a person who had been captured and kept for an extended period among non-Navajo returned, a ceremony was performed over her or him before the individual could associate with family members. Benally explained the case involving his grandmother:

While she was walking in, the family started preparations for the ceremonial. Upon her arrival she undressed some distance from the hogan where the ceremonial was to take place. The medicine man came out of the hogan, singing and carrying a prayer stick in one hand. He extended one end of the prayer stick to her, and together they walked into the hogan where yucca soap was ready. She bathed and then dried with white cornmeal. The medicine man started his prayers, which continued until evening. When they were over, she was greeted by each member of the family. Tears of joy were shed, and they were happy. Together they shared the blessing of yellow corn pollen. (Benally quoted in Johnson 1973:72)

This ceremony is still used today to purify Navajo who have lived among non-Navajo for an extended period. As Mae Ann Bekis described, it is deemed especially appropriate as a cleansing ceremony for veterans returning from military service:

MAB: [T]hey have to come back in their uniform and, well, if one was living in Lukachukai[, Arizona], they have to stop over—in their uniform—in Tsaile[, Arizona,] and if it [the ceremony] was being done right here . . . the medicine man could be called, and then he would go over there and have everything ready. And . . . they would get [the sand] from the field, put it down, and then they would smooth it out and bless it and then put the basket on it and put the yucca in there and have it all ready. You know, soap suds all ready. And then [put] the tádídíín [corn pollen] on it. . . . You do the blessing of the basket, put it [the corn pollen] around it. And then make a footprint and a handprint [out of corn pollen]. And then you have to have four footprints right there, by the door. And that is where he steps in and walks back in. And then he steps over to where he is going to be washed off. And then he takes all of his clothes off and then gets draped around as a woman and then gets washed up—everything is washed off of him. And then he gets into his civilian clothes. So, in that way the flashbacks won't bother him. There [are] a lot of flashbacks. You know, whatever happens over there. . . .

MS: But what are you cleansing away from the veteran?

MAB: Well, what he has been in over there. All the experiences that he has been in, in the military. . . . And all the shooting and all, whatever he has done over there. Killing other people, if he did. We're trying to wash it off. *Even the dirt that he has been stepping in over there.* And his mind, and we do the smoke right after we bless him with the cornmeal. For a lady, you put on yellow cornmeal. Like a powder. You can rub that on, and he is blessed with that again. Like he was pure, they were pure. And for a man, it is white cornmeal.

MS: And this is a form of Blessing Way?

MAB: It is a regular Blessing Way. (Bekis, July 15, 2004)

This cleansing ceremony is the first order of business upon an individual's return to the Navajo. It will remove all offending substances from him or her and protect the individual's family and community. Resonating with Sheila Goldtooth's commentary on foreignness and the significance attached to land, Mae Ann Bekis pointed out that as part of the process of purification, "even the dirt he has been stepping in over there" is washed off (July 15, 2004).

In many cases, however, ceremonial intervention will not stop there, for contamination by non-Navajo will have deeply infiltrated the individual. Family narratives document how women sometimes had sexual relations with non-Navajo men while slaves during times of warfare with the Spaniards and the Mexicans or, more recently, while holding off-reservation jobs; alternatively, a soldier might have killed a non-Navajo while in the military. Interventions to correct problems resulting from such situations can take many forms depending on the particular circumstances; they range in intensity from short prayers to a nine-day ceremonial event.

In sum, although all stories from Navajo oral history and Navajo exegeses concerned with enemies have something to do with conflict and contamination, in most cases of contamination from contact with outsiders the accounts associated with monsters deal with death and conflict while those connected with the Gambler focus more narrowly on issues of control. The contamination in cases of both monsters and outsiders is fundamentally derived from power and control. The issue of control is vital to keeping monsters at bay because Navajo people need to exercise self-discipline—abide by the diné bike'ji—to prevent their return.

MONSTERS

> TD: They didn't have cancer, they didn't have diabetes. They didn't have these things until recently. Even amputation, they didn't have that back then. . . . I have been doing a lot of prayers for different problems and especially looking at a lot of different ceremonies, especially looking at the Squaw Dance, the Enemy Way. We are messing around with something that is really supposed to be sacred for us Navajo. And yet, we are playing around with it, we're having Song and Dance for a fund-raising [event]. And that is where we are asking for problems. . . . A lot of these ceremonies are only supposed to be performed in the summertime. Now we have these so-called Song and Dance. At the Enemy Way ceremony now people say, "We love our veterans." In what way do they love their veterans? By messing around with something that is really sacred? That is supposed to be for protection. . . . Way

back the stories say we had a different kind of monsters, and the two Twins got rid of it. And the old people say, "It's gonna come back. But it's not gonna come back as monsters, diabetes, cancer, AIDS, it's gonna come back in that way [as disease rather than child-eating monsters]." And that is the way the story goes, I understand it in that way. That is where a lot of diseases come from. (Deschene, June 15, 2005)

Thomas Deschene, Jr., was referring to the portion of the Navajo origin story in which the world's natural order was disrupted as a result of the sexual aberrations and excesses of the last underworld. The women who had masturbated with unusual objects gave birth to misshapen creatures that grew huge and preyed on healthy children. The Holy People intervened by arranging for Changing Woman to be found as an infant and for her to give birth to twin sons who, upon maturity, worked together to slay the monsters. As Deschene noted, prophecy dictates that whenever Navajo people fail to follow the diné bike'ji established by Changing Woman and the other Diyin Dine'é, monsters will again walk the earth. Deschene is not alone in connecting contemporary diseases to the monsters of oral history. Consider, for example, the comments of Kenneth Black, Jr.:

> MS: What do you think has caused the Navajo people to face the crisis they do today with diabetes, cancer, and heart disease?
> KB: I think there are several reasons. . . . I can think of three or four different reasons why it could be that way from different perspectives. This one has to do with the Monster Slayer story. The Monster Slayer story has to do with how they're called Nayéé' and there was a prophecy that at some point in time, in the future, they will come back [and] take things away again and try to kill off people. But that is one concept. The other one is—(Black, June 16, 2005)

Before he could go further, I interrupted Black because I knew enough to know what his offhand allusion to the return of monsters might mean, and I wanted to hear all he had to say on the matter.

Years previous, Harry Walters had demonstrated that the relationship between origin stories and current events is not self-evident. The stories compress historical knowledge and human experience into vivid narratives that can illuminate and educate. As teaching tools, or parables, they are open to different levels of analysis. In the Navajo world, the stories are useful because they contain numerous messages at twelve separate levels of interpretation, depending on the degree of analytic abstraction applied by the Navajo listener (Walters, August 12, 1993). The child-eating monsters described in the oral histories, for example, are metaphors for things such as improper or immoral behavior and are believed to have come back in the form of hantavirus as recently as 1993 (Schwarz 1995). I asked Mr. Black, "Do please follow that one along for me. What would be the monsters today?" He responded: "Well, the monsters could be the uranium, diabetes, cancers, alcoholism. When we say monsters there are people who think in terms of an actual monster like you see on TV, but Nayéé' is like hunger, poverty, cold—[that] is what I am told. And they were able to exist today because they were allowed [to do so]. But there was a prophecy [that] at one point *in the future those Nayéé' will be there again to kill off people.* And these are just probably speculations that cancer [comes] from the uranium, diabetes is probably what it is to this day, [that] is what I am being told" (Black, June 16, 2005). The notion that Navajo people brought this upon themselves, or caused the monsters to return, fits the traditional paradigm wherein illness comes from immoral acts or internal imbalance rather than being brought from outside. Navajo people can be said to have caused the monsters' return by forsaking the old ways—traditions and practices.

Despite the fact that the twelve monsters who terrorized the earth were not entirely outsiders—they were born to women ancestral to Earth Surface People—the Enemy Way ceremony proved the only ritual capable of healing Monster Slayer. Sheila Goldtooth related how this ritual came to be the intervention appropriate for contamination associated with outsiders, whether based on death or combat: "It goes back to our stories, our origin stories. And I guess it actually deals with when they [our ancestors] had to go to war or when they had to kill other tribes. . . . That is where the Enemy Way ceremony came about. Up where they got sick, after they killed off all the monsters. And so they had to have an Enemy Way ceremony done to get rid of the ill effects of the ghost of that. So it all goes back to the Twins becoming ill after they slew the monsters" (Goldtooth, July 18, 2005).

As this event is recounted in oral history, the Twins lost consciousness after slaying Yé'iitsoh, their first kill. To restore their health, they were treated with a Hóchxǫ'jí (Evil Way) (Haile 1938:22). Each campaign to destroy a monster left them progressively weaker. Oral tradition emphasizes how the smell of both the monsters' and the Pueblo warriors' blood had a profoundly debilitating effect on each of the Twins (Haile 1938:22). As the aggressor, Monster Slayer was especially affected when he destroyed the monsters terrorizing the earth (Nettie Nez, July 10, 2000). Monster Slayer "felt distressed and lacked peace and harmony" (Yazzie 1971:72). Not surprisingly, therefore, Monster Slayer was the first patient to receive the Enemy Way ceremony (Yazzie 1971:72).

In accord with Sheila Goldtooth's commentary, Don Mose, Jr., maintained that the contemporary series of ceremonies that includes the Evil Way, the Blackening Way, and the *Anaa' jí ndáá'*, or "Enemy Way," is a "reenactment of what the Hero Twins went through" (June 13, 2005). Mose learned that this ceremonial cycle was specifically taught to Navajo ancestors when the world was given over to them because the Holy People anticipated how much it would be needed. He explained:

> DM: *All these ceremonies were brought back by the Twins*, they learned all this. And so . . . each gift of the medicine man, the way of life, is brought back by the Hero Twins. All those ceremonies that we have [are] a reenactment of what the Hero Twins went through. . . . And that was to help us deal with being here on another world. Heaven knows, they saw what we would have to go through. They knew there was trouble ahead. It wasn't going to be a happy trail, but they gave us something. In other words, we were placed on this Mother Earth for a reason. We can't fight the unknown, but there were weapons given to us to fight fear itself. (Mose, June 13, 2005)

The close connection between contemporary ceremonies and the primordial ceremony involving the Holy Person for whom it was first performed is emphasized in Harry Walters's explanation of why Monster Slayer had to have multiple ceremonies performed before he fully recovered from slaying the monsters.

HW: Monster Slayer had four Enemy Way ceremonies. The first one he didn't have any blackening ceremony, for it was just him. The second time his mother, Changing Woman, was blackened and he was OK, but he was still ill. The third one, I forgot who the third one was. But the fourth time his cousin was blackened and he got well. So, this was when they said if a male patient is unmarried, his cousin will serve. All ceremonies are, if you are married, your spouse takes part in it. . . . You are never treated by yourself. Your spouse always has a [part] because whatever is affecting you, you have contaminated that with yourself.

MS: So that explains why when there is the male patient, the wife is blackened?

HW: Yes.

MS: And then all the female relatives in the shade [house] are blackened?

HS: Yes. And then you contaminate these [relatives] through, they call it *na'iiskáą,* [it] means you're contaminated through sexual relations. So, illness works that way. . . . So, if you are a male patient, you don't have a wife, then your father's sister's children are your cousins. Or somebody from your father's clan, those are your cousins. [One of them] will stand where your wife is. Monster Slayer did that. . . . And so she plays a role in it: to make it whole. . . . To make it workable. (Walters, August 10, 1993)

The principle of na'iiskáą introduced by Walters dictates that illness based on contamination from an enemy can also derive from intermarriage (Black, June 16, 2005; Deschene, June 15, 2005; Goldtooth, July 18, 2005; Shay, June 15, 2005). Thomas Deschene, Jr., pointed out that "people used to have to teach their kids and grandkids not to get involved with different nationalities relation[ship]-wise and [through] intermarriage, and that would cause that [illness caused by contamination]—if you get involved with different nationalities. And that would somehow come back to that person, and the only way to cure that is to have an Enemy Way ceremony" (Deschene, June 15, 2005). Shelia Goldtooth elaborated: "It goes back to . . . our origin stories. So, [it's] pretty much the same way with intermarriages; if one was married to an Anglo and later on the Anglo spouse passed away, then the wife would need to have an Enemy Way ceremony done. Just to get rid of the spirit or the ill effects because that person is no longer there" (Goldtooth, July 18, 2005). And importantly, as Kenneth Black, Jr., noted, such ceremonial intervention is needed because commingling of bodily substances during marriage results in spouses having the same blood (Black, June 16, 2005).

As a result of the principle of synecdoche, commingling of bodily substances through less intimate or prolonged contact can also result in contamination. Goldtooth noted, "If a person goes through an accident where some Anglo or [a member of] some other tribe were killed, and they go where the accident had occurred, and if they get blood on themselves, then they will be affected because that person is deceased and the person's ghost is still affecting that person" (Goldtooth, July 18, 2005).

Influence from a deceased individual can result from even more remote contact. Echoing previous accounts of children becoming sick from wearing clothing donated by Anglos, Leroy Nelson stressed:

> LN: We can't use materialistic goods that are passed down from a dead person or that that person used. We can't live in a place or work in an area where . . . someone died in that area or that place. Like a living quarters of some sort. . . . Like a bed or a couch or a chair to where this man, woman, boy, girl, baby died in that chair or that bed. And some of these [goods] they've been donated elsewhere and people get it, and then they use it. And a diagnostician would say, "Well . . . this is what you are looking at. This is where this is coming from." You want to question this then. This is evil. This is the black spirit, the dead spirit of this dead person. That spirit is haunting [the item], this is why you are feeling this way. Even to talk about it in such a way that this vehicle was running good and then all of a sudden something happened, maybe an accident or this man died in this vehicle. And then it was taken in and remodeled, repainted, and it went back to the lot and some individual came in as a Navajo and bought it and . . . was driving it again. . . . So that diagnostician had diagnosed, saying, "It is because that person is still holding on to this vehicle. This is his vehicle." (Nelson, July 20, 2004)

The potential contamination relayed through exposure to an enemy's death is deemed risky even to unborn children, which accounts for cautions shared with pregnant couples and other young adults during their child-bearing years to be careful not to expose themselves to dangerous situations. Thomas Deschene, Jr., insisted that "[t]he only way to cure that [such exposure] is to have an Enemy Way ceremony. . . . When you don't have it done you will have health problems" (June 15, 2005).

ENVIRONMENTAL POLLUTANTS

An additional by-product of the marked change in their lifestyle and loss of traditional values is a breakdown of the Navajo relationship with nature and Mother Earth; that is, a loss of respect for, and awareness of the place of Nihookáá Dine'é in, the environment. As Donald Denetdeal explained, Navajo epistemology focuses on the maintenance of harmonious relationships between humans and other entities within their environment as well as with the Diyin Dine'é. Importantly, this must be undertaken with the full knowledge and humble realization that humans are but one component among many:

> DD: [We need] to be healthy and . . . know that man is only another species. . . . That we as Navajo are only another small species that [has] to be codependent with other species that have to be inter-dependent with other species. And so, how well we do that balance is a challenge, and that's an area where we are really falling apart. Our people today have no respect for the environment, they have no sense that we are only one small particle of what we see the world is made up of. And people have no respect for the Earth, people have no respect for little things: trees, bushes, and rocks, and different things. And thus resulting in a trashy and very filthy Navajo Nation. . . . You'll see a lot of shiny glass bottles and trash along the highway. You'll know that you've come onto the Navajo reservation. . . . We're not supposed to do that as traditional people. We are not to throw things away and not to be trashing, but we've lost that, and so that's another imbalance. (Denetdeal, July 11, 2004)

Echoing the concerns of Denetdeal and other consultants, Ursula Knoki-Wilson maintained that the diseases plaguing contemporary Navajo people are the result of what she termed "an imbalance in many things." She singled out one particular area of concern for special consideration: the relationship between people and Mother Earth. According to Knoki-Wilson, "The Earth has been violated so many times you might say people are mining her and all kinds of things. A lot of the sacred sites have been mined" (July 5, 2005). While Knoki-Wilson diplomatically avoided placing blame in this statement, the message is clear. Mother Earth has been violated by the mining of sacred sites, where offerings and prayers should be left rather than anything being taken. These actions have broken down the intricate web of relations vital to maintaining balance in the Navajo world.

Larry Todachinee considers treated drinking water another source of health problems. He explained: "So I think this disease come[s] from—like today the traditional people say that a long time ago they never had treated water, they usually got it from the spring and . . . from the earth's dam, the water. And at that time they don't have that windmill, but today they have [the] windmill and now we have running water. And most people say that it [disease] comes from water because we use a lot of this treated water. So I think that is where it is coming from. That is what the older people say" (Todachinee, June 28, 2005).

Fred Laughter is also concerned about Navajo drinking water. He cited environmental pollutants caused by uranium mining as a critical contributor to contemporary illness: "And some illnesses are from nature. One way is by uranium. It gets to us through the ground and also through the air. Uranium mining, blowing that certain type of toxin, chemicals into the air we breathe, and the other way [people get sick] is . . . by drinking contaminated water" (Laughter, June 16, 2005). Again, Laughter left unsaid the details of how uranium and other chemicals get into the air, ground, and water of the Navajo environment (on these matters see Brugge et al. 1997; Eichstaedt 1994; Florio and Mudd 1986; Spieldoch 1996). Larry Todachinee also attributes contemporary diseases to pollutants and chemicals. He directly links them to the Gambler's descendants when he identifies them as by-products of fuels used to operate modern conveniences:

LT: [Illness comes] from these propane stoves. [A] long time ago we
    used to chop wood and build fire, then we cook on this regular fire

and charcoal. But today it is different, we use propane a lot. . . . The propane is from uranium. This [is] where it's coming from, so that's what they use. They say, "The uranium is some kind of chemical. We shouldn't use it. That is where . . . the heart attack comes from," that is what they say. And these are coal mine[s] and these are uranium mine[s] and [this is] pollution that we have in the Navajo reservation. They used to only use horses, but today it is a vehicle. So all these kinds of pollution, that is where these things come from, that is what they tell us. So . . . that's what I think, that is what the older people talk about, that's where it comes from. (Todachinee, June 28, 2005)

In addition to environmental pollutants, consultants pointed to contemporary foods as a source of chronic diseases such as high blood pressure and diabetes. By the late 1960s, approximately half of school-age Navajo children received all their meals at boarding school, and the remainder ate lunch there. In addition, roughly half of Navajo families received surplus commodities from the Commodity Food Program, introduced in 1958. When it began, the program offered only four foods—flour, cornmeal, rice, and dry milk. By 1965 the number of foods had increased to as many as twelve, depending on whether the family lived in New Mexico or Arizona. In contrast, the Donated Food Program, which replaced the Commodity Food Program in 1971, made up to twenty different food items available, including sugar, syrup, lard, peanut butter, dried beans, rolled wheat, and, in some areas, butter and cheese; limited quantities of canned goods— fruits, juices, meat or chicken, and vegetables—as well as macaroni, cereals, and dehydrated products (Kopp 1986:12–13). Some, such as Don Mose, Jr., consider these foods to collectively represent one of the prophesied monsters come to destroy contemporary Navajo people.

Mose was taught that included in the teachings Changing Woman gave to the Nihookáá Dine'é was a plan for proper nutrition, with information on the amounts of proteins, grains, and vegetables required for healthful living:

DM: Changing Woman, when she sent the group of Navajo back to their homeland, she specifically gave them, ah, have you ever seen one of those pyramids? A health (motions a triangular form with his hands)—

MS: The food pyramid?

DM: From back in the old grade school. She gave them that. And we don't really realize [that Changing Woman offered nutritional guidance]. They said, here is the water, water is important. And so that is what we use. In other words, before we eat, sometimes they used to put tádídíín in there and pass it around and then you have your little feast, and water was important. And there was vegetation that was given to them and there was protein, which was jerky. And I think there was beans, squash, and corn. Corn was important because tádídíín comes from that, see? And tádídíín is important; that is your offering. . . . Then the sacred tobacco. Of course, you make an offering as well as the prayers. And so they say you have to be cautious of your health. . . . Take this and use this for your health control. But now our foods have just completely gone out of control, and they think flour—even the doctor once told me they think white flour is one of the biggest causes of diabetes. There are things that are not supposed to be. . . . [I]t is hard to say, but if you really look at it, what you need is your greens, your protein, and your waters. . . .

MS: So, are you saying that a lot of foods like chips, soda, and fast food are one of the monsters?

DM: Yeah, certainly, these are just not things to eat, it brings unhealth to your body. It does something to your blood, it is not good for you. Cigarette doesn't belong in your body, a great amount of sugar doesn't belong in your body. It rejects it, and above all whiskey . . . does something to Native people. It just doesn't connect with them because we never had it before. It is an unusual kind of food. . . . [S]ome day look back at the old pictures back in the 50s and even to the 40s, you will see how slim and tall the Navajo ladies and men are. You think at that time they weren't healthy, but now you start looking at pictures of modern day, you see how huge kids are. Way out of control because of this chips, candy. (Mose, June 13, 2005)

Mose raises important points concerning the association between spirituality and food, as well as its consumption. This is foregrounded when he mentions putting tádídíín in water and passing it around for all those present to consume before a meal, as well as the importance of home-grown tádídíín and sacred tobacco for use as offerings. Clearly, these were some of Changing Woman's teachings at the time the world was turned over to the Nihookáá Dine'é that some contemporary Navajo feel are now slipping away.

Ursula Knoki-Wilson also shared personal recollections of her grandmother cautioning her to "be prayerful . . . before meals and after meals" (July 5, 2005). These observations offer insight into the inextricable connection that exists between spirituality and food in the Navajo world. Knoki-Wilson continued, "And then she taught me that fixing food for her family was a sacred responsibility, and when you were preparing food you have to have good thoughts for your family and those who you are preparing food for because when they took the meal then they would take it in a good way" (Knoki-Wilson, July 5, 2005).

Denetdeal pointed out that another important area of spirituality associated with harvesting food is being neglected in the contemporary world: showing proper respect to animals before they are butchered. As he delineated: "We don't take the time to pray with the food that we eat. We don't take the time to pray to nature when we want to partake of nature for meals. We don't take the time to pray to a sheep before we butcher [it]. We don't take time to say a prayer before we butcher a cow or a horse or whatever it may be. We just go to a shopping center and buy meat. Who knows how these things are slaughtered? And so we're not eating right" (Denetdeal, July 11, 2004).

Mae Ann Bekis warmly recalled the variety of corn dishes her mother made and other foods she enjoyed while growing up in the late 1920s and early 1930s, especially the special sweets she earned as treats.

> MAB: At the stores they have all these good foods that [are] good for us, they are way in the back. And potato chips, candy, and all these goodies they are in the front—and they are the ones our children grab for. You know, potato chips and pop and candy and all these. And way back when I was a little girl, we never had that. Once in a great while we would have some pop, which used to come in [a] small jar or bottle. And you'd drink that and it lasts you a long time. . . . But we never got candy. If we did, that is *a treat*, my dad would keep it. We live in [a] hooghan and there would be a little

corner somewhere. He would hide it up there and once in a while, after we herd sheep, we would come back and we'd be given candy. Just a small piece for my sister and me. . . . [O]ne of our friends from down at Round Rock[, Arizona,] they made a yucca fruit. She made it into a roll maybe about three inches, about that round (indicates with her fingers) and about a foot long. . . . And that was our candy. . . . And we ate a lot of cornmeal and corn mush and [our] mother would cook it different ways. (Bekis, July 22, 2004)

Ursula Knoki-Wilson bemoaned the fact that traditional foods, such as those made by women of Bekis's mother's generation, are becoming increasingly scarce. She attributes this to many variables, including the fact that "no one plants anymore. There is no place to gather the traditional foods, the vegetables and fruits that we used to be able to gather. There are no gathering places anymore, partly because of population growth and the other is . . . the change in weather patterns. . . . And then the trend of all the fast food availability and the USDA [U.S. Department of Agriculture] foods availability" (Knoki-Wilson, July 5, 2005). Leeanne Johnson agreed with this assessment, noting: "We have changed our eating pattern 100 percent, we have made a turnaround. We have gone [to] fast food totally. And then even [at] home I would estimate . . . that people eat in Gallup[, New Mexico,] 75 percent of the time in a given week foods that are not healthy. Nobody has a cornfield. I am going to say nobody because the percentage is very small. Maybe 2 percent of the families still have cornfields. I think that is the reason diabetes has come to overtake our lives" (Johnson, July 3, 2005).

This trend in food consumption has had a devastating effect on what Navajo people eat on a daily basis. Donald Denetdeal was insistent that "we have a high cholesterol diet, we have a high fat diet, we eat a lot of sugar, a lot of artificial stuff that leads to physical imbalance. And that's resulting in a high level of diabetes and high level of hypertension, high level of heart attacks, high level of cholesterol, clogged arteries, and on and on" (Denetdeal, July 11, 2004).

Other consultants agreed. Kenneth Black, Jr., noted: "There are so many conveniences nowadays when people go to Farmington[, New Mexico,] Gallup[, New Mexico, or] whatever. They stop at Thrift Way [a chain of convenience stores] there and load up on chips and pop. And that is a contributing factor." Black closed by stating, "We need to know more about dietary [requirements]" (Black, June 16, 2005).

Eleanor Begay agreed with Black that Navajo people must educate themselves about their nutritional needs. In contrast to the many consultants whose views have been stated, Begay did not lament the loss of traditional foods and eating practices. Instead, she actually attributed the increased incidence of diabetes to those traditions while crediting the Indian Health Service's efforts to educate Navajo people about nutrition and the importance of exercise in avoiding the disease. Begay is correct in identifying mutton and fry bread cooked in lard as high cholesterol foods, and people are in fact encouraged to eat huge portions at ceremonial feasts. She overlooks the fact, however, that these events play significant roles in building and sustaining reciprocity and solidarity within families and communities, which have much to do with Navajo collective notions of identity. She told me:

MS: What do you think causes the sugar diabetes like you have?

EB: Well, at that time [when she was younger] we didn't even know what diabetes meant. We just ate like our mom and everybody else. "Let's go, they're having a Squaw Dance." Then they're having a Yé'ii Bicheii or other things. I didn't care what I ate until I started working over here [at the BIA school in Lukachukai]. That is where I started having trouble. So, you never had any counseling, and people walk and things like that now. But now . . . I have to gather all those papers from the nurse and go to all those meetings about being diabetic, this is what you eat. I still like to eat stew and fry bread, but not all the time, even candy and pop, but not all the time. I had to cut down. So, I start using diet and all that. Now when I buy it [food] I have to look for fiber and all that, but before I didn't know what calcium and all those [things] were. I didn't know until . . . I gathered all those papers from Chinle and I start reading. I had to read over and over, some of them different words, and then I had to go for a dictionary. That's how I know it now. (E. Begay, June 10, 2005)

Mae Ann Bekis contextualized the explanation offered by the Indian Health Service—in which food is a prime factor contributing to diseases—

within traditional Navajo logic about illness causation. She conjoined store-bought meats such as hamburger with the causative factor most frequently mentioned in accounts by traditional diagnosticians, practitioners, and patients—lightning. Bekis explained:

> MAB: And sometimes the lightning strikes the fields where we get the corn and our food like watermelon and all that. Sometimes they get struck by lightning. . . . That will cause sickness too, if you eat something like that. And even at the slaughtering. My brother was watching TV, he said "this is in Texas at the slaughter-house. There was a bunch of cows that are ready to be slaughtered. They're in groups, fifteen different pens, and the first group went in, the second group is about to come in, the third group is about to come in, here the third group was striked by lightning. There was maybe six or seven killed, and all they did was just take them out with a tractor. Took them away, the rest of them went in before any-thing was done." So he said, "This might cause us to have diabetes too. Something [a religious rite] should have been done. But we don't know what is coming to us through [the] store. We don't know if it came through lightning, or . . . certain things could be there in the herd. And one of them might've got bitten and it will spread to all that is in that group. That would cause us to have something like that [diabetes]." Because if you got bitten by a snake, it gets rotten right away.
>
> MS: The meat gets rotten?
>
> MAB: Yes. The meat gets rotten right away. So if it [the snake-bitten animal] was with the herd, and then all the herd mix[es] together and you walk among them, it will be dangerous to our health. The whole thing's got struck [the whole herd has been struck by lightning], but the rest of them lived. But still, you cannot eat that herd until something is done, in Navajo. If our sheep were under a tree and lightning struck the tree and killed [some of] the sheep . . . you just don't bother those sheep that were there. . . . You don't move them [those struck and killed] because they are already struck, hurt by the lightning. And so the herd gets away from it [the tree], and then you should do a prayer right there and give that lightning

some pieces of jewelry. And after four days you can eat them [the surviving sheep] again. That is how it is done. But if it [meat] is from the store, they were already hurt by the lightning. And they say, "It is no wonder a lot of the meat you buy from the store, like hamburger, doesn't keep long." [It] gets rotten right away or smells right away. So they say, "Some of them [the animals] are probably at the slaughteries that have been hurt like that." So, we eat them and we never know what we are eating. (Bekis, July 22, 2004)

At the risk of restating the obvious, I asked Bekis:

MS: So, you think that because the meat hasn't been properly cared for in the process of being slaughtered, that this is contributing to the ill health of Navajo people?

MAB: Yes. And even that [it] is the way that it might come—death. We might have all these [diseases] like cancer, like diabetes, and things like that are from that. And it wasn't good for our health, and here we are eating it. (Bekis, July 22, 2004)

Lightning is not the only source of power believed to have the innate ability to bring about illness. Electricity used for lighting, cooking, and operating household appliances, nuclear radiation, and sunlight are all classified as aspects of "lightning" by contemporary Navajo and, as such, are deemed potential causes of cancer (Csordas 1989:476). In a similar vein to Bekis's commentary, Csordas reported that a consultant told him "one should eat home-grown meat rather than store-bought meat, not because the latter contains chemical preservatives as Anglo-Americans might fear, but because commercial livestock is sometimes subjected to electrical stimulation to enhance growth" (1989:476).

• • •

Navajo narratives on traditional sources of illness reveal that it can be derived from inappropriate contact with elements of nature such as lightning or tornadoes, contact with snakes or bears, contact with the monsters of old, or from contamination by any contact with death. In contrast, many of what are perceived to be recently introduced diseases such as diabetes, cancer, and heart ailments stand for social change, loss of tradition, and conflict with Anglos, or white people—their colonizers, descendants of the Gambler. This is the inverse of the way Navajo consultants portray health, which entails living according to age-old traditions. Conflict with colonizers has manifested itself in multiple forms of contamination, which can sicken people and be rectified only through ceremonial intervention.

Fundamentally, the forms of contamination at play in illness narratives come from contact with the dead and contact with outsiders—that is, enemies, alive or dead—or with their products, such as convenience foods, processed waters, environmental pollutants, and fuels. Contact with outsiders plays out in many important areas of Navajo life, including intermarriage, warfare, and, most relevant to our purposes, surgery. Contamination caused by contact with the dead—whether Navajo or non-Navajo—plays an extremely important role in organ transplantation as well as in the transfer of bodily substances through CPR and blood transfusions.

CHAPTER FIVE

The Exchange of
Life Substances

*I went over there [to the Indian Health Service Hospital in Fort
Defiance, Arizona] Sunday morning while I was in labor. They
say they don't do surgery on Sundays, so they transported me to
Gallup. . . . This was early in the morning when I went to
Gallup. At 12:30 [P.M.] I had him. . . . The next morning they
kept telling me to walk around. So, I got up and I was walking
around. And . . . there was another lady, she was a diabetic,
and she had a baby too. . . . It seems like we were all forgotten,
but they were really having problems with that lady. And they
got all kinds of fluid on the floor, she was on IV. So they told me
to get up. I got up and I slipped and fell. And it didn't bother
me, I just got back up. . . . I told one of the nurses, "I just fell
down because there is water on the floor." They brought one of
the janitors in and cleaned it up. And still they were telling me
to walk around. I walked down the hallway, and I blacked out
right there. I didn't remember nothing until I woke up and I saw
a bottle of blood. It was hanging . . . right there. I guess they
were giving me a blood transfusion. It was so cold, too, that
thing, they just shot it up my vein. . . . I could feel it running*

*down my veins and up to my head. . . . I told that lady, "This
thing is hurting me." "Well, it is like that, it has to be like that.
You need to have a blood transfusion." So they put about two
pints in me. It was two bags. . . . And a couple of years later I
started having dreams about the Anglos and the blacks. . . . It
didn't really get to me until a few years later. . . . I started having health problems. And I didn't know what it was, and I never
did connect it to the blood transfusion. This is when I was
working at Navajo Communications. I used to get dizzy, and I
would start vomiting. I was having a hard time. Sometimes I
would . . . go to the hospital and they would tell me, "There is
nothing wrong with you." . . . And then out of the clear blue sky
I would just get sick, I would get dizzy—it was something else. So
we went to see a medicine man down in Gallup[, New Mexico,]
and went to see this man whose name is Alfred Thompson. . . .
"What happened to you?" he said. "Did you get a blood transfusion?" I said "Yeah." "Well, that blood transfusion they gave
you, it was a black lady's blood," he said, "and that lady is
gone, that is why it is bothering you," he said. And that is where
he saw that [that she was sick as a result of a transfusion]. . . .
For maybe about two or three years I felt better after he saw
what was bothering me. (Jackson, July 20, 2004)*

Sarah Jackson's therapeutic narrative (see Early 1982), in which she recounts
the biomedical procedures she was subjected to surrounding a cesarean
delivery, complications that arose, and some of the traditional interventions
she and her husband sought to bring her relief, introduces us to the first topic
addressed in this chapter—blood transfusion. The inextricably linked topic
of the donation of life substances (blood as well as breath) will also be discussed. Jackson's narrative serves as a connecting strand within this chapter,
and segments of her story are told throughout. This opening account raises
two important points about blood transfusions that are applicable for all
transfers of life substances—that problems may develop with donations from
non-Navajo and with donations that involve death. Critical to each of these
issues are the tenet of synecdoche and concerns over various forms of contamination, discussed in earlier chapters. A new element, which this particular

procedure brings to the analysis of how Navajo accommodate biomedical technology within the framework of their medically and religiously pluralistic lived-world (that is, a world in which they make choices between multiple religious and medical options on a daily basis), is the need for an appreciation of Navajo notions involving blood.

In undertaking this aspect of the project, my understanding of Navajo views on blood was greatly expanded. Previously, I had learned that Navajo people have traditionally distinguished between two types of menstrual blood—that shed during a woman's first two periods (positive) and that shed during all subsequent periods (dangerous), the latter of which can cause health problems. They have also distinguished between two kinds of animal blood—that shed while butchering livestock (benign) and that shed while butchering game (dangerous); the latter is linked to the birth of monsters in the underworld (Schwarz 2001). The commentaries of Sarah Jackson and others regarding transfusion indicate that Navajo people likewise divide human blood into two categories: Navajo and non-Navajo.

That distinction not only marks Navajo collective identity, it also plays a key role in recipients' preferences for sources of blood and—as will be shown in chapter 7—has implications for the acceptance of organs. Each of these distinctions must be understood as a component of a whole, however, rather than as an isolate. Navajo understandings of blood are therefore summarized here to provide an overview of the collective implications of these divisions.

BLOOD

It is said that half of our blood veins are blue, the other half red. I do not recall which side is red. It divides right in half from the head down between our legs. The two colors join in the middle. Each side of the blood veins do their work for the body. When it comes together it just automatically turns to its own color fast. All these blood vessels are called "earth veins" (*Nahasdzáán bits'oos*). When digging in the damp ground you will find these long worms, which we call earth worms. The blood flows in these throughout our system. The fluid that we call blood has its work to do to purify our system to keep us alive. (Mustache 1970)

In Navajo cultural logic, blood is understood as fundamentally life-sustaining. Nora Young of Chilchinbito, Arizona, stated it simply: "Blood . . . that's the element that makes our body function" (June 14, 2005). According to Navajo exegeses, human blood is understood to have two primary functions—it aids in development and, as Curly Mustache, a well-respected elder from Tsaile, Arizona, pointed out in the preceding quotation, it cleanses the body (Mustache 1970).

Various Navajo consultants' statements clarify the exact role blood plays in cleansing the body. Regarding the blood shed during menstruation and nosebleeds, Mae Ann Bekis commented: "That is the bad, it is not really bad bad, but that is what you get rid of for your health. . . . They are both to cleanse the body (Bekis, March 22, 2005). Comments by interviewees indicate that blood is deemed capable of absorbing contamination. In his explanation of the long-term influence marriage to a non-Navajo can have on an individual, Kenneth Black, Jr., stated: "When we live together, [if] something happened to her it will still affect me because my body makeup has still, *the blood; it still is one*" (June 16, 2005). Other testimony supports the idea that blood has the ability to purge unhealthy elements from the body. Consider this statement made by Don Mose, Jr., while discussing the drawbacks to consumption of contemporary convenience foods such as soda pop, chips, and fast food: "it brings unhealth to your body. *It does something to your blood*. It is not good for you" (June 13, 2005). Likewise, while discussing the means by which patients are healed with herbal remedies, Jonah Nez noted: "we brew the herbs into a tea. And we use that. It will really clean you out right away—*whatever bad stuff that is in your blood*. It only leaves the red blood cells, the white blood cells, the oxygen" (June 12, 2005).

In terms of development, the Navajo theory of conception clearly distinguishes the act of conception from the maturation of the fetus (Knoki-Wilson, August 10, 1992; Walters, August 18, 1992; Schwarz 1997:68–69). After conception, blood from the mother's body and two types of fluid contribute to the child's growth and development in the womb. The growing fetus is nurtured by blood supplied by the mother—the blood that would have become menstrual fluid if conception had not occurred (Knoki-Wilson, August 10, 1992; Walters, August 18, 1992). In addition, both *tó ał'tahnáschíín*, "all different kinds of waters come together," identified as male, and *tó biyáázh*, "child of water," identified as female, play a fundamental role in the proper maturation of the fetus, for they foster the development of the person's contrasting aspects—male-female (Aronilth 1990:33). Personal identity also comes into play in regard to inherited substances and lifelong influences from one's clans.

The profound influence of the clan system in the Navajo world cannot be overstated. As Avery Denny, a Night Way singer from Low Mountain, Arizona, told me, "To us the clan system is the foundation of our generations" (August 11, 1993). Navajo people distinguish four types of blood that run through every individual's system. Development is enhanced and individualized through the assistance of what are referred to as "clan bloods" representing distinct groups from which a child claims genealogical heritage (Denny, October 8, 1993).

DANGEROUS AND BENIGN FORMS OF BLOOD

> MS: I am trying to figure out a way to ask this question. It is having to do with menstrual blood and the danger. Some people call it danger. What makes it dangerous?
>
> MAB: I don't know, I think it is just that, in Navajo, we are back to a kinaaldá. *She is pure, nobody [has] bothered her.* But her first blood that you see? You are not supposed to put a pad on her. That is supposed to have been pure for two times, the first one and the second one. And then the third one, and that's that. She is a woman, she can conceive now. (Bekis, July 28, 1993)

The blood shed during a young woman's first and second menstrual periods signifies her reproductive capacities and energies (Bekis, July 28, 1993). Ideally, every Navajo girl is to have two Kinaaldá, or "puberty ceremonies," while in this state. In earlier times, young girls were considered eligible for marriage after their second Kinaaldá (Bailey 1950:12; Frisbie 1993[1967]:348; Leighton and Kluckhohn 1947:77). Thus, the distinction between different kinds of menstrual blood theoretically correlates with the pre-sexual and sexual phases of a woman's life. That is, the blood shed before a girl ideally marries or otherwise becomes sexually active is not dangerous; the blood shed after a young woman ideally becomes married or otherwise sexually active is very dangerous. Madalin Chavez clarified the reason for the distinction between these two forms of blood: "The first Kinaaldá, *there isn't a penis yet.* A man hasn't opened it yet. That is a *kinaaldá's* [pubescent girl's] blood, and she makes the *chiih dik'ǫ́ǫ́zh* [antidote for *aadi'*, polite term for menstrual blood shed by a Navajo woman after her first two cycles] because she is a virgin" (Chavez, June 29, 2000). This explains why different terms are used to refer to the blood shed during the first two menstrual cycles and that shed during all subsequent cycles, as well as for a length of time following childbirth. It also clarifies why young women are carefully trained to properly dispose of all personal products used during menstruation, for contact with aadi' is dangerous to everyone (Schwarz 2003:77–94).

When a girl sheds blood during the pre-sexual phase of her life, she has the ability to foster the growth and development of children (Bekis, August 5, 1992; Dooley, August 19, 1992; Kee, August 3, 1992; Walters, August 10, 1993), to heal problems related to exposure to menstrual blood shed during the sexual portion of a woman's life by means of massage or the laying on of hands (Bekis, July 23, 1998), and to produce an essential component of chiih dik'ǫ́ǫ́zh (Bekis, July 28, 1993; Agnes Dennison, July 27, 1998; Alfred Dennison, July 27, 1998; Mace, July 23, 1998).[1]

According to Ursula Knoki-Wilson, chiih dik'ǫ́ǫ́zh is ingested or aspirated to "contain the power of the menstrual blood" (August 10, 1992). When used correctly, it forms a barrier to protect vulnerable individuals from aadi'. It is sprayed from the mouth onto the interior of a room that contains a vulnerable person, or it is put on, or ingested by, individuals to correct several problems. For instance, chiih dik'ǫ́ǫ́zh is placed in the mouth and blown on a person to "help him or her come out of unconsciousness" (Chavez, June 29, 2000). Menstruating women use it when they are tending to the needs of infants or sick people. All menstruating visitors use it in the homes of the terminally ill (Bekis, July 28, 1993). If a person is hospitalized, it is used to counteract any potential ill effects from menstruating nurses and other medical personnel (Chavez, June 29, 2000).

A comparable distinction between benign and dangerous forms of blood exists for boys and men as well. As detailed in the next excerpt, Louva Dahozy of Fort Defiance, Arizona, was told by her grandfather that when a boy's voice begins to change—the culturally recognized sign of the shift from the pre-sexual to the sexual portion of their lives for males (Leighton and Kluckhohn 1947:77; Reichard 1950:39; Schwarz 1997:156–73)—he is required to go on a hunt and kill a deer. If he has a *né'édił*, or "nosebleed," while on this hunt, it is considered equivalent to a girl's first or second menstrual cycle—that is, sacred. She explained:

> LD: When they go hunting, when he is a young man, just when he is going to change his voice . . . they know that he's becoming a man, and then he has to kill a deer. My grandfather used to say that a man when he is hunting, [if] he has a nosebleed that is what that represents. . . .
>
> MS: He would have a nosebleed, and what did that represent?
>
> LD: That he is the same as a kinaaldá. (Dahozy, August 19, 1992)

Subsequently, Navajo people shared personal accounts in which they said it is inappropriate for anyone to have contact with the blood from a nosebleed except the person from whom it originates. I sought clarification from Mae Ann Bekis after a woman told me that when her husband has a nosebleed, he will not allow her to help him clean it up. Bekis explained that like the menstrual blood shed by women after their first two periods, the blood shed in nosebleeds after a young man's voice begins to change is deemed dangerous. As a result, from that time forward men must clean up their own nosebleeds. She insisted that men must take care of their own nosebleeds the same way a woman takes care of herself during her menstrual period:

> MAB: They said you are not supposed to clean somebody else's nosebleed. . . . That is what you get rid of for your health. . . .
>
> MS: So it is a cleansing?
>
> MAB: Uh huh.
>
> MS: Is menstruation a cleansing thing?
>
> MAB: Menstruation and the nosebleed.
>
> MS: They are both to cleanse the body?
>
> MAB: They are both to cleanse the body.
>
> MS: So, what would happen to a woman if she helped clean up a child's nosebleed?
>
> MAB: Well, the child [is] different. . . . It is cleaner than the older people.

MS: Is it a difference between before and after puberty?
MAB: Yeah.
MS: So, you could clean up a nosebleed?
MAB: Yeah, a nosebleed from the baby or the little child, up to
    puberty. (Bekis, March 22, 1995)

The cleansing function alluded to by Bekis corresponds with the explanation offered by Curly Mustache (1970) and the examples offered by Don
Mose, Jr. (June 13, 2005) and Kenneth Black, Jr. (June 16, 2005). If an antidote commensurate with chiih dik'ǫ́ǫ́zh exists to counteract the negative
effects of the blood shed through the nose by sexually mature men, however,
I have yet to learn of it.

Taken collectively, these accounts and bits of information offer insight
into why a girl's menarche is celebrated, yet strict guidelines aimed at controlling the potential danger of menstrual blood from subsequent periods
exist. The fact that sexual purity and a woman's ability to conceive are the
distinguishing factors between the menstrual blood shed during the first
two cycles and that shed during all subsequent cycles indicates that Navajo
views on the relative danger of menstrual blood are centered on sexuality
and fertility. The statements of consultants suggest that the danger associated
with the menstrual blood shed by a Navajo woman after her second cycle is
directly linked to issues surrounding normative and non-normative reproduction and sexuality. Navajo people have strong opinions about these issues.

In addition to cautions against holding hands with, kissing, or fondling
a sexual partner in public (Billie, July 23, 1992; O. Tso, July 18, 1992),
Navajo people reported that it is inappropriate to dance with a clan relative in ceremonial or social contexts (see also Kluckhohn and Leighton
1974[1946]:201). Extreme personal modesty is the ideal, with emphasis
on concealment of body parts, especially the genitalia. Even among sexual
partners, exposing the sexual organs is considered shameful and embar-
rassing (Dyk 1951:108–10, 112). Sexual relations are to take place during
darkness "to insure privacy and protect personal modesty" (Kluckhohn
and Leighton 1974[1946]:91) and because indulging in sexual intercourse
during daylight hours is "said to cause damage to the sperm" (Csordas
1989:478). Sexual excesses are included in the norm which holds that
excess of any form is dangerous (Reichard 1950:80). As Mary Shepardson

explained, "Excessive sexual activity by a man or a woman is deplored. . . . Excessive sexual activity with promiscuous partners for whom one takes no responsibility is labeled 'just like dogs'" (1995:168).

The lasciviousness and inappropriate sexual acts documented in the Navajo origin story resulted in strict rules for sexual behavior, regulations surrounding the butchering of game animals and the handling of blood from nosebleeds of sexually mature men, and regulations for women surrounding the care and disposal of menstrual blood shed after the first two cycles. Conversations with Navajo people who have had transfusions shed new light on Navajo views on blood. Like Sarah Jackson, many Navajo people are apprehensive about this procedure—often declining blood transfusion when doctors recommend it because of the influences they anticipate it will have on them.

TRANSFUSIONS

> BA: I know that transfusions are looked upon askance; a lot of people will refuse transfusions even though their blood count is quite low because you do not know where the blood comes from, and if you accept the blood of an enemy then you have *contaminated your own body,* and that's very bad. That requires a major ceremony. I know people that have had transfusions and they're pragmatic about it. If you have to have it or it has been done, then there is nothing you can do about it later except to undergo the ceremonies; or if those people are not traditional, then generally speaking they have heard comments about it but they don't feel particularly one way or the other for themselves. (B. Allen, June 10, 2005)

Commensurate with concerns about contact with menstrual blood shed by a sexually mature woman, Navajo consultants are apprehensive about accepting blood donated by non-Navajo because doing so will contaminate the body (B. Allen, June 10, 2005). Nora Young said simply that "accepting blood from another ethnic group is unacceptable" without elaborating on the matter (June 14, 2005). Others, such as Larry Todachinee, stressed the difference between the blood running through the veins and arteries of Navajo and that running through the bodies of non-Navajo. Blood offered in the form of transfusions is a sign that marks the difference between health and danger as well as between Navajo and non-Navajo, which, as will be shown, supersedes biomedical technology in immediacy of concern.

> MS: How about blood transfusions? . . . Are there any prohibitions against having them? I mean taking blood from someone else.
> LT: Well, if you get a blood transplant from another person, it is like from bilagáana and even from Mexican blood, it is a different kind of blood, so it wouldn't work for you. . . . That is what they tell us in our traditional, the old people, if you get it from [a] Mexican, then the blood will be different, so it wouldn't work for you. . . .
> MS: So you should only take a transfusion from another Navajo?
> LT: Uh huh. (Todachinee, June 28, 2005)

Echoing this view, Kenneth Black, Jr., explicated what he understands the consequences for a Navajo will be of having blood from a non-Navajo in his or her system: "It will affect you physically and it will affect you mentally. That is just how you are, that is how you are different" (June 16, 2005). Don Mose, Jr., recalled an account told to him by a friend: "My wife not too long ago when she was having a child, she bled a lot so we have to give her somebody else's blood [from the blood bank] so that she can survive all this, and before that she was such a healthy women. She did everything, but now she says, 'I break out in hives. I'm not as healthy as I used to be. I was told not to do these things when I was a young child. Is this the price that I have to pay? It has an affect on me. I don't see as good'" (June 13, 2005). Without specifying the exact nature of the physical complication she believed would arise from having different blood in one's body, Eleanor Begay stated: "I never had that one [blood transfusion] because they have different nationalities, and when they put it in you, *you start having problems elsewhere in your body*" (June 10, 2005).

In regard to the mental side of the equation, Thomas Deschene, Jr., noted, "If it is crossing different nationalities, then it gets complicated. . . . It starts haunting you. The person that received the blood transfusion, it's gonna start haunting them. It can't always be cured" (June 15, 2005). It is little wonder, therefore, that blood is only deemed acceptable if it comes from someone "within the same bloodline" (Deschene, June 15, 2005). Some, such as Rose Mary Wade, a devout Catholic from Pine Springs, Arizona, who practices what she refers to as traditional Navajo religion, made it clear that knowledge about the source of the blood, rather than the procedure itself, is by far the most critical issue surrounding blood transfusions. Like many Navajo families, hers prefers to exchange blood among family members when it is needed rather than accept blood from a blood bank.

> MS: How about blood transfusions?
>
> RMW: They say it's a no-no, but there is no way it is a no-no because we don't know who the blood is coming from, but for survival purposes the family just agrees to it. . . .
>
> MS: But is it a no-no to take a blood transfusion from anyone? . . .
>
> RMW: Within the immediate family they can.
>
> MS: Could you take blood from any Navajo?
>
> RMW: I think you could. There's enough relatives to give blood, so that shouldn't really be a question. (Wade, June 17, 2005)

Like Wade, many Navajo consultants consider blood from relatives the best option for transfusions. As Ursula Knoki-Wilson recalled, this has been the case for decades: "Back in the early 70s, when there was a blood transfusion that needed to be done people used to ask, 'Well, can one of my family members donate blood to me instead of just [getting it] from the blood bank?' They used to be afraid of blood banks because you could get blood from, they don't know what nationality this person was or what race or whatever. So they would be more afraid of the blood bank than they were with their family giving their blood to them" (Knoki-Wilson, July 5, 2005). Nora Young reported that whenever her father needs blood, one of his children supplies it (June 14, 2005). Julia Mathis expressed the desire to have blood from relatives on hand when she has her liver transplant in case she needs a transfusion (June 11, 2005).

Not all transfusions are planned. Emergencies occur on a regular basis, and relatives who are the right blood type are not always available to offer blood when needed. Yet, only one person shared an account with me about receiving blood from a Navajo who was a stranger. Mae Ann Bekis lived for many years in Colorado while her husband, Jim, worked in the uranium mines. While there, she bore most of her eight children. She told me about a complicated birth during which hospital staff found a Navajo miner who matched her blood type and agreed to provide blood through a direct transfusion. The miner who donated blood to Bekis took a great risk because she was in the prime of her life, when her inner form was most strongly attached and her reciprocal relationships at their height. It is at that point in life that an individual's death is deemed most potent, so the man could have suffered grave consequences if Bekis had succumbed to complications related to the birth. Following the transfusion, the miner stayed nearby for the remainder of the night as she lay unconscious, just in case she needed more blood. She recalled:

> MAB: I hemorrhaged. And so the doctor got someone off the street. . . . I met the man afterward. It was OK for me to get that. I don't have any problems with my transfusion. . . . The reason why is that I hemorrhaged real easy. So that is why my doctor, Doctor Meredith, said, "Mae, I know you don't want this, but I don't want you to die in my hands." . . .
>
> MS: So, you said they pulled a man off the street.
>
> MAB: Yes.
>
> MS: He was a Navajo man?
>
> MAB: Yes. I imagine he was from Aneth, Utah. And he had the same blood [type] as mine. (Bekis, July 15, 2004)

I wondered if the exchange of blood would be considered a form of incest should the donor and recipient be related by clan. I asked Bekis:

> MS: Was he related to you by clan?
>
> MAB: No. I never asked him about clan or anything like that. I just met him, he [her physician] just brought him over to me, "This man gave you the blood." So, I just thanked him. That was it. I didn't even ask him any questions. . . . I accept it and then, afterward we always pray with tádídíín or early in the morning with white cornmeal to protect us, and that's how I use mine. (Bekis, July 15, 2004)

Bekis's lack of interest in the donor's clan affiliations surprised me given the importance the Navajo people I know place on clan exogamy. She reports never having had any ill effects attributable to the transfusion. As noted, these may have been warded off by the prayers she makes regularly with corn pollen or cornmeal. Many Navajo who have received blood transfusions have been less fortunate.

In many cases, transfusions occur while individuals are serving in the military. This was the case with the brother of Ambrose Shepard, a Native American Church (NAC) road man from Ganado, Arizona. Shepard's older brother Bill became ill after being given blood from a non-Navajo: "Just like my brother, his name is Bill. . . . He has been in the wars, the Korean War. He got shot up . . . been wounded over there. So he was losing a lot of blood. At the time they did the transfusion of blood from another person. So all he remembered was a Mexican, a *Naakaii*. His blood was being put in[to Shepard's brother]. So it got to him, he was getting sick. They found out that he had the blood transfusion from another nationality and that is what is causing it [his illness]" (Shepard, June 3, 2005). Shepard explained that his brother experienced horrifying dreams, night terrors, and other symptoms after returning from his tour of duty (June 3, 2005). Sarah Jackson also experienced disturbing dreams, dizziness, vomiting, blurred vision, and partial paralysis because the person from whom she received donated blood had died.

These physical symptoms are not uncommon and are easily recognized by healers. Thomas Deschene, Jr., recalled discerning this problem while conducting NAC meetings. Patients frequently came to him suffering from fatigue, nightmares, and what he called "seeing things"—that is, encounters with ch'įįdii. After cautioning that the condition is often not curable, he remarked on the similarity between the symptoms experienced by Navajo who have had blood transfusions and those diagnosed as diabetic by biomedical doctors.

> TD: A lot of times people, when they go through surgery they lose a
> lot of blood, and then they get blood from [a] blood bank.
> MS: Blood transfusions?
> TD: When you perform ceremonies you come across these things
> [meaning he discerns through coal gazing that patients have had

transfusions]. . . . Whoever donated that blood could have gone [died], too. And that would determine the Hóchxǫ'jí, the Evil Way. You will have a sickness like that and [it] seems like there is no way of curing that person. Only through a certain ceremony they can heal.

MS: That was one of my other questions about blood transfusions because blood is taken from living donors.

TD: That person might have passed on, later on. And then they [the original patient] would have had that person's blood—have received blood from that person.

MS: Have you had any patients who have had this problem?

TD: Yes, a lot of them.

MS: What types of problems do they have when the donor has passed on?

TD: They would have a sickness, an illness. They will get real fatigued all of a sudden. . . . Like it had been the same thing as diabetes, and I think that is where a lot of diabetes comes in, a lot of things. And people start having nightmares and they start seeing things. Or if they go into a dark place, there will be somebody standing there or sitting there. Or have somebody go across a door or behind a corner. You start seeing things like that or having problems with the dead spirit. Especially when it gets to be around this time of day (dusk), and when it gets dark they don't want to be alone. They don't even want to go out. They get scared or something. It can affect their health. They get really sick, too. . . . In the case of a blood transfusion, if a person receives it and the person is still here and somewhere along the way that person dies—the one that gave the donation for the transfusion—somehow it's gonna contaminate the other person who received the blood. (Deschene, June 15, 2005)

Recipients of blood transfusions who are plagued with bad dreams or delirium can have their conditions transmute into other types of illnesses if their problems are not addressed. Some, like the woman discussed by Ursula Knoki-Wilson in this narrative, end up suffering from severe depression.

UKW: One was a postpartum patient that got transfused, and the doctors said she had a prolonged postpartum depression; that was the clinical diagnosis. But from the Navajo side, they said her symptoms were caused by the transfusion that she got, and she got nightmares almost on a nightly basis. She imaged people coming to her and the dark side, she dreamed about things like that, and that led to aggravating her fear and she was fearful of going to sleep at night. And so she was consequently not getting enough sleep. Which consequently zapped her energy level, and she was very afraid to be alone and she wore people out for having to tend to her needs. And so she withdrew, and then she went deeper into her depression by withdrawing. When she would come to the clinic they would say she had prolonged postpartum depression and send her over to mental health for counseling sessions. Which really did not help her address her fears because I think she was afraid to tell the mental health worker, who was not Navajo, about them. It didn't address the problem from her belief system because I think she was afraid to tell the provider that her symptoms were related to getting a blood transfusion. Or if she did, I think the provider told her something like, "Well, how would that affect you? That doesn't have nothing to do with your issues. Your issues are mental problems." So she didn't go there anymore. . . . She confided in me what she was going through, and I said, "Oh, you absolutely have to go through traditional diagnosis and care and have the problem dealt with in a traditional way, and you have to make that a priority for yourself." . . . So I sent her to a social worker who helped me to put her into some things [programs] where she could get help. (Knoki-Wilson, July 5, 2005)

Disturbing dreams or nightmares are the signature symptom associated with blood transfusions gone wrong. The case of Ambrose Shepard's brother Bill, who suffered greatly after receiving blood in Korea from a fellow soldier who was of Mexican ancestry, is typical among Navajo men who serve in the armed services: "There are a lot of military personnel or soldiers where it [nightmares] had to be corrected after they come back.

Some of them, it went as far as making them go crazy. They wanted to commit suicide. That is how powerful it is" (Shepard, June 3, 2005).

The central role of dreams in illness narratives of Navajo patients who have had transfusions is culturally significant because, as Gladys Reichard noted, "[d]reams have much to do with disease and curing" in the Navajo world (1950:550). Navajo people rarely comment on their dreams other than to note whether they were good or bad; if the dreams were bad, they assume something undesirable is going to happen (Morgan 1932:391). This is so because, as detailed in this passage from the Blessing Way story, dreams have special power in the Navajo world. Coyote said:

> "You see, whenever dreams are bad a ceremonial for it [to counteract them] should be performed. In such cases the no-sleep [ceremonial] should be held and prayers should be said," he explained. "You see this mind and thought part [of humans] was made only for thinking of things which can be seen with the eyes," he said. "But as one goes along in life, future conditions ahead of a person and accidents with which a person may meet in the future, how could they be recognized if there were no such things as this [dreams]?" he said. "You see then that dreaming will occur in sleep, it will search ahead in one's future for that purpose. Anything ugly, which wants to do a person deadly injury, it will see ahead for him," he said. "For this purpose prayer and song came into being. Thus, if a dream should be bad in this manner and if Blessingway is performed, [one] will not suffer an accident. Thereby it will become well again," said Coyote. (quoted in Wyman 1970:431–32, brackets in original)

For these reasons, dreams are granted prognostic power. As forewarnings, they must be heeded (Kluckhohn and Leighton 1974[1946]:204; Wyman 1970:224, note 168). In Sarah Jackson's case, her disturbing dreams could be seen as alerts about the woman from whom she had received blood's death.

Disturbing dreams, night terrors, and nightmares are not the only symptoms experienced by those who have had transfusions. In addition, the man described in the next account suffered from night sweats and nausea. He also became violent and vicious—personality traits he had not previously demonstrated but for which a Navajo diagnostician found an explanation. Ursula Knoki-Wilson recalled the case:

> UKW: This was a man who had night sweats, and he would get nau-
> seated and he had deliriums, dreams, and he attributed that to having
> a transfusion. And the other thing was that he believed that he took
> on the personality of the person whose blood he got. And appar-
> ently that person whose blood he got was a very angry person, and
> so he for no reason would get very violent and kind of vicious and
> his family said that was not the kind of behavior they were used to.
> So . . . I got involved. I was a public health nurse. . . . I had to give
> him his medication out in the field. The kind of ceremony that he
> needed was a little more involved, so his family took almost a year
> to plan an extensive ceremony that he was supposed to have on a
> mountain with chanters because the blood of the person that he got
> used to be a bear hunter. So he got that bear energy in him, so he
> had to have a Mountain Way chant to get rid of that spirit that was
> in that blood. . . . He went to a diagnostician [who] told him, "You
> have got the blood of a white man that used to hunt bears and so
> the spirit of that and incidents from that man [are now in you]."
> The white man was very short tempered and he would get violent.
> Almost take on the personality of a bear because he would go and
> hunt bear. In fact, he would eat the bear too, [which] in our culture
> is taboo. . . . He eventually had [the ceremony]. And to this day he
> is fine. . . . He is back to his sweet old self. Because he was a very
> compassionate, sweet man, and all of a sudden he would be out-
> raged. (Knoki-Wilson, July 5, 2005)

This is not an aberrant case. Other consultants reported that they were warned against accepting blood transfusions because of the potential that they might take on aspects of the donor's personality. Consider how elders in the community cautioned Amelia Benally, a devout Catholic from Klagetoh, Arizona, and her daughter La Naya, neither of whom had personal concerns about transfusion, against the procedure while Amelia was preparing for her heart transplant:

MS: Why did you say that you were told not to accept blood transfusions?

AB: I guess because . . . it comes from a different body.

MS: But blood transfusions most often come from a living person,
not a dead person. So why the restriction on—

AB: A lot of people get transfusion. . . . I guess some that are really
traditional are against that.

LNB: Yes, a lot of it has to do with it [the blood] coming from somewhere else. A lot of times maybe they think we have picked up
another person's spirituality or personality, and they are really
afraid of it. And I don't understand it because I am not traditional.
I don't know what their thinking is. But I always say, "Well, if it
is going to save me, fine. If I don't get sick from it, it's OK." (A. and
L. N. Benally, July 13, 2004)

When I asked Amelda Sandoval Shay her views on blood transfusions,
she replied, "I think everybody is against that. . . . They had to know where
the blood comes from" (June 6, 2005). She later told me that she had
accepted a blood transfusion after a miscarriage. Out of fear of disapproval
from her family, especially medicine men who are close relatives, she kept
the procedure a secret. Knowing the traditional warning against transfusions, to this day she wonders if hers caused the onset of her diabetes. Her
concern echoes Thomas Deschene, Jr.'s, suspicions about whether blood
transfusions are a source of diabetes (June 15, 2005). Shay has also begun
to wonder if her donor is still alive; she sensed that he is not, and her intu-
ition was confirmed through traditional diagnosis. She explained:

ASS: I did have a blood transfusion.

MS: You did?

ASS: Uh huh. Because it is from a living person. So I told them,
"Make sure there was nothing wrong with it. Make sure that that
person you got it from, they were healthy." So there was nothing
wrong with it. . . . Nobody knew, not even my mother, because I
had a miscarriage and I lost a lot of blood. So [I had] no choice. It
was a matter of life or death. . . . So they did the blood transfusion.
And now I wonder [if] maybe that is how I became a diabetic.

Maybe that is how it happened to me, but nobody knew that . . . I
had a blood transfusion.

MS: Why did you not tell them?

ASS: Because I might have to deal with the medicine man and he
was against it. . . . He would get mad at me for it, but it was
already done, so why fuss over it? So it was just as well that they
don't know it. . . . So I always think, "I wonder if it was an
Indian's blood that I got? Or is it from somebody else?" . . . I was
very sick, and I just said, "OK." Because the doctor explained to
me that it was a matter of life and death. . . . So I was wondering,
"Is that person still alive, or is he dead?"

MS: The donor? Have you ever gone to a hand trembler or anyone
and asked about that?

ASS: (Nods in affirmation). There was a lot of answers to questions
like this one—the blood transfusion? They say that person might
be dead. "Maybe they were alive when they gave you the blood,
but to me they are gone." (Shay, June 6, 2005)

It comes as no surprise that Shay sought insight from a traditional diagnostician about the fate of the individual from whom she had received blood.
After gaining no satisfaction from the Indian Health Service clinic about her
repeated episodes of vomiting and dizziness, Sarah Jackson and her family
sought help from a diagnostician in the Gallup, New Mexico, area. Even
Kenneth Black, Jr., who brings a very modern perspective to blood transfusion and has experienced no complications as a result of his own transfusion,
included a visit to the diagnostician as a foregone conclusion in his commentary on the matter: "Let's say that whoever's blood was transfused into my
body, it was probably a healthy person, hopefully he is still alive now.
And . . . I survived and I am alive; we are OK. His blood probably got out of
my system now. And whatever is in my blood is probably my own blood
now because it takes about thirty days for your own blood to reconstitute
into your own body. . . . So I am probably OK, but if I was getting ill, the
diagnostician would always see that. How is it that you are ill? Something
happened, you know what I mean?" (Black, June 16, 2005).

As these narratives demonstrate, individuals experiencing disturbing
dreams, fatigue, night sweats, vomiting, or visitations from ch'įįdii most

often seek help from traditional diagnosticians, which Frank C. Young told me is the only way to determine the cause of such symptoms (June 14, 2005).

TRADITIONAL DIAGNOSIS

> "*Tiníléí*," it is Gila Monster. You know what that is, don't you? Well, the hand trembler is called by the [name] Gila Monster. That's an ugly-looking thing. It's a slow-moving thing. It's poisonous, but to the Navajo people this is a very important reptile. He is the—I don't know if I should say magic, but he is the leader of diagnosing a patient or what's ailing them. . . . That's why he is the god of diagnosing. . . . The Navajo people believe this is an important reptile. (Mose, June 13, 2005)

Diagnosis is attained traditionally by three separate means. The first type is *'iists'áá'*, or "listening," whereby the relevant information is heard. Listeners are rare today. *Déest'įį*, "star or crystal gazing," is the second type; in this method the practitioner looks either directly at a star or through a crystal and receives insight into the patient's condition. (The third method, hand trembling, is discussed shortly.) While educating me on the uses of various herbal remedies, Jonah Nez shared information his father had taught him about the use of crystals when dealing with broken bones: "'Way long time ago there were no hospitals like today,' he used to say. 'If a person had a broken bone or fractured muscles, they got a crystal,' he said. . . . 'If you got crystal, it is like using a magnifying glass, you can see that bone; through that crystal you can see where the bone is broken.' And then you can put the [appropriate] herb on it" (Nez, June 12, 2005).

Don Mose, Jr., a teacher in the Kayenta school district, shared a vivid account of how a crystal gazer located the cause of excruciating pain that had virtually incapacitated him:

> DM: I walked into the main office. I was just as pale as the walls. Everyone started asking, "What has happened? What is wrong with you? Are you OK?" I said, "I am sick. I can't even straighten up.

There is something wrong." "We will get a substitute." I [asked] this liaison worker . . . [to] take me to a medicine man. "Let me go to a medicine man before I go to a doctor. I don't want to be cut open." . . . So he said, "Let's go see this healer. It's not too far." So he took me to see him. And I was just like this (doubles over to demonstrate). . . . I finally got there, and . . . I told him what the situation was and he said "sit down." So he takes out this quartz crystal. Puts it right there (motions in front of him). . . . He takes his glasses off. . . . Blesses me with this eagle feather, and then he takes the eagle feather and he holds it like this (mimes holding the eagle feather in his right hand in front of the crystal). Imagine he can't see it with his naked eye, so he places this (indicating the imaginary crystal on the table in front of him), he looks through it and it reflects back to what's ailing—he won't see my whole body, he will just see the object. So he does that for a few minutes, and then he went behind my back. He pinches like this (pinches my arm), and then he begins using his mouth to suck it out. Right between here somewhere (touches his back just above the waist), then he went off to my side. It looked like some kind of a stone. . . . When he got done, he blessed me. By the time we were leaving, I was straightening back up. I was OK. I didn't have to have a substitute. I taught that day. (Mose, June 13, 2005)

It was Mose's good fortune that the crystal gazer was able not only to diagnose the problem but also to extract the offending agent, thereby allowing him to return to work. While this narrative offers insight into a patient's perspective on the experience, it does not provide perspicacity as to exactly how a crystal gazer accomplishes such a diagnosis. Such insight is provided in the next account.

Larry Todachinee grew up just north of Jeddito assisting his grandfathers, both prominent medicine men. His maternal grandfather was also a diagnostician in the gazing methods, and he taught Todachinee about crystal gazing. He is thus in a good position to educate others about star and crystal gazing. Todachinee was taught that there are irreconcilable differences between the two forms of gazing, requiring diagnosticians to choose between them. He explained:

LT: It is just a light, a small light comes into that crystal and you can diagnose people with it—just like an X-ray.

MS: Can you do it inside? In this room? I thought you had to be outside and have the stars shine into it.

LT: Well, that is a stargazer. That is another, different thing. There is crystal gazing, you can do it inside. The stargazing, you can do it outside. There is two different gazing[s] that we can do.

MS: Do you do both?

LT: No, I only do it inside. The crystal gazing that was given to me by my grandfather. But he said, "Leave this other one, stargazing, alone. That is two different things." That is what he told me. If you can do both of them, there is going to be a conflict between one another, so it has to be one of them. That is what he told us, to do the crystal one. (Todachinee, June 28, 2005)

Both types of diagnosticians are usually men who have learned the practice (Levy, Neutra, and Parker 1987:30).[2] Julia Mathis has both a sister and a brother who are stargazers. According to Mathis, "They use a crystal to see the different things that would help you in your healing process. And they provide prayers, so they have done that for me and different prayers" (June 11, 2005).

The third method of diagnosis is *ndishniih*, or "hand trembling," whereby the diagnosis is ascertained through an involuntary motion of the right arm. It is the most commonly practiced form of diagnosis on the contemporary reservation and is conducted by both men and women. In addition to involving a mild trance state induced through possession by Gila Monster, this form of diagnosis is understood to be an unsolicited gift; that is, a talent that cannot be developed but that occurs spontaneously. Upon discovery of the ability, a ceremony must be performed under the guidance of an experienced hand trembler to "control" the involuntary shaking and induct the novice into the status of diagnostician (Wyman 1936a, 1936b; see also Levy, Neutra, and Parker 1987:30–31; Milne and Howard 2000:549).[3]

When an ill person comes to a hand trembler for help, accompanied by concerned relatives, the diagnostician first washes that person's hands and forearms. Then, using one of a variety of designs and methods, pollen is sprinkled on the right forearm from the elbow along the radial margin, around the hypothenar eminence of the hand, along the palmar surface of the thumb to its tip, along each finger, and on the center of the palm. A prayer is then said to Gila Monster asking for information concerning the specific problem. Sitting with eyes closed, the diagnostician sings one or two songs, during which his or her extended hand begins to shake. During the shaking the diagnostician thinks of various problems that might be the cause of the patient's symptoms. The hand stops shaking when the mind focuses on the correct problem. Don Mose, Jr., an individual who possesses the gift of hand trembling, spoke about this form of diagnosis. His right arm began to tremble as he explained:

> DM: But this hand trembling, he [Gila Monster] is the authority of diagnosing what ails a person. When the hand trembler begins, that is what they [hand tremblers] do, they do a figure drawing of the Gila Monster on the palm of their hand and then often they use lightning to guard [the people involved] while the diagnosis is taking place (using his finger to mark where these images would be drawn on his hand). . . . And when the hand trembling begins they often sing a song. There is a song I've heard sung; they mention the name of the Tiníléí (begins to sing). Tiníléí, Tiníléí, Tiníléí, you hear it used when the hand trembling begins, suddenly the hand becomes the eye of the thinker and they [hand tremblers] will diagnose. It is just like a picture here (touching his forehead), and he will diagnose what will make the person heal. We don't know how to understand [the phenomenon], but we know it is powerful medicine. (Mose, June 13, 2005)

Diagnosticians often inform patients of consequences beyond those surrounding the source of the blood they accepted. They frequently have information concerning blood or wind that has been donated as well.

DONATION OF LIFE SUBSTANCES

> KB: I was in ICU [intensive care unit] one time. And I don't know how many quarts of blood they had to (motions injecting with his

hand into his arm). . . . And with that experience, off and on I donate blood.

MS: You do?

KB: Yeah, but I was telling that to someone, a medicine man. . . . Then he says, "OK, you donate blood. Your blood probably went somewhere. . . . Let's say it goes to a university hospital, a big hospital, a big ICU. Now your blood is there and someone is dying; critical, real critical condition. Do you feed some of that blood into that patient? It is not his blood, it is your blood that is in there now. What if all of your blood is still in there and the patient dies? The patient dies with your blood?" That could have a critical impact on my life. *I am half dead now. My blood is dead with that person.* That is how it is viewed. And with that thought in mind they say, try to refrain from that [donating blood]. (Black, June 16, 2005)

The Navajo individuals with whom I consulted agreed with this ceremonial practitioner's assessment that if donated blood is in someone when he or she passes on, that individual's death will have consequences for the donor. Amelda Sandoval Shay put it succinctly: "If you give this person your blood and then they are dead, then you are dead with it" (June 6, 2005). Thomas Deschene, Jr., noted, "If a person gives blood to a certain person and then they die, it's gonna affect the person who gives the blood too because they [the deceased] have that person's blood in them" (June 15, 2005). This sentiment is not new, for in an account published in 1962, Dr. Paul Mico wrote, "The Navajo has a fear of giving blood transfusions also, since it is believed that if the recipient of the blood dies, so will the donor" (1962:16).[4]

Interestingly, along with blood, Navajo individuals also find it problematic to donate their wind, or breath, while administering cardiopulmonary resuscitation (CPR). Moreover, as Leroy Nelson and Larry Todachinee made clear in their discussions of CPR, their objections are based on the same rationale as that offered against donating blood.

CPR

LN: If that person dies, it is going to come back to haunt you. . . . But if that person lives, then it is good. Then you saved a life. But it is between if that person lives or if that person dies. It is between there—that is the understanding.

MS: So, if you give your breath to someone else and they live, that is good?

LN: That is good.

MS: If that person who dies comes back, who comes back?

LN: That person's spirit will come back . . . and haunt you. It is kind of like [a] curse and sickness. Not saying that he is going to be around right here picking on you. All of a sudden you are going to get sick. . . . It is like people that are in that career or profession as working with [the] human body do CPR, a lot of them went too deep and need to go through a ceremony to be all right. But a lot of them changed their career after what they were exposed to. . . . One thing we say, it is all of us [in] today's world; we have to know it because one day we may need CPR ourselves.

MS: Do you know what ceremony you have to have to correct the problems?

LN: That is the Evil Way, Hóchxǫ'jí, the Hóchxǫ'jí sets the pace, Hóchxǫ'jí sets the scale . . . for everything having to do with death. (Nelson, July 20, 2004)

This commentary was offered in reply to my asking Leroy Nelson why it is a problem to give one's breath to another individual. Echoing similar sentiments in regard to prohibitions against CPR, Larry Todachinee offered these comments. Whereas Nelson provided information on which ceremonial is called for to alleviate complications brought on by the death of the person in whom one's breath has been placed, Todachinee discussed what ceremony should be done if the person to whom breath is given survives.

LT: Our traditional way is if somebody has [an] accident and is going to die, we never CPR them. That is our tradition. Because once that person dies, the air is gonna come up and you won't breathe. If you put it back in there, you gonna get [an] effect on that. That is what old medicine person say.

MS: If your air is inside that person when—

LT: If they die, it is going to affect you. So you never do that, that is what they tell us. Then if the person gets all right, then it is OK, but you have to have a blessing with singing. The blessing is the bottom thing to have. . . . Just like when you give air back to that person and that person is well, you should have a blessing singing, Blessing Way. The bottom line a Blessing Way, singing, would be like you can live a long time with that. (Todachinee, June 28, 2005)

If the person in whom you place your breath dies, her or his death can have a variety of influences on you. Mae Ann Bekis explained that one of the reasons she objects to CPR is because it can cause convulsions.

MAB: When I was taking first aid up in Colorado . . . we were supposed to all take CPR, and . . . I said, "I object." And the teacher said, "Why?" I said, "I believe in my own belief. And even a dummy," I said, "I would not blow in it." He says, "Why?" "It's gonna bother my voice. And I'm gonna breath all the air that I have into that dummy or a person that is dying and he is gonna die with my breath. And so is the dummy—somebody else will use it again. I don't want that. That's my belief."

MS: Can you explain a little bit more about that?

MAB: See, it happened to my brother. He was a policeman and he shot a man that was running from policemen down at Round Rock[, Arizona]. And when that man was dying, they had to use CPR. He [her brother] was breathing in it, and that person died. He was bilagáana. And he [her brother] goes into convulsions. And the crystal gazer and then the hand shaker and then other [diagnosticians] that we know of, you know how they try to find out what is wrong with him? They said, "That bilagáana died with your breath, you were blowing in it. There is no way we can fix it. You can have an Enemy Way dance [done] for you; still, it is in the man that died. Your breath is within him. He died with it." So that is why I would not take CPR, even in the dummies. (Bekis, July 15, 2004)

Administering CPR can also result in asthma, as in the case of Florence Sandoval of Valley Store, Arizona. She has personal experience with the effects of CPR because she worked for many years as an emergency medical technician (EMT). She explained why Navajo people are cautious about performing CPR:

> FS: They believe that you are not supposed to do CPR. It will affect you. It will affect your breathing, and it turns out to be asthma. . . . I did a lot of CPR, and when I got into high school I got certified to be an EMT. I started making my runs, and I used to do a lot of CPR and it started affecting me and I was getting asthma, and I was like, "I didn't have asthma as a child, why am I getting it now?" And that went on, like I said, I didn't know the traditional way. And then when I came back out here [to the reservation] I was told that they were saying that I ate something. . . . I said, "What did I eat?" And they were saying, "Cactus?" I said, "OK, I did have some cactus." And that was it, and I had ceremonies done but it didn't help. And then one of my nephews, they were up in the sheep corral with my mom when he fell over and stopped breathing. I got up there in time to revive him, and we left and when we had gotten to Chinle and put oxygen on him that happened [she had an asthma attack], and then it really started affecting me and I didn't know [why]. In all the years I just lived with it. I was using inhalers and everything until he [indicating her husband, Ronald Sandoval, a Chiricahua Wind Way singer] came about. After I met him I was telling him I have this problem. "I have asthma." I said. "If I should stop breathing, you will rush me up to the hospital or [get] my inhalers, this is what I use." And he was saying, "I know what is wrong with you." So he took me to—he can't perform the ceremony on me.
>
> MS: I understand.
>
> FS: So he took me to another medicine man, and he did . . . a short version of the Wind Way, and after that it calmed down and then later on I had the whole thing [full ceremony] done on me. Now I don't have asthma. I don't have allergies. I don't use my inhalers anymore. That is how it [doing CPR] affects [you]. You have breathing problems. (F. Sandoval, June 25, 2005)

Not all accounts about CPR shared by consultants had totally negative overtones. While discussing her ten pregnancies, which included several miscarriages and one stillbirth, Amelda Sandoval Shay shared this account of delivering a breech birth at a small dispensary in her home community with the assistance of a midwife. Shay believes CPR saved her child's life, but not without complications. She explained:

> ASS: We didn't have a ride to go to anywhere. My husband was always away to work on construction, and he was never home with us and I had these kids. . . . We had a small dispensary we call it, and they had a maternity ward there. . . . So I went over there . . . where the church is there is a maternity ward next door to it. So when I went in labor . . . I walk across to get to the dispensary, the maternity ward. . . .
>
> MS: So you delivered a breech birth?
>
> ASS: Yes. And it took about three to four minutes for that baby to cry. So, there was about three or four nuns that were there. . . . One was mainly a midwife, and the other one is just a helper. And these two were kneeling there on the floor in the delivery room with their rosaries, praying to have that child cry and here I was, I can't pray. All I could think is, "I want my child to, oh please." So finally he cried a small cry, so I don't know, back then we never think of CPR, that was something that we don't know about. But that is what she [one of the nuns] was doing to the baby. . . . But he cried. (Shay, June 15, 2005)

Because of the child's innocence, performing CPR on a Navajo infant would not be deemed problematic for the person doing it, even if it was a Navajo, because if the child died, no negative consequences would befall him or her. In the case of Shay's son, however, the by-product of the procedure—having a foreigner's breath infiltrate his body—appears to have had lasting consequences for him. Shay explained tearfully, "My son got into drinking, drugs, and [hanging] out with the wrong crowd. And to this day he is still in prison in Tucson. And that kills me" (June 15, 2005).

Dr. Buella Allen initially noted the connection between CPR and death and dying pointed out by many other consultants, but she quickly brushed these concerns aside and refocused the discussion. She gently redirected me to think of breath in the larger context of the importance attributed to wind and air in the Navajo world.

> MS: Several Navajo people have told me they will not perform CPR.
>
> BA: That's because of the breath. If you do CPR, then the breath of the person that is perhaps dead already or is in the process of dying, that breath is going to be taken into your body and that becomes a problem.
>
> MS: Oh, so the breath of the dying person would be in your body.
>
> BA: Uh huh.
>
> MS: OK, so then you would be in contact with the dead or dying.
>
> BA: Uh huh. You know that life comes to us as a result of breath, which is like the winds. When the winds come into your body, that is when you begin to live, and so a child is thought to be alive when he begins to breathe. So, if a baby is born never having taken a breath, then that baby is traditionally disposed of or is buried in a different fashion. . . . So, it's very important that the breath not be taken into your body if you are going to be doing CPR, and that is why they wouldn't do it. (Allen, June 10, 2005)

As it did in the creation of the first Nihookáá Dine'é, air plays a pivotal role in the animation of every contemporary human being. Wind gives life and breath to Earth Surface People. The essential elements shared by all made forms in the Navajo world constitute every component of the human body—internal organs, flesh, bones, muscles, and skin. The winds that enter the body at birth animate and firm the outer body, leaving it in part during dreaming and permanently at death. The locations of the entrance and departure of the winds are evidenced on the body surface by the whorls on the fingertips, on the bottoms of the feet and toes, and at the top of the back of the head (McNeley 1981:35; Bekis, July 28, 1993; Denny, October 8, 1993; Walters, August 18, 1992). In each case, spirals mark the entrance of the animating winds into the person's body.

As Gladys Reichard learned more than half a century ago, the components of the Navajo body interconnect to create an intricate series of layers with spaces between them: "The body is composed of skin, flesh, bones, and internal organs—all considered layers, each tissue carefully fitted to those next to it. Nevertheless, between the layers are interstices ('atatah) through which ghosts [winds] may travel. They enter the body where there are whorls—for instance, at the fingertips and hair spirals—as frequently as through orifices—mouth, nose, ears" (Reichard 1950:31–32).

Navajo infants are soft at birth. Once an infant breathes and cries, the constitution of its body begins to transform. After the child emerges from the birth canal, internal contact with air through respiration, along with contact between air and the outer surfaces of the child's body, begins to firm the infant. The air that initially enters every Nihookáá Dine'é at birth permeates its interior, filling the 'atá't'ah, or "interior recesses, pockets, and folds," between the internal organs and the layers of the body surrounding them, gradually allowing the child's body to become firm (Bekis, July 28, 1993; Denny, October 8, 1993; Walters, August 18, 1992). Fully cognizant of how being born soft and needing contact with air to attain firmness serves as a hallmark of Navajo collective identity while simultaneously differentiating Nihookáá Dine'é from bilagáana and other non-Navajo at the most basic level, Mae Ann Bekis stated: "I don't know if the other way is different. Your way. I don't know" (July 28, 1993).

Once the child's body is filled to capacity, fine hairs emerge from pores all over its surface (Reichard 1950:497). These hairs and pores are believed necessary for proper functioning of the body, "for it is through [them] that air comes out of the body" (O'Bryan 1956:103; see also Goddard 1933:147). As Wilson Aronilth of Tsaile, Arizona, explicated, the hairs on arms, legs, and other parts of the body are the means by which the "physical body breathes" (1985:147). Because of their characteristics, these hairs and pores can also allow potentially harmful substances to permeate the body.

The air circulating in, through, and out of the body maintains the constant connection between individual Nihookáá Dine'é and their world. Small winds form over the entire surface of the body wherever air flows through the tiny hairs and pores covering its exterior. These animating winds make moving, talking, and thinking possible. Exactly when these all-important winds will leave an individual decides that person's life span, which, as will be discussed more fully, is believed to be determined before he or she enters the Navajo world. Both Amelda Sandoval Shay and Johnson Dennison raised the issue of how administering CPR can cause someone to live past her or his pre-determined lifetime, thereby interfering with the plan negotiated with the Holy People. Shay pointed out:

> ASS: Maybe it was meant for him to die right there, so why should we give this person our breathing? It was already dead. And part of you is gone if you give it to them. . . .
>
> MS: Does this have more to do with not interfering with what is meant to be?
>
> ASS: Yes.
>
> MS: Or does it have more to do with not giving up part of yourself?
>
> ASS: Both. To me it is both because . . . maybe it was meant for him to go right there and then. Then you're trying to save him. And all your breathing and your air—you are giving it to them and they'll be gone with it. And here you are up here [on the earth].
>
> MS: And you think it would cause you harm?
>
> ASS: Yes. Later on.
>
> MS: What type of harm would it cause you?
>
> ASS: Because you might be thinking about it mentally. . . . Who wouldn't think about it? I would. I'd wonder what happened. If he lives it would have been OK. But [if] not, there is no way to get your air back because it is already in his system. And then you start to wonder about it. I guess mentally it will affect you. (Shay, June 6, 2005)

Johnson Dennison agreed with Shay about why Navajo people should not perform CPR: "Because if your time is up for the Navajo, then you do the CPR and then the person's heart begins beating again and it's kind of like going beyond the point [restarting the person's heart, causing him to live beyond the point intended; see chapter 6]. That is one part" (June 22, 2005). He cautioned that "your wind spirit" goes into the person upon whom you perform CPR, and if they expire afterward it will affect you, "then you get sick, ill" (J. Dennison, June 22, 2005). He also pointed out, however, that ceremonial interventions can be done to reconcile the situation.

INTERVENTIONS

> And then I went to see a medicine man down here (indicating east
> with her chin), toward Low Mountain[, Arizona]. I went to see him
> again, and . . . I couldn't even see, everything was blurry. I couldn't
> even move, I couldn't even get up. . . . We had a hard time finding
> that medicine man, so we went to see him in the morning and then I
> told him [what was bothering me]. "Well, I can do it right now, I can
> sing on you right now," he says. Then my husband goes, "Well, do
> you want to have it done right now, or do you wanna wait?" I said,
> "I want it done right now. I am not going to wait." So he [the medi-
> cine man] says, "Go over to the hooghan over there." So we went
> over to the hooghan. Then he brought his stuff in and he just started
> singing and then he—way in the middle of it, I don't know how
> many songs he sang, [after] about four songs I could see. And my
> vision, it seems like it was clear. And here I couldn't even eat or
> anything, I didn't even want to drink any water or nothing. And he
> gave me all that herb [an herbal medicine to consume], and then he
> sang about four songs, and this was maybe an hour, maybe forty-
> five minutes singing and stuff like that, and after that we left . . . we
> stopped at Chinle[, Arizona]. . . . I got hungry, and then I ate and I
> felt a lot better. Until to this day I feel fine, but just once in a good
> while. And he wants me to have the rest of the stuff done [the pro-
> scribed ritual], but I haven't done that yet. So, that is what happened
> and here I am. (Jackson, July 20, 2004)

Sarah Jackson reported feeling much better for two or three years after her
condition was diagnosed as having been caused by the blood transfusion;
however, it did not last. Her condition gradually deteriorated until she suffered loss of appetite, partial paralysis, and blurred vision. That is when
her husband took her to a ceremonial practitioner near Low Mountain,
Arizona, who—as she described in the preceding extract—performed the
short version of the Enemy Way ceremony over her, whereupon she recovered immediately. The ceremony was intended to simultaneously cleanse
Jackson of the negative effects resulting from two forms of contamination:

first, that of an outsider—the African American donor's blood—and second, the donor's death.

The cleansing ceremony Jackson described is the first level of business when a Navajo individual returns after a separation from the community. The power of the Holy People brought to the sanctified hooghan through the ceremonial practitioner's voice, the belief of the patient and all those present, and the faithful following of every detail of ritual proscriptions— including walking on corn pollen footprints, ritual bathing in yucca suds, drying in cornmeal, and dressing in new clothing—will collectively remove all offending substances from the individual and protect her or his family and community (Bekis, July 15, 2004; Johnson 1973:72; Tinhorn, June 14, 2005).

In many cases, however, ceremonial intervention will not stop there, for contamination by non-Navajo will have deeply infiltrated the individual. This is true in situations ranging from automobile accidents to those of most concern to this project, such as surgery or when a Navajo individual has received a non-Navajo's blood or, conversely, has given blood to a non-Navajo. More extreme forms of intervention will be called for in these cases. Depending on the situation, the interventions range in intensity from a nine-day ceremonial event like the Enemy Way to a one-day Hóchxǫ'jí to various forms of prayer, as described by Rose Mary Wade.

Wade had this to say about blood transfusions:

> MS: If you take blood from a non-Navajo, is it a no-no?
>
> RW: Outside [from someone other than a Navajo]. Maybe from a white person? Or a black person?
>
> MS: What would you do if you did take blood from outside?
>
> RW: You'd have to have a clearance prayer done so that whoever gave the blood will be at peace with the [portion of his or her body] within you. With whoever got the transfusion.
>
> MS: So, this prayer is so the donor will be at peace with the blood he [or she] has given up?
>
> RW: Uh-huh.
>
> MS: Do you know what it is called?

RW: It is just a clearing. It is called the forgiving Hóchxǫ'jí. (Rose
Mary Wade, June 17, 2005)

Wade stated that a primary motivation for conducting the "clearance
prayer" is to make sure the donor is at peace with the part of him- or herself
that is now in the recipient. This sentiment is similar to the motivation
Thomas Deschene, Jr., claimed for performing Native American Church
meetings or prayers in circumstances where the donor has died and the
recipient is suffering physical or mental effects. He considers his responsibility to be one of negotiation:

TD: You negotiate like we do and ask for forgiveness because as
Navajo, we are not supposed to do these things [have blood transfusions or organ transplants]. And it is just like making a prayer
to people that go to church, it is just like making a prayer to Jesus
and to God. You do exactly the same thing to the person that has
passed on. You talk to him, to the spirit that has passed on: "You
wanted to donate your blood or your organ. . . . That is what you
wanted, to help a person to live." You make an offering right here
to the fireplace, sometimes it releases that person so that they can
go on to live. (Deschene, June 15, 2005)

For others, such as Larry Todachinee, the only viable form of intervention
for donated blood that now resides in a dead person is Evil Way. He firmly
maintained:

LT: From Anglo to Indian, it wouldn't work for you, that is what
they say.
MS: What if you donate blood and then the person that your blood
goes into dies?
LT: Well, you have to have an Evil Way doings. That is all it takes, Evil
Way, then Blessing Way. That is it. (Todachinee, June 28, 2005)

Sheila Goldtooth concurred, noting that if the person from whom you received
blood or to whom you donated blood was a Navajo who passed away, the
Navajo recipient or donor would need an Evil Way ceremony (July 18, 2005).

EVIL WAY

> The singer and his assistant took the patient out by the ash pile north
> of his mother's hooghan and had him strip down to his shorts. . . .
> The singer's assistant twirled a bull roarer in front of the patient, to
> the north. The singer carefully helped the patient bathe in the water
> prepared with an herb collected from the base of a tree that had been
> struck by lightning. Once he was done washing, they turned to enter
> the hooghan. . . . Neat piles of ash [sat] at each of the cardinal points
> around the woodstove.
>
> The singer, his assistant, and the patient entered. The patient took
> his position on the west side of the hooghan to the left of the singer.
> The patient sat with his legs and arms outstretched. His feet were
> flexed and his hands were lying on his legs with the palms up. The
> singer began a series of songs, using a gourd rattle. After one or two
> songs he stopped and crushed some herbs into water in a coffee can
> and then put the bull roarer in this [mixture]. Then he dug through
> his paraphernalia bag [an old suitcase] and removed some arrow-
> heads, herbs, and rocks. (Field notes, August 8, 1993)

Hóchxǫ'jí is required to restore health when a person has been contaminated
by harmful factors such as contact with the death of a Navajo. Its purpose is
to expel the influences of the ghosts of Natives to whom they appear in
dreams "in the shape of fiery balls which elude search, or in shadowy forms
which leave no tracks, or at best some animal tracks" (Haile 1950:viii).

After being ritually bathed, the patient is marked sequentially with black
tallow, ocher, white tallow, and charcoal—from his or her toes to the top of
the head (Field notes, August 8, 1993; Haile 1950:239–40). Every substance
or artifact with which a patient is ceremonially painted or dressed provides a
layer of lifelong protection to the surface of the body (A. Denny, October 8,
1993; Walters, August 10, 1993). Individuals acquire an additional layer of
protection each time such items are ceremonially applied to them, accumu-
lating multiple layers of protection during their lifetimes.

Depending on the nature of the ceremony, the singer starts with either
the right or the left side when applying blessing or protecting materials to
the patient. Manipulations begin on the right and move to the left during

ceremonies associated with blessing, such as the molding and painting of a young woman during her Kinaaldá. Application of materials starts on the left and moves to the right in healing and protection ceremonies (H. Ashley, July 27, 1993; Walters, August 12, 1993), as in the portion of the Hóchxǫ́'jí described in my field notes:

> Next, the patient was treated with ashes from the piles around the fire with an eagle feather fan. The singer began a new series of songs as he dipped the fan into the ash pile on the east. Starting on the patient's left, the singer tapped the patient on the soles of his feet with the feather fan. He dipped the fan into the ash pile on the south and tapped the patient's knees and palms. He continued singing. Next, he dipped the fan into the ash pile on the west and tapped the fan against the area over the patient's heart and on his upper back. Then he dipped the fan into the ash pile on the north. With this ash he tapped the fan on the patient's shoulders, on the sides of his head, along the crest of his head from the nose backward, and then on the top of his head. Finally, the singer made a clockwise circular motion around the patient's head with the fan, concluding his song as he clapped the feather fan to the north [the patient's left]. In each case, the singer started on the left and moved to the right [left sole, right sole, left knee, right knee, and so on] tapping twice at each location. (Field notes, August 8, 1993)

A vital shielding layer is acquired in the Evil Way after the evil has been expelled from the patient's body, when she or he is dressed in shoulder straps that have protective materials such as arrowheads, deer hooves, bear claws, shells, and ntł'iz attached to them. As Harry Walters explained, in this context these artifacts are used to dress the patient in the image of Monster Slayer, thereby instilling lifelong protection:

> HW: To protect [the patient], just like a coat of armor, like a soldier will put on. There was a ritual involved in that, so even if you take it off, you still have the armor.
> MS: You always wear it?
> HW: Yes.
> MS: You always have it?

HW: You always have it.

MS: As a protection?

HW: Yes, just like the yé'ii [supernaturals] mask when once you put it on, and then you take it off. You have been initiated, and then you are blessed with that. You have certain [privileges]. You can dance in it. When there is a ceremony involving someone to be dressed in a yé'ii to treat the person, you can do that. . . . Otherwise, you can't do this. That is what it symbolizes. The place when you put that armor on, and then after the prayer is said, and then you can take it off, you always have that protection. (Walters, August 10, 1993)

The singer next motions his eagle feather fan in a clockwise direction over the patient's head, raises it upward to the smoke hole, and then claps it sharply to the left of the patient to direct the harmful factors leaving the patient. Some Navajo believe the singer directs his motions to the left of the patient at this juncture in the ceremony because negative elements must leave the body through the fingertips of the left hand (Knoki-Wilson, July 29, 1993). Others are of the opinion that malevolent factors are perceived to be leaving the body from the left side at this point in the ceremony only because of the patient's position in the hooghan, not because the fingertips of the left hand provide the point of departure (Walters, August 10, 1993). If a patient is sitting on the west side of the hooghan facing east, her or his left side is to the north. Therefore, the singer motions to the left as he uses his eagle feather fan to drive the malevolent factors leaving the patient's body out of the hooghan to the north.

ENEMY WAY

MS: What does the death of the person who has your blood do to you?

KB: Well, you have to have a big ceremony. Sometimes it will work, sometimes it wouldn't.

MS: What ceremony?

KB: Because your blood now is six feet underneath [the ground]. You have to have some sort of Hóchxǫ'jí, that blackening ceremony, the

Evil Way. Or if it is contaminated with another race, let's say like a
white race, you have to have Anaa' jí ndáá', the Enemy Way. (Black,
June 16, 2005)

Sheila Goldtooth agreed with Kenneth Black, Jr.'s, assessment regarding
what ceremonies are appropriate in particular cases of blood transfusion
or donation. Like Black, she pointed out that if the person from whom you
received blood or to whom you donated blood was a non-Navajo who died,
the Navajo recipient or donor would need an Enemy Way ceremony rather
than the Evil Way, which would be needed if the person from whom you
received blood or to whom you donated blood was a Navajo who had
expired (Goldtooth, July 18, 2005). Ambrose Shepard reported that this
ceremony had helped his brother Bill, who became ill as a result of a transfusion from a non-Navajo while in the military, return to a normal life:
"They did a Squaw Dance [Enemy Way] to make that correction. He got
well" (June 3, 2005). Shepard elaborated: "A person is getting out of line,
getting to drink, do[ing] crazy things. . . . You ask for a Squaw Dance to be
performed over him. And that is how they correct them. They get cleared
up and they live again. They get out of that misery. That is what I know.
I've seen some people that has gone through that, like my own brother had
that problem" (Shepard, June 5, 2005).

According to Johnson Dennnison, these two ceremonies are also the
appropriate forms of intervention for health problems caused by having
performed CPR on someone who subsequently dies. He noted:

> JD: And then the other part is that your wind spirit goes into the
> body. And then if he or she dies with it, then you get sick, ill, that
> is why. So then there is this ceremony that corrects that. . . .
> MS: What is the ceremony that you can do?
> JD: The Evil Way for the Navajo and then the Enemy Way for a
> non-Navajo. (Dennison, June 22, 2005)

Although blood and wind are clearly considered analogous in terms of
these forms of ceremonial intervention, no Navajo consultant ever differentiated human breath on the basis of either pre-sexual versus sexual maturity
or any other basis.

Ronald Sandoval, a Chiricahua Wind Way singer from Valley Store, Arizona, informed me of one other possible intervention for cases in which one's blood has been given to someone who subsequently dies:

> RS: Going back to that blood transfusion, there is a very special prayer for that. Not many medicine men are left who can do that now. With this prayer that they can do, they get it back from way down under, in the First World, where people go after they die. There used to be different prayers that would bring it back up. That is how they believe it, that they'll talk it back up for the person.
>
> MS: Talk what back up?
>
> RS: The blood. By saying this prayer for the person that donated his or her blood, for the donor, if they are having any complications or if they are having, say, nightmares or something like that, they can do that prayer to overcome that. . . .
>
> MS: So, if, let's say, if you donated blood and the person that had your blood in his or her body passed on, then certain practitioners can do special prayers to correct the problem and bring your blood back up from the First World?
>
> RS: Mm hmm.
>
> MS: To correct the problem because the person with your blood has it in the First World.
>
> RS: Yeah.
>
> MS: And do they use this prayer to correct problems related to CPR or organ transplants?
>
> RS: No, it is just the blood transfusions because it's a fluid, like water. That way they can get it back up, but the other ones are just there forever. (R. Sandoval, June 25, 2005, with translation assistance by Amelda Sandoval Shay and Florence Sandoval)

As Sandoval noted, this rare form of intervention does not help with CPR or organ transplants, the latter of which will be taken up in chapter 7.

• • •

Navajo views on the transfer of life substances—blood as well as wind or breath—offer the opportunity to more fully explore traditional views on identity, contamination, and human physiology. Navajo people divide human blood and wind into the categories of Navajo and non-Navajo. Based on the tenet of synecdoche, problems may arise as a result of the transfer of life substances through donation, CPR, or transfusion. This may be so because the person to whom a Navajo's blood or breath has been donated later dies; alternatively, it may be the case because the organ or blood donated to a Navajo is from an individual who was dead at the time of the initial donation or who has subsequently passed on.

The distinction between Navajo and non-Navajo blood and breath not only marks Navajo collective identity, it also plays a key role in recipients' preferences for sources of blood or wind. In any event, contamination by a non-Navajo's blood or wind, by the breath or wind of a dead person, or by having one's life substances in the body of someone who dies can be rectified by a range of interventions, including but not limited to a cleansing or protection prayer and/or a cleansing, Evil Way, or Enemy Way ceremony.

CHAPTER SIX

Surgery and Disposal of Body Parts

I was brought up traditionally. The old Navajo traditional prayers and ceremonies, I was brought up with that. My mother used to teach me, she had certain things done for me to bring me up. A lot had to do with the Beauty Way because they say with the Beauty Way you should have it at least once a year, and that is what I did is have a ceremony done maybe once a year. And then when you get an ailment, you go get a medicine man or either a hand shaker or [a] stargazer. They tell what was wrong with you. So they had different types of ceremonies for a person to make those corrections. So I had those kind of ceremonies performed for me. And I believed them, that [was the] way I was brought up. And when I went to school—when I went to BIA [Bureau of Indian Affairs] School—there were a lot of things that was mandatory. You had to choose a religion to go to. My father and the church that was here already [in Ganado, Arizona,] I knew a little bit about it so I became a Presbyterian. I went to that church, and then later on I wanted to know something about the other religions so I went and learned something about the Catholic Church, and now I believe in both of them.

And then later on I picked up another traditional ceremony
which became available. Navajo had a real correlation to that
religion. It is called Native American Church [NAC] and I went
into that because my brothers and sisters were going to that. . . .
I was drinking a lot . . . when I left and I came back from the
military. And I wanted to try and quit, but there was nothing
that could help me quit, and then I went to this church [NAC]
and start giving up my drinking for it. So I went deep into that,
exploring into that church, and I look at various angles of it.
And it then became a reality that I should practice that [reli-
gion]. And the songs and prayers were so beautiful that I wanted
to be a road man. They're called road man, it is like a priest. I
went and did that, got the ceremony, and I did a lot of perfor-
mance of ceremonies for people around here. . . . Also another
religion that I kind of learned about is the Mormon Church. . . .
Altogether I feel that there is no church that is different, even
the Navajo traditional ceremonies is still, with the teaching and
the stories, related. There still is a God, there still is Jesus. That
is what I found out.

(Shepard, June 3, 2005)

When I met with Ambrose Shepard of Ganado, Arizona, he provided the
typical Navajo greeting: he introduced himself by clan affiliations. After
graduating from the Phoenix Indian School, he served in the U.S. Air
Force. After returning home, he married and secured work with the public
school system. While raising a family and working, he moved into tribal
government. Ultimately, he served at all levels of the government, including
an undisclosed period as the chapter secretary-treasurer, eight years on the
Navajo Tribal Council, and twelve years as a county supervisor. As a result
of diabetes-related complications, Shepard has had five major operations.
After having the toes and other portions of his left leg removed, he had the
leg amputated from the knee down. Subsequently, he progressively had
portions of his right foot and leg amputated; the section below the knee is
now completely gone. He has also had his right kidney removed. He spent
almost two years in the hospital for the surgeries on the right side of his
body, recuperation, rehabilitation, and physical therapy.

A major concern of this project is to learn how patients validate the moral worth of each health-seeking decision and chosen therapy, as well as how each type of healer justifies his or her moral worth and legitimizes his or her therapeutic power. Shepard's story of his battle with complications associated with diabetes thus serves as a connecting strand throughout the chapter as a means to nuance several issues pertaining to the relationship between the Native American Church (NAC) and traditional Navajo ceremonies as they coexist today. These include the idiom of helplessness, the sacred and secular nature of medications, an attempt to understand to what church members and officiants credit moral validation, and the power dynamics of cures. Segments of Shepard's account appear in the text as topics relevant to it arise.

Because of the inherently syncretic nature of the NAC, moral validity can be derived from multiple sources, including Christianity, traditional Navajo beliefs, and other indigenous belief systems. As a result, in the case of Ambrose Shepard and other members of the Native American Church, to address the concern about how patients validate the moral worth of chosen therapies and how healers justify or legitimize their therapeutic power, we must first sort out the basic tenets of the peyote religion and, when possible, determine which are derived from Christianity and which from Navajo traditions or perhaps another source, such as an alternative indigenous system. Second, we must determine when a patient or a road man is validating a personal or ritual decision on the basis of a Christian or Navajo tenet.

Following Rosalind Shaw and Charles Stewart's suggestion (1994:7), special attention is given to the workings of power and agency within this particular syncretism. Near the end of the epigraph that opens this chapter, Shepard espouses religious relativism, or the notion that all roads lead to one God or at least to the same source of supernatural power. This is a fundamental tenet of the Native American Church. According to David Aberle, "In theory, peyotism preaches the equality and humanity of all mankind under God, and seems to teach that all religions worship the same God and are therefore equal" (Aberle 1982b:181). Consider Larry Todachinee's interpretation of this principle:

> LT: My mother would go down to Keams Canyon and the Hopi, they
>   have a Catholic Church there, and she used to sing in the Catholic

Church [choir]. So, later on we go to church over there, then all of us, maybe all my sisters, we were baptized there. And my grandfathers, they usually do the crystal gazing, so we joined in. And my uncle, my mother's brother, back in 1939, he is the one that started peyote, Native American Church religion [in the Jeddito area of the reservation]. So later we started using this peyote and then we were raised by that too. So it is all into one, the way I look at it. Christianity and traditional and this peyote, they are all into one. What they do is pray, that is the main one, prayers. And they do songs—like traditional we have songs, and in church school they have songs, and Native American Church they have songs, so it is all in the one. That is the way I always think about it. (Todachinee, June 28, 2005)

Todachinee's family history alerts us to another long-recognized NAC tenet, which is also evident in Shepard's testimony. As Aberle noted, "Since all men worship the same God, it is acceptable for a peyotist to join with any congregation in their worship of God." Thus, "Exclusive membership in the Native American Church is not demanded" (Aberle 1982b:181).

HELPLESSNESS

And another thing that I grew up with is what they call peyote, peyote ceremonies. . . . My brother who used to live here used to perform ceremonies. When I was 'round about nine or ten years old . . . my dad and my mom and me and my little brother . . . were just sitting in [on my brother's NAC meeting]. . . . Toward morning he got me up and he set me over here (indicating where the patient sits during a ceremony) and he talked to me. I really remember that one, too. And what he said to me was, "Your mom and your dad are not educated. They cannot help you, but your dad always says go as far as you can with education no matter what." So, he was saying this to me—to every one of us. All my brothers and sisters, they all went to school. . . . And my brother said, "Sure, you have land down there, and you have cornfields. You have livestock, horses, sheep, and those things.

And whatever tools your dad has" . . . and then he said, "those things belong to your parents; they are not yours. Those things were just there to get you ready to live your own life and grow up. And if you want those things, there is the door, from that door out that way maybe you will find work and get those things on your own. . . . They call this the peyote ceremony, they call it the fireplace, and this fireplace and this medicine that is right there, that's the only one that is gonna help you. It's gonna guide you." (Deschene, June 15, 2005)

This notion of guidance and help coming from the fireplace and peyote is derived directly from NAC oral traditions. Despite the fact that the historical account of how peyote came to the Navajo from the Ute, who acquired it from the Comanche, is widely acknowledged in academic circles, members of the Native American Church hold sacred various accounts of what is best termed the peyote origin story. The next account encapsulates the fundamental elements:

A long time ago there were some people traveling around. There was an old woman with these people and she was very sick. She had sores all over her body and wasn't going to make it. . . . They left her there to die and this woman all of a sudden heard this voice. This voice came from a plant and it said, "Eat me!" So this woman looked down and there was this plant there and she ate it. It was the medicine.

She ate the medicine and all her illness went away. Then the medicine told her, "Go back and join your people. Follow the tracks that you see before you." And when she looked on the ground in front of her, she saw the shoe prints that the horses of her people had left as they traveled on. In this way she was able to find her way back to her people. (Anonymous road man quoted in Quintero 1995:82)[1]

Featured here is the fact that the peyote religion is a means by which individuals can find their way back to their people. This resonates with the claim made by the Chiricahua Wind Way practitioner interviewed by John Garrity who stated that finding peyote as the lost ceremony would enable the Navajo to "come home" (2000:531). Of greater significance for this analysis is the primary idiom of the NAC revealed through the plot of the peyote origin story, which in essence documents a female hero being spoken to by a peyote plant after she has been abandoned by her family because of extreme illness—sores all over her body—or, as demonstrated in the next account, because of wounds incurred in an ambush by enemy warriors. In each case the plant tells her to eat it and she will recover, thereby disclosing the idiom as "help is always there when you need it on the road of life." To emphasize its willingness to help, in the next narrative the plant itself reaches out to her. She partakes of it and is healed. Thus, an exemplar button of peyote sits on the ridge of the crescent moon altar throughout every Half Moon ritual, in the middle of what is known as "the road of life," as if to forevermore relay the message that it is available to help when needed (Calabrese 1994:513).

In addition to expanding our understanding of helplessness as a primary tenet of the NAC, the next account by Wilson Aronilth, a faculty member at Diné College in Tsaile, Arizona, and a NAC road man, introduces an important additional tenet through his language choice: that of suffering. Recall that this concept was also central to Thomas Deschene, Jr.'s, rendition of the restoration narrative. As will be clarified, these points are germane because Christian ideas of *redemptive suffering*—the sacrifice of Jesus for mankind (Porterfield 2005:131)—are paramount to the Navajo version of the Native American Church. Aronilth explained:

> As the story goes, this woman was participating in a hunting trip with fellow hunters from her tribe. . . . A group of warriors attacked these hunters and in the process many were unfortunate and others ran to safety. Among the unfortunate was this one woman. She was wounded from the war party, and was left behind by her people to die. Through all of her suffering she became lost and helpless in the desert. But, out of this desolation and terror this woman heard a voice speak to her first through a dream and after she woke from the dream. The Voice said, "Eat the sacred plant that is growing beside you, that is life and all of the richest blessings for you and your Indian people." Weakly, this woman turned her head against the earth's surface and saw the herb. Its head was divided into five points. These five points are the symbol of man, his beliefs and his religion. She reached for the plant and it seemed to extend outward to meet her fingers. She

pulled out the herb and partook of it. Through the partaking of this plant her strength returned and she was healed and cured from her suffering. (Aronilth quoted in Calabrese 1994:517)

Aberle maintains that, like the protagonist in Wilson Aronilth's account, peyotists are helpless before the form of supernatural power they recognize (Aberle 1982b:154). The implied comparison in Aberle's claim raises more questions than it answers and causes us to contrast the notion of helplessness attributed to members of the NAC with the attitude with which traditionalists approach the Holy People when seeking aid.

In her discussion of the nature of ritual power and the process of its acquisition, Katherine Spencer pointed out that in every oral tradition accompanying a Navajo ceremonial, the hero is faced with the problem of securing supernatural aid to accomplish his or her rescue or restoration. While on occasion the Diyin Dine'é may freely offer assistance or secret information about how to gain access to the particular supernatural that can cure the hero, for the most part the Holy People are reluctant to contribute aid until *compelled* to do so; in other words, they must be approached in the proper ritual manner with suitable offerings (Spencer 1957:33–34).

This notion of compelling is based on understandings of a system of reciprocity, whereby the quantity of goods is not important; rather, only the *correct goods* will induce a Holy Person to act. *This is therefore a situation of ceremonial prestation that compels reciprocity* (Aberle 1967:17). As a result, Navajo people negotiate for aid with full confidence that assistance will be forthcoming *as long as protocol is followed*. In contradistinction, a sense of helplessness arises from perceptions of having no control.

Aberle maintains that "[t]he prayers of the peyotist, then, express a feeling of helplessness. The language and the tears clearly indicate this. But the prayers are intended to alleviate the anxiety of helplessness through the aid of an all-powerful God" (Aberle 1982b:154). Because it is through peyote that Native Americans are able to communicate with Him, "God and peyote are to be approached humbly and besought for help. . . . The peyotist is like a child crying to its parents for something that it wants" (Aberle 1982b:180). In fact, although it is decidedly uncharacteristic for traditional Navajo to shed tears in a public venue (Schwarz 2001), as other scholars have noted, "[c]rying and other forms of emotional expression are common and even encouraged in peyote meetings" (Lewton and Bydone 2000:486; see also Aberle 1982b:153–54). The infantilization of pleading patients and the uncharacteristic emphasis on crying that is frequently evident in Native American Church meetings reflect the peyotist's relationship to the supernatural.

In Christianity, supernatural power is transcendent rather than immanent, as it is in Navajo ontology. As previously noted, Navajo oral history documents that all animals, plants, mountains, and people within Navajo sacred geography were endowed with spiritual power at the moment the Holy People took their places as the inner forms of key environmental features (Wyman 1965:91). This tenet of a transcendent God is one of the fundamental Christian influences inherent in the NAC; thus, while considering themselves to be embedded in nature, Navajo peyotists believe God is above all and rules both man and nature (Aberle 1982b:195).

The terms used for God by peyotists Aberle interviewed during his fieldwork circa 1950 reflect a monotheistic ideology (Aberle 1982b:153, 376). This was also true among the members of the Native American Church with whom I consulted. The two groups did not use identical terminology, however. Whereas those Aberle interviewed used "Our Heavenly Father," "Our Lord," or "Our Savior," those I interviewed were more likely to use "the Great Spirit" (J. Nez, June 12, 2005; see also Aronlith cited in Calabrese 1994:513), "God" (Deschene, June 15, 2005; Shepard, June 3, 2005; Todachinee, June 28, 2005), or "the Creator" (J. Dennison, June 22, 2005; Deschene, June 15, 2005; see also Goodman cited in Calabrese 1994:508; Garrity 2000). Other spiritual beings such as "Jesus" were referenced as well (Deschene, June 15, 2005; Shepard, June 3, 2005). The traditional polytheistic perspective has not disappeared, however, for Navajo deities such as Mother Nature, Father Sky, the Holy Spirits (Deschene, June 15, 2005; J. Nez, June 12, 2005), and simply the Holy People (Deschene, June 15, 2005; J. Nez, June 12, 2005; see also Garrity 2000:529) are still very much a part of the spiritual world for Navajo members of the NAC with whom other scholars and I have recently consulted.

Aberle stressed that "[i]t would be a mistake to think of peyote curing as operating only through the spiritual power of peyote, only through communication with God through peyote, or only through peyote as a substance. Peyote is a power; God is a power. In the curing ceremony the prayers of the officiants (road chief and others), of participants, and of the patient; the singing and drumming; and the ingestion of peyote by the patient and the others are all contributory to a cure" (Aberle 1982b:181–82).

Jonah Nez, a Native American Church road man from Luckachukai, Arizona, shared numerous accounts about remarkable cures of every conceivable problem, from broken bones to life-threatening diseases such as throat cancer and diabetes. When I asked Nez what it is that brings about a cure in a Native American Church meeting, whether, for instance, it is the peyote or the prayers, he replied as follows:

> JN: You really have to have faith in the Great Spirit. That is how I believe. You don't just go to the person and give them medication. . . . You got to know just how much medication to give to a person to deal with that cancer. And then sure enough, that person might get well.
>
> MS: What do you think it is that makes the cancer go away? Is it the peyote? Or is it the prayers the people are saying who are in the tepee?
>
> JN: It could be both, the peyote and the prayer. They say that there is Holy People, there's four of them standing, facing each other from the east, the north, the west, and the south, and then right there in-between. And those are the ones that know the whole population of Diné because we have that color turquoise, red, and black; if we have that color the spirits can know. And through the prayers that we say, the sacrifice that we make to the Holy Spirits, there is a man and a woman facing each other and then the other ones [other Holy People previously mentioned] too. And you learn to believe what we are saying for a person.
>
> MS: So, what is the sacrifice you are making?
>
> JN: There are different types of sacrifices. You can make a sacrifice with the tobacco. Not with the tobacco you buy in the store. Like over here in Durango, up there on Durango Mountain there's tobacco. Not only one kind but there is five different kinds of tobacco on that mountain. And you have to know just what you are coming for. And you make an offering to Mother Nature. To the Male Rain and the Female Rain and the Great Sun, and you

make an offering to those when you go to get that tobacco. And then use that. So, you can use that tobacco to make a sacrifice or white shell, turquoise, abalone, jet. . . . Or there is corn pollen, too, put it on the ground and say it is a sacrifice for Mother Nature. But when you do that you don't use the white shell.

MS: What about the people who are with you in meetings. They are consuming peyote while they are praying. Is that a form of sacrifice too, that they are sitting up all night praying?

JN: Well, it is really up to a person that's sitting in a peyote meeting, and if you're a road man praying for a patient, your job is right here (indicates the area between where the road man and the patient sit in the tepee during a curing meeting) to make the patient well. And each individual, he is in here for his own special purpose. If they want to pray for the patient, they are more than welcome to do that, but if you are sitting here for a person doing your job for the person, that's how you can really help a person. Those are some of the things that I was taught. (J. Nez, June 12, 2005)

Jonah Nez's insistence that both Holy People and Native American Church powers are present and essential during NAC healing meetings is not an aberrant occurrence or an isolated event; rather, it fits within the broader scope of what Roland Wagner referred to as a series of "syncretic experiments" documented since the mid-1940s (Wagner 1975). Nez's description of the conjoined powers of the NAC and Holy People in one healing ritual is highly engrossing, however, because it raises cogent issues surrounding Aberle's point regarding supposed inherent differences between the NAC and traditional Navajo ritual patterns. Aberle maintains that the NAC calls for spontaneous prayers that beseech God within a generalized frame, while Navajo ceremonies call for rigid formulaic practices, songs, and prayers by means of which the Holy People are compelled to offer assistance (1982b:154; Aberle and Stewart 1957:33). The individual syncretic experiments described over the past few decades offer an opportunity to reconsider Aberle's hypothesis.[2]

In the case of the road men with whom Garrity consulted between 1993 and 1997, who had begun to creatively integrate traditional diagnostic techniques such as listening and stargazing, or, alternatively, those conducting peyote meetings that correspond to Blessing Way, Lightning Way, Evil Way, and Wind Way or who integrate traditional dry paintings into their NAC healing meetings (Garrity 2000:527), the presence of the associated Navajo Holy People would certainly be required for efficacy.

Navajo women who practice these traditional ceremonies outside the context of the NAC candidly discussed this point with me. Gladys Denny, a practitioner of the Fire Dance from Low Mountain, Arizona, explained: "When you are getting ready to sing, that is when you say aloud, 'All the people that are in here'—you are not really saying it to the people in the hooghan, you are really saying it to the Holy People—'help me to perform this singing tonight.' The Holy People are present. . . . They are the ones you are really talking to. When I say 'help me perform the singing tonight,' the Holy People know I am not saying it to the Navajo there. They know I am asking them to help me keep everything in order and keep my voice strong" (G. Denny, July 17, 2000).

Practitioners' personal narratives reveal that they are cognizant of the Holy People's presence throughout the ceremony. Jean Mariano, a Blessing Way singer from Mariano Lake, New Mexico, stated, "They are around me. . . . I can feel them surrounding me. That is how I know that I am being helped when I am singing. They help me put the songs in place" (June 29, 2000). Keeping the songs "in line" (Edison, July 17, 2000), "in order" (G. Denny, July 17, 2000; Edison, July 17, 2000), or "in place" (Mariano, June 29, 2000; Nix, July 10, 2000) is vitally important because for the ceremony to be effective, the practitioner must carefully follow all of her or his mentor's instructions and present each song, prayer, and procedure in full, as well as in the correct sequence. Collectively, a singer's verbal and physical expressions form an incantation compelling the Holy People to assist. In fact, errors or departure from this rigidity may result not only in failure of the prayer or ceremony but also in harm to both the patient and the ceremonial practitioner (Aberle 1982b:153).

In marked contrast, within Native American Church meetings "[t]here are, of course, numerous slight tribal and even intra-tribal variations. In fact, each leader conducts the ritual as he wishes; consequently, no two meetings are identical, but all conform to a standard" (Stewart and Aberle 1984:36). This raises the issue of how both types of prayers and powers can be successfully conjoined within one ritual.

Since peyote meetings remain idiosyncratic rather than formulaic, their very presence at NAC meetings indicates that Navajo Holy People do respond to non-formulaic beseeching. Moreover, once present, they take on considerable roles in the healing drama. This will be well evidenced in the section Redemptive Suffering wherein Thomas Deschene, Jr., further elucidates the interplay among Navajo Holy People, the Creator, and a road man in NAC curing meetings, but first we examine more immediate concerns related to amputation.

"NAVAJO BODIES MUST NOT BE CUT"

I've sought a lot of help from different religious groups. When I was first having problems with my leg—the sores were beginning to develop in my toes and all that. And they said, "We are going to have to send you to the hospital. You might have to amputate the leg." So, I had a brother, he is a lay minister. His name is Tom White. He lives in Gallup and I always call on him because he used to do a prayer for me when I was on the [Navajo] Tribal Council. . . . I called him, I said, "I have a problem. They detected a problem in my legs and say I might get one amputated. I am going to the hospital in Flagstaff and [would like to] see if I can get some help from you." . . . The day I called, that evening he came, showed up at the hospital. And he kind of counsel me on my being afraid and about getting my legs amputated. So he said, "Seventy percent of what you are told is not going to happen. The 30 percent is all in your mind and your beliefs. If you can go over the hump, it is you that is going to do it. How you believe in it. How you are going to go through the surgery. I will help you with the prayer, but a lot of times it is going to be up to you." So the 30 percent I looked for while he did the prayer for me. And while I was in the hospital, I always thought about what he told [me], the 30 percent that I help myself to get over that hump, I am going to survive the major surgery. (Shepard, June 3, 2005)

Among the first decisions a Navajo individual must make when faced with the possibility of an amputation is how to reconcile this invasive biomedical procedure with cultural and personal beliefs about the body and healing. In the case of Native American Church members such as Ambrose Shepard, these beliefs could be derived from traditional Navajo teachings, Christian teachings, or an alternative source in addition to those available through the NAC. I asked Shepard what he believes about the interior of the body in terms of having surgery. When I asked if the body is considered sacred, he replied:

> AS: Years ago there was no doctor, no nothing. All they relied on was the [traditional] medicine, the herbs and the sing [traditional ceremonies], all that. They depended on that. And they don't want to have anything come into their body with anything inside, to cut. That would be against the principle or the belief.
>
> MS: Why?
>
> AS: That is the principle and the belief, and the way the belief used to be was to have a sing and a ceremony and the medicine to cure that [the problem]. When the white man came over with the medicine and the surgery methods and all that, I guess they [Navajo] were kind of reluctant to have that done. Anything cut, you know. (Shepard, June 3, 2005)

Jonah Nez provided more expansive testimony about these healing techniques, which further elucidates the points raised by Shepard. Nez also discussed Navajo use of herbal remedies that can prevent the need for surgery—especially important for those who wish to follow the diné bike'ji prohibiting cutting of the body to which Shepard referred—but he additionally described the use of herbs to speed the recovery of surgical patients. While Nez testified to the power of herbal remedies in the hands of highly qualified ceremonial practitioners, he bemoaned the loss of such healers in the contemporary Navajo world.

> JN: Well, this mesa right here (pointing with his chin)? . . . On top of that mesa is sacred ground, they say. My father was a medicine man. And these birds, they travel south in the wintertime and then come back north in the springtime. . . . And you don't see those birds around here that often. Whenever they started being around here my old man would go up there [and say], "I want to learn

that prayer." They say like if a person falls off a horse, and if he fractured his muscles or if he fractured his bones, or a person might go to the hospital and the doctor cuts him open, cuts his body open, takes out some bad stuff, how it's gonna affect that person, how it's gonna get put back together without any kind of infection? "These birds up there, they know the prayers. If you see them birds, they know. That's how come I'm gonna go back up there and learn some more prayers." He used to say that. He used to go up there. . . . That is the medicine area, and they know where to get it. Not a whole lot of them used to do that on the sacred ground. They roll that medicine into a ball and then give it to a person. . . . And the medicine will understand just where that pain is. And if the medicine man knows which way that infection is, he takes a little bit of that herb and through the mouth he could shoot that medicine to just where that infection is. And use that whistle to guide that medicine to . . . anywhere in the person's body. . . . The whistle guides the medicine to just where that infection is. And the medicine dissolves it [the infection] and it purifies. But we don't have that kind of medicine man no more, I don't think so.

MS: You don't?

JN: Un-uh. Seems like there's some medicine men doing—they call themselves medicine men, but it seems like they just want to get a hold of some of that green stuff. (J. Nez, June 12, 2005)

Many Navajo would agree with Nez that the more esoteric knowledge—known only to the most learned ceremonial practitioners—is disappearing at an alarming rate. Some such as Tso Allen, however, who has dedicated more than forty years to health issues on the Navajo reservation, maintain that the fundamental tenets of Navajo philosophy given to the Nihookáá Dine'é by the Diyin Dine'é remain a common denominator by means of which multiple generations of Navajo can communicate—at least within the contexts of health and illness where decisions are made collectively. As Allen explained, in her former capacity as a public health nurse she found the teachings and traditions taught to her when she was a child of immeasurable value because they served as both a foundation for communication and a bridge for building culturally sensitive health care solutions:

TA: I am really very thankful that I learned a lot of these [teachings and traditions] when I was small. And I always refer back to it because many of the elders now, and maybe I say fifty years old and over, are very influenced by traditional beliefs, so they still are very affected by the traditional upbringing, the way they were taught by their grandparents. . . . When I came to work in the community, I just work with people and just build on what I knew, what I learned from my parents, and the families share with me what they do, and so I just build on what they knew and what practices and what beliefs they had to change whatever is happening in their home, to build on what they know and to be healthy again. So, that is how I have used my traditional upbringing and traditional belief. (T. Allen, July 15, 2005)

An excellent example of the type of issue Allen regularly faced in the field is the one raised by Shepard—whether surgery should be allowed when a philosophical tenet disallows cutting the body. Consultants' accounts offered greater perspective on this prohibition as well as related issues.

PREDETERMINED LIFE SPAN

SJ: At one time my husband said that one of his neighbors, I guess he was a diabetic and then his leg just turned into cancer. But he didn't want to have his leg amputated. So he just left, he told the doctors, "Just leave it like that. If I have cancer, *let it be*. I don't want my leg to be cut off and stuff like that. I just want it like that." So, they just left it like that. . . . But some of the Navajo, they get their legs amputated and stuff like that, but this guy, I guess he didn't want anything to do with that. He didn't want his leg took off. So he just lived with it. "Well, it's already there, and what are they gonna do with my leg if it gets amputated? Where are they gonna put it? I don't want my leg to get amputated and then just have them throw it away. If my cancer is there, let it be. See how far it is gonna take me." That is what happened, and a couple years later he was gone. (Jackson, July 20, 2004)

When I asked Sarah Jackson if she had any experience with amputations, she replied with the previous story. When an ill patient says *"let it be,"* meaning he or she will let the disease take its course, the individual is falling back on a lesser-known element of Navajo epistemology. It is commonly understood that "according to our beliefs" an ideal age exists: "you are born to live 102 years; that is our goal" (Denetdeal, July 11, 2004; J. Dennison, June 22, 2005). Avery Denny contextualized this belief within Navajo oral history:

> AD: We believe that we come out of Mother Earth. From the Father Sky. They are facing one another, in between there we are the child of the Holy People, and in there we have mountains that we live by. That is our body and soul, that is our flesh and blood, too. And then there is the water. Nahasdzáán áádóó Tó Asdzáán [Mother Earth and Water Woman] . . . we believe that is where we come from. *Áádóó, eiya ei Nílch'i dóó* [and the wind also]. . . . The Holy People made it so people can be born and live the full extent of their life as a human being. We have 102 years old, that is how far we have to go. So, there is a road of life. It is set aside for us that on these sacred mountains we are going to go on our road of life to make our complete cycle. (A. Denny, August 11, 1993)

Johnson Dennison explained that if "there is a time within our life where our time, our number is up, that is where we stop. We don't go beyond that" (June 22, 2005). As Kenneth Black, Jr., put it, people have traditionally accepted that "when your time comes, your time comes" (June 16, 2005). Such acceptance is based on the premise that every Navajo life has a predetermined time span (Johnson, July 3, 2005; Shay, June 6, 2005). As previously mentioned, Don Mose, Jr., lost his brother at a youthful age to pancreatic cancer. Mose's recollection of the advice a ceremonial practitioner in the community gave him at that time sheds further light on this belief:

> [The medicine man said,] "It was he who decided when he stays or goes. . . . It was when they got together with the Holy People . . . when they sat down with the Holy People." He says, "It was he, it was you, it was everybody that decided how long it's gonna last,

when he is going to go, before you came into this Mother Earth. You decided what your plan is. What all these four directions' plan was. You decided what needs to be done and—when you said this is it, the deal isn't where you are going to live on forever. No." He said, "You cut your own line somewhere, and you said that would be it. . . . You make that plan. . . . But when that time comes, that is it." (Mose, June 13, 2005)

Delano Ashley, a twenty-something-year-old man in the prime of his life, further clarified this concept:

> DA: This oral tradition was told to me by my grandfather and my grandmother and my other grandfather, his brothers, and some of my uncles that are traditional. Those are the stories, we call it diné ba' hané, history, oral history. The way the story goes, it tells us the different worlds, the different processes, and the different events that took place in each phase of life in the Navajo culture. . . . The spiritual beings got together, saying "We are going to make some of these lives, these people, this Navajo, the Diné." So the story of that and how they give a pattern or plan, a life-hood for each individual, and once that is set, that's that. It's set. It's kind of like a story that I heard all the time, so that is how I understand it and how I perceive life. . . . So if it is time to go, then you know it is time. (D. Ashley, June 16, 2005)

Numerous stories were conveyed about Navajo people who, when faced with surgery as the preferred medical option for coping with a life-threatening disease, chose death instead. Ambrose Shepard expressed this view as follows:

> MS: When I asked you about the interior of the body, you said it was against the Navajo way, your old traditions, to get cut open. Did your grandparents or anyone ever explain to you why that is against the old traditions?
> AS: I talked to a lot of people about that. And they said the stronger the belief that you have that you don't have it done, try to correct

it with the medicine and the ceremonies. If that doesn't work, *a lot of people just decided that they much rather die than get cut open.* That is some of the belief that I know of. If it is a strong belief, then the last resort is death. They can live with that. (Shepard, June 3, 2005)

AUTOPSY

DM: My father, when he pass away, we don't know exactly how. He was coming back from Chinle[, Arizona,] and he ran off the road. We don't know if he had a heart attack or if he fell asleep. . . . The doctors, of course, the police, they say, "Let's do an autopsy." My grandfather, my mother, my family say, "No, he's gone. Why do you need to go dig into a man to find out what killed him? He's gone." He said, "That's not our way. Let it be. When his time came, that was it. He was the one who planned out his life before he came and when his time is up, he says 'This is what I am going to do. And when this day comes, that's it for me' he said." So my grandparents on this side said, "No, let's not bother to find out what killed him, let it be." Here's this fine line. This side is dark line, this side is white. You belong, if you're standing right in the middle here you stay with this side, this side doesn't belong to you, this is the dark side. That belongs to the Holy People. That is death. They deal with that now. You just stay on this side. . . . They [family members] said, "That really does belong to the Holy People 'cause you don't know what takes place afterward, so just let it be and accept it." In other words, be respectful for the dead. (Mose, June 13, 2005)

For his part, Don Mose, Jr., used his father's death as an example to convey the depth of feeling his family members have against the notion of being cut. In this case, what was at issue was an autopsy. This account simultaneously provides insight into beliefs against being cut *and* so-called taboos about contact with death.

Conversations with other Navajo consultants revealed that autopsy is an extremely touchy subject for many Navajo people (Bekis, July 22, 2004;

Black, June 16, 2005; Todachinee, June 28, 2005). The primary concerns center around having the body cut up and having parts removed. As evidenced by the accounts shared by Mae Ann Bekis and Larry Todachinee, the latter issue focuses most specifically on organs. Todachinee stated that people in his community believe that in the process of a routine autopsy "they get some of your organs and save it for somebody else" (June 28, 2005). Bekis divulged this account:

> MAB: This is just rumble, people talking, talking, all that. I don't know if it is true or what. But this guy, he died over at the store somewhere and they took him in for autopsy. And the parents, they got a call and they went over there and then—I don't know if they saw the body or if he gave his heart or whatever it was, or maybe he didn't sign [an organ donor card], maybe he did. And here it broke out that "people at the hospital in Albuquerque are taking the good parts of the body and whatever our son is left with. Whatever part they took out," and they were just talking among themselves. "They shouldn't do that" and stuff like that. That broke out for a while, now it is quiet about it. (Bekis, July 22, 2004)

Todachinee insisted, "Our traditional [belief] is against that [autopsy], so we're not supposed to do that" (June 28, 2005). Kenneth Black, Jr., acquired firsthand experience with autopsy at a young age when his wife was killed in a tragic automobile accident near Holbrook, Arizona. He candidly shared his views on the subject.

> KB: Several times it is necessary to have the autopsy. But that is beyond the family's control. Like when someone is in an automobile accident, there is a state law that says you don't have a say. We will have to do an autopsy to determine if there was alcohol involved. It is allowed, so in those situations you don't really have a say.
>
> MS: They had to do a full autopsy to find out if alcohol was involved?
>
> KB: My question is, why did they have to do an autopsy?
>
> MS: Can't they just do a blood test?

KB: Why can't they just do a blood test? That is from my experience.
My first wife . . . was in an automobile accident by Holbrook, and
when she passed away it was like [people at the] medical center,
they had to take her to the town coroner or something like that.
They said she had to have an autopsy even though I said, "No, it is
against my heritage, it is against my tradition. It is in our culture
that we don't practice that." And apparently their law meant more.
So I didn't have a say. They didn't find nothing; they released the
body back after so many days. (Black, June 16, 2005)

Leroy Nelson put being cut by a coroner or a surgeon into the context
of Navajo perspectives on hunting and warfare to elucidate some of the
beliefs on which these decisions are made.

LN: The individual as a person should never be cut open. . . . This
body shouldn't be cut whatsoever; otherwise it is like being on
the warpath. I guess that is one way to put it. . . .

MS: Could you explain more about going on the warpath? Like how
to be cut is like going on the warpath?

LN: OK. Going on the warpath is like saying that the enemy is there.
So a lot of times, then, I guess being a warrior in the old days,
what they used to do is cut the scalp. Make a scalp, get the scalp.
Bring the scalp back to show it is like, this is it. And then they
would take the tongue, get the tongue, cut the tongue out. And say
this is it now.

MS: Show that you killed . . .

LN: Yes, to kill the enemy. And then another way is to get the heart.
Cut open the body and then get the heart and put the heart on the
body. . . . Like, this is it. It is not going to haunt us. So to express
that, this is what it is. . . . So that is an old story coming from a
hunter. A hunter [is] like a warrior. Saying a warrior today, we
don't know what we are saying. A true warrior, in our ways it is
like they used to wear paint. They used to wear certain things to
not be seen. They spoke certain tongues. Certain ways they used
to go on the warpath. And then when they came upon the enemy,
it is like their enemy didn't see them in the area. When they do,

all it takes is just one look and that is it. And that is how they used
to go on the warpath. (Nelson, July 20, 2004)

Such background information puts into perspective the decisions of those
who told Sarah Jackson's husband (July 20, 2004) and Ambrose Shepard
(June 3, 2005) they would rather die than be surgically cut. Additional
insight is gained from the account of Johnson Dennison, in which the individual also chose to die rather than have surgery. Dennison recalled: "Some
patients believe and say, 'I don't want that. I don't want that surgery of
removing my breasts because the Creator has created me as such and I
want to go back that way, like that. So if I have to die because of my breast
cancer, then I have to. But I don't want [them] removed, and the removal
would be part of my body so I just—' you know. . . . Some believe in [that]
and record that on their wills as such" (J. Dennison, June 22, 2005).

In Dennison's account, the patient's apprehension was clearly focused on
not being able to return to the Creator as she was made. This same concern
was conveyed as a prime motivator when Thomas Deschene, Jr., painfully
recalled learning of his brother's decision: "They told him he needed a heart
transplant; my brother, the one that had the heart disease. He said he 'would
let it go,' what he had, that he 'would rather die than have it done—being cut
and all of this.' On account of he didn't want anything to do with a transplant.
He'd rather 'go in one piece.' So he just died" (Deschene, June 15, 2005).

These testimonials demonstrate that this belief crosscuts traditional and
Native American Church boundaries, for it is held by congregants in both
faiths as well as by traditional practitioners (Johnson Dennison and Leroy
Nelson) and NAC road men (Thomas Deschene, Johnson Dennison, and
Jonah Nez).

BODY INTEGRALITY

The previous comment attributed to Deschene's brother hints at an additional
trepidation about surgery over and beyond being cut, which is wanting to
"go in one piece." Kenneth Black, Jr., who agrees that Navajo people
should not be cut, captured the essence of the fundamental tenet alluded to
by Deschene's brother when he said, "Once you open up someone, I think

they are gone. They are not complete no more, that is my perception" (June 16, 2005). Ursula Knoki-Wilson elaborated on the issue of completeness as a major concern for Navajo people:

> UKW: They don't want the surgery because they want their bodies to be complete. They don't want any scars on their body when they go to meet their maker. And then some people believe that they don't want any intentional scars on their body when they go to meet their maker. They want to go as natural as possible. They don't want things done to their body. Some people believe that.
> MS: And would it matter if anything had been removed from inside their body?
> UKW: Yes.
> MS: Like, if they took a gallbladder out?
> UKW: Yes.
> MS: What would happen if something had been removed?
> UKW: I don't know that anything would happen. I guess the feeling is like they are not a whole person before they went to meet their maker. (Knoki-Wilson, July 5, 2005)

As Knoki-Wilson pointed out, many patients arrive at hospitals across the reservation apprehensive about prescribed surgery because they do not want to have any part of themselves removed, and they do not want their bodies marred when they die. Rose Mary Wade told me this is so because "your whole body is a sacred gift. It is a gift and you have to preserve it" (June 17, 2005). Tso Allen went a step further when she noted: "You're considered to be a spiritual being and sacred. . . . Your whole being, you are a spiritual person because the term the people use is Diné, we're sacred, is how they use it" (July 15, 2005). Sheila Goldtooth explained:

> SG: Every part of the body is sacred in the way that we were made. We are sacred, and that is why grandma always says, "Don't cut your hair. Don't cut your nails, don't paint your nails. Don't do this to your body. Don't put tattoos on, don't pierce your body." And that is because our bodies are considered sacred in the way that we are made. Special representations went into how our bodies are

made. And so because of that, the body is considered sacred. The Changing Woman is the one that made us. . . . She used sacred items, sacred materials to make us; because of that we are considered sacred inside and outside. (Goldtooth, July 18, 2005)

Don Mose, Jr., agreed that the body is sacrosanct. Significantly, he specified that bodies are only to be marked in ceremonial contexts with impermanent pigments, for in essence they belong to the Holy People and therefore must not be permanently altered. In his words:

DM: Yes, it [the body] is sacred; it doesn't really belong to you. It belongs to the Holy People, that is why you take care of it. Your body is like a hooghan, it is like a temple, it is here. You take care of it, it belongs to them, the Holy People. . . . And when they created, they made sure that there is a male and female part to this. . . . So you take care of it. . . . Don't even go as far as to defile it by being tattooed all over your body. That is not right. *The only time you should mark your body is during a ceremony.* But not to where it stays intact because that is not good. . . . You don't mark up your body. Those are only done for sacred purposes. Don't defile your body. And that was the strict ruling of it, don't defile it. (Mose, June 13, 2005)

In regard to this prohibition against marring or modifying the body, Amelda Sandoval Shay added:

ASS: I was told that the man upstairs gave us only seven holes. I was told that is all we should ever have. We should never make another hole on our body. When these guys are making these ear piercings and the belly button piercings, my grandchildren got kind of interested and I told them "no, we are only allowed to have seven holes on your body. That is how you people are put here on earth. You are not supposed to put anything or another hole on your body yourself. That is one of the sacred seven holes you have on your body; you should treasure that for the rest of your life."
MS: What are the seven holes?

ASS: Well, the seven holes, you start with the lower (indicating the genital and rectal area), there are two down there [obviously from the male perspective]. And then our mouth and our nose, then our ears and our eyes. (Shay, June 6, 2005)

Johnson Dennison said bluntly, "You should go back into the spirit world with everything that is in your body" (June 22, 2005). Borrowing a phrase from Kenneth Black, Jr., this could be termed the "you come in one piece, you go in one piece concept" (June 16, 2005). Time and again, when this topic was broached, people were adamant on this point. Julia Mathis recalled that when her father faced the prospect of surgery, he said, "I came into this world with all of my parts and I am going to leave this world with all of my parts that were given to me" (June 11, 2005). And that is exactly what he did.

I was told that not leaving this world as a whole entity is considered a breach of a "taboo" and that such an action will "hinder the journey process" after death (Black, June 16, 2005). Thomas Deschene, Jr., elaborated on the consequences of this action, noting that in addition to influencing the level of respect one engenders from one's relatives, the condition in which one leaves this world affects one's condition in the hereafter:

TD: When they go back to the Holy People, when they leave this world, if part of their body is missing, that is how their body is going to be there, too. Even way back in [the] traditional way, when they buried them, along the side they would kill a horse, and with the horse they would journey back into the spirit world. And when they get back over there, there should be relatives there, and if they see you come in with a horse they would be happy for you, and if you don't come in with a horse, then your relatives that are still living don't really have respect for you and they don't love you. Probably some of them believe that, and that is why [it is important not to have missing body parts].

MS: And so when they greet the Holy People they don't want to have any missing body parts?

TD: Yes. That is their belief and they want to stay like that, and that is how they go. (Deschene, June 15, 2005)

Ronald Sandoval clarified the full significance of being complete when one dies: "The Holy People, they will turn away from you [if you are not complete]. And turn against you and not really accept you back" (June 25, 2005).

Further ramifications were made evident when Sandoval and Larry Todachinee pointed out the potential influence not being whole could have on one's relatives for generations to come. Sandoval noted: "I don't want any part of my body taken out because I want to go back as a whole if I have to go. . . . We believe that if any stray body part is still here, it will affect the people—my kids, my brothers and sisters who still are here—it will affect them. So that is why I say that" (June 25, 2005). Todachinee provided further elucidation:

> MS: What would happen if you left this world and you weren't whole?
> LT: Well, it wouldn't do anything [to you], but your niece, your aunt, or your grandkids, they're gonna be affected by it because you are not holy and that area—
> MS: If you are not complete when you leave, then you are not holy?
> LT: Uh huh. Then it is going to affect your grandkids, your children, and other family. Your whole family, it is going to affect them. That is why they have to have a traditional ceremony, for protection. (Todachinee, June 28, 2005)

In addition to these many beliefs, every individual faced with such an illness has to choose whether to pursue some form of religious healing to supplement her or his biomedical care.

REDEMPTIVE SUFFERING

> TD: My brother that used to live here was a road man too. And he used to tell me, "It is good to learn, there are a lot of teachings out there, but don't ever become a medicine man, don't ever become a road man. Look at me healthwise; look at me." He was a diabetic and he had a heart condition too. And I always wondered where it came from. And he had a lot of different ceremonies done for

him. He had just barely turned fifty when he passed on. He had a
heart attack. Before I started running meetings, I was really healthy
too. And after so many years running meetings, I understood what
he meant because people that come to me had different kinds of
sickness. Let's say a person needed help with Lightning Way; it had
something to do with the lightning. And that would get them sick
and they would come to me wanting a ceremony to find out what
caused it [their illness]. Being a road man is just like you're a nego-
tiator. You negotiate with the Creator and the Holy People. And all
you do with the instruments, the paraphernalia that we use, [is] just
take care of those [illnesses]. And you kind of communicate with
Mother Nature and the supernatural power that we have. You need to
understand those things. And if there is nothing wrong with you and
you perform a ceremony for a person that is ill from the Lightning
Way, you negotiate with the Lighting People—the Holy People
from that side, they will release that person, now he [or she] will get
well, but then they will turn around and say "Who are you?" In a
traditional ceremony, you have a ceremony in the Lightning Way,
that ceremony takes five days and every day you have to make different offerings, but on the final day they put a painting on you and
they do a big sand painting. And you sit on that sand painting and
they give you herbs and they put a bead right here (touches the left
side of his head with his fingers), a seashell, and a turquoise, and
they tie a small feather in your hair. They initiate you that way so
you communicate with the Lightning People and they recognize
you by that bead that you have on your hair. And they say, "Who
are you? There is nothing wrong with you. Now we are going to
get to know each other." And that is when you start getting sick.
Start having health problems, and we've had little ceremonies performed to fight certain aspects of it along the way.

MS: What types of ceremonies are you having performed on yourself to take care of this problem?

TD: I had a Lightning Way. I had to be initiated in that, and then the
Wind Way, then this one, I don't know how to say it [in English],
it is for people that have passed on: Hóchx̨ǫ'jí. (Deschene, June
15, 2005)

Like his brother before him, Thomas Deschene, Jr., can be said to be literally making a corporeal sacrifice when he heals others; that is, he is offering up his own health. This fits well with Christian ideas of *redemptive suffering*—the sacrifice of Jesus for mankind (Porterfield 2005:131). These are not completely new ideas within Navajo thought. First, it is a foundational principle of Navajo curing practice that the ceremonial practitioner stands between a patient and the source of his or her illness (Schwarz 2001). For all intents and purposes, it can be said that a practitioner is the one who stands between a patient and his or her illness as well as between the patient and the Holy People who have released their claim over her or him—whether the ceremonial practitioner of record is a man or a woman. This is true because the primary culturally sanctioned role for men is that of protector (Schwarz 1997:159–60, 162–63), while that for women is nurturer. This means Navajo women are to be mothers whose most important responsibilities are to foster and sustain the development of children (Schwarz 1997:26–27, 238–39). This role distinction is symbolized by the traditional weapons of each gender: the *ádístsiin* (stirring sticks) for women versus the bow and arrow for men. As Mae Ann Bekis detailed, "Men can do everything because they have a bow and arrow. That was given to the men, and then the bow guard. These weapons were given to them to fight the war and to face the war . . . so that's why they can do all the things. And a woman, she was only given a stirring stick for her weapon, and so she can just do so much, that's her weapon. . . . And so there's a lot of difference right there for man and a woman" (Bekis, July 31, 1998).

Both women and men can be ceremonial practitioners; however, the majority view is that men must initiate all apprentice ceremonial practitioners (Bekis, July 31, 1998; Nix, July 10, 2000; Shorthair, July 11, 2000; Yazzie, July 30, 1998).[3] According to Mae Ann Bekis, men must initiate women practitioners because the initiator provides a shield against every illness-causing element encountered throughout the women's years of practice. That shield is not unlike the protection a warrior offers to kin and community. Only men have the power to wield such a shield and thus to stand between a patient and the source of his or her illness (Bekis, July 31, 1998). As Bekis explained, it is a man's warrior status that enables him to stand up against danger, whether in the form of illness, lightning, or the fierceness of a bear or other animal: "Only a man does initiation because he's got the authority, like having a gun, bow and arrow, and he can kill animals and things like that. Whereas a lady can't kill animals. All she has to do is stay home and take care of her children and the house. And that's the reason why she can't. . . . See, a man stands up against the bear, the snake, the danger. He stands between you and the danger of a snake, lightning, and bears or lions" (Bekis, July 31, 1998). It is in this position that the healer—or, if the practitioner is a woman, then the man who mentored and initiated her—routinely takes on the illness (Deschene, June 15, 2005) or claim, as Navajo people often refer to this aspect of the negotiation (F. Young, June 14, 2005).

Buella Allen compellingly described how, as a Navajo person who is also a biomedical physician, she understands herself to be absorbing her patients' ills over time: "Part of being the physician is taking into yourself all of the illness of the people that you treat. Working in the emergency room you become spiritually congested with the pain and frustration and the anger and the violence. And when that happens, I go to the medicine people. Every four years I'm told that you're supposed to have a cere- mony to get rid of all of that. You don't want it to be left inside because that affects your own health. So that is what I do. My spiritual balance gets taken care of" (B. Allen, June 10, 2005).

Echoing what Allen and Deschene had to say on the issue, Frank C. Young reported that Navajo biomedical surgeons also periodically need ceremonies to counter the effects of curing patients:

> FY: You wouldn't have that offering done all the time when you are
> doing a surgery but [only] when you feel that you need that spiritual
> strength to perform the surgery. But after you are done you will
> also notice, let's say, maybe the person was struck by lightning
> and you save that person, the effects from the lightning will also,
> now that you have fixed it, it has claimed this person's body but
> you restart that person's body, so you kind of took that claim
> away, so you also need to every now and then have each one of
> these ceremonies done depending on the type of surgeries you
> have performed. A lot of Navajo people just say "you can't do
> that," or they mention all these taboos. But if you are a medicine

man, you operate the same way [as a biomedical doctor], and if
you are well versed in these ceremonies it is like being a physician, yes. So it would be nice if you know those ceremonies too.
(F. Young, translated by Nora Young, June 14, 2005)

TO SUFFER, TO SACRIFICE

TD: The only way to understand it is to dedicate yourself to it. And
your faith will be your shield. The faith you have in it. That is the
only way it is going to work with you. A lot of students come to
me, especially Navajo, they're researching this and they want to
know about the ceremony. I tell them, you have to suffer from it.
If you suffer from it and get well, then you don't want to go out
into the open with it because if it falls into the wrong hands, they
are going to start making money off of it. If that happens, you are
going to be in trouble and it will cost you your life. (Deschene,
June 15, 2005)

It is the intentional language of Native American Church road men Thomas
Deschene, Jr., Wilson Aronilth, and Jonah Nez that sets their narratives or
personal testimonies apart. Aronilth used the terms "suffering" and "helpless" in his version of the peyote origin story. Nez pointedly distinguished
between what are commonly called offerings by English-speaking Navajo
people and what he calls "sacrifices." The distinction is significant because it
indicates that for Nez it is a form of redemptive suffering to climb mountains
in Durango in search of tobacco to be used as sacrifices in peyote meetings.
Deschene also distinguished between offerings and sacrifices. Moreover, in
his view, one must "suffer" to learn how to conduct a NAC meeting.

On the basis of these Navajo exegeses, I suggest that the notion of the
necessity to sacrifice or suffer is another NAC tenet *derived from Christianity*. In this case, it comes from Christian ideas about the redemptive
suffering of Jesus. Amanda Porterfield has demonstrated that in the version
of the Sun Dance promoted by Black Elk, flesh cutting and piercing evoked
the crucifixion of Christ as well as the bravery of indigenous people, thereby

bridging their suffering and the redemptive suffering of Christ (2005:131). In the case of NAC practitioners, their word choices of "suffer" or "sacrifice" also evoke such linkages, thereby empowering their practice with the aid of the transcendent God.

Participants in those meetings make a sacrifice by sitting up all night to sing and pray on behalf of the patient. And while road men also sit up all night singing and praying, as Thomas Deschene, Jr., vividly described, the primary sacrifice for them is absorbing the pain and illness of the patient as well as negotiating with the Diyin Dine'é, such as Lightning People, who are in control of the cause of the illness or disease.

PRAYERS AND CEREMONIES SURROUNDING SURGERY

> AS: And they gave me some shots in both legs, into my main artery, right here where my leg was. . . . While they were doing that I was looking at the screen, and I saw that the blood flow is up to where this amputation is now. That was a good flow of blood. Beyond it, down to the end there was nothing. So I ask them, "Where would be the best place for me to get cut?" He says, below the knee. So I said, "Go ahead, let's do it." So, all that I was told [by the lay minister], I still believed it when I went in surgery and I survived it. (Shepard, June 3, 2005)

Once Shepard and his family made the decision to go ahead with the surgery on his left leg, they, like other Navajo families, had to determine how to fit the surgery into their world given their philosophical beliefs about health and contamination. Personal convictions play a large role at this stage in the process. The issue of belief or faith arose time and again in consultations with Navajo road men, patients, Christians, and traditional practitioners (G. Davis, July 18, 2005; Deschene, June 15, 2005; Nez, June 12, 2005). In the case of Native American Church road men, it became evident that the recurring emphasis on the necessity of faith in their testimonies is derived from Christianity (Porterfield 2005:116).

The importance of a patient's allegiance to a particular canon or cure was never more evident than in the testimony of Billie Davis, a lifelong sheep-herder from Lukachukai, Arizona, who described his battle with diabetes. He methodically explained that he had previously had approximately a quarter of one foot amputated as a result of diabetes-related complications. When Davis excused himself to look for documentation of his birth date, his daughter shared the sobering news that the next morning she would be taking him to the hospital so another segment of his foot could be removed because of progressive degeneration. In spite of these hard, cold circumstances, when I asked "Have you sought guidance from anyone in the Native American Church [for] your illness," with the assistance of Amelda Sandoval Shay he replied:

> BD: I believe in this Native American Church. It heals me. I believe in the peyote tradition. It heals.
> MS: I would like him to tell me more about that, how he was healed of diabetes with NAC.
> BD: During the meeting they were doing all the prayers, the healing prayers that they say, and all this. (B. Davis, June 11, 2005)

Choices regarding what, if any, type of religious healing option to try are not made alone but rather in consultation with members of one's matrilineal family network. As is routinely done by Navajo people of nearly all religious persuasions, except fundamental Christians of some denominations, Davis sought advice from a traditional diagnostician about his deteriorating medical condition immediately after a biomedical doctor had recommended surgically removing a portion of his foot.

Alternatively, diagnostic assistance can be sought from Native American Church road men trained in this area. Sheila Goldtooth described a version of NAC diagnosis done for her in which the road man looked at a bowl of water to ascertain her problem. She told me she found it to be like "crystal gazing," one of the traditional forms of diagnosis described in chapter 4 (Goldtooth, July 18, 2005; see Frisbie 1992; Milne and Howard 2000:567).

Thomas Deschene, Jr., explicated how as a NAC road man he routinely aids those who come to him seeking an understanding of what ails them by means of a crystal in combination with burning embers from the fire. The latter element is derived from an alternative diagnostic method known as fireplace, or "coal gazing."

> TD: Yesterday I had this one patient, a young lady, twenty-one years old. She came to me with her boyfriend. She came from the clinic. She's been going to the clinic for the last month. She gets migraine headaches. Goes to see the doctor, the doctor can't find nothing, keeps telling her, "There's nothing wrong with you." So they came to me and said, "You need to find out what's wrong with her." So we came over here and we did the ceremony, and I used that peyote. I set it right there and made the offering. With that cedar, I made that offering right there. The main reason why I used that sacrament of peyote is that this person is having migraine headaches and the doctor doesn't know what is going on. "We need to find that out, and we need to help her." . . . And through the instruments that we have, through that crystal? Through that and through the charcoal, we can see things and tell the patient what is wrong. All the way from when she was in her mother's womb and up until today, tell her what is wrong with her and what she did. . . . Maybe she injured a plant or certain insects or reptiles, and then we would make an offering to whatever was doing that. And give her that medicine, like an aspirin, to cure her. And that is how it is used as a medicine. (Deschene, June 15, 2005)

Derek Milne and Wilson Howard, who conducted a comparative analysis of diagnostic methods practiced among the Navajo, offer further clarification of the specific process of coal gazing:

> Here small burning embers are viewed and interpreted by the diagnostician, similar to some extent to the way stargazing works. Of course, interpreting the embers replicates diagnosis as it might occur in a NAC prayer meeting, and some road men who are coal gazers also diagnose in this way in the context of a meeting, using embers from the central fireplace. However, diagnosis of this type most commonly

occurs outside of the all-night meeting, usually prior to the decision to hold it. In these cases, either the diagnostician or the patient may ingest peyote medicine, with the decision usually made by the patient. In most diagnoses we observed, peyote was not taken as part of the rite. The ritual itself is not elaborate—small embers are taken from a fire and placed on the ground. A prayer is made, and the embers are then blessed with cedar placed on them (a common procedure in the NAC). The smoke is then wafted onto the patient. Following this, the road man stares at the coals and interprets images. The cedar blessings and prayers continue through the rite as the coal gazer interprets the meaning of the images in consultation with the patient. (Milne and Howard 2000:551–52)

Diagnosticians recommend treatment based on their individual epistemological persuasions. In Billie Davis's case, a traditional ceremony was recommended for him. He reported, "It was the five-day Lightning Way that was done on me. That was before the surgery. That is how it is done in the healing way" (B. Davis, June 11, 2005). Other consultants agreed that whenever a Lightning Way is recommended it must be performed *before* any surgery, for if the surgeon "touches the sores" before the ceremony, the growths or disease will continue to progress (Shay, June 6, 2005). After his consultation with a diagnostician, a similar recommendation was made for Chee Tapaha of Greasewood, Arizona, a longtime member of the Native American Church, who—like Billie Davis—lost a limb as a result of diabetes-related complications. He reported, "The diagnostician had told me that I could get some help with the Lightning Way ceremony, and so we did seek someone from the Jeddito area to come and do this ceremony, but the guy never showed up. We paid him. We did make a down payment, and the rest was going to be given to him when he arrives, but he never made it. Six years, I guess. We've never tried again with another practitioner" (Tapaha, June 2, 2005).

Tapaha also reported seeking and receiving treatment through the Native American Church. He offered valuable insight into the type of advice given by a road man to a NAC member facing this crippling disease, which by extension offers a glimpse into NAC views on illness causation, progress, and healing and provides another example of how medical and religious pluralism is routinely navigated.

> MS: What medical condition is it that caused you to need the amputation?
>
> CT: I was a bad man. Too much booze, that's what.
>
> MS: Drinking alcohol caused you to need the amputation?
>
> CT: Yeah. There are a lot of effects of that stuff. . . . Diabetes.
>
> MS: The doctor said it was diabetes?
>
> CT: Diabetes, yeah.
>
> MS: When you were first diagnosed, did you seek help from the Native American Church?
>
> CT: Yeah. I was participating in the Native American Church. . . . After the meeting I had experienced chest pains and . . . the following day I had more chest pains, so that is when I went into the hospital and the chest pain, have to be heart attack, mild heart attack I was having. And it was at that point that my high level of sugar was discovered, when they diagnosed the heart attack. That is when I was first diagnosed with a high level of sugar. . . .
>
> MS: And did you seek any help from the Native American Church?
>
> CT: I was given some peyote as a healing sacrament.
>
> MS: And was the understanding that consuming the peyote would eliminate the diabetes from your body?
>
> CT: "You have to take care of yourself and control your sugar intake" is what I was told. They say, "It is not curable; diabetes is not curable," but they would use peyote "as a help."
>
> MS: So members of the Native American Church would say it is not curable?
>
> CT: "It is not curable," that is what I was told. "Even though we will give you peyote and it will help you deal with the sickness, try to keep your health," but the diabetes is not curable. "This is not the cure." . . .
>
> MS: What kind of guidance did they give you about taking care of yourself?

CT: Eating right, and then you can use the [traditional] herbs for sugar diabetes, and I did have some control of my sugar level, but then I kind of got away from using the herbs and that is when it really went. (Tapaha, June 2, 2005)

Tapaha pointed out the significant role methodical use of a traditional herbal remedy played in maintaining his health, noting that from his perspective it was only when he stopped using the herbs that his diabetes went completely out of control. The sores led to gangrene on his leg, and in time it was clear that he would have to be admitted to the hospital for amputation.

Despite the fact that she presents herself with a stoicism expected from Navajo adults of her generation, Eleanor Begay of Lukachukai, Arizona, clearly conveyed her fundamental fortitude upon realizing that she would be losing a body part: "There is another guy that lives over by Tsaile school. He is the one that did a crystal gazing on me and he told me, 'Aunty, I am sorry but you are going to lose one of your legs.' So, I said to myself, 'Uh oh. Well, that's OK, I will deal with it.' So, that is what I did" (Begay, June 10, 2005). Ambrose Shepard's account from this same stage in his illness narrative, captured in the first quotation in this section, echoes Begay's resignation while revealing that he was struggling to remain in control, hence his comment, "Go ahead, let's do it" (Shepard, June 3, 2005). This sense of composure is also apparent in his description of events surrounding the right side of his body.

AS: It kind of got routine. So when I got to the right side, I got the same feeling. That is why I asked the doctors, "Can you do the amputation on my right leg and then remove my kidney on the same day?" He [the doctor] said, "It can be done." "What are my chances?" "Your chances [are] good." So I said "Let's do it." I went in and had it done. I had that leg amputated and [they] took my kidney out. So that was the most painful thing I have ever experienced. But I get supplied with all this medicine that they have, pain medicine. And I survived it. And this lay minister . . . comes in and prays for me just about every day and the different people. There was this old lady, a white lady, but she really spoke Navajo. And she came in and gave me all the packets and everything, and

the Bible and all that. So I read up on it. I had a feeling that somebody is watching over me and I shouldn't be afraid. So that is how I
went though all these surgeries. And the healing ceremony in
between was done for me. And it helped, brought me back up, my
mind, putting everything back together and being able to do what I
need to do in order to survive and be able to walk again. I had a lot
of help from the Navajo tradition and the Christianity and [the]
Native American Church. Everybody seemed like had a hand in it
and helped. (Shepard, June 3, 2005)

Like Ambrose Shepard, Eleanor Begay found solace in Christianity.
As she explained, for her, solace came in the form of her long-standing
association with the Catholic Church in her home community: "Most of
the time I would go to the Catholic, the mission out there (indicating with
her chin its location in the community). So I just pray. . . . I used to feel
way down, but ever since I got my divorce from my husband [I have felt
different]. So that is when I got really sick. But I went back to church and
the father counseled with me a lot of times. I mean even about how I
should feel and everything else, so that is what I went through. Now I am
fine" (Begay, June 10, 2005).

John Porvaznik, a biomedical physician, documented that Navajo
patients often had Blessing Way ceremonials performed as a prophylactic
before surgery when he provided care in the Tuba City area during the
1960s (1967:180). Although some of those with whom I consulted mentioned the desirability of a Blessing Way before surgery (Bekis, July 15,
2004; Hale, June 15, 2005; J. Nez, June 12, 2005), the majority told me
about what they termed "protection prayers." What appears to be a marked
procedural difference is likely no more than a confusion in terminology
stemming from the fact that a series of protection prayers is actually a
component of the various versions of Blessing Way (Bekis, July 15, 2004;
Denetdeal, July 11, 2004), although such prayers can derive from other
sources as well. As the name implies, protection prayers are most often done
before the medical procedure to protect the patient. As Julia Mathis, Buella
Allen, and Ursula Knoki-Wilson explained in excerpts cited next, a second
intent is to ensure that the procedure is properly performed. Mathis described
that after such a prayer, the Holy People are compelled to enter the operating

room in front of the surgical team, where they will remain throughout the procedure as a protective force.

> JM: What usually happens is that if you are going to go through a major surgery, they do a prayer for you, they do a prayer, which is like in my Navajo culture they call it *ach'ááh sodizin.* Meaning protection prayer. . . . A protection prayer is supposed to protect him [or her] from anything that will harm [the patient]. . . . The prayer itself is to help the doctors. To oversee over the surgery— that the Holy People will all be there before and the doctors will be right behind, and while they do their surgery that everything is to go well. And that's the kind of protection prayer that they usu- ally do. (Mathis, June 11, 2005)

Buella Allen clarified that this protective force is put into place without the knowledge of the biomedical health care providers. Their unawareness does not inhibit the efficacy of the Holy People's protective powers, however.

> BA: It's particularly the case that if someone is going to be undergo- ing surgery or if they're going to be undergoing a consultation off the reservation, if they are going to go elsewhere for medical care, the patients will often have a ceremony to make sure that every- thing goes well. And . . . the surgeons do not realize the prayers have been said for them too. So that when they come in to do surgery that their hands will be steady and their minds will be clear and they will be able to do a good job. So it is not just for the patient for his [or her] good health but also for the circumstances of the treatment and making sure that those people that are applying the treatment are in good shape. (B. Allen, June 10, 2005)

Unbeknownst to the surgeon, the prayer effectively puts into place a protective shield to guide the surgeon's hands. This ensures that no mistakes are made during the procedure. Ursula Knoki-Wilson explained: "The pro- tection prayer, in that case it is called a shielding prayer. See, they do the shielding or there will be a shield, an invisible shield there to guide the surgeon's hands. It would be kind of like putting an extra pair of gloves on so there is no contact with the person. . . . That provider actually doing the surgery would be [encased by] this invisible shield. So they will do the shielding prayer for that one ahead of time" (Knoki-Wilson, July 5, 2005).

Navajo people following traditional practices are not the only ones who provide prayers for family members destined to undergo surgical procedures. Indeed, Rose Mary Wade reported that her family uses both Catholic and traditional prayers to protect family members before surgery:

> MS: Are there any special preparations that you had to have done before you go in for surgery?
>
> RW: Yeah. We usually have a protection prayer before, and they just pray that you are going to get well after your surgery or whatever. It is just like the Catholics, they say "put everything in God's hands, and God will guide the doctor's hand, and then everything will be peaceful within the guidance of God." That is the same way. And then afterward you can have a thanksgiving type of a prayer done for you too.
>
> MS: Do you know what this type of protection prayer involves?
>
> RW: It is just a protection prayer. We call it sodizin, ach'ááh sodizin, same thing, protection prayer. (Wade, June 17, 2005)

Paulla Damon Henderson, a devout Baptist, also discussed a Christian form of prayer used before surgery. While in her case these prayers are firmly rooted in Baptist beliefs, they are based on a similar ideology as that noted by Wade regarding the Christian notion of surrender to the transcendent God epitomized by the statement "put everything in God's hands." Henderson explained: "We pray for the medical teams, we pray for those working in the health care field—that nothing will go wrong, *that their hands are guided,* and these people were blessed with the knowledge and wisdom to know what to look for" (July 14, 2005). And increasingly, people call on Native American Church road men or women to perform a protection prayer before surgery (Long, July 13, 2005; Mathis, June 11, 2005).

Ideally, such prayers should be completed before surgical procedures, but this is not always possible. In that case, as Eleanor Begay noted, they are sometimes completed afterward: "Johnson Dennison, he said a prayer for me after I came back [from surgery]. . . . He . . . came over and he said a protection prayer first and then after that he said he will put it in a good way, so he said another prayer for me" (Begay, June 10, 2005).

THE CARE OF SURGICALLY REMOVED BODY PARTS

> MS: What about disposal of amputated body parts?
>
> TD: Amputations, I am not too sure with that, we have a lot of those things. One person that I used to work with, he was kind of a tough guy. He was diabetic and lost his leg. He was saying, "My leg's already dead and went to Hell." He was saying this.
>
> MS: That his leg already went to Hell?
>
> TD: Yeah. "My leg's already in Hell where all the dead are. . . . And how am I supposed to take care of something like that?" (Deschene, June 15, 2005)

Once an appendage has been surgically excised from the body, the patient and his or her family are faced with an additional problem—how to dispose of the severed body part. Dealing with detached body parts is nothing new for Navajo people. Logically, accidental loss of fingers, toes, or limbs must have occurred as far back as anyone can remember. Indeed, when asked about the care of surgically removed body parts, Nora Young retold the account of such an incident in her family, which served as a paradigm for her father when he faced the situation as a result of diabetes: "My grandma Isabelle, she lost a finger. . . . She was roping a cow—this is when he [Young's father] was young and he said they had to find . . . the finger. . . . They couldn't find it, but she still went ahead and did that ceremonial prayer to the tree. And he said that what she was going to do was . . . place it in the tree. They have a certain procedure that they go through. They would give it [the severed appendage] back to the tree with ceremonial songs and prayers. They never found the [whole] finger, but they found just a piece, so they did the ceremony, gave the piece to the tree" (N. Young, June 14, 2005).

Young insisted that "we cannot leave a piece anywhere" (June 14, 2005). This sense of stewardship is based on a fundamental tenet of Navajo ontology dictating that parts of the body, bodily fluids, and offal offer the potential for positive or negative effects throughout a person's existence. Parts of the body and bodily substances can affect the health and welfare of the individual and, by extension, those of her or his kin and community, long past detachment or elimination. The extension of influence on the basis of synecdoche so crucial to understanding Navajo views on blood transfusion and cardiopulmonary resuscitation (CPR) is also essential to comprehending Navajo perspectives on biomedical procedures such as surgery and amputation, as well as organ donation and transplantation. Detached body parts such as skin cells, blood, umbilical cords, saliva, hair, fingernails, and toenails retain a lifelong connection with the person from whom they originated and can therefore be manipulated for good or ill. Such body parts are easy fodder for witchcraft (Kluckhohn 1944). Paul Mico found that this sinister use was the source of greatest fear for Navajo patients requiring surgery in the Many Farms area of Arizona when he undertook his study circa 1960 (1962:32).

Because intentional amputation is a relatively new phenomenon with which Navajo people are learning to cope, many Navajo amputees, such as the man quoted by Thomas Deschene, Jr., in the first excerpt in this section, find themselves at a philosophical and religious impasse when faced with issues such as how best to care for a severed appendage. When new problems such as this arise, individuals and families across the reservation turn to trusted leaders within the community, such as traditional practitioners or Native American Church road men. These counselors draw on their experience with other detached body parts to reason out the best answer to this modern dilemma. Because this reasoning is done on a case-by-case basis, as Donald Denetdeal noted, "There is a difference of opinion depending on who you talk to" (July 11, 2004). From his perspective as a traditional practitioner:

> DD: Amputation, the way I understand it here in the middle section of the reservation, at least some of the people that were in my life, the elders that were in my life, medicine men that were in my life, they've always said that a human body . . . well, if the person had a very healthy lifestyle and they die, then their physical body should be all together. On the other hand, if the person did not have a healthy lifestyle, where this person may have had their limbs amputated, let's say a foot or a hand or whatever, they say that once that amputation is done, that the part that is cut off should be

retrieved from the doctors, and that this hand or finger or this part should be buried in Mother Earth and given back to nature, and that later on [when] the person dies, you don't bury the person where you bury the limb, you just bury it in a burial ground because in due time they'll meet up again because all parts are going to the same [place]—to the earth. (Denetdeal, July 11, 2004)

This seems perfectly congruent with Navajo philosophy, since as Nora Young described, "when a child loses his teeth, there is a certain procedure that we go through—giving it back to the land or giving it back to Mother Earth" (June 14, 2005). This is also true for other body parts—placentas, umbilical cords—that routinely detach from the body and, deemed vital to the proper development of Navajo personhood, are also routinely buried in Mother Earth.

This is far from the majority view, however, when it comes to *surgically removed* body parts. Regarding the pros and cons of burying severed limbs, Leroy Nelson reasoned, "This person is still living, we can't take it to the gravesite. That is taboo for us—to take a body part or limb to the gravesite. It shouldn't be so" (July 20, 2005). Johnson Dennison stated pointedly: "If you do that, then you're half buried. . . . A part of you is buried. . . . And when that happens, then part of your body is dead and buried. But there is no way you could be alive too" (June 22, 2005). Jonah Nez, Larry Todachinee, and Anna Laughter, an eighty-some-year-old wife and grandmother from Shonto, Arizona, agreed with Dennison on this point. They each insisted that burying an amputated limb will have grave consequences for the person from whom it originated. Nez noted that the severed limb is considered to be dead, and he added that burying it will cause one's life to end (June 12, 2005). With the help of her grandson Delano Ashley, Laughter agreed, supporting her statement with examples of people in her community who died immediately after their amputated appendages were buried (June 16, 2005).

Fred Laughter, an eighty-five-year-old crystal gazer from Shonto, Arizona, pointed out that there is at least one option for circumventing the danger associated with having part of one's body buried while the individual remains living: "The best way to do it is if any part of the body is amputated, if an amputation takes place, you store it [the amputated appendage] or keep it in a place where it can be kept until the individual passes on or deceases, and then that amputated part is brought back and then buried with the rest of the body—everything together" (June 16, 2005). Thomas Deschene, Jr., also mentioned families employing the same option. In this case, cold was used to preserve the body part: "I do know some people, they would put it [the appendage] away in a freezer until they die. Then they would give it back to them so they can bury it with them" (June 15, 2005).

These responses corroborate received wisdom about how Navajo people treat other detached body parts. It has long been known that loving family members simultaneously use their understandings of, or access to, the Navajo philosophical system to make daily choices to foster desired traits in developing Navajo persons at critical points in the life cycle through the manipulation of detached body parts. This begins at birth.

Staffs at reservation hospitals are sensitive to family concerns over the care and disposal of parts of the body that are important to the child's safety and future. Particular concern focuses on the placenta, the water used for the child's first bath, and umbilical cords. Placentas are taken home from the hospital to be buried so they can "become one with Mother Earth again" (Knoki-Wilson, August 10, 1992), or they are placed in another location of special significance to the family. Because of Navajo beliefs about the life-long relationship between individuals and detached body parts, such place-ment of placentas results in a lifelong connection between newborns of either sex and their matrilineal homes.

The teachings of the Holy People governing the development of person-hood dictate that the umbilical cord be placed in a location the parents and grandparents consider most beneficial to the child's future. Its placement has a profound effect on the child's future occupation and personal procli-vities. It also establishes a child's relationship to his or her physical landscape, anchoring individuals of either sex to Mother Earth and to the customary use area of their maternal line. Thus, umbilical cords, placentas, and teeth are the de facto exceptions to the rule against burial of body parts; according to the majority of those with whom I consulted, other means are preferred for all other parts (Schwarz 1997:138–41).

While burning hair and fingernail and toenail clippings is deemed accept-able when accompanied by prayers and herbs (Bekis, July 28, 1993)—similar to the burning of blood from a child's first bath (Knoki-Wilson, August 10, 1992)—the burning of severed limbs is deemed highly controversial by the Navajo people with whom I conferred. According to Johnson Dennison, burning a severed limb will cause undisclosed problems that can be reconciled only through traditional ceremonies (June 22, 2005). Jonah Nez, in an excerpt recently quoted, cautioned that burning a surgically removed appendage would have the same consequence as burying it: it would bring the person's life to an end (June 12, 2005). To this list of consequences, Larry Todachinee added stomach problems and changes in skin color. He clarified:

> MS: How about when someone has to have a limb amputated? . . . What is the proper way to dispose of the limb that has been removed?
> LT: Well, way back there we never heard about that. But today, they talk about that. And sometimes when you're doing the crystal gazing it comes out, like if somebody has an amputated leg, "What did they do with this leg? Did they burn it or did they just put it in their trash and maybe they went and cover it with dirt," so we don't know where it went. So sometimes they [the person who had the amputation] get affected on this. Part of your life is still on this earth and the amputated part, if it goes underground, then it is going to affect them just like Hóchxǫ'jí [Evil Way]. Or if they burn it, then . . . you going to be becoming a dark color. Just like somebody who'd been hit by lightning, then their complexion will be dark. . . . I guess that is why they're not supposed to burn your body, so it is against our tradition. But nowadays they do that. . . . They're supposed to just put it away, but sometimes they just burn them.
> MS: How are they supposed to put the limb that is removed away?
> LT: Well, they can't put it underground. Before that, in our traditional way, they just usually put it between them, like tree branches, they put it between there . . . but nowadays they just give it to the hospital and they burn them.
> MS: And that will cause your body to darken?
> LT: Uh huh. Then they [the amputees] can be affected inside their stomach or inside their body, so they have to have Hózhǫ́ǫ́jí done for that too or maybe Evil Way [done] first and then Hózhǫ́ǫ́jí, the Blessing Way ceremony. (Todachinee, June 28, 2005)

Eleanor Begay had her leg removed from below the knee in two separate surgeries. The first, to remove her foot and ankle, took place at a hospital in Flagstaff, Arizona. She recalled: "That time they asked me, did I want it [the amputated part]. I said, 'No. I don't want that. I suffered too much. Just do whatever you are going to do with it. I did not want that back.'" (E. Begay, June 10, 2005).

In like fashion, Billie Davis, a portion of whose foot had been removed, reported: "I just let them dispose of it, however they do that. I was asked, 'What would you like done with it?' and I said, 'Well, it was bothering me, maybe it was gonna kill me.' Why bother taking it home? So, I just gave it back to them to do with it whatever they do" (B. Davis, June 11, 2005). Chee Tapaha, who also did what the hospital recommended and let them incinerate his amputated leg, quickly learned that this was not a culturally appropriate action. He related:

> MS: What were you taught? How was the amputated limb to be disposed of?
> CT: I didn't even know. When I asked my doctor, Dr. Wood, what he did with my leg, he told me they just destroyed it. 'Cause it's all covered with sores and gangrene. "Put it in the incinerator, burned it," he told me. "So they just burned the leg." But after I came back later, the diagnostician asked me what I did with the leg, and so I told him what the doctor had said and the diagnostician said, "That is inappropriate. The leg should have been brought back and disposed of properly in [the] Navajo way."
> MS: Which is what?
> CT: It would be to bring it back and then offer it back to nature appropriately through a ceremony. So I kind of worry about that. (Tapaha, June 2, 2005)

Leroy Nelson witnessed a ceremony for an amputee who also suffered from complications brought on because his severed limb had been incinerated at the hospital. As Nelson recounted, through traditional diagnosis it was determined that the surgically removed body part should have been treated like a stillborn child.

LN: A lot of these individuals that went through these proceedings [amputations] were complicated . . . due to they were feeling the limb and then dreaming about it, and then it was haunting them in various manners. And the reason was that [it] was burned. And . . . I questioned it. I was there at the ceremonies. I said, "Well, what is the right proceeding?" So the diagnostician did a diagnosis and it revealed it. And it was said . . . "This woman was pregnant, but then she got a miscarriage. So if there is a miscarriage, the family is oriented, then they bring a medicine man in. And the medicine man does a chant and then they get the miscarried baby. They take it up into the hillside; they take him into the mountains. And then they put it between cedar branches. That core of the cedar branch, they open it and then they put it in between the cedar branches. And then they place it back, and then the tree grows with it. And the tree all of a sudden adopts it; the tree grows with it. And then people observe that tree." So . . . the same proceeding should happen. That is what we were told. They should get the limb back and put it [the amputated limb] in . . . the core of a cedar tree and let it grow with the tree. That way it is like the prayers and the song, everything is there—toward that cedar tree. That is the information I have about a limb. (Nelson, July 20, 2005)

This concurs with the procedure followed by Frank C. Young, who according to his daughter, after having a toe amputated, "gave it back to a tree with ceremonial songs and prayers" (N. Young, June 14, 2005). As Mae Ann Bekis denoted in her explanation of how to properly dispose of an amputated limb, treating it like a stillborn is equivalent to offering it back to Mother Earth or to nature, as Chee Tapaha was directed to do, for that is what allowing it to be adopted by a cedar tree constitutes.

MAB: They say you should do an offering like a fetus, like an offering to Mother Earth; [that] is the way it is supposed to be done. In that way the person wouldn't feel so much hurt. Because a lot of them, they said, after they saw they didn't have a leg [it was a shock]. And this one lady . . . told her son, "I want you to do [the] offering the right way. I want you to put it [the leg] back in the mountains somewhere. Where there is nobody around. Put it in there and then just pray for it. Wrap it in something. Don't leave the shoe on, leave the shoe somewhere else. Don't burn the shoe. Just put it in a bush somewhere over there where you put my leg." So they did it that way for her. So it is not a shock to her. She knows that it is put away right. (Bekis, July 22, 2004)

Ambrose Shepard added his thoughts about the disposal of severed limbs: "See this river here? . . . When I nodded in affirmation, having noticed the wash on the way into his homestead, he continued. "When it is high water, drop it in there. Offer a prayer with it. It is gone. Let the water clear everything, let the water take care of it. That is what I was told and that is what happened. I went up here by the lake and just put that [severed limb] in the water. That is the way of disposing of any part of your organ. Or just put it to rest they said in a rock, layers of rock, in between the rock. Or a tree trunk, that is the other way to dispose of these kinds of things" (Shepard, June 3, 2005).

Jonah Nez offered insight into an alternative method by which to offer surgically removed body parts back to nature. He advised that the severed limb be taken to sacred ground and left for the Holy People:

JN: There are some sacred places up here on the mountainside. It's really hard to deal with for us Diné because you are talking about our culture, our traditions. So let's say they cut a person's leg off, OK?
MS: Uh huh.
JN: The bad part of your body, you cannot put it in the ground, you can't do that, they say. There are some sacred places in our community out here (indicates east with his chin). Especially on the mountainside right here. There is a real nice place there with a different type of plant with this flower. If you go in the morning there will be some of these flowers, they're a real whitish color. And they're along the mountainside. They only bloom early in the morning. When the sun comes, they unfold themselves then. The dead part of a person's body, you can just lay them there in that flower. But you can't put it in the ground and you can't burn it. If you burn it,

you can't do that while a person is still alive. They say that there are Holy People that are out there, and they come across these kinds [the severed limbs], and they're the ones that know how to go about it [dealing with the limbs]. But if we burn it or put it in the ground, that's it. Your life will be ended right there. They say that. So, I guess that is what should be done. Take it over here on top of the mountain and put it away where there are no sheep or no horses or no people go there for their livestock. A lot of flowers there, and that is where they should be put. That's all I know. (J. Nez, June 12, 2005)

Despite these many warnings, Thomas Deschene, Jr., recalled a patient who found particular merit in allowing the hospital to burn his body part: "This one man came to a peyote meeting. He was making a prayer, he didn't have a leg, and he was saying part of his body was burned: 'Put it back in the fire so nobody can mess around with it'" (Deschene, June 15, 2005). In this case the amputee was referring to witchcraft; he didn't want anyone to be able to perform witchcraft on him by using the detached body part. Deschene was the only person I consulted about amputations who specifically mentioned witchcraft. His commentary does coincide, however, with an issue raised by Paul Mico who, when discussing Navajo apprehensions about surgery, pointed out Navajo concerns over the disposal methods of "surgically-excised organs, which conceivably could fall into the hands of witches" (1962:32).

Unless some form of storage is involved, disposal will likely take place long before the patient returns home from the hospital, for patients frequently spend months or years recovering from amputation surgery and subsequent physical therapy. If a patient's recovery runs into complications, family members can petition health care providers to allow their loved one to return home for ceremonial treatment. This was the case for Ambrose Shepard when gangrene began to set in on the remaining portion of his right leg.

THE LIFE WAY CEREMONIALS

AS: It is called "Iináá'jí [Life Way]." Survival, it is called a survival. They give you medicine while they're doing the three-night performance. For three nights they have this medicine, kept putting medicine in me. . . . Whatever is done will purify me, and that is what happened here. That was done for me after the surgery. The healing was not taking the right course. I had to prompt the healing. That is when I had that done and . . . pretty soon it [the area of the amputation] started healing. The sore was there, and one time I could smell the deterioration, I guess you might call it. The bad tissues and all that became a smell to me, and that is when I had it [the ceremony] done and then I went back in the hospital. I asked for a leave over the weekend to have that [Life Way] done, and they gave me time to have that done. And when I went back over there [to the hospital] it began to heal. . . . I was so frustrated, all of this time I spend in the hospital, and one day I said "this home." [Overcome with emotion, Ambrose begins to weep.] This house we lived [in], it really got to me. I got lonesome so I said to the doctor after this was done [indicating his missing right leg], "I have to go home. When can I go home?" He says "Next week or maybe two weeks." I said "I want to go home next week." So he said I can go next week. I was the happiest person coming home. That is when I had a lot of the ceremonies done again. It is not only a one-time thing, but it has to be repeated. And different medicine men, they came over and gave me medicine and people helped me with those kinds of herbs that people know about. And I took anything they gave me. And that is how I began to heal, and I healed up. (Shepard, June 3, 2005)

Shepard refers to a group of ceremonials known as Iináá'jí, or the "Life Way" complex, which are documented to have been routinely employed for decades as emergency or first aid measures for treatment of injuries (Franciscan Fathers 1910:354; Haile 1943:39; Wyman and Kluckhohn 1938:30). The individual ceremonies that make up the Life Way group are *Na'at'oii bika' iináá'jí,* or Life Way Male Shooting Branch; *Na'at'oii ba'áád'jí iináá'jí,* or Life Way Female Shooting Branch;[4] *Ndishniih iináá'jí,* or Life Way Handtrembling Branch; *Béeshee bika'jí,* or Flint Way Male Branch; *Béeshee ba'áád'jí,* or Flint Way Female Branch;[5] *'Akaz bika'jí,* or Stalk

Way Male Branch; and *'Akaz ba'ááď'jí,* or Stalk Way Female Branch (Wyman and Kluckhohn 1938:6). While known to be quite ancient, these ceremonies are not static. One of the ways this ceremonial complex has changed is that some of the component ceremonies, such as 'Akaz bikạ'jí and 'Akaz ba'ááď'jí, have disappeared since documented by researchers in the 1930s (Frisbie and Tso 1993).

In the contemporary world, the Life Way group predominantly consists of two separate but integrally conjoined sets of ceremonies—those seeking connection with the powers of life medicine and those seeking the powers of flint. Donald Denetdeal noted that the first cluster "is designed for minor physical injuries to restore the person's injury—injuries such as a broken limb, minor fractures on the person's physical body, a broken finger, or maybe a dislocated shoulder or a dislocated hip or something along those lines. To speed up the recovery . . . the medicine man would sing a day or two *depending on the severity of the injury* and administer certain herbs, prayers, and all of that to restore the person to physical healing" (Denetdeal, July 11, 2004). In such cases, Life Way medicine in conjunction with songs and prayers provides the needed healing. Ceremonies in the Life Way group associated with flint "have to do with major physical injury such as multiple broken parts, multiple broken bones, a head injury, a major head injury, or things like that. This ceremony is also done by a medicine man for a number of days, two or three or four days, administration of herbs, prayers, songs, and so on. That is the only ceremony that we have that has to do with physical injuries" (Denetdeal, July 11, 2004).

One point Denetdeal mentioned that is worth further consideration is that unlike other Navajo ceremonials, Flint Way is not performed for a proscribed set of hours or days; in fact, it has been documented to have been performed for as few as two and as many as sixteen days. Once begun, it continues "until relief occurs or until that particular form of treatment is given up as useless" (Wyman and Kluckhohn 1938:31).

When consulted about this complex, Leroy Nelson concurred with the basic points Denetdeal raised, adding that Flint Way is specifically called for in the case of surgery (July 20, 2004). This is not a new practice, for it coincides with a case, documented by John Adair and colleagues in *The People's Health,* of a prominent medicine man who by his own account had "the Flint Way ceremony [usually conducted for wounds or internal injury], in order to help heal the incision made by the surgeon" after an appendectomy in 1959 (1988:171).

This ceremony is specifically called for in the case of surgery because, as Ursula Knoki-Wilson illuminated, as a substance *flint has the ability to counteract contamination*: "They use the arrowheads to chase off the enemy. That will cut that contamination. So they use flint. It is part of a shielding ceremony too. What they do is, they blacken the body with ashes and then put that invisible shield on the patient . . . so the enemy gets chased off, so to speak. And then the black shield, if the enemy tries to come back they can't enter that black space and the patient's body. And then after they do the shielding, they have a cleansing ceremony to erase all that contamination, so to speak" (Knoki-Wilson, July 5, 2005).

As previously discussed, Navajo who undergo surgery performed by non-Navajo surgeons need ceremonial assistance to counteract the contamination incurred during the surgery. Thus, the significance of Flint Way ceremonies in such contexts is easily understood. The ceremonies that constitute the other side of the two strands that make up the Life Way group are equally important to Navajo recovering from surgery. In a clear demonstration of how these ceremonials interrelate, Frank C. Young offered further insight into how contact with Europeans and their metal weaponry led to what could best be termed a fluorescence of the Life Way group.

> FY: We Navajo are aware that we went through colonization, and at that point in history we considered each other enemies. *That was the first time we came into contact with metal things like rifles, swords, and what not.* Prior to that, it was a different type of warfare; with these weapons, when a person got wounded or cut, it created in the wound bacterial growth and infection. Infections resulted from gunshot wounds and all that stuff. So that is when we began to heavily rely on herbs. And in the ceremony that we go through, there is a mixture that you make, it is freezing cold when you sprinkle it on a person or when you apply it; that mixture, it kind of freezes the bacterial growth or infection.
>
> MS: Do you know the name of the ceremony?

FY: Yes. . . . Iináá'jí, "Life Way." It has a lot to do with herbology. That is what they apply to freeze it. It is really cold. It freezes the infection. That is the procedure that was enhanced during that time [colonization]. . . . I guess before that they didn't really rely on herbs because it wasn't necessary, but during this period it caused a need to use it. . . . So what they do today is when you go through surgery they follow that same procedure. And it works. . . . The herbs are cut and that mixture is put together, and then it is applied to the incision. (F. Young, June 14, 2005, translated by Nora Young)

Larry Todachinee alerted me to important differences between biomedical and traditional medicine from a Navajo perspective, which specifically focuses on the *tools* used in patient care.

LT: Well, our traditional [belief is that] they are not supposed to cut, the bilagáana surgeons? They are not supposed to cut you.

MS: Why?

LT: Because our traditional way—we have herbs. So if you don't believe in these herbs, when you have this surgery, then it is going to affect you. That is what they tell us.

MS: Why will it affect you?

LT: Well, these tools and these bilagáana, it comes from Anglo people, that is what they say. That is why it is going to affect you. So . . . you have surgery, then you're supposed to have this Life Way singing, then it wouldn't affect [you], that is what they say.

MS: But why will Anglo doctors and Anglo tools—

LT: Well, they have their own tools and we have our own tools. . . . There is two different things.

MS: Exactly.

LT: So that is why. We have different tools, we have traditional and these Anglo, they have different tools. So if they use their tools to cut you open, then it is going to affect you. But if you just use this herb, it wouldn't affect you. So there is two different things. That is how it is going to affect you.

MS: I am trying to understand this. Would I be right, or would I be
    even close, if I said something like the Holy People gave you songs
    and prayers and herbs to heal, and it is right to use those and it is
    not right to use the tools the Anglos have.

LT: No, not really.

MS: I am not right when I say that?

LT: Not really. Well, these bilagáana tools, they make that up of metal,
    but they use silver and all those, it is a metal. . . . But our tradi-
    tional way is normal herbs. . . .

MS: Prayers and songs.

LT: Uh huh, they only use arrowhead to pray with when it had some-
    thing to do with surgery, it's what they use, so . . . if they use
    Anglo tools, *it came from metal, so it is going to affect you*, so
    that is why they have to have a prayer done for them. (Todachinee,
    June 28, 2005)

Building on the insights offered by Young and Todachinee, Julia Mathis
reported what her mother taught her about use of the Life Way complex
after surgery. Echoing Young's account of wounds incurred in battle, her
explanation reinforces the significance placed on the fact that the instrument used to cut or wound the body is metal:

JM: And then after the surgery there are healing ceremonies, and I
    don't really remember what it is called, but I know my mom used
    to say *Béeshee*, meaning, Béeshee is like a medicine. They sing
    for you, they feed you herbs, and that is the healing.

MS: What about you, Amelda [Sandoval Shay], do you know what it
    is called?

ASS: Iináá'jí.

JM: Iináá'jí, yeah, that one. And she also called it *Béeshee k'ehjigo*,
    meaning they use their scissors, their knives. So, for where they
    cut you, where they stitched you up, that's the healing ceremony
    for that.

MS: Can you say that again, please?

JM: Béeshee k'ehjigo, meaning using tools, scissors, knives. Because
    that is what the surgeons use—surgical tools. (Mathis, June 11, 2005)

From her choice of words—Béeshee k'ehjigo, or "in the way of flint"—it is clear that Julia Mathis's mother was actually referring to the flint side of the Life Way complex. This seems appropriate since *béésh*, the Navajo word for flint, is the term used to refer to metals introduced by Europeans and Americans, and surgical tools are constructed of such materials.

Mae Ann Bekis generously shared her personal experience with Béeshee bika̧'jí, which was performed for her after a hysterectomy. Importantly, her account points to concerns with sharp metal instruments following the ceremony:

> MAB: Flint Way is for if you get cut by a scalpel and a bilagáana cuts you. You have to have a Flint Way, it is called, it is one of our traditional sings. They sing for you maybe five nights, five days. They just keep on singing. . . . It's done in there, in the hooghan (indicating the family ceremonial hooghan). And he sang for me for five days and five nights, and then he made me some medicine. And I started drinking that medicine until it was gone. And that was to help me so I wouldn't think about my being cut. But there are certain things you cannot do. And I watch it all the time. Like when somebody is cutting a cake, they can't pierce the cake with a knife because I had that Flint Way—that is cutting. And I don't want to have myself pierced again like that . . . and so I have to watch when somebody is cutting something. They have to cut it the right way. . . . Like one time we went up to Mesa Verde . . . and when they come out with the food this man, he had a little cutting board, about like that (indicates about 6 × 10 inches with her hands). They put a little loaf of bread on it, and here he went and pierced the bread with the knife and then they let the knife down. And he brought it over and I said, "You pierced that bread. I cannot eat that. It is against my religion." And he said, "I am sorry." Then he put it back and he gave me another piece. And I said, "Just don't put the knife beside it, carry the knife on the opposite side." . . . There are all kinds of rules on that. (Bekis, July 15, 2004)

Thomas Deschene, Jr., agreed that ceremonial intervention is needed to rectify contamination from contact with an enemy surgeon who operates on a Navajo (June 15, 2005). He also made clear that the purpose of the ceremony is in part to heal the surgical incision and—as noted by Julia Mathis, Larry Todachinee, and Frank Young and implied by Leroy Nelson—in part to counteract the influence of the metal surgical instruments (Mathis, June 11, 2005; Nelson, July 20, 2005; Todachinee, June 28, 2005; F. Young, June 14, 2005). Significantly, this clearly indicates that contamination can come from foreign materials, such as metal, just as it can from foreign people (Goldtooth, July 18, 2005). Deschene further wanted to convey that the ceremonial intervention for such contamination does not have to be a Flint Way or an Enemy Way; it can also be a Native American Church meeting (June 15, 2005).

The use of herbs stands out as a critical element in all accounts of the Life Way complex; however, herbs are not limited to this group of ceremonies. Rather, herbal remedies play important roles in many other forms of healing in the contemporary Navajo world.

HERBAL REMEDIES

JN: So, all types of people come looking for help.

MS: Tell me about if somebody comes to you and the person has diabetes.

JN: We have herbs to care for diabetes.

MS: What type of herbs?

JN: If the diabetes is just starting, we just deal with it. But if the person is too far gone, if somebody has removed their toes and some of their body, that is really hard, it is really complicated to deal with. But if the diabetes is just starting, there are herbs for it. I mix it, gather it right there (indicating a mesa on the mountain across from his home). . . . I measure it, and we brew the herbs into a tea. And we use that. It will clean you out right away.

MS: So, how do you gather the herbs? Is there a certain way?

JN: Yeah, you got to make a sacrifice because you just don't go over there and pick that herb up. . . . You have to make a sacrifice, out of the white shell, turquoise, abalone shell, or jet—and corn pollen if you have that. And when you do that, you talk to the

herb and talk to nature and Father Sky and the Sun. The Sun and
Father Sky and Mother Nature, they are the main ones. And so that
is how come you make the sacrifice. You talk to that herb like
you are talking to a person. You don't give the patient a whole lot
of that medicine, just a little bit of it at a time, and you have to stay
with that person and pray all that bad stuff is washed away. . . .
And the person is gonna know too because it's gonna go through,
then stop. . . . And you give them something good to eat. And
then after four days, you want that person to come back to you
again and check out how well he is doing, if everything is normal.
(Nez, June 12, 2005)

Healers such as Jonah Nez, known for their expert use of herbs, have
patients at all stages of diabetes seek help from them. Nez eloquently
described the collection of herbs for treating patients with diabetes. Again,
his choice of the term "sacrifice" for what traditional Navajo would refer
to as offerings is emblematic of his involvement in the NAC, which has
syncretized the tenet of redemptive suffering from Christianity. Suffering
is a trial of faith and a noble burden in the Christian tradition.

The choices of patients who seek out Nez for herbal treatments instead
of, simultaneous with, or after allopathic treatment shed light into the social
biography of medicines in the Navajo world—the full spectrum, from their
production to their marketing, sale, preparation, and actual consumption,
which lays the foundation for their social and symbolic power (Brodwin
1990:34). All choices in health care options are highly politically charged
decisions and actions, even medication choices. In thinking about the
social life of these various forms of medication, we must consider if they
are sacred or secular. In what contexts are they deemed efficacious? Moreover, what does someone's choice of one type over another tell us about his
or her alignment within the social fabric of the contemporary Navajo world?

As is clear from Nez's description of treating a diabetic patient with an
herbal remedy, the primary function of the procedure is to purge the patient's
body of any "bad stuff." In addressing the topic of traditional cleansing
practices, Kenneth Black, Jr., offered an explanation for the holes in the
body mentioned by Amelda Sandoval Shay. As he detailed, in combination
with carefully selected herbs, these orifices are critical to age-old purging

methods—which remove what he also refers to as bad stuff, as well as "toxins" or "plaque" that cause imbalance or dysfunction in the body. According to what he was taught:

> KB: When they [the holes in the body] get clogged up, that is when you will have problems. And they will convert to other things. And he [the ceremonial practitioner who offered Kenneth this guidance] says stress is one of the prime motivators of that and also grief. Hóchxǫ'jí, it would be called Hóchxǫ'jí, there is a ceremony for that too. All those things can cause things to get plugged up in your system. But a while back he says we used to utilize herbs. Everybody utilized herbs to cleanse yourself out. You need to go and have a chant that cleanses yourself out. A lot of these ceremonies still utilize that, but I think it was on day three and four they partake of a lot of herbs that cleansed them out. And it makes them kind of nauseated; it doesn't taste that good, but it takes out the bile, the acids, and it cleans out the stuff from the other way [through the bowels] too. It makes them weak and all that. I experienced it once. It is not a good feeling. But the overall benefit of it is good health. That takes out all the toxins. It takes out all the bad stuff, and he says, "Grief and stress and bad thoughts can somehow develop something in your intestines. Low creatines will cause a plaque of some sort and that will cause imbalances in your body and that will cause certain dysfunctions. If you don't heed and take care of yourself, that can result in a diabetic. Or that can result in some cancerous form or hypertension, heart disease. So that is why cleansing used to be an ongoing thing for Native Americans a while back. So there was never ever a need for surgery." I guess when you break a bone, then you have to [have surgery], but as far as cancers and all that sort of stuff, heart disease, that is how it was dealt with. But I don't think people really use herbs anymore. They don't really use the traditional concept of a sweat bath or a sweat lodge ceremony. Hardly anybody does that anymore, and maybe even the ceremonial practice of it . . . is lost. But that is the holistic approach, with some prayer and some cleansing and all that sort of stuff. It is all-involving, too, that counseling,

talking to the patients to revibrate their self-esteem. All that takes place as a whole treatment to that person. And that is how it is utilized in Native America. . . . And if it is a broken bone or other stuff, there are other herbs. There are so many different herbs for alternative medicine. (Black, June 16, 2005)

When I asked Jonah Nez how his treatment methods varied for patients with advanced stages of diabetes who need amputations, he provided testimony on how essential his will to believe is to the agency through which healing occurs. Marking yet another connection between the NAC and Christianity, this response resonates with Amanda Porterfield's commentary on modern faith healing, where she noted that the believer's devotion—or will to believe—is vital to the agency through which healing occurs (Porterfield 2005:116). Nez's commentary, therefore, likens NAC curing meetings to modern Christian faith healing. Some NAC road men such as Thomas Deschene—whose account appears immediately after Nez's—agree with Porterfield's stance that it is the patient who must believe for a cure to occur. In contrast, as is made clear in his statement, Nez maintains that the burden of belief falls fully on the shoulders of the healer:

> JN: If a person, let's say he has lost his toes. OK, we can use the herb that grows over here on the mountainside and then take that person into a sweat [bath].
>
> MS: And what will that do?
>
> JN: If you take that person into a sweat and give them that medication, it seems like there is going to be a big shock in there, and those red stones that are sitting in front of you, you can actually know just how much medication you can give to the person. If *you learn to believe* that . . . it is going to be like a cherry red piece of stone—
>
> MS: You mean the stones are so hot that they look red?
>
> JN: (Nods in affirmation.) But if you know what they are for, I mean the prayers and the songs that go with that stone, if you understand that you need to do something using stone, then you go according to that [meaning he acquires guidance through the stones—perhaps a vision]. You give your patient just so much medication. And

you don't have to have it too hot. You got to have just so much . . .
heat in there. . . . One of my nieces from over the mountain was
getting herself shocked, and a month later she came back and she
was fine. If it is an early case it's OK. But if a person goes too
deep, then you have to go maybe two, three times into the sweat.
But there are lives that we've saved. (J. Nez, June 12, 2005)

Nez added regretfully, "But some we couldn't, then there is nothing that
you can do, it's too complicated" (June 12, 2005).

Larry Todachinee spoke about the overarching importance of herbs,
including peyote, to efficacious healing. Like Nez, Todachinee stressed
the vital connection between the will to believe—in this case the patient's—
and the agency through which healing occurs:

LT: The crystal gazing, that was given to me by my grandfather. . . .
He told us to do the crystal one. . . . I don't really know about the
church. . . . If you just talk to God and pray to Jesus, it is going to
take time to do that [heal] because there was no herb involved. If
there was traditional herb involved, it is going to happen then, but
if there is no herbs involved, just talking straight to God, it is
going to take longer to heal a person. That is the way I notice in
the crystal gazing. And then this peyote ceremony, if you . . . talk
to this medicine, then if you give it to the person [it is dependent
on the person's will to believe], if he really wants to get well, *it
has to be him again, but if you have belief in this medicine, peyote,
then if you pray for this medicine, give it to him, then he is going
to get well too.* There is Evil Way and maybe Mountain Way . . .
all kind of different effects, but they can get well through this
medicine [peyote] in one night. (Todachinee, June 28, 2005)

All members of the Native American Church attest to peyote's sacredness
as a sacrament. Like members of Native nations as diverse as the Delaware,
Comanche, Shawnee, and Aztec (Schultes 1938:711), Navajo members of
the church refer to the peyote consumed in meetings as a medicine. In most
cases, road men purchase peyote for meetings from middlemen who buy it
from peyoteros in southern Texas who harvest it for a living. Some Navajo

do, however, make a point of going on a pilgrimage to the peyote fields at least once in their lives to ceremonially gather and dry their own buttons. Importantly, peyote is typically referred to as an herb by Navajo peyotists when its use is described in the context of a Navajo herbal medicine (Aberle 1982b:179; Calabrese 1994:508–509; J. Dennison, June 22, 2005; Deschene, June 15, 2005; J. Nez, June 12, 2005; Todachinee, June 28, 2005).

This sacred herb has a dual presence in every Navajo NAC healing meeting. It is present in an ingestible form, to be consumed by each person who wishes to partake. Moreover, it is featured in the form of an especially large button, a perfectly formed cactus that each road man keeps among his paraphernalia to place, as described in the account by Calabrese and Goodman (Calabrese 1994:508), on the center of the crescent moon–shaped mound of earth that forms the altar. The road man explains the patient's problem to the exemplar button during the opening minutes of a healing meeting, makes his plea for help, and then makes a sacrifice or "offering" of mountain tobacco. Interestingly, this performative speech directly parallels that of a Navajo herbalist during the collection of traditional Navajo medicinal herbs.

For an herbal remedy to be efficacious, it must be properly gathered and prepared in a multistep process, which includes explaining the specific need to an exemplar specimen. As Mae Ann Bekis explained, a critical factor is placement of *biyeel 'áshłééh*, or "the proprietary offerings made to a medicine plant from whose species one wishes to collect." She noted:

MAB: You have to get the Navajo given name of your patient, and then she [the healer] puts down the sacred stones, the four stones—white shell, turquoise, abalone shell, and jet. And then she puts down what we call, it's the blossom of blue flowers. And then cattail pollen, and then the regular pollen, you put all those down, and then the corn pollen. You put them on each side, hide it up on the sides of your precious stones, this side is your corn pollen (indicating east with her finger). Then you wrap it up and take it up there [to the place where the herbs will be harvested]. And then you're gonna say your patient's name that you're gathering the medicine for. And then you put the precious stones down and the others down too, like the corn pollen and the other pollens . . .

and then you say a prayer that you're gathering herbs for this person. And . . . then you start picking here and there, all over. And then you bring it back and you split them, and then you wash them good, and then you give it to the person. And I don't use a hammer or any sharp article, like a knife or hatchet or anything like that. (Bekis, July 28, 1998)

Like the archetype button cherished and brought to each meeting conducted by a road man, the exemplar specimen of the desired herb is sacrosanct; it must be kept holy and therefore will not be ingested or used in any other manner. Because of its status, the button takes its place at the center of the altar during each NAC meeting; the altar reminds all those present of the cultural ambition to attain a long life, while the exemplar button reminds them that peyote will be there to help whenever the need arises along the road of life.

Consultants such as Ambrose Shepard, Chee Tapaha, and Eleanor Begay freely discussed the use of herbal remedies to combat their diabetes. Their descriptions from the patient's perspective complement the narratives from a healer's perspective, such as those provided by Jonah Nez and Larry Todachinee. Begay reported that a specialist came to her home to say a prayer and mix an herbal remedy designed precisely for her needs, directing her to drink it around the clock (June 10, 2005). Mae Ann Bekis provided background information on the physiological reasoning behind that dosage:

MAB: You can drink it like you drink water. . . . And then it will be in our body, in our vein system. That is the only way you can get your medication. . . . The medicine, you can drink it any time you want. And one of my, my brother that died two years ago? (I nod in affirmation.) He was a medicine man. I had a problem with my leg, and he made some medicine for me. He told me, "It has to get into all your smallest veins—up to your toes, up to your everywhere. It will go through and then it will work for you. Otherwise it won't work for you, if you just drink it once in a while," he said. So that is the way the medicine would work. (Bekis, July 28, 1993)

Although not a first-person narrative from the patient's perspective, Don Mose, Jr., provided an account of how traditional herbs healed his aunt during a second bout of cancer. His explanation sheds light on how the Navajo healing system's focus on harmony and balance enhances the efficacy of its cures. Mose also offers insight into the power dynamics not only between traditional herbalists and biomedical providers but also between any form of traditional Navajo or Native American Church healing practice and biomedicine in the Navajo world.

> DM: I have an aunt, she got colon cancer. When she got back where they were planning whatever needs to be done, they spotted that she has liver cancer and they told her, "We are going to have to go back as soon as you get up [recover from the colon cancer treatments], we are going to have to come back and . . . clean that up too." She said, "No, I've had it. I don't want to go to the doctor no more. I just can't anymore. It's weakened me. . . . I know that it's helping me to live some, but I'm sick, let me just go home." She went home. Her daughter was like, "Mom, I'm going to take you to the medicine man." . . . So she takes her mother. She went all over until she finally found one in Klagetoh[, Arizona]. . . . He said, "I will make you medicine that will help you." So they go out somewhere toward the Grand Canyon where plants hardly grow anymore. . . . He does it. The plant, they got it and she's there with him and [he] tells her exactly what to do. It is a medicine man and a patient's thing: they come together and they go back to Mother Earth for guidance and for help. From above Father Sky and from Mother Earth you see two humans standing there asking this plant for guidance, and so they [make an offering]. And then he gave her a whole bottle of herbal medicine and said "drink this, it is going to be your food." Two months later she got used to drinking that stuff. *Two months later she went back to the doctor, the doctor can't figure out where the cancer went.* But if it [the herbal medicine] were just pulled out and made into a pill, I don't think it's going to work. It has to be this ceremony, this balance thing. It has to be the Father Sky and Mother

[Earth] coming together with the two human beings, and then it works. (Mose, June 13, 2005)

As in the case of Mose's aunt, after being treated by traditional herbalists, ceremonial practitioners, or Native American Church road men, Navajo cancer patients frequently return to allopathic doctors for rechecks, whereupon they learn that the pathology can no longer be discerned by available biomedical technologies (Schwarz 2008).

Eleanor Begay was willing to go to the Indian Health Service clinic for her diabetes but not for her high blood pressure. Moreover, she refused to take the pharmaceutical drugs prescribed by the doctors at the clinic for her diabetes, preferring instead (since those prepared by the ceremonial practitioner had run out) the herbal remedies available at the flea markets in Chinle, Window Rock, or Shiprock (E. Begay, June 10, 2005). As discussed in the next section, many consider the flea market a controversial resource from which to secure herbal medicines. Begay is not alone, however, in avoiding the prescription drugs proffered at the Indian Health Service hospitals and clinics. Time and again, stories were relayed about individuals who threw out their prescriptions after returning from the clinic.

SECULARIZATION/DEPERSONALIZATION OF MEDICATION

In marked contrast to the remedies gathered by traditional herbalists, over-the-counter medications—previously available only at trading posts, currently available at grocery and convenience stores—prescriptions from Indian Health Service hospitals and clinics, and herbal remedies from flea markets are decidedly secularized. This may be their primary appeal for some Navajo patients because their commodification not only depersonalizes the experience but also removes it from any religious context.

Consultants had numerous problems with the notion of purchasing herbal remedies from a flea market. In Navajo tradition, after an herbalist has been requisitioned by a concerned family member, given a detailed account of the patient's condition, and been told the patient's sacred name, he or she goes to the location where the needed herb grows, prays to one specimen of the species, mentions the patient's sacred name while explaining the illness as the need for the requested amount of plant substance, makes an offering (or as Jonah Nez prefers, "sacrifice") of precious stones and various pollens to that specimen, and gathers plant matter from other specimens of that species in the area. Upon returning home, he or she sorts, divides, and washes the plant material before preparing the tea or other form of remedy needed. The most frequently mentioned steps presumed to be left out by those selling herbal remedies at flea markets are mentioning the patient's name, explaining his or her need, and making offerings. Thomas Deschene, Jr., remarked, "In the traditional way, we always make offerings" (June 15, 2005). Sunny Dooley quipped, "You have to make offerings to it [the selected plant]. You just don't go dashing over there and pull something out of the earth and pound it and boil it" (August 21, 1992).

It is deemed imperative to meet the person who will be gathering herbs on behalf of the ailing relative. As Dooley clarified, this is so because the physical condition of the herbalist will be transferred to the individual consuming the remedy: "You really have to know the condition of the person who is going to be getting the medicine. . . . And . . . you have to be in a well place in your own life, the herbalist. You cannot have an injury and make medicine for somebody else because you are putting your own weakness into that medicine. So when the person [herbalist] picks it [the herb] up, that person [the patient] will not get its full recuperative strength" (Dooley, August 21, 1992). If a buyer does not know who gathered the proffered herbs, he or she might inadvertently purchase herbs that will cause the patient's condition to worsen.

Mae Ann Bekis also objected to the sale of herbal remedies at area flea markets. She noted that given the sequence of events—when illness occurs, patients encounter herbalists and herbs are secured—the medicines sold at flea markets cannot possibly be properly prepared. She added that it is inappropriate to keep such remedies on hand just in case a need should arise: "What you buy at the flea market, I don't really go for that. That is not done right. They are just doing it for the money. Even the herbs that they have there, it is not right. You cannot have some herbs kept around, you cannot just keep it" (Bekis, July 28, 1993).

Bekis's comments seem provoked at least in part by the sheer volume of herbs in the possession of salespeople at flea markets. This apprehension stems from the fact that excess in any form is considered dangerous in the Navajo world (Reichard 1950:80). The birth of child-eating monsters that threatened the survival of Navajo ancestors (Fishler 1953:38–39; Haile 1938:77–79; Witherspoon 1987:15), which was the consequence of the sexual excesses that took place during the separation of the sexes in the last under-world, stands as grim testimony to this philosophical tenet. Hence, Navajo people are taught from early childhood to do everything in moderation.

In commenting on why he opposes those who proffer herbal remedies at flea markets, Thomas Deschene, Jr., further nuanced Bekis's point when he implied that making a surplus of medicine in advance of a real need in effect brings an urgent need into being. This rationale, which clarifies matters considerably, is based on Navajo understandings of the power of language. As he explicated: "When you are gathering the plant, it is only usually for the patient that is sick. . . . Now you go to the flea market and you see people that are selling a lot of medicines. They have a lot of different kinds. When I look at that and the person that is selling it for a purpose like that, [I question] 'Is this person asking for sickness for a lot of people just to make money?' That is the way I look at it. Way back, the way the older people did it, you are not supposed to do that. Just only use it [medicine] when it is needed for a person with a different kind of illness" (Deschene, June 15, 2005).

Deschene is alluding back to the previously described vital step in the process of making an herbal remedy—when the herbalist verbally explains to an exemplar specimen why the particular plant matter is needed. Con-joining two fundamental philosophical tenets—prohibitions against excess and beliefs about the innate power of language—Deschene is arguing that using the Navajo language to request healing herbs in such excessive quantities essentially constitutes calling for an epidemic of each illness for which remedies are proffered at flea markets across the reservation.

PHARMACEUTICALS

Hastiin Lonewolf's family avoided all contact with traditional Navajo cere-monial matters because of their religious persuasion. Because no hospital or clinic was within a reasonable distance by wagon or horseback, he recalled using over-the-counter remedies as a child growing up along Canyon de Chelly in the 1950s, including what is affectionately referred to as "Ben Begay" on the reservation today.

> HL: At that time the family had a good friend that runs the trading post. Old Man Garcia, Hernando Garcia. He used to own that. He'd supplied some medicine like that because he learned it from their own white man's side; from that side he brought some medicine back to the trading post. Now we did use for certain things, like aspirin, like that, and then there was Ben Gay and all those kind for muscle-ache and all those. . . . Actually, I have never been to any kind of medicine man style or anything like that, their way [Navajo ceremonial]. I never got into that too much. So, I stayed on this side of the medicine up to this day. So, that's the way I grew up and my parents were going to church and all that. And they don't use any kind of ceremony or religious [events] like that. At that time they live in their love of Jesus Christ, serving the Lord with all our love. We're still serving the Lord. We trust him, he can heal us. (Lonewolf, June 10, 2005)

Another side of the same story was discussed by Dr. Buella Allen, who routinely encounters patients who resist being seen for their health problems or, as in the case of the female patient described in the next account, do not comply with treatment recommendations even after they have been sent home following amputation of a limb. In this case the woman lost a leg as a result of complications related to diabetes, yet she refuses to take medications prescribed by allopathic doctors. As a result, her remaining foot has developed sores, and doctors have had to remove part of it:

> BA: She [the patient] is up and around, she is mostly in a wheelchair. I don't think she is walking, but she moves her wheelchair around and she does household chores, and she and her husband are quite close and they talk a lot about what's going on in the community and so forth. He's with her almost all the time when she comes in, but the last time I saw her she had a real bad problem with her surviving foot, and without one leg the other foot

then becomes—you really have to preserve that other one. I think she may have lost another section of that foot. But she told me that she didn't take any of her medicine, she didn't believe in it, she wasn't going to take it.

MS: But you told me she was taking traditional herbs?

BA: Yeah. She has ceremonies and she takes her herbs and when she gets sick she comes into the hospital, but then we have no control over what she does at home.

MS: Does that frustrate you?

BA: Yup, sure does. We have a number of patients that are like that. I had one lady that would come in repeatedly for medical care and was always out of control. We would give her medicines and then she would go home and she said no, she wouldn't take them. One time I asked her, "Why don't you take your medicine" and she said "the medicine man told me just to throw them away. That they weren't any good for me." Now, I don't know whether that's true. (B. Allen, June 10, 2005)

The topic of cooperation between biomedical and traditional practitioners came up frequently in discussions with consultants. Kenneth Black, Jr., reported that a ceremonial practitioner once cautioned him: "These medicines that you go to the hospital and get, you get a whole bunch of different medicines—even aspirin—[and it] causes a lot of acid. It does you more harm in the long run. It is not good. You know if you run, get up early, like the philosophy says, you get up early in the morning and greet the sun. If you live by those examples, you will live long. You take care of your body and treat it like it is holy, you will live long. If you watch what you eat, you will live long. And if you pray, if you have a belief, you will overcome a lot of things" (Black, June 16, 2005).

In counterpoint, Leeanne Johnson emphasized that in most cases of which she is aware, it is a patient's decision, rather than the recommendation of a traditional practitioner, not to comply with a biomedical doctor's advice:

LJ: Usually, this is the prescription of a medicine person, when they do your ceremony on you they will say, "You also keep your appointment with your doctor. And if that doctor sees an emergency, you listen to that doctor. Because I don't know what your doctor is telling you. I am only giving you a prescription on what you are telling me now. But you will also have to listen to your doctor." That is what I always hear. So there is really no medicine practicing person that I know of today that will go against a doctor's opinion, but it is the patient that will decide. The patient will say, "I will only take the prescription from my traditional medicine man, and I will discard my medication."

MS: Unfortunately, a lot of patients are doing that. They throw out the medicine from the clinic.

LJ: But that is not the prescription of the medicine man. That is the choice of the patient. (Johnson, July 3, 2005)

It was clearly Josephine Whitegoat's own decision not to comply with her allopathic doctor's recommendations regarding prescription medication. Given that she insisted that she has not been involved in any "traditional doings" since her husband passed away decades ago, I was hard-pressed to understand her refusal to take the pharmaceuticals routinely prescribed at Indian Health Service clinics and hospitals. With the help of Amelda Sandoval Shay, she told me emphatically:

JW: All us Navajo are guinea pigs to the doctors. At this time those doctors and other medicine people are only learning further by using us. From our perspective, we have never been told that right here, this exact spot, is the place that is causing your ailment, this is the place where your illness "resides." They have not said this is the right and exact medicine that would heal what causes your illness. We have never been told that. It is unknown from where they obtained their medicines. Some might have been from various insects that they create medicine and mixed it up with other medicine and they offer that to us. That causes us dizziness and keeps us in a confused state. In return, they walk away from us with lots of monies. In exchange, we are used as their experimental subjects. That is what I say now about bilagáana medicine. (Whitegoat, translated by Amelda Sandoval Shay and Wesley Thomas, July 17, 2005)

Despite her claim that she is a devout Oodláni who no longer holds to any traditional Navajo beliefs, I suspect Whitegoat's apprehensions about ingesting medications she considers may contain insect body parts might stem from some version of the restoration episode in Navajo oral history documenting the close connection between human and insect physical makeup (see Haile 1943:60–76; Reichard 1944:7–11; Spencer 1957:100–102; Wheelwright 1946:5–6). As Thomas Deschene, Jr., detailed, such connections make Navajo people hypersensitive to medications that contain those particular types of ingredients:

> TD: There's all different kinds of plants. We have plants that you only see one time out of a year. There is the tumbleweed. It grows and gets big, in the autumn it dries up and starts getting really big, it starts rolling, all those seeds coming out, it goes about ten miles and then pretty soon something crushes it. Then you have plants like these trees (indicating deciduous trees outside) that go to sleep in the wintertime, they bloom in the spring all green again, autumn comes around [and] all the leaves fall off. Then you have another plant that is green all the time like sagebrush, cedar, Christmas trees. The evergreens, they are green year-round. Then you have plants where there is no air, where there is no sunlight, that are beneath the ocean, on the ocean floor. These are the kinds of plants that we have to use. And sure, these people that make pills, like painkillers and all these things, they use those. But they also use other things like body parts of insects. And the painkiller, I guess they get it from snake venom, to numb the skin to do surgery— *but they don't make offerings.* And they use that, but if we use that as Navajo, we are in trouble. 'Cause we don't know where it came from and it can contaminate us. . . . Maybe that's why a lot of people, especially Navajo people, they get pills—like diabetics— and then they don't want to take them. . . . It would cause something like the same thing as when the snake swallows something. Their whole body or their organs slow down because they are crushing that animal. They will start lying down and lay there for, like, six days until it digests. And some of them will get something like that from taking diabetic pills, it gets them constipated. That's

why they don't want to take those pills because they know what
is going to happen. (Deschene, June 15, 2005)

Not all traditionalists oppose biomedical care. In fact, Buella Allen has
found traditional practitioners to be some of her most methodical patients.
She explicated:

> BA: We have other people that are absolutely religious about taking
> all of their medicines, traditional people who take their medicines
> religiously and who follow our advice. I have a patient who is a
> medicine man who's had open heart surgery and who has high
> blood pressure and he is extremely well controlled, he takes very,
> very good care of himself. . . . And he is precise in the taking of
> his medicines. He brings them in every time he comes in. He is
> very compliant. I asked him one time, "You are so good about
> this thing, how did you come to this" and he says, "well, I think I
> need to take care of myself like I talk to my [own] patients." (B.
> Allen, June 10, 2005)

Like those patients of Buella Allen's, ceremonial practitioners frequently
make use of biomedical care as well as traditional healing. Mae Ann Bekis
applies the same philosophy to pharmaceuticals prescribed by a doctor at
the Indian Health Service clinic that she applies to herbal remedies:

> MAB: I had a problem with my knee. And the doctor gave me some
> medication and I put my mind on it, set my mind on it. He made
> this, he prescribed this medicine for me, and if I take it [every]
> four hours a day, after I eat . . . and if I do that the way he pre-
> scribed for me, and if I take it like that, it will work for me. I have
> to set my mind on it. . . . The same way with the herbs. If it is
> made for me, I have to use it the same way. I have to drink it, if
> the medicine man told me "drink this all the time" I have to do it
> that way and set my mind on it. That is the only way it will work
> for me. Otherwise, it won't work for me if I just take it here and
> there, like three times a day or something like that. I have to drink
> it all the time.

MS: So, you have to focus on it.

MAB: I guess your thinking and your illness works together. (Bekis, July 28, 1993)

Rather than pick between the two, many Navajo, such as Ambrose Shepard, find ways to incorporate both medical worlds—using medicines prescribed by both traditional and biomedical specialists. Shepard explained:

AS: I was told I am at the verge of getting to be a diabetic. . . . I try and take care of myself by not eating too much and try to control it. And I just lost a handle on it because I love food, so it just got deep into it after maybe twenty years. . . . The way it attacked me was that my eyes, I was beginning to see double. So I went and seen a medicine man and he gave me some herbs, medicine too. And it worked, it cleared up my eyes and it focused back into one vision. So then I also sought [allopathic] medical assistance and they give me some medicine, and that is how I got cured. And then . . . it's getting to be seeming everyday I am having little problems, so they gave me some oral medicine, pills. I have been taking that for at least two or three years. And then one day one of the nurses or the doctor wanted [me] to try giving myself a shot, insulin. So I tried that and it seemed like it was a lot better. So I started that, giving myself a shot. Once a day in the morning and then [again] in the evening. And that seemed to really help. Today I am on that. (Shepard, June 3, 2005)

* * *

Testimonies by Navajo amputees and those facing other types of surgery offer a chance to gain insight into how NAC members understand their personal and collective identities and use their personal agency to navigate the contemporary moral and political landscape, particularly Catholic services and traditional ceremonies. Specific topics that arose included idioms, tenets, the sacred or secular nature of medications, the forces to which church members and officiants credit moral validation, and the power dynamics of cures.

Religious relativism is a distinguishing tenet of the NAC; as a result, moral validity within the NAC can derive from multiple sources including Christianity, traditional Navajo beliefs, and other indigenous ideological systems. A primary idiom established in the NAC origin story is that help is always there when needed on the road of life. The Christian idea of redemptive suffering is of paramount concern in the Navajo version of the Native American Church. Traditional tenets of profound concern to Navajo people grappling with recommended amputation or other types of surgery maintain that the body should not be cut, that every individual has a predetermined life span, and that body integrality should be retained.

Should surgery be chosen, protection prayers are done prior to the procedure. The principle of synecdoche dictates that special care must be taken in disposing of the severed body part, or grave consequences may result. If healing is delayed, in addition to allopathic treatments, herbal remedies are frequently used along with a ritual from the Life Way group to seek connection with the powers of life medicines or flint to speed recovery.

CHAPTER SEVEN

Transplants

*We lost our son back in 1994. My kidney failure was in 1993,
and the following year Dean left us and I was very, very sick. . . .
You have a lot of energy when your kidneys are working. When
you have a kidney failure you have no energy at all; everything
just kind of shuts down. So one day I was feeling really bad. I
was lying on the couch and I went into a trance or I passed out
or I don't know what words you would use. But I left and there
was a big old funnel, blue light. Big bright light, and He said,
"Put an end to all this. Come into the funnel." And the light was
so pretty. It was really blue, but it was really pretty and it was
burning, He wanted me to go inside and I think my son was
present there. You know when you have a dream you always
think someone is there but you really can't identify them, but I
think it was my son that was there and somebody else was talking
to me, and I don't know who that other person was. I started for
the funnel and then I pulled back, and the minute I pulled back
the light disappears and that was it. I didn't go. And I said,
"Oh, something wonderful would have happened if I did continue—just gone for it." I felt a little more refreshed. . . . I have
often thought to myself, if I had gone that way [into the funnel
of blue light], would I have left? And I don't know the answer.*

(Watchman, June 21, 2005)

The fact that Harrison Watchman thought his son Dean was waiting for him in the funnel of blue light is not unusual; according to Navajo custom, deceased relatives usually come to guide the dying to the afterworld (Wyman, Hill, and Osanai 1942:38). According to Navajo tradition, though, they do not stand at the end of blue funnels. The combined accounts of Harrison's and his daughter Gwen Watchman's experiences with kidney failure and kidney transplants serve as the connecting strand for this chapter. As is evidenced by his narrative, Harrison is a devout Christian, while his wife, Eloise, relies on traditional Navajo religion. Like the Watchmans, all of my Navajo consultants seek explanations for the cause of illness as well as cures from religious sources. Pentecostals and other Evangelical Protestants credit Jesus Christ as the sole source for cures. Catholics, traditionalists, and members of the Native American Church (NAC) combine religions and credit each with helping combat the cause of illness.

The Christian Navajo organ recipients or those awaiting organs with whom I spoke represent a variety of denominations. Lonewolf, a heart recipient, was raised Presbyterian; Paulla Damon Henderson and her brother Chancellor Anson Damon, who have exchanged a kidney, are devout Baptists; Harrison Watchman, a kidney recipient, Eugenia Bert, a liver recipient, and Asdzaan Taachiini, who awaits a kidney, are Pentecostal. Amelia Benally, a heart recipient, Julia Mathis, who awaits a liver, and Rose Mary Wade, who shared the story of her brother who has received two kidney transplants his body rejected and is awaiting a third, are Catholics. These denominations provide different moral compasses and have very different influences on individual and collective identities.

In the throes of socioeconomic changes, discussed previously (Frisbie 1987:197; Iverson 2002), Navajo people turned to Christian denominations in record numbers from the 1930s onward. Christian churches appealed to Navajo for pragmatic reasons, such as acquiring increased social and political skills, 9-to-5 work values, contact with the outside world, and acceptance by Anglos (Aberle 1982a; Blanchard 1977; Frisbie 1987:197; Rapoport 1954). Moreover, Christian faiths offered access to a transcendent form of supernatural power as opposed to the immanent form available through Navajo traditional religion (Aberle 1982a:219).

Over a third of all churches established on the Navajo reservation since 1950 are Protestant; of these, most identify themselves as Pentecostal, of which there are "myriad . . . denominations and sects" (Frisbie 1987: 203–204; see also Dolaghan and Scates 1978:27, 41). Pentecostalists believe they have recovered the healing power of faith that was lost for centuries (Porterfield 2005:180). Modern prayer and Pentecostal healing are self-consciously personal in their focus on the power of faith and their understanding of the coincidence between faith and the Holy Spirit. According to Amanda Porterfield, "The modern concept of faith healing implies that the believer's devotion, or will to believe, is essential to the agency through which healing occurs" (2005:116).

Hence, this religion is distinguished by "spiritual healing" and "glossolia," or speaking in tongues, either languages that are unintelligible or not consciously known by the speaker (Pavlik 1997:49). Pentecostals consider speaking in tongues a sign of the individual's baptism in the Holy Spirit (Frisbie 1987:203). According to William Hodge, Pentecostalism appeals to Navajo people because it offers access to "power flowing out of an ultimate source," which can be accessed by those who are "saved" through prayer or speaking in tongues (Hodge 1969:90).

We must not lose sight of the fact that changes in religious affiliation can tear families apart. Charlotte Frisbie commented on siblings whose differences of opinion over peyote use have resulted in deep-seated conflicts and strained relations that last for decades (1987:198). Louise Lamphere found instances where Pentecostals were "condemned by traditionals and peyotists for their refusal to participate in Navajo ceremonies, to help in preparatory activities, and to contribute food" (1977:29). An important point is that not being able to participate in ceremonial events cuts Navajo individuals off socially from networks of relatives with whom they share reciprocal relations vital to the perpetuation of individual and collective identity. Thus, participation in these alternative religions can break down family ties and erode Navajo collective identity.

Evangelical Protestant opposition to Navajo traditionalism is legendary. In many cases congregants are required to excise all traditional paraphernalia from their lives and stop participating in any traditional religious activities (Frisbie 1987:206; Lewton and Bydone 2000:488). Given this intolerance, how are we to understand interfamilial relations when different segments of a family select contrasting religions? Moreover, how are we to understand successful intermarriage between Christians from these denominations and traditionalists? Recent research indicates that the picture is less black and white than often depicted.

Elizabeth Lewton and Victoria Bydone pointed out the existence of more centrist views when commenting on their study of Navajo Pentecostals:

> While some Navajo Christians adopt entirely new identities, many do not reject traditional Navajo culture and are less exclusionary in their approaches to the other two religions [traditional Navajo religion and the Native American Church]. Many Christians take great pains to point out how Christianity fits with many aspects of traditional Navajo lifestyle and value orientations, including humility, hard work, and deep spirituality. In fact, there is often an ambivalence or tension among Navajo Christians as they struggle to reconcile the foreign roots of Christianity with their own Navajo perspective. They allude to Biblical analogies of sheep herding and the desert environment and associate Biblical parables with the Navajo creation story. (Lewton and Bydone 2000:491)

Echoing what Harrison Watchman said in differentiating himself from "a born-again Christian" (June 21, 2005), Lewton and Bydone continued: "Navajo discourses on Christian religious practice thus specify a variety of identities that may be negotiated—from a 'born again' Christian to one who draws parallels to traditional Navajo teachings" (2000:491).

While none of my consultants drew parallels between the Navajo creation story and biblical parables, several people clearly saw connections between elements of Christian doctrine and Navajo teachings. Some, such as Asdzaan Taachiini, spoke of being raised with a solid foundation of the fundamental principles of Navajo life but within a Christian faith (June 7, 2005). Her perspective and practices are similar to those of the Navajo Christian ministers interviewed by John Garrity, who "nurture a deep sense of pride and respect for their Navajo cultural heritage and concern for the preservation of the Navajo language and traditional way of life, both of which are intrinsic to their self-identity, save for their religious orientation" (2000:528).

Most compelling were stories from people grappling with how best to accommodate diverse religious beliefs within one family unit—especially between husband and wife. Watchman told me, "In the Pentecostal Way they said that you pray hard, and you ask the Lord for forgiveness and you receive what they call the Holy Ghost or the Holy Spirit, and you have probably heard of people speaking in tongues and shaking and dancing. But I never went that far" (June 21, 2005). Watchman has, however; felt that the Lord has answered his prayers with visible signs, such as the funnel of light described earlier or by other means on separate occasions when he has felt the Lord close to him.

PRAYER AND SURRENDER

Two consistent themes running through the illness narratives of Christian Navajo are the "power of prayer" and the notion of "giving it up to the Lord." Prayer is the means by which their needs are conveyed to the Almighty and cures are manifest. Giving it up to the Lord is the means by which they surrender their fate to the transcendent deity. Christian healing prayer is a prominent feature of church services, tent revivals, prayer meetings, counseling sessions, and camp meetings. Prayer can cure all ills (Hodge 1969:77, 79). Hodge reported that individuals can request prayers from the pastor for recovery from sickness and that relief is certain for those who request aid (1969:87). Ministers reported that prayers from the congregation are preferable to individual prayers by the minister. As in traditional Navajo religion and the Native American Church, the power of prayer is believed to increase proportionate to the number of participants (Lewton 1997:236–37).

For Christians such as Paulla Damon Henderson, who shared the account of how she came to donate a kidney to her then-estranged brother Chancellor Damon, all major decisions are ultimately given over to the Lord.

> PDH: My brother had a mass found behind his liver. . . . He went from Fort Defiance to the Gallup Medical Center. . . . The physicians there worked with getting him transferred to Baylor Medical Center [in Dallas, Texas]. . . . So his daughter who was twelve at that time . . . she and I boarded the plane to go to Dallas and we waited for him to undergo this liver transplant. . . . He went into surgery, we waited. . . . There were cubicles in his transplant

facility. One of the family members says, "We've been here for over thirty days, my brother has not woken up in thirty days since the liver transplant." And I wonder what is going to happen to my brother. And the woman on this side of him had just expired. And it's like, what in the world? Well, *it's all in the Lord's hands.* . . . He stayed at Baylor Medical Center for a good period of time because they have to wait to see if it's going to reject and the after care and all that. . . . Shortly thereafter was when his kidney started failing and they put him on dialysis. They said . . . if we could, among the family members, discuss if there's anyone that wants to donate one of their kidneys. And to me there was no hesitation, and the interesting thing about this is that *the Lord had his hands in all this.* See, when my mother died in 1981, my brother and I's relationship had really widened. There was a big gap, and we would only talk on special occasions. . . . We didn't talk at all until the brother next to me [in age] died in an accident. . . . My brother died in May and I realized that my brother [Chancellor] was sick, and in June [1992] is when they sent him to Baylor Medical Center. . . . He had four girls. . . . They all underwent the initial testing as well as myself, and it came back to where he had his oldest daughter and myself. . . . We were the candidates for a kidney transplant. . . . And I said, "My oldest niece has yet to have her family . . . so let it be me." I said, *"The Lord's got his hands in this and he'll make it well. It's all at his will."* So they flew me to Dallas. (Henderson, July 14, 2005)

Facing the reality of the potential negative complications of such a major procedure on the eve of the surgery in which she would donate a kidney to her brother caused Henderson to rethink her own life, past wrongs, eternal life, and what she termed "glory." She described the experience: "The night before my surgery, I called my uncle who is a pastor at Ganado, [Arizona,] and I asked him, 'This is where I'm at in my life. I just really want to recommit myself to the Lord, and if anything happens, I want to go to heaven. I want to have eternal life.' So he started the prayer chain out there too. And next morning we went into surgery, and I woke up and my husband was there and everything went well. . . . My brother was up before I was, and he came down and we prayed and thanked each other, and it was good" (Henderson, July 14, 2005).

I asked, "What happened the night before the surgery that made you know the Lord was there?"

> PDH: I reevaluated my life. See what I've done. I took an inventory of the people that I hurt, people that I took for granted. My children, my older children, how I did not make them a priority in my life, my earlier life, and it was like, if . . . something were to happen in this surgery and you died, where are you going? So that really . . . knocked me to my knees, just to say that I don't want to spend eternal life in hell. I want to spend eternal life in glory. And that's what prompted me to call my uncle in Ganado. And we had prayer over the phone. My husband was there and it was a relief, and he told me, "You'll be OK, you'll be all right. I'm gonna be right there." So there's other times that I felt the Lord's presence because he promised he'll never leave us or forsake us, he's always there. And with him all things are possible, and that's what Chancellor and I prayed about that night before our surgery. (Henderson, July 14, 2005)

Testimonials such as this one from Paulla Damon Henderson reveal that for Navajo Christians, the moral force that allows prayer to heal comes from Jesus Christ. This shifts a central focus of their individual and collective identities away from a core element of Navajo culture—the oral tradition that establishes them as the people chosen to live in Diné Bikéyah following the diné bike'ji provided by Changing Woman and the other Diyin Dine'é—to an outside source: the Lord, Jesus Christ. Henderson's turn of phrase indicates that she sought validation that the Lord was truly involved in what was happening to her family. This reveals a noticeable disquiet within her faith, which seems to have been alleviated by the call to her uncle.

Asdzaan Taachiini, the mother of two, has nonfunctioning kidneys. She was on CADP (Continuous Ambulatory Peritoneal Dialysis) for two years until complications caused her to convert to dialysis.[1] She was on the kidney transplant list until she developed a heart condition that required installation of a defibrillator. When we met, she was hoping to regain sufficient good health to be placed on the transplant list again. A devout Christian, she attends the Church of God Holiness in Vanderwagen, New Mexico. Taachiini says that what has brought her this far is the power of prayer.

> MS: When you were told that your kidneys had failed, did you seek help from a religious source for your medical problems?
>
> AT: I did receive some help, a lot of help. I was helped by the church group, and I know that it's helping me and that the only thing that is pulling me through at this point is prayers—*the power of prayer.* When I go to church and all the congregation, they hold special prayers and they support me with their prayers, and so in my way of looking at things the only thing that is pulling me through at this point and I've gone this far with is the power of prayer, and they help me a lot with prayers from attending church, so that is what's helping me. (Taachiini, translated by Donald Denetdeal, June 7, 2005)

While pregnant with her third child, Eugenia Bert, who is originally from Nazlini, Arizona, began to develop symptoms that eventually revealed a rare liver disease. She suffered from jaundice, loss of appetite, and constant gastro-intestinal upsets throughout the year she waited for a donor organ. She described the role her Pentecostal faith played in her illness, both before and after her surgery:

> EB: Well before, I didn't want anybody to know that I was sick. I just thought that maybe it would heal on its own, but eventually it got worse. . . . And by the time I ended up in the hospital, nobody knew I was sick. But my mom told our pastor, and my father-in-law, they would put in prayer requests because they are Christians too. And they would have other people pray for me, and I didn't know that. . . . And people that I didn't even know were praying for me. So, *I think that with all of that, with all of those prayers, that is what got me through.* The thing was that I had gotten so sick that the doctors were expecting me to be dependent on a wheelchair and a walker by the time I ended up in the hospital. . . .

And my surgeon, when he got my liver, he said that my liver was
as small as a prune. And he was saying that it was really amazing
how I was still walking. And that to me was a miracle. And my mom
called me the miracle child . . . and I think about that all the time.
God brought me all this way to keep me strong. (Bert, July 22, 2004)

Pentecostals are not the only Navajo for whom prayer is a critical aspect
of healing. The topic played a central role in the narratives of other consultants such as Josephine Whitegoat, who stressed the importance of
prayer in the fellowship of her Oodláni congregation. She pointed out that
"they exchange prayers. Our pastor tells us to pray for one another. Even
when we leave the church, he asks us to pray for one another from our own
homes. The church people tell us to do that for one another" (Whitegoat,
July 17, 2005). Furthermore, she noted that if congregants have individual
needs during church services, "he tells us to come to the front, one by
one"—that is, to the altar at the front of the church where the pastor will
personally address them—"he himself does prayers for us. At the end, each
person is prayed for" (Whitegoat, July 17, 2005).

Using the example of a hypothetical individual who enters her church
seeking assistance, Whitegoat made clear the importance of belief and
commitment for healing in the sect's canon. She noted, "If someone new
came in requesting prayers, he has to completely commit himself, give of
himself, and literally face the Lord. Then he can be healed. If he comes
with false pretense, with no belief in the church, he will blame the church
for not being healed. . . . He has to fully commit himself and offer himself
to the church, thrusting himself onto his knees. Then and only then can he
be healed" (Whitegoat, July 17, 2005, translated by Amelda Sandoval Shay
and Wesley Thomas).

Paulla Damon Henderson, who attends the nondenominational Community Bible Church in St. Michaels, Arizona, was also eager to elaborate on
how the power of prayer works. She explained: "We resort to prayer, we
get on a prayer chain, we attend prayer meetings for any problems, not
necessarily medical. It has to do with financial and educational, whatever
the needs of our family members are. And co-workers, friends, whoever,
take their needs or their petitions to prayer and have other people join us

in prayer" (Henderson, July 14, 2005). I asked Henderson to provide a detailed explanation of how a prayer chain worked:

> PDH: It's when you can get on the phone to your Christian family members and tell them your need for prayer. You don't have to go into specifics. It might be just saying a general statement like, "My son is ill and he really needs prayers." And it's amazing to see how many people [respond]. It's just like a chain letter. It just goes on and on, and people really pitch in. And then, too, when they have needs, they call and they ask, "Can you please pray for me?" or "Can you present this petition at your prayer meeting?" I have co-workers here in the building come to me and say, "I'm having this problem, can you pray about it?"
>
> MS: So a prayer meeting is when your congregation meets.
>
> PDH: We meet every Wednesday.
>
> MS: And then Wednesdays you meet, and somebody mentions that there is this particular individual that needs mention and prayer, and then everyone there concentrates their prayer on that individual?
>
> PDH: Uh huh. . . . You'll find that the churches around here, like the Nazarene Church, the Baptist, Methodist, Christian Reformed, people meet weekly and they have their prayer services or prayer meetings, and then too, especially this time of summer, there's camp meetings and revivals and you see these tents pitched here and there. People go there and they provide a time for Bible study, kids to go to vacation Bible School, and there is also a time for prayer, and that's usually when people come forward and present their needs. (Henderson, July 14, 2005)

Lonewolf, a devout Presbyterian who received a heart transplant, reported that according to his faith's philosophy: "A person can go to the doctors for the healing because they were given the knowledge to know what to do. And they can use the modern medicine and the doctors to help them get their healing" (June 10, 2005). He also mentioned the importance of prayer meetings and the prayers of his fellow congregation members: "They say we'll be praying for you and all that. I believe, myself, I believe in the

Lord. He can heal if you truly believe in him and trust in him and in the word and all that" (June 10, 2005). When pressed for a fuller explanation of how prayers were solicited, he mentioned that prayer requests among Presbyterians involve congregations in multiple states: "They have, like, one church will have prayer meetings, and every so often [they will hold such a meeting] for that person in need, and if they know somebody in other churches or other states, they will notify them and they can put up prayer meetings also. . . . The prayer can really help. All different people. I have some friends from Pennsylvania, Kentucky, Louisiana, Michigan; they help me in support with the prayers and all that" (Lonewolf, June 10, 2005).

In marked contrast to the majority of Evangelical Protestant missionaries, who are characterized as attempting to discredit or suppress traditional culture, Catholics in general have a reputation for working with, rather than against, traditional beliefs and practices. As a result, being Catholic does not tend to erode one's Navajo identity. The Navajo consultants who practice Catholicism identified themselves as firmly entrenched in Navajo society. Their fundamental religion is the Navajo traditional ceremonial complex, to which the Catholic faith is seen as ancillary. In addition, some also practice the NAC. Julia Mathis, patiently awaiting a liver transplant, provided a clear statement of how Catholicism supports, rather than undermines, her Navajo identity:

> JM: I feel that I am a strong Catholic because not only do I pray in the church, but I pray here at home. Not just through the Lord God, but when I am here I use my corn pollen, I use both the corn pollen, and then I go to church as well. So, I pray with different things in mind—the Lord, Jesus, and then all the Holy People. I have asked for prayers from the church, and they help me. Just like, I went through a real bad depression. I hit bottom. And I was almost over the edge. And I sought help not only from the Catholic Church but the Baptist Church, the different churches that offer prayers. . . . And my mom, that is one of the things that she always said, "You never condemn other people's religion. Because we are all here for a reason and we all pray to one God whether it be through the religious, the church, or through the ceremonials, we pray to one God. If it wasn't for that God, we wouldn't

have our traditional ways and we wouldn't have our church."
(Mathis, June 11, 2005)

This is not to trivialize Catholic belief and practice or to say they are
not given credit in securing a cure; rather, multiple sources are seen as
individually contributing to one outcome. For Amelda Sandoval Shay, a
devout Catholic who also relies on traditional Navajo ceremonies to meet
familial medical needs, prayer is a deeply personal ritual undertaken daily
for the good of the family. Like many Navajo consultants, however, she has
benefited from congregational-wide prayer requests as well. She explained:

MS: I am wondering if when you or someone else in your family
goes through some kind of illness, you seek any kind of help from
the Catholic Church in terms of healing.

ASS: In my family I use a Navajo traditional Blessing Way. I do
that, and then at the same time I pray. I don't go to church, but I
pray day and the night to have my family get healed.

MS: So you use Catholic prayers and traditional [methods].

ASS: And then later on, if there is anything that needs to be done in
a traditional way, then I will go with that. Nobody knows that I
pray at night before I go to bed. I bless myself and I have a holy
water, and I do that in my private way for me and my children.

MS: But are there any prayer groups? Do you tell the priest that your
family is in need and the priest can have others members of the
congregation pray on behalf of your child or anything like that?

ASS: No, but the ladies that I go to church with, they are meeting
with the church and they are the ones that will offer to pray for
you. Then I say OK. I don't ask them, but they tell us to, they tell
me, say, "We will pray for you," then I say "OK." . . .

MS: So, if you tell them that one of your children is ill or something
like that, then you know they are praying for you?

ASS: Yes, but they let me know. Well, "We will pray for you," so I
say "OK."

MS: And do you feel that helps in the healing?

ASS: Sometimes I wonder. Yes, sometimes I wonder if everything is
OK if they get well, or I will think, sure, that their prayer work,

but if nothing happens I don't say anything about it. I don't say "your prayer doesn't work." (Shay, June 6, 2005)

Eleanor Begay cherishes the solace she receives from her frequent visits to the Catholic mission in her community, where she can pray and be counseled by the priest (June 10, 2005). Rose Mary Wade combines her devout Catholic faith with traditional Navajo religion and biomedicine to meet her medical needs. Interestingly, the only prayers she mentioned were traditional protection prayers. In regard to the role Catholicism plays in healing and spirituality, she noted: "The Catholic is kind of like internal feelings that you have. Or, I kind of think that it is in line with the traditional, too. . . . And the church is like your peace within yourself. You go to confession and just live the right way and mind your own business" (June 17, 2005).

In addition to prayer, Navajo Pentecostals may use discernment to determine an individual's problem, as well as the "laying on of hands," a type of healing described in the New Testament.[2] Several members of the congregation surround the patient, laying their hands on him or her with each person beseeching God to "help" the patient, often weeping, and saying "Praise God" or "Thank You Jesus" (Lewton 1997:236–37).

At least a third of Pentecostal churches on the reservation have Navajo pastors (Dolaghan and Scates 1978; Pavlik 1997:50). Pastor George S. Davis, who leads one such ministry in Lukachukai, Arizona, denied using the laying on of hands for healing and described his form of curing as based on the word of God. He stressed that in his Pentecostal ministry the believer's devotion is fundamental. No healing of any kind can happen without devotion, for it is essential to the power by means of which healing occurs.

> GD: The word of God, they believe it. If they begin to believe, God himself will bless them. If they bless it, the people start crying. At that time there is healing and [people are] delivered. If they don't cry, they go around like this and go, how can God do that? . . . If you believe the truth, the truth will set you free. If you believe it, it means if you believe Christ, Christ will heal you and set you free from all kinds of sins and things like that. . . . You just can't see. Just like God, you can't see God now. You don't see Jesus.

You can't see the Holy Spirit. Only the word from belief that he will, for the people, you can see that, God's blessing, right there. People get healed, get delivered. (G. Davis, July 18, 2005)

PLURALISM WITHIN FAMILIES

The complexity of religious and medical pluralism on the Navajo reservation is profound. One aspect of the entanglement is that individuals experience this pluralism as members of large, multifaceted families rather than in isolation or as nuclear families. So we must gain an understanding of the intimate negotiations that take place within such families. Several examples from the consultations offer a glimmer of insight, but this topic is worthy of further research.

The first example centers on Eugenia Bert, the young mother who received a liver transplant, but it actually involves multiple generations of a matrilineal family. This is fairly typical of a family in which some segments are Christian while others remain traditional. Bert's mother is Irene Gorman, who converted to Christianity as a child after her family had sold all their livestock and pawned all their jewelry to compensate ceremonial practitioners in an effort to cure her polio. Irene married another Christian with whom she returned to live at her matrilineal home. They raised Eugenia and their other children in the Pentecostal faith. Irene Gorman's parents and her siblings, who live on adjacent land, remain committed to the traditional religion. In discussing her personal reaction to the life-altering experience of her illness, Bert confided that the full significance of the event evaded her:

> EB: Until that day I was getting ready for my operation, that is when it hit me. And I thought, "If I die during this operation, where will I go? What will happen to me?" That's because during my whole life I was raised like a Christian, but I really wasn't into it like I am now after what has happened to me. And I really don't know anything about the Navajo tradition and stuff. I would ask people, why? Why they would do this and that? But it seems from looking at other people, they would tell me that when they were sick and stuff, they would have ceremonies, and then they would tell me

that they didn't get anything out of it, that they just lost money from it. And . . . I just watched that during the whole time I was getting sick, it seemed like it opened my eyes to what I should believe in. As I was lying in the hospital I thought, "Where would I go? Would I go to heaven or would I go to hell?" I was scared. All I could do was pray, and *I gave my life to the Lord.* And I just wanted to make sure that I was going to make it to heaven. . . . I used to think, "Who would take care of my daughters" and things like that. I thought, "If I weren't to come back, what would that have done to them?" . . . That's all I would think about. It was really interesting, what I had to go through, to experience. Just to depend on God, and just to learn to have faith and all that. (Bert, July 22, 2004)

Bert pointed out that although she had been raised in a Christian home, she had never made a personal commitment to the faith. Her illness gave her reason to consider her religious options. After giving some thought to the efficacy of traditional Navajo ceremonial practice, she had come to her own decision about what faith to chose. She continued reflectively:

> EB: I heard from a cousin that my nephew would talk to my grandma, my mom's mother lives down here (points east to a house on the adjoining property), that she would mention to my aunts that they should have something like a ceremony for me. My aunts would tell her, "They [Eugenia and her family] don't believe in that, and we shouldn't be doing anything for what is going on." So, they didn't bother with that, with the Native traditional stuff. Because I guess they have seen miracles also and they know what we've gone through and what they've gone through, with just our praying with them. So they didn't try to push it or anything.
>
> MS: So, when you say "they've seen miracles," do you mean from the Christian faith or—
>
> EB: Yeah, that's what I mean. I think they have seen it but they try not to mix it, the Navajo tradition with Christianity. They respect our religion for us.

> MS: But they were concerned about you, so they wanted to have a
> Navajo ceremony for you?
> EB: Yeah, but my aunts told my grandma not to have anything like
> that for me. (Bert, July 22, 2004)

Clearly, her grandmother was on her mind while she was wrestling with her decision regarding whether to fully accept Christianity. She seemed touched by her grandmother's concern and a bit perplexed by her aunts' intervention. Eugenia's father, Eugene Bahe, who was sitting in on the interview, brought our thoughts full circle back to his wife's childhood experience when he interjected: "Yeah, they kind of wasted it all, pawning their jewelry and selling livestock for ceremonies. So one day we just changed everything and put our trust in God. And after all these years, they are still doing that. See, that is why we don't trust in the traditional ceremonies" (Bahe, July 22, 2004). Evidently, this family has decades'-old unresolved issues over religious choice.

As difficult as such relations are to navigate between parents and adult children or between siblings, imagine the delicacy required to successfully negotiate them between spouses. Asdzaan Taachiini's husband of twenty-five years comes from a traditional family. She mentioned that it was difficult when they first met because he was a traditionalist and that even after a quarter century, "I still have some difficulty in trying to connect with traditional values or traditional ways of believing, and ceremonialism is kind of hard for me; however, I continue to believe in Christianity and my children are all Christian, and we attend church and we continue to do so. But for my husband's side of the family, they are traditional practitioners and so we just kind of work around that, but for myself, I'm still Christian and I don't [plan to] change to any other's [religion] at this point" (Taachiini, June 7, 2005, translated by Donald Denetdeal).

Since she first became ill, she has been aware that her husband's family has had various traditional ceremonies performed on her behalf. While fully understanding that they do this only out of concern for her, she noted that she does not concern herself with these religious activities, focusing instead solely on the Christian beliefs and prayers with which she was raised: "From the other side, I don't know and I don't have much understanding of the old ways. But I do know that they must also want to help me. They

pray for me and that's all I know, but exactly how or any details about how
that is done, I don't know. I do know that they must pray as well, but the
bottom line is that I believe my Christian belief and my Christian prayers,
and the people that are helping me at the church is what's pulling me
through at this point" (Taachiini, translated by Donald Denetdeal, June 7,
2005). In contrast to Navajo Catholics who would welcome spiritual aid
regardless of its source, as an Evangelical Protestant Taachiini outright
rejected the aid proffered by her traditionalist in-laws.

The final example involves the Watchman family. Because of the agreement between Eloise and Harrison Watchman regarding each other's choice
of religious practice, when his kidneys failed they asked for prayer requests
at the local Assemblies of God Church as part of their healing strategy.
Eloise noted, "We chose to strengthen ourselves with the help of God. And
I think that was probably the best decision. . . . There were times when I
actually think that God himself presented himself to Harrison" (June 21,
2005). Consider this account in which Harrison Watchman described
experiencing the Lord as a rush of warmth:

> HW: I had the kidney failure, and they were asking me if I wanted to
>   get a graph where I go get it done by a machine. You can go—
> MS: Dialysis?
> HW: Yes. And I chose CAPD [Continuous Ambulatory Peritoneal
>   Dialysis]. So they put me on [a] cart for the surgery, and . . . one
>   of the nurses asked me, "So, what are you doing?" I knew her
>   years ago and I asked her if she recognized me, and then she
>   asked me [again] what I was doing and I said, "I've got kidney
>   failure and I'm going to get my CAPD." And she says, "Kidney
>   failure! CAPD! You're not going to live over a year. . . . Most
>   people that get the CAPD, within a year from starting most people
>   die." And what have I got to lose? If I die I die. And when I had
>   that kidney failure and I was growing so weak that I didn't think I
>   was going to make it, *that's when I asked the Lord* because if I go
>   I go, but *I put everything in your hands.* And when I was lying
>   there and that lady told me that I wasn't going to make it no more
>   than a year, I thought to myself, "I'm going to make a liar out of
>   her." So they put me in and I felt this warm rush in my body, and

I remember that. It was just like somebody putting a warm blanket over you, and then I felt real comfortable and then they put the CAPD in me, and it was no problems after that and the oil changes, I mean my CAPD changes, I went through it perfectly well. When I had my kidney transplant, I went back to this lady and I said, "You want me to throw this out the window? [referring to his CAPD catheter] Put a rock on it and throw it out the window?" I thought I would throw it out the window. (Laughs). And she said, "No, you can't do it that way. It has to be undone surgically. How long you been on it?" I said, "I've been on it a year, two weeks, two hours, and thirty minutes." She got a big kick out of it, that I kept track of it, but that's how terrible it was. ... I think it's really up to you if you want to live, then go for it. Or you can give up. At that place when I prayed to the Lord and then that warm rush of air came over me. I believe in the Lord, I believe in the Lord. (H. Watchman, June 21, 2005)

The Lord is clearly Harrison Watchman's moral compass, providing him with the power to heal.

In marked contrast, when their daughter Gwen Watchman was diagnosed with kidney failure, a different treatment route was selected. Interestingly, although Harrison identified Eloise as a Catholic, Catholicism was never mentioned as part of the treatment plan selected for Gwen. Instead, as Eloise Watchman explained, "There are purification ceremonies for it [organ transplantation] afterward and in my tradition there's protection prayers, there's ceremonies, and then you just, like I was telling my daughter, just thank your donor" (June 21, 2005). Therefore, the family addressed Gwen Watchman's kidney failure and subsequent kidney transplant through traditional ceremonial intervention.

EW: With Gwen, when she got sick, she got sick for a whole week or two and finally we went to the hospital, we resorted to the hospital. And they found out that she had kidney failure. Just like that, she just had kidney failure. And it was when she was in the hospital and I was at the hospital with her in Albuquerque, and all my family came back and they had two ceremonies done for her,

and they said this is the cause of why she had this kidney failure
and there were several things that needed to be taken care of.

MS: Can you tell me what ceremonies you had done?

EB: The Lightning Way, the Bear Way.

MS: What did they think had caused the kidney failure?

EW: The Lightning Way is used with that. Eventually, with a lot of
people that is what affects their body. It starts burning the insides
of their body, the vital parts. They say that if you were struck by
lightning or if lightning struck outside your house and you absorbed
the fumes or if you walked into a place that was struck by lightning or if electricity, that's part lightning, if electricity zapped you
or you were electrocuted, that eventually starts burning out the insides
of you, basically. Like your kidney, your lungs, and that's why
they say that the majority of people have cancer and you can be
affected by the Lightning Way. And I had to think about this for her.
A Snake Way, that could be another cause to having kidney failure.

MS: Did you take her to a diagnostician, I mean like a crystal gazer
or a hand trembler? And they are the ones that figured this out?

EW: Yes, a crystal gazer. We still use him, he's our medicine man or
my medicine man, and he lives right down the road from us, and
after her transplant for about four years straight, I don't know if it
was the medication, I don't know what it was, but she had a whole
different effect on her body compared to what her dad had gone
through. Maybe he didn't share with me some of the things that she
shared with me, but she experienced headaches. She experienced
vomiting. She experienced foot swelling, especially migraine headaches, that kind of thing, and she would cry at night and sometimes
I would sit up with her, but when she was going through her CAPD . . .

HW: Oh, the oil changes. I call them oil changes. It's a simple way
to put it.

EW: When she was going through a lot of that there were a lot of
nights . . . she would get up at maybe 10 o'clock at night and I'd
sit with her, and she experienced more symptoms than her dad
did and like 5 o'clock in the morning she would finally go to sleep;
and most of the time I got up early, praying for her [referring to
the tradition of greeting the dawn with corn pollen]. And there

was an understanding between Harrison and I, whether or not I should practice Navajo religion, and with Gwen that is what I used was Navajo religion, and with Harrison, he says to me, "Just leave it in God's hands." That's how we did it. (E. and H. Watchman, June 21, 2005)

For Eloise Watchman, healing power comes from the Diyin Dine'é. They are the ones who can diagnose and cure. Out of respect for her wishes, the family had this series of ceremonies performed for Gwen. For each ceremony Eloise Watchman would depend on the support of her siblings and their married children. The ritual would therefore reinforce Navajo collective identity, strengthen bonds among family members, and bring the powers of the Holy People to aid Gwen.

Curious to know if this was the full extent of religious-based therapy chosen by the family, I asked Harrison, "When your daughter Gwen was diagnosed with kidney failure, Eloise said there were several ceremonial interventions your family had for her. Did you also pray for her?" Without hesitation he replied: "Yes, definitely. We found out that she had that, it was probably the worst news I've heard, when we took her to the hospital and the doctor says 'your daughter has kidney failure,' it was like being hit with a sledgehammer. It was the last thing I wanted to hear because I know what she had to go through. And . . . the whole picture just kind of clicked right in front of me. And I prayed and prayed and prayed, and I think our prayers were answered because she got hers [kidney] about a year and a month later" (H. Watchman, June 21, 2005).

Like Asdzaan Taachiini's in-laws did and Eugenia Bert's grandmother wanted to do, Harrison Watchman used his chosen religion for the benefit of an ailing loved one who practices a different religion. These few examples shed light on the intricate negotiations made within families over the extremely personal and emotionally wrought topic of religious belief.

DONOR PREFERENCE

MS: When did Navajo people begin to have organ transplants? What is your experience with that?

TA: Well, the first transplant that I became familiar with was corneal transplants. I knew by going to school and by profession that transplants can be done, but when I came and was working in the community, there was a lot of problems with trachoma. When the eyelids turn inward, [it] causes scarring on the cornea of the eye, and so people went blind because they had sores and scarring on their eye and there is scarring where they're supposed to see. So what has happened is the cornea has to be removed, and at that time the only thing available was if somebody gave up a cornea to be transplanted onto your eye.

MS: When was this?

TA: I would say when I [first] dealt with one was around the late 1960s and early 70s. . . . I remember dealing with a woman whose eyes were so scarred that she had to be led by her children to go places. . . . She said, "I want to see again," so the ophthalmologist said, "The only way she can see is if she wants to sign up for corneal transplants." . . . And the doctor said, "The only way that they get it is from another person." So it has to be cadavers. But because this person was an elder, I had to say that "at this time, the only way you can get it is from another human being that has died," and that was not what she was going to have, so she said, "No, I don't want it," . . . because her belief is that she didn't want to have a part from another body, and so she said, "No, I will stay the way I am rather than get the pieces from another person." . . . So she just shook (demonstrating a full body shiver) and she said, "No, I don't want to do that." So I said, "OK, that is fine."

MS: She didn't do it?

TA: She didn't do it. So, that was my first experience with a transplant. (T. Allen, July 15, 2005)

Navajo consultants had strong opinions about whether they are willing to donate or receive organs through transplantation. They had equally strong views on whether they would accept organs from non-Navajo people or deceased donors. Regardless of their perspectives, Navajo people in need of organs only have choices on the latter issue in specific cases. Such decisions are dependent on the type of organ needed; kidneys and livers can be harvested from living donors as well as cadavers, while hearts and corneas, as Tso Allen pointed out, can only be taken from cadavers.

When asked without qualification if they are willing to donate or receive organs, non-Evangelical Protestant Navajo consultants were uniformly negative in their initial responses. Ursula Knoki-Wilson responded, "Well, traditionally it is taboo" (July 5, 2005). Larry Todachinee said, "It is against our tradition" (June 28, 2005). Kenneth Black, Jr., replied, "I think traditionally that is prohibited" (June 16, 2005). Ambrose Shepard stated, "There is opposition against it because you don't know who that organ is coming from, a white man, a colored, a Mexican. And in order to survive it has to be done, but it is going to hunt you down" (June 3, 2005). Sheila Goldtooth emphatically said "No," continuing, "I was told not to donate, do not donate an organ or blood" (July 18, 2005).

The Navajo notion of a life plan is also extremely relevant to this discussion, for as Kenneth Black, Jr., pointed out, organ transplantation goes directly against the age-old philosophical belief that each life has a predetermined limit. He reiterated that death has a predetermined line, and no one is intended to go beyond it.

> KB: It is when your time comes your time comes, is their philosophy.
>
> MS: Why is that the philosophy?
>
> KB: Well, death has a line. And in a lot of cases that is not something to be scared of. If you know that your body can only take so much, you have to accept the fact . . . that is what your line is. Is what was explained to me.
>
> MS: So even if it is someone young and something goes wrong with their heart or liver?
>
> KB: The way it is explained to me was that *'iinaa' ał'ą́ą́ 't'éego ndiit'ééh,* "life has different endings." And they say someone as young as one day old can only live to one day old. And that is how it is meant to be. And that is how God intended and that is how God made it that way, and there are some that are lucky enough to reach 100 years old, old age. And that is the intention. So there is a belief that there is a time, in different stages of your

life, everybody has different perimeters that you have to know
and accept. That is how it is. And people I think pretty much lived
with that over the years. But now, organ transplant[ation] has
taken place. (Black, June 16, 2005)

Regardless of whether it brushes up against the diné bike'ji given by
Changing Woman and other Diyin Dine'é, contemporary Navajo people
do donate and receive organs. Don Mose, Jr., offered valuable insight into
transplantation in the form of what he terms "the loophole."

> DM: The Navajo say, "No, don't do that." If I should take a kidney
> from a dead person and have it implanted in me, some medicine
> men probably say "It's not good. It's not our way of life. Don't
> place that in yourself." Well, some do today, so they prolong
> their lives. But the medicine men say "Well, it has its price, too."
> Oh yeah, you got to live on, but somewhere there's a price for it
> and what is that price? I really can't say. . . . I don't know how
> they explain that. Just that it will have some kind of ill effect on
> me. But I notice there is always a loophole. [I go to a] Navajo
> medicine man [saying] I don't feel good at all. . . . They'll probably
> find out because "you had a transplant. Let's have a ceremony
> for you." And so they go back and do this. It always goes back to
> the ceremony. There is always a loophole for something. (Mose,
> June 13, 2005)

Mose's commentary reveals an inherent flexibility in Navajo traditional
religion enabling it to accommodate the unexpected. He contends, therefore, that traditional healers can find a means to treat someone in such a
way as to offset the ill effects of having had someone else's body part
inserted into them.

Asked why they were unwilling to donate organs, some consultants such
as Mae Ann Bekis, Leeanne Johnson, Florence Sandoval, Ambrose Shepard,
Larry Todachinee, and Eloise Watchman provided insightful commentary.
Bekis interjected her typical humor to explain that if one of her organs
happened to be donated to a problem drinker, she would hound that individual to quit drinking and thereby make his or her life unbearable:

MAB: I would not [be willing to be an organ donor] because I don't want to cause anybody problems.

MS: How is it causing problems by being an organ donor?

MAB: It's the same purpose, and they might say, "You got an organ from so-and-so and it's within you and it might not help that person." Because I am already dead and they got my organ.

MS: But some organs, like, for example, kidneys or livers, they can take while you're still alive.

MAB: If it's in my own family, yes. But right now, I would not part with nothing. I want to live as long as I have. Even if I have to give up on my children. Hope I don't have to.

MS: So, you wouldn't give up an organ for your own children?

MAB: No. When I do my Social Security, they always ask me, "Do you want to give your organs to anybody?" I always say "no."

MS: So, you would not donate an organ to anyone.

MAB: I would not. I am just as traditional as traditional.

MS: I know you are. So, you wouldn't donate an organ. Can you explain why?

MAB: Well, I might come back and haunt them. Ghost. That is the only thing that I can come up with.

MS: Let's say, for example, that you did decide to donate your organs when you die. Do you think your organs will cause problems for somebody?

MAB: Yes. For somebody.

MS: How so?

MAB: Well, I don't know how this person is . . . . Maybe he was a drunk, maybe she was a drunk or anything like that, and I don't go out in public and do this and that, and so if they use mine [organ] that is why I would come back after them (laughs). In their dreams.

MS: So you mean that if they put your heart in the body of a drunk, then you would torment that person to change his or her life in their dreams?

MAB: Might be worse than how he is now. (Bekis, July 15, 2004)

Larry Todachinee turned the conversation back to traditional teachings by saying, "They said not to. If they transplant anything from this person but this person dies [the donor], then it is going to affect this person [the recipient], that is what they were saying. So never do that" (June 28, 2005). Our conversation continued:

> MS: You were saying that if someone gives up an organ, that will affect them when they die. Why will it affect them when they die?
>
> LT: Well, it is going to be at that person's one side and the other one [the donated organ is] not of that person, so the evil people's going to come around inside when you donate this thing to this person, but this person [the donor] died, so the other person [the recipient] is going to get affected from that evil.
>
> MS: So, you mean the person that received the organ would be affected by the fact that the person from whom they took the organ is dead.
>
> LT: Uh huh. But if both of them [are] alive, then it wouldn't hurt them.
>
> MS: So if they took an organ from a living person, like a kidney or liver, it would be OK?
>
> LT: Uh huh. It is OK, but one of them is going to pass on, and then it is going to affect the other person.
>
> MS: The living person?
>
> LT: Only if one of them dies.
>
> MS: How will it affect the living person if the organ they take is from a deceased person?
>
> LT: It is from evil, it is kind of like against our traditional [ways]. That is why the evil is going to come. But they have another doings like Evil Way prayer, they can have that and then they will be all right. (Todachinee, June 28, 2005)

Considering the topic from the reverse position, Florence Sandoval cautioned against donating organs because of the influence the process can have on the donor: "Like people that get kidney transplants and then if they die they take the kidney with them, and the person [who donated the kidney] will still be out here, and they say it starts affecting them after that. And the people don't live long after the other person goes with their, whatever part of their body goes, whatever they donate to the person that died, and then the other person, I don't know if they think about it or they go under stress. Somehow they just keel over" (F. Sandoval, June 25, 2005). This sentiment is directly linked to concerns voiced by Eloise Watchman, Ambrose Shepard, and numerous other consultants having to do with organs and the contamination associated with death.

Eloise Watchman pointed out: "Death is kind of a no-no if you are a Navajo. So I think that is why Navajo don't believe in getting or giving an organ to another person. In a way, I guess it is like you're carrying a dead person's body parts in you" (June 21, 2005). Ambrose Shepard offered further clarification when asked, "Do you have any idea whether Navajo people are willing to be organ donors?" He replied:

> AS: It depends on whether the person is a believer in the culture and Navajo tradition. Some who don't believe in it would probably say, "Go ahead. I will be doing it. Whatever happens, just donate my organ." And I wouldn't want to do that.
>
> MS: Do your traditional beliefs prohibit you from being a donor?
>
> AS: Yes, that is the belief that it's your organ and your body and you shouldn't hurt it and do anything with it, and if you die, that is it. Everything is dead. It becomes a bad thing. The ghosts and all that. That happens, you know. Giving the donation, it is not proper, it is not appropriate for the belief to do that. But I think it goes back to how your belief is, the person that it is being done to. If he wants to do it, it is his body and he wants to donate them [organs], some do, I know, some Navajo donate.
>
> MS: What I am trying to understand is why they would not want to donate—
>
> AS: It becomes a ghost . . . and a belief probably would be if the man is dead, his organ is a ghost, and if you put it in someone else's body again to make it live, then you have to do something to correct that. And there is another traditional ceremony in all of that, it is called the Ghost Way, the Ghost Way ceremony Hóchxǫ'jí they call it. That is the ceremony that can be done so that if somebody got an organ from another nationality, those kinds of ceremonies can be done to do away with the ghost part of it. The

[donor's] body and your body can make that correction so that
you can use that [organ]. (Shepard, June 3, 2005)

One elder whose name—for reasons that will become apparent—I felt
it would be inappropriate to include told me a story that poignantly reveals
the depth of her convictions against parting with any portion of her body
as well as the extent of her concerns over contact with death. These beliefs
prevented her from donating an organ even to a beloved sibling.

MS: Would you be willing to donate organs?
AE: No.
MS: Why not?
AE: Because that was mine, I was put here on earth with it and I don't
    want it, part of me, giving it to someone. Even though my sister
    was, that was some years ago that they asked me if I could give
    one of my kidneys to my sister. I said, "No." I didn't give it to her.
MS: You had a sister that needed a kidney?
AE: Uh huh, she was a dialysis patient. The one that died not too
    long ago.
MS: So, she needed a kidney transplant?
AE: From me, if it matches. I said, "No." She didn't know that, the
    doctor asked me privately. That was way back when she first
    started [being ill]. I said, "Don't ask me, no. She has daughters;
    she has several girls, she can get it from them, not from me."
MS: Well, that is an organ transplant. And your sister was willing to
    accept an organ?
AE: Yes. I think she needed it. But she never got it.
MS: There are lots of people on the waiting list. But that is different,
    accepting it from a living donor rather than from a dead person.
AE: From a dead [person]. But still, she died. She probably would
    have been dead with part of me over there [on the other side] and
    . . . it scares me. I know I am going to die someday, but I would
    think about it if she died with part of me over there. Part of me is
    dead now. Those are the things that would go through my mind.
MS: What would that mean? Part of you was dead inside your
    sister's body?

AE: I don't know, a lot of things. I think it would bother me.

MS: What might it do to you?

AE: It would probably kill me. I think worrying about it and thinking about it, and even though I didn't give her part of me, I dream
about her now and then.

MS: Now? You dream of her since she died?

AE: Since she died. With my mom, she comes to me in my dreams.
One time I got mad at her and I said, "Leave me alone. You be
happy where you went. Maybe someday I will catch up with you.
But you can kill me there. When I catch up with you, you can kill
me over there" (Anonymous Elder, June 8, 2005)

Fully cognizant of traditional views, Leeanne Johnson made it clear that
there is one case in which she would be willing to make an exception regarding
transplantation. As she explained, she would gladly donate an organ to an
infant or a young child should the need arise.

MS: I am trying to learn more about Navajo views on organ transplantation. Is this a topic that has ever come up in your family?

LJ: In my family among maybe one or two members it has, but not
as a whole family. Not like Mother and Dad talking to you about
it. It is between me, my two sisters or something. We would talk
about it and we would say that if it was a Navajo child, a Navajo
infant that needed a piece of my organ, I would give it because
that child will have a long life with it. We discuss things like that,
but if it was somebody that was an elderly person or something,
why would we give it to an elderly person? I usually tell them if it
was a child I would because it changed my whole life. Having a
child changed my whole life and [my] perspectives of children. And
that is where my heart is making sure that the children are safe,
the children are healthy. It is taking me to that side of the fence. And
my sisters and I talk about it. It is a hard subject to talk about.

MS: Why?

LJ: Because I think a lot of the people in my own family or my two
sisters that I talk to, we talk easily about it because we are more
informed. We read a lot and there are groups out there that get

together for the goodwill of people. They donate their organs because you can save somebody else's life. Just as you would [want] somebody saving your life. . . . But with my family outside of my two sisters, I think they are in question because they feel that your body was given to you just for one time, for one use of somebody's life. And that was the way the maker, the Creator, meant for it to be. And they don't see why a part of their organ would save another person. To them, their understanding is that it was only meant to be used in your lifetime, and that is the cycle of life. So you get caught in the middle of those two [viewpoints].

MS: So, you are referring now to what would be considered a Navajo traditional view?

LJ: Uh huh. I think that is what some of my family members believe. And if it were not meant to be a cycle of life, then nobody would have to face death, is what they are saying. But *the cycle of life is that people will come and people will leave, and our body parts were given to us just to live that life that we were given in the length of time we were given.* So, that is another perspective and that is pretty powerful too.

MS: That is really powerful.

LJ: And when you look at it and say well, I believe that if a child was born with some sort of serious health problem, I would give my organ to that child so that child could live, isn't that the same thing? And I don't know, I don't have answers for it, but these are two thoughts that we are challenged with. (Johnson, July 3, 2005)

What Johnson diplomatically left unsaid is that her risk would be minimal in donating an organ to an infant. If that child perished, little, if any, harm would come to her from its death, as the baby would have had little time to think, speak, acquire knowledge, or do evil (Davies 2001:7; Wyman, Hill, and Osanai 1942:17; see also Kunitz 1983:123).

One evening the Bekis family and I were discussing community goings-on. The conversation turned to an area family that was being criticized for having planned a relative's funeral before the individual's demise. Because of the power of Navajo language, this is seen as equivalent to calling the death into being. People were upset by such thoughtlessness on the part of the ill elder's children. Mae Ann Bekis brought the discussion around to organ donors when she said "and the organ donors are probably the same way, too." I asked, "Do you mean the fact that they agree to be organ donors is like planning their own deaths?"

> MAB: Uh huh. If you are going to plan to give your heart or something, if you knew ahead of time you could have some Blessing Way or something done so it would not affect you or whoever is gonna get your heart or your kidney, especially kidney.
> MS: Why especially kidney?
> MAB: Especially kidney because if I was to give my daughter a kidney, I would have a prayer and then I would have a Blessing Way done for me so it will help her. That is another way to do it.
> MS: But are you saying that someone signing an organ donor card is like calling your own death?
> MAB: Yes. . . . That is what I mean. Like if I was to give my daughter a kidney, I would do it but I would have to do something for myself before I go in and do that, have a prayer and have a Blessing Way done and say out loud that "I am giving my daughter my kidney so that she could live." And that prayer would be pertaining to that [transplant], not [to] anything else. That is the way I would give up my kidney. If I am alive, I don't think I would give my heart away (laughs). If I am alive, no way. Kidney is about all. (Bekis, July 15, 2004)

This exchange offered critical insight into the reality of Navajo organ donation. Based on Bekis's commentary, it appears that some Navajo are unwilling to sign up to be donors on their driver's licenses because they would not be comfortable having a card that essentially "calls their death" on a daily basis. When the need arises within the family, however, many are willing to donate as long as they are given the opportunity to verbally explain what they are doing to the Holy People.

In fact, many consultants maintained that Navajo-to-Navajo donations are best. Larry Todachinee told me that a Navajo donating an organ to a Navajo is "all right" and if the type of organ needed necessitates that it come from a deceased person, the recipient only needs to have a Hóchxǫ'jí performed to correct the situation (June 28, 2005). Leroy Nelson agreed that it is best for Navajo recipients to take organs from Navajo donors, adding "if they are Navajo, then the transplant, that donor should be Navajo to Navajo, that is what we are saying. Navajo to Navajo, that is healthy. And then knowing that—the lineage, too, bloodline of this Navajo—even better" (July 20, 2004).

Relatives who are acting on behalf of the ill patient also consider the best interests of the entire family. This is demonstrated in the next account, relayed by Tso Allen. Such consideration can result in a decision to have required blood or organs come from within the family. Allen advanced this line of thinking by making it known that in many areas it is not only acceptable but actually preferable for donated organs to come from within a family. She shared this story:

> TA: I know of one [case] where when the individual expressed to her siblings and her parents and relatives in a family meeting that the only way that she could get better, for her kidneys to get better, was to have a transplant and that she agreed to have [a] transplant. . . . So she said, "I am going to go ahead and get on the donor's list," and the family had a discussion and said, "No, we don't want you to sign up for donor's list. We think it will be better if one of the family members could [provide the organ]." So they asked . . . what had to be done to approach it that way, that if . . . one of your family members was willing to donate, could they be tested, and of course they can. . . . To the family that was much more acceptable . . . because it's relatives . . . and *they are from the same blood system.* (T. Allen, July 15, 2005)

Key to understanding this preference is the underlying belief that the fundamental mother-child relationship, which serves as a model for all other genealogical relationships, "is identified and defined in terms of life[,] particularly its source . . . and sustenance." Those with whom you share k'é are first and foremost to "sustain life" (Witherspoon 1975:15). Thomas Deschene, Jr., used this logic when he first defined the connection between mother and child as life-giving and sustaining and then agreed that it is now acceptable for donations to come from siblings or even clan relatives.

TD: I would understand if a mother wanted to give one of her kidneys or [part of her] liver to one of her children or another person to continue to live.

MS: Sisters and brothers can do it too?

TD: Yeah.

MS: So, is that OK?

TD: And that would be OK if it was within the same bloodline. (Deschene, June 15, 2005)

This makes cultural sense within the Navajo world, for, as noted by Gary Witherspoon, "[j]ust as the mother is [the] one who gives life to her children through birth, and sustains their life by providing them with loving care, assistance, protection, and sustenance, kinsmen are those who sustain each other's life by helping one another, protecting one another, and by giving or sharing food and other items of subsistence" (1975:22).

In regard to knowing the bloodline, Larry Todachinee concurred that it is now acceptable for donations to come from clan relatives and siblings:

LT: Today they say that you can donate [to] your same clan, like a brother and a sister, they can do that, that is what they say. In the same clan.

MS: So a brother and sister, members of the same clan, can donate kidneys?

LT: Uh huh. Same family, they can do [it], that is what they say.

MS: That is OK?

LT: That's OK. (Todachinee, June 28, 2005)

Without doubt, the donation of a body part to someone in the prime of her or his life is simultaneously the most generous and the most dangerous gift one Navajo can give to another, for that is when the recipient's death is most potent (see chapter 4, Death—Dangerous and Otherwise).

Concurring with the view that it is best for donations to come from clan relatives or siblings (T. Allen, July 15, 2005; Deschene, June 15, 2005; Nelson, July 20, 2004; Todachinee, June 28, 2005), Frank Young said it is optimal to have organs exchanged within the family, such as from a child to a parent (June 14, 2005). How do Navajo people negotiate these preferences within the context of incest taboos?

NAVIGATING INCEST TABOOS

> A long time ago, even sitting close to your brother (including a clan brother) was not permitted. Some people owned harden[ed] rawhide. These rawhides were placed between opposite sex siblings to prevent any physical contact. You were not permitted to talk to an opposite sex sibling too much. Only limited words were exchanged. One never dipped a cup of water in a bucket and handed it to her opposite sex sibling. That was never done. Now, we do not even take that into consideration. We were told that contact causes problems later on. . . . Bothering female relatives was prohibited since it causes mind loss or you "go crazy." It ruins your thinking. Your body parts would begin to function on their own, as if they have their own minds. It disfigures your body. That is what we were told. . . . If a male makes his female relative his wife, that causes arthritis. That is why he has to make the correction [Unraveling Ceremony] if the woman has arthritis. (Mace, July 23, 1998, translated by Wesley Thomas).

Although, as Anna Meigs and Kathleen Barlow have noted, the incest taboo (or any consciously articulated set of rules that forbid sexual relations between certain closely related individuals) "is to anthropology what Shakespeare is to English literature," widespread agreement exists within the discipline that analysis of the phenomenon is stalled (2002:38). Scholars writing on the subject tend to recite the litany of arguments proffered by Edward Westermarck (who argued that the taboo, rather than the behavior, is natural and that proximity in childhood leads to sexual aversion), Sigmund Freud (for whom the taboo is an instrument essential for becoming human), and Claude Levi-Strauss (for whom the taboo exists to promote the broad networks of relations and economic exchanges that constitute the social world), concluding only that no universally acceptable explanations exist for the fact that all societies ban incest (Meigs and Barlow 2002:38–39). Classical theories of incest do not strictly require that incest be pervasively and powerfully tempting; they require only that it be tempting enough to be detrimental to a group's chance for survival.

John Ladd has pointed out that the common Navajo chastisement "you ought not 'bother' your close relatives" is the incest prohibition that applies to siblings, parents, and children, as well as members of the same clan (1957:230). As will be shown, however, among the Navajo, sibling incest and clan incest are the most important types (Levy, Neutra, and Parker 1987:150). Moreover, brother-sister incest is the form of greatest concern. In their analyses of Navajo incest taboos, scholars have relied heavily on Levi-Strauss's theory that incest interferes with the proper functioning of social groups and that the incest taboo is intended to compel the reciprocal exchange of marriage partners (Levi-Strauss 1969[1949]—except that in the Navajo situation, it is marriageable men who are exchanged rather than women. The transhuman pastoral and agricultural economy developed by the Navajo after contact with the Spanish depended on an isolated, extended matrilineal family group, which needed to operate as an integrated and, to a great degree, self-sufficient unit.

Pursuant to Levi-Strauss's theory, Katherine Spencer has noted that the form of matrilocal residence creates inevitable tension points at which disruption of the family unit will occur: (1) when the sons reach marriageable age and are ready to seek wives, and (2) when family members need to adjust to sons-in-law who have just married into the family (1957:36). An often cited feature of Navajo ethnography known as the mother-in-law avoidance rule has relieved some of the strain arising from this situation. It dictates that a man must not look at the mother of his spouse, and she must not look at him (Franciscan Fathers 1910:447; Kluckhohn and Leighton 1974[1946]: 105). The usual reasons offered for this prohibition are that if either party looks at the other, they "will go blind" and their "body will be weak all over" (Ladd 1957:230). In fact, this rule also forbids any kind of contact, touching, speaking, as well as seeing—with seeing deemed less dangerous than more intimate forms of contact (Ladd 1957:230).

Differences in gender that are so important to the primary solidarity formed through marriage weaken secondary affinal solidarity and all genealogical solidarity. Brothers and sisters, mothers and sons, and fathers and daughters must not joke with each other about sexual matters (Witherspoon 1975:51). A brother is prohibited from using any type of sexually explicit language in front of his sister (Ladd 1957:230). Taken collectively, incest rules are best understood as a mechanism to encourage sisters to attract young men from other families and communities for the overall economic health and welfare of the isolated matrilineal family unit.

The greatest concern among Navajo centers on sibling incest (Levy, Neutra, and Parker 1987:150). Hence, as Juanita Mace noted in the first quotation in this section, rules are in place dictating against opposite sex siblings being found alone together or having any direct physical contact. A tendency to generalize the source of the danger is evident. For example, this prohibition covers a variety of acts of familiarity besides sexual intercourse. Siblings are taught to avoid face-to-face physical contact. If a brother asks for a shoe, a cup of water, or another item, a sister cannot hand it to him but must set it on the ground and allow him to pick it up himself (Ladd 1957:230; Witherspoon 1975:51). *Placing the requested cup of water or other item on the ground between them eliminates the risk of brother and sister having their fingers touch in the process of passing it;* thus, the space between them can be understood as a neutralizing force. Sexual continence rules apply to brothers and sister, fathers and daughter, mothers and sons, as well as those who have exchanged ceremonial knowledge for the purpose of healing.

Oral history dictates that a practitioner and his or her patient are considered related after the practitioner has performed healing acts over the ill person; marriage will not be allowed between a practitioner and one over whom he or she has sung. If a practitioner has cause to sing over his or her spouse, they must thereafter behave as close relatives between whom any sexual contact is strictly forbidden (Kluckhohn and Leighton 1974[1946]: 198; see also Spencer 1957:63).

On a related note, if spouses are patients in the same ceremony, a prepubescent boy is assigned the role of the "one-who-sits-between." To explain this custom, Sadie Billie of White Valley, Arizona, drew on her own experience from a time when her husband, Ray, was a patient in an Enemy Way.

> MS: One time you said, "If it was a married couple, there had to be a young boy to sit between them."
> SB: Yeah.
> MS: Could you tell me about that?
> SB: Well, it differs from area to area, and we had a totally different clan that played a role in between me and Ray. . . . His name is Orlando, he was in between us.

MS: And he was unmarried?

SB: Uh huh. He was just maybe eight years old then. (Sadie Billie, August 24, 1992)

When asked for clarification regarding the purpose of this third party, Harry Walters offered this explanation. As he noted, the one-who-sits-between is to serve as an intermediary between spouses to alleviate the need for them to have any direct communication throughout the ceremony:

HW: You're not to communicate. You don't talk to your wife during the ceremony, and so if you want to say something to your wife you tell it to him, then he relates that. Like that.

MS: He acts like as a go-between?

HW: Yeah, go-between.

MS: Is there ever a young girl that they choose as a go-between?

HW: No, it is [always] a boy. (August 10, 1993)

The existence of such a role in ceremonial contexts alerts us to the significance placed on the distinction between *direct versus indirect contact,* which mirrors the importance placed on direct versus indirect contact in sibling incest rules—best exemplified by Juanita Mace's story about passing a cup of water. The special importance of sibling incest is also marked physiologically; that is, by illness.

Unlike other forms of incest, sibling incest is directly associated with a form of "mental derangement" (Franciscan Fathers 1910:350), understood in the contemporary world as a particular seizure disorder colloquially referred to as Moth Madness. Ursula Knoki-Wilson explained that chiih dik'ǫǫzh (the antidote for contact with aadi'), which is constituted in part of a kinaaldá's saliva, is used on patients who are overcome with a "frenzy disorder" caused by "their guilt over [breach of an] incest taboo that only they know about" (August 10, 1992).

The most frequently mentioned cure for this illness is the Moth Way.[3] Mae Ann Bekis described treatment for a young man who became ill with Moth Madness after having sexual relations with his sister. He was the only one of the pair to develop symptoms. As Bekis explained, he had a moth lodged in his forehead that would periodically flap its wings, causing him to go mad:

MAB: You can't bother your sister, your brother. . . . There is this boy. He was going crazy, and then they told him he was married to his own sister. And that is why he is getting crazy. And so he went over to Alfred Leonard and said—he was the only one that used to do that [the Moth Way]—and they gave him money and Alfred went somewhere where he found some Egyptian flowers and brought some back. And he cut out two about half an inch [long] and a small one, put it in his [the patient's] nose, and then he was singing and all of a sudden he sneezed and both of that Egyptian root came back out and then a fly came out or a moth.

MS: A moth came out?

MAB: Uh huh, a moth came out. It was through the nose. He said that is what causes it [Moth Madness] if you are running with your sister. Your niece is different, but your sister is really a no-no. You can't hold hands with her or, you know. . . .

MS: Did he mean that this young man was having sexual relations with his sister?

MAB: He was married to his sister . . . and having intercourse with his sister. That is what he meant.

MS: So he actually went crazy?

MAB: Yes. They say it, from here, the hole is up into your head. . . . He said that. And then he said, "Then later years, it won't happen right [away], maybe right at that time. But in later years." I guess there is a moth up here (touching her forehead) and they flap its wings, and that is when he got crazy. . . .

MS: You are saying the moth was in his forehead?

MAB: In his forehead and flapping its wings when he goes crazy.

MS: So whenever he is going crazy, that is when the moth is flapping his wings?

MAB: Uh huh. It was lodged there and doing his sister, all that is what caused it.

MS: Did the sister also have a moth in her forehead? . . .

MAB: No. Just him. He is the only one—for doing his sister. . . . Just one came out, he said.

MS: Just one. Do you happen to know which side of his head?

MAB: He didn't say which side, but he said just one. And I heard
before that [that] it happens. They used to tell us, "Don't bother
your brother." It was really preached when we was little. And my
dad and my mom said, "Don't marry [a member of] the same
clan." So that was really a no-no. (Bekis, July 22, 2004)

In contrast, father-daughter incest is not thought to cause a specific disease; nor is it given as salient a position as sibling incest in Navajo oral
history (Levy, Neutra, and Parker 1987:15–16).[4] The concerns associated
with incest and blood transfusions are also associated with human organs,
which are harvested from living or deceased donors depending on the specific organ required.

Navajo consultants, as discussed, overwhelmingly rejected the notion of
contaminating themselves with organs from non-Navajo, preferring instead
to receive organs from members of their own families; that is, from child
to parent or from sibling to sibling. Puzzlingly, these are the individuals
who fall into incest dyads in which sexual contact, speaking to each other,
and even touching are prohibited. This seemingly imponderable contra-
diction is nuanced through a consideration of distinctions between Navajo
understandings of genealogical solidarity versus affinal exchange.

The fact that motherhood and kinship are synonymous in the Navajo
view is the lynchpin for understanding why Navajo people prefer to accept
organs from those to whom they are related genealogically. Because of
their life-sustaining qualities, organs are shared by kin who routinely seek
to support each other's lives by giving or sharing food and other items of
subsistence. Furthermore, incest prohibitions focus on controlling or preventing direct actions: sexual intercourse, touching, dancing, speaking, and
seeing. The exchange of organs constitutes passive and indirect contact
rather than personal action by donors or recipients. Siblings and children
do not hand over organs directly; instead, like the requested cup of water
described by Juanita Mace, contact is neutralized by intermediary hands and
space. In the case of organ transplantation, physicians and other hospital
staff serve as intermediaries, similar to the one-who-sits-between in ceremonial contexts. It is they who excise the needed organ from one family
member and surgically integrate it into another—thereby alleviating the

need for direct contact between individuals who fall into culturally determined incest dyads. Concern over incest is only one among many factors influencing Navajo willingness to accept organs. Another involves whether the organ is offered or must be requested.

OFFERED, NOT REQUESTED

> MS: If you were faced with a kidney transplant, what would you do?
>
> EB: I would say yes in my own relatives.
>
> MS: From a living donor, from one of your relatives, you would say yes. What if there was no relative who was willing to give you a kidney?
>
> EB: I would just let it go. And let the Lord take care of it.
>
> MS: Why would you not be willing to take a kidney from anyone else?
>
> EB: I did enough suffering, so why suffer any more. So that would be it.
>
> MS: Why would you be willing to suffer more if you could get a kidney from a relative?
>
> EB: That is if they say, "Here, take this, I will give you one of my kidneys." Then sure, I will take it and I will be glad.
>
> MS: But why wouldn't you be as glad to receive a kidney from a non-Navajo?
>
> EB: Just like I told you about the blood transfusion. Just like a different nationality. They have a kidney, and they put it in you, and sure you can live, but maybe later on you get sick again. (E. Begay, June 10, 2005)

Begay's point regarding asking versus accepting is vitally important. As previously noted, k'é is differentiated from affinity—the major form of nonkinship solidarity—by the fact that the former is distinguished by sharing or giving and the latter is marked by exchange; that is, direct reciprocal compensation. Other consultants, such as Frank C. Young, also reported that they would never ask a person for an organ; they could only accept a proffered organ (June 14, 2005).

Yet I learned of situations in which children of people in need of transplants did exactly that—offered their organs—only to have the.parent refuse.

Two of Tsosie Long, Sr.'s, daughters and a son offered to donate a kidney to him but he declined, saying, "no, if I take one of your kidneys I might shorten your life, and I never thought that way so I want you to be full in every way, to move on." He ultimately accepted a non-Navajo organ instead of taking one from within the family (Long, July 13, 2005). In fact, he, Chee Tapaha (June 2, 2005), Ray Francisco (July 7, 2005), and Frank Young are some of the consultants who noted that in their opinion it is acceptable for a Navajo to use organs donated by non-Navajo. Young did, however—like most others of his persuasion—qualify his position by saying that it is only acceptable if the donor signed paperwork agreeing to donate before his or her death (F. Young, June 14, 2005).

In explaining why she would only accept an organ from a Navajo donor, Eleanor Begay alluded back to her statement regarding the negative effects of non-Navajo blood on Navajo people; that is, they will "start having problems elsewhere in your body" (E, Begay, June 10, 2005). Thomas Deschene, Jr., echoed this belief when he cautioned that "crossing different nationalities" when matching donors and recipients "gets complicated" (June 15, 2005). Begay and Deschene are not alone in this sentiment. Larry Todachinee also maintained that organs used in transplantation must come from fellow Navajo, noting that donations from other "races" simply will "not work."

> LT: Traditional medicine people say if that person is an Anglo and he donated, like, a liver or a heart, and they put it in [a] Navajo, then it wouldn't work for them. They are different races. . . . Different kind of race. . . . So it wouldn't work for them.
>
> MS: So you are thinking that it [a transplanted organ] is only from a Navajo. That is what you are saying?
>
> LT: Uh huh, from Navajo to Navajo. . . . And Anglo and Anglo, I guess they can work too. . . . But if you get a heart from a Navajo and put it in a bilagáana, then it wouldn't work. If they get it from a bilagáana and they put it in a Navajo, then it wouldn't work. It has to be same race. . . . Like, it's like a colored [African American], then it wouldn't work for the Navajo. (Todachinee, June 28, 2005)

The fact that the belief in inherent differences between Navajo and non-Navajo is profound enough to require that Navajo refuse organs donated by non-Navajo speaks volumes about notions of collective identity. Biomedical administrators are committed to seeing Navajo patients as the same as other patients within their national system. They therefore stress similarities rather than differences. It does not behoove Navajo individuals interested in maintaining tribal sovereignty to dilute the bodily differences that mark Navajoness from non-Navajoness; rather, it is in their best interest to perpetuate these differences to promote Navajo collective identity.

Whether the organ comes from a Navajo or a non-Navajo, the next big consideration in transplantation decisions has to do with the role death plays in the negotiation. As consultant after consultant pointed out, even if the donor is alive at the time the transplant occurs, one or the other member in the transaction may die anytime thereafter, thus causing ill effects for the surviving partner. According to Johnson Dennison: "The tradition and the belief is that it is a transplant of a person, so if the person dies and you still have his organ within yourself, that could cause illness. That organ is not yours, it belongs to him. So when the illness occurs the ceremony is there, but it might be so severe that it [the ceremony] may or may not be successful. So, in other words, you will have part of the other person's body [inside your body]. . . . One illness may be taken care of, but it creates another illness. So another medicine man gets involved" (Dennison, June 22, 2005).

Ursula Knoki-Wilson explained her thoughts about organ donation and transplantation: "If you knew a family member was donating an organ, it would probably be more acceptable than if it was unknown. I think some of the traditionals would think it was taboo to get cadaver organs in particular." She continued:

> UKW: Because there is a concept which is hard to translate, it is sort of because a cadaver is already in a state of imbalance. It has already passed on, so it is in a state of imbalance. One translation could be a state of chaos. . . . And so if you put that state of chaos into, try to put it into another state here (touching her chest), you don't know what kind of chemistry it is going to create. It is—
>
> MS: So, taking an organ from a cadaver—which is in a state of chaos—is adding a piece of chaos into the living body?

UKW: Yes, and it could go either way. It could add life to the person *but at a cost,* so to speak. And it could end a person's life, too. It could go either way. So that is what they were afraid of. (Knoki-Wilson, July 5, 2005)

Rather than chaos theory, Amelda Sandoval Shay offered what she considers a religious explanation for not wanting someone else's body parts inside her. Her reasoning hinges on the belief that donors retain claims to their body parts.

MS: What do you think that body part will do to you?

ASS: It will kill me, even though maybe I was dead already.

MS: Do you think there is some kind of ceremony that could be done to make it OK to have that body part inside you?

ASS: I don't think so. I would never accept that; that is just me thinking. I don't know about the other people, but I would never.

MS: This is what we are trying to find out about. Because there are lots of people who are accepting these organs, and they are dealing with just what you are talking about. They have to figure out, how can it work? And if they can make it work. And there are lots more who are not accepting organs.

ASS: Like, if this person has given you a heart or a liver or something, they give [it to] you when they are dead without their permission because they are dead. And then from the grave they might think that you belong to them because part of theirs is in you. So who knows, they might be in hell and you wanted to go to heaven. And you might end up in hell, in a burning hell. They might be down there and you might end up there with them. That is the way I think. And the Catholic way and the religious way, that is how I feel. So to me if I wasn't allowed to go to heaven, I would rather end up in purgatory than go down [to hell]. . . .

MS: What does the Catholic Church say about organ transplants?

ASS: I don't know. I never asked. (Shay, June 6, 2005)

While discussing his transplant experience, Ray Francisco mentioned that his kidney came from a deceased individual. Unlike Shay, this fact does not bother Francisco. He has his own theory about why the matter need not concern him:

> RF: This individual gave away their parts and I take the position that they have given that away willingly, therefore there is no connection that we have to each other. They have just separated themselves from that particular part. And so now I have it and it doesn't bother me. I don't think about it and it hasn't bothered me yet. No diagnostician has made reference to it, so if the diagnostician doesn't make it known and I don't feel any side effects, then I don't worry about that. Maybe there will be a time down the road that the diagnostician or some illness, side effect, may involve that, may be traced to that, at which time maybe it would be appropriate for me to have traditional ceremonies, but at this point in time I am happy with everything and don't worry about it. I don't let that bother me and I just live, and I just enjoy life every day. Just keep praying. (Francisco, June 7, 2005)

The belief that the deceased will return to claim his or her missing body parts is a long-standing tradition among the Navajo. While the notion originally pertained to parts disassociated through grave robbing, witchcraft, or both (Wyman, Hill, and Osanai 1942:23), it has been transferred to surgically removed body parts and remains a viable idea in the minds of at least some Navajo. Billie Davis told me that if it were medically called for, he "would be glad to have" an organ transplant "as long as it's a good fit." He added, "It won't bother me, not even if it comes from a dead person." In regard to donating an organ he stated, "I would give an organ like my heart or liver or kidney, but if I catch up with that person after death I would ask for it back" (laughs) (Davis, June 11, 2005).

PERSPECTIVES ON INTERVENTIONS

Any time that there has been [an] invasion of the body, then you certainly have to put that to rights. So the ceremonies that are conducted for that will take place following. There are acute interventions, minor interventions, and the major ceremonies. And those things are done according to a person's wealth and when it is convenient, but the immediate intervention is usually prayers and herbs that are provided afterward. (B. Allen, June 10, 2005)

When asked about organ donation and transplantation, Leroy Nelson was adamant that they violate traditional tenets regarding prohibitions against contact with death. He explained: "Like organ donation and organ transplant . . . it shouldn't be done. It shouldn't be done. I guess one way to explain it would be, we can't crisscross the dead. . . . A live body, human body, it is all right to be among. But we as Navajos have a taboo in place to where we can't really crisscross the dead—meaning we can't touch a dead body. Having to get somebody's donated organ to be transplanted into us, it shouldn't be so" (Nelson, July 20, 2004).

Understanding that the world is constantly changing and that, for better or worse, such biomedical technologies have become part of Navajo contemporary reality, Nelson offered insight into the sequence of traditional practices and ceremonies needed before and after a transplant:

> LN: I guess between donating body parts, donating or getting a donation, the bottom line is it shouldn't be so. You say no. It is not possible. It shouldn't be because it is not our way of life. But *today in society we are choosing between life and death.* We are saying give this a chance. Give this chance to this person to live. So that is how they are getting this donation. . . . Technology is going to help someone, is going to help me, give me a body part, and then what I would do is go to a diagnostician. And then a diagnostician would give me a prescription and then maybe a ceremony, a healing ceremony. One way would be a Blackening Way. And then thereafter would be Protection Way. Then after would be a renewal, a Blessing Way. It is like that Blackening Way would wash off all the evil. Nothing would exist. The Protection Way would be reidentifying oneself and then being in a mood to where you need to think this way. You need to act this way. You need to be careful of this. You need to understand this is

the way you need to live. So Blessing Way is like, there is a road here to [allow you to] look at that rainbow, look at that sun, smell the flowers, look at the trees, look at the mountains, look at this now. It is like you are being reintroduced to nature. So that is the standard that we need to observe. We need to understand. It is healthy. I say it is healthy because we choose between life and death. We are choosing life. (Nelson, July 20, 2004)

For Tsosie Long, Sr., accepting a transplant was not his first choice. When initially diagnosed with diabetes, he disregarded the doctor's warnings; when told that he had kidney failure, he scoffed at the notion of a transplant because of his traditional beliefs about the problems caused by having a deceased person's body part inside you. Finally, after four long years on dialysis, he surrendered to the inevitability of a transplant. As documented in his narrative, he used a combination of traditional and Native American Church rituals to cope with diabetes, and eventually he did have a successful kidney transplant.

> TL: At the time that I was working, sometimes I felt real—my body had some ailments here and there, so there was times that I went to a clinic and . . . I was diagnosed to have diabetes, but I didn't accept that. So as time went on finally it started getting to me. And at a time when I worked in Globe, Arizona, at an acid plant, that is where it really got to me. So I had to get away from that, and then I was told that one of my kidneys was malfunctioning. So through clinic they told me I had to stay home—not work. Then I got on disability and started to go to a dialysis clinic for four years. Then I was told that I need a transplant but I said, "No, I don't need it."
> MS [to HA]: Can you ask him why he was not willing to get the transplant? . . .
> TL: At the time that I refused to have a transplant, I was thinking about our tradition that that can't be done. If, let's say with this kidney, if it is from another [person] or from a dead person, it was like a "no-no." Because if it has been transplanted from another person and you live with it, it is going to cause a lot of problems

or it is going to affect you psychologically in a lot of ways, so I refused. But I went on with the dialysis, so that kept on until I got tired of it. [It went on for] four years and I was restricted on a lot of food that I can't eat certain types of, and in other words I had to change my life. So I got tired of it. Traveling back and forth every other day, and I lost a lot of weight and all these things, so finally one day I said I want to quit that dialysis, but by that time one of my kidneys was to where it wasn't functioning. . . . So I made up my mind, "I am going to go with a transplant." Then I asked one of my relatives to have another NAC meeting, so within that they prayed, even though it was really difficult to put prayers in a way where we need a kidney from someone. I am sure bluntly you say, *"We need somebody to die in order to get the kidney."* It was a real difficult way to pray about it, but they went through that. Then within a couple of weeks in the policeman came and told me that I had to report to the hospital, that there is a kidney. . . . That person took me all the way to Phoenix, and that is where I underwent surgery. And they replaced that kidney and during the operation, during that time the relatives over here had another NAC prayer service to have me go through the operation in a way it will work for me. So within two days I woke up and then I stayed [in the hospital], almost every day they check and the physicians, the surgeons, they were surprised. I guess they had other operations like that, but a lot of times the kidney was rejected or can't work. But for me they even told me that the kidney and the vessel in every way was all matched up, and they all healed together well. So they were really surprised. Then they asked me, "Why is it like that?" And that is how I went through that kidney transplant. So as time or the days go by, my whole body started to come back to normal in eating and drinking water and everything. I started normalizing again. (Long, July 13, 2005, translated by Hanson Ashley)

In this narrative the surgeons' amazement at Long's quick and uncomplicated recovery as well as the success of the transplantation is attributed to the Native American Church meetings held both before and while he was undergoing surgery. This subtly legitimizes NAC therapeutic power over that of biomedicine.

Most surprising to me was Long's discussion of the Native American Church meeting called for the sole purpose of requesting a kidney. In addition to healing, scholars have documented peyote meetings arranged for a wide spectrum of events, including the celebration of marriages and the protection of schoolchildren or soldiers journeying to or from home (Aberle 1982b:196), as well as the celebration of birthdays and anniversaries (Schwarz field notes 1993, 2005). Other consultants have mentioned holding meetings for relatives in the hospital, especially while they are undergoing surgery (Knoki-Wilson, July 5, 2005; Shepard, June 3, 2005). I know of no previous account, however, of a Navajo NAC meeting requested for this specific purpose.

Thomas Deschene, Jr., provided testimony on a Native American Church meeting held for a heart transplant recipient, who chose not to simultaneously seek ritual healing from any other source.

> TD: There was this man down in Cameron, young man thirty-six years old, had a heart attack. He was working in Phoenix as a crane operator, those cranes on skyscrapers. And that guy used to be in rodeos and do calf roping. And he had a heart attack. And they told him, "You need a heart transplant," and he kind of got lucky. There was this Mexican guy about eighteen years old, got in a car accident and died, he was a donor and they put it [his heart] into that man who had the heart attack. And my brother was asked to do the peyote ceremony up there at the heart recipient's home]. And that young man didn't have any hair, but [after] he received that heart he started growing a lot of hair; it got thick and started curling. He had to take a lot of medicine, maybe within twenty-four hours he would take sixty pills, and they put him on a strict diet and he had to have this liquid that looked like oil. And they said, "It lasts two weeks and it costs six hundred dollars and he has to have that for life." All the family came in at the beginning of the ceremony, all his brothers and sisters. They said, "He can't take peyote, he is strictly under doctor's orders." My brother

told him, "You wanted the ceremony, so it is up to you. When we start the ceremony, you can eat a lot of medicine and see what happens." So when we started the ceremony, he started eating a lot of peyote. At midnight he . . . asked me to roll a smoke for him, that mountain tobacco. So I did all the rolling and everything for him. He was all right toward morning. And we got a call a week or two later that they had cut back on all the pills, that he was only taking about six or seven pills [a day]. And they got rid of that bottle, too, that they said he needed for life. And he went back to work as a crane operator and started roping again. And he wanted another ceremony and those ceremonies you call appreciation ceremonies. He wanted that, but his family didn't want to. He tried to have it done, to have another member of the family do that ceremony for him again, but they never got to it. So everything was all right with him; he was in good health. For a final checkup he went to Tucson. He signed his name, sat down on a chair to take a little nap, and never woke up. He passed on. (Deschene, June 15, 2005)

Deschene carefully explicated that in such a case a NAC road man "makes an offering right here to the fireplace. Sometimes it releases that person so that they can go on to live" (June 15, 2005). His brother had done that for the young man who had received the heart transplant from the young automobile accident victim; presumably, his brother's actions had successfully released the heart recipient from the accident victim's grasp. Deschene further emphasized, "He wanted a peyote ceremony again, but nobody wanted to help him. And I guess he got kind of fed up—gave up" (June 15, 2005).

Ambrose Shepard is a NAC road man who, as a proponent of religious relativism, also partakes of traditional Navajo religious ceremonies and Christian prayer. He explained that in regard to the possible interventions done to correct problems that arise as a result of organ transplants, the *Hoozhónee*, or "Beauty Way" (not to be confused with the Blessing Way), is appropriate before surgery, if time allows; otherwise, an Enemy Way can be done afterward. He noted:

AS: Then you have a sing . . . performed to make those corrections . . .
with the organ transplant. That is being done now. I know of some
people that have organ transplants in order to survive and continue
for at least several more years of life.

MS: What ceremony do they use to make those corrections?

AS: Well, if it is . . . a sudden thing you don't know about it until it
is done, and that way it is different. Then they do it at the end by
performing the Enemy Way ceremonies to make those corrections,
but before it is done, if you know about it, if you are going to go
in the hospital and get an organ transplant, then you have that ceremony done before you go in and make the Beauty Way and make
sure things come out right for you. And then at the end, if it starts
bothering you, then it is the Enemy Way ceremony [that] is going
to make those corrections. (Shepard, June 3, 2005)

Donald Denetdeal refined this analysis by pointing out that Enemy Way
is needed to correct for an organ received from a foreigner and Hóchxǫ'jí
is needed if one has received an organ from another Navajo.

DD: From the Navajo point of view, that would affect the recipient
and to correct that *Ndáá'* [Enemy Way] [is performed] if it is a foreigner's organ. Ndáá' would be a way to correct that. But if it is
from another Navajo, then Hóchxǫ'jí [Evil Way] would be the ceremony to correct that. So that accepting this physical part from
another person will be in harmony with the receiving physical body.
Now the key for the ceremony is [that] these connections would
be in harmony, that they would be compatible. . . .

MS: And what about after the surgery?

DD: After the surgery, yes, ceremonies could be performed if they
wanted to. And from a Navajo point of view they would have any
number of ceremonies, one would be Ndáá', another one might
be Hóchxǫ'jí. . . .

MS: So, you mean Enemy Way or Hóchxǫ'jí depending on who the
donor was.

DD: Right, exactly, a foreign donor would have an Ndáá', or Enemy
Way, and the Hóchxǫ'jí would be [if] the organ, the donor would

be another Navajo. And it doesn't matter which donor it may be to have Life Way or Flint Way, that would be the aftermath. (Denetdeal, July 11, 2004)

Sheila Goldtooth was very explicit in her explanation as to which ceremony would be needed after an organ transplant and why it would be needed. She first indicated that an Enemy Way would be needed as a result of contamination by a non-Navajo.

> SG: You were cut by a non-Navajo and they actually worked on your body and they have gone inside, and that is why they feel that you need to have the Enemy Way ceremony.
> MS: So, it goes back to the contact with non-Navajo?
> SG: Uh huh.
> MS: So, is it an issue of contagion?
> SG: Yeah. (Goldtooth, July 18, 2005)

When I pointed out that certain types of organs can be obtained from living donors, Goldtooth noted that problems will arise should the donor subsequently die while the recipient remains dependent on his or her organ. Fortunately, ceremonial interventions will offset the ill effects in such cases. She pointed out: "Probably just the Evil Way. That is probably the only one and also the Enemy Way if the person wasn't a Navajo" (Goldtooth, July 18, 2005).

This ceremonial prescription was duplicated by many consultants. Chee Tapaha, who is using CAPD while awaiting a kidney transplant, said he will be happy to accept a kidney from any available source. He reported that if he receives a kidney from a living Navajo he will need no ceremony. He will, however, have the Hóchxǫ'jí if it comes from a deceased Navajo and an Enemy Way if it comes from a deceased non-Navajo (Tapaha, June 2, 2005). For Navajo people operating within the traditional ceremonial system or the Native American Church, decisions are made about preferences for organ donations within the context of the choice between contamination by death and contamination by outsiders; this information is also germane to diagnosticians when they are selecting appropriate interventions such as the Enemy Way for ailing Navajo.

ENEMY WAY

Way from the beginning, for whatever *Naayéé' Neezghání* [Monster Slayer] did down below, the name naayéé' is attached. We use it in Blessing Way and for some of the prayers too. He [Naayéé' Neezghání] brought it back with him. He did a lot of killing; Naayéé' Neezghání did everything. And after he did the killing, Naayéé' Neezghání got affected by *'ana'ị* [enemy]. When he killed all the 'ana'í, that is how he got affected. The *Tsé Naagháii* [Rolling Rock] and the *Tsé Nináhálééh* [Monster Rock Bird] and *Tsédahódziiłtáłii* [the Monster That Kicked People off the Cliff] and *Jádí Naakits'áadah Naajeehi* [Twelve Running Antelopes] and *Yé'iitsoh Dá'í Naagháii* [One Walking Giant] and *Bináá'yee Aghánii* [Eyes That Kill] and *Shash Na'ałkaahí* [Tracking Bear]. He was living in the midst of all these. He killed all these monsters, so that was when he became affected. He got crippled; he was crawling around. So that was why they decided to have an Enemy Way for him. They kept having Enemy Way for him, but he did not improve. They performed Enemy Way for him three times and he was still the same, crippled. The *Tsé'édọ'iitsoh* [Big Rock Fly] kept flying around. He was hunting for the cause of Naayéé' Neezghání's illness, and when he came upon it he said, "We have to make a shade house. That is the only way he is going to get well. A lady has to sit under the shade house and they will dress her. Naayéé' Neezghání needs to shoot the enemy that is bothering him. And the lady, when she is all dressed, *she is going to walk behind him to erase his footprints*. After they do this, he will get well and it will not bother him again." That is what Tsé'édọ'iitọ soh said. They did that over there [in the past], so we do the same thing today for our people. (N. Nez, July 10, 2000, translated by Mae Ann Bekis)

The Anaa' jí ndáá', or Enemy Way, often referred to locally as the Squaw or Warrior Dance, is a complex event frequently performed in the summer and autumn months to cure Navajo of contamination acquired through contact with non-Navajo. As illustrated by multiple Navajo consultants throughout this text, illness requiring this intervention may result from a variety of circumstances, including combat situations (B. Allen, June 10, 2005; Shepard, June 3, 2005), automobile accidents (Goldtooth, July 18, 2005; Nelson, July 20, 2004), intermarriage (Deschene, June 15, 2005; Goldtooth, July 18, 2005), contact with human skeletal materials in burials or archaeological ruins (B. Allen, June 10, 2005; Nelson, July 20, 2004), *or surgery*.

Patients are treated within the privacy of the sanctified hooghan. Although I was never invited to witness the healing that takes place inside the hooghan, Jonah Nez offered a wealth of insight into how being cut by a surgeon is linked to being injured in battle.

> JN: If the person starts having complications [from surgery], that is what the Squaw Dance is there for. . . . When a doctor cuts your meat open with the instrument, it is just like getting shot, they say. Like using a weapon. That shoots you. That is how come your body kinda gets like you're getting shot. That's where that Warrior Dance comes in, the Squaw Dance. . . . To purify. Let's say they do get shot by a rifle. And that shell might stay in your body, but that's got to be removed somehow. Even if you remove it. And they lay in some stuff, and at that Warrior Ceremonial they use herbs there too. Almost like the kind they got with diabetes, the white chicory and the piñon and the pine and the spruces. And they mix it and make it into a tea. With all that, you are gonna purify, with that herbs. Clean the patient out. . . . After they get done doing it, they put ash over it. Like maybe the second night of that War Dance they put ash over it. Then whatever the bad stuff that comes out of the patient, they put it way out there. They use that ash again, so that it is not going to come back.
>
> MS: And this is to purify the patient?
>
> JN: Yeah. For a person who has had surgery, who is having some problems, some complications with their surgery. (J. Nez, June 12, 2005)

According to some Navajo consultants, the rising need for Enemy Way as a result of complications after surgery has contributed to an undue increase in the overall number of ceremonies performed per year. Ronald Sandoval noted: "That is why there is a lot of Enemy Way going on every weekend. A lot of people have a lot of surgery and that is why these Navajo have [a] lot of Ndáá' every weekend and some of them are sick, are really sick" (June 25, 2005). Indeed, without mentioning any specific cause, Billie Davis demonstrated marked concern over what he considers an excessive number of these ceremonies being performed.

> BD: When I was growing up, there weren't very many Squaw Dances, only a few a year in the summer. But nowadays there is always a lot. Seems like every week or every other week. So, they cut off the cedar branches. And it shouldn't be done. . . . In Navajo traditional way, it is always four. It is four days, or anything that has to do with a traditional ceremony is always four. And that shouldn't be cut more than four branches a summer. But it seems like there is a lot. Not just in one area but across the Navajo reservation. That is all you hear about is a Squaw Dance here and then going on over there and over here. So there is a lot more than four that's being cut in one summer. (B. Davis, June 11, 2005)

Based on an event in Navajo oral history involving an illness the culture hero Monster Slayer incurred while killing the child-eating monsters who threatened the survival of the Navajo ancestors (Fishler 1953:38–39; Haile 1938:77–79; Witherspoon 1987:15), the Anaa' jí ndáá' involves two groups that play critical roles as warring factions in a series of requisite events over a period of nine days (Franciscan Fathers 1910; Haile 1946). Through this process, the illness-causing enemy is slain.

The first group centers on one or more patients. Navajo people are bound by duty to assist clan relatives hosting Enemy Way ceremonies with food preparation or prestations of food products, livestock, and other necessities (Jacobson 1964; Lamphere 1977). The second group centers on the recipient of a rattle stick—a vital element of the ceremonial that is transported to the recipient's place of residence and to the main patient's camp. Group interactions include travel to and from these and other camps, feasts, gift exchanges, and social dances at multiple locations; they also feature ceremonial rites conducted over the patients within a sanctified hooghan, including blackening just before the enemy is slain.[5]

In preparation for this vital component of Anaa' jí ndáá', a "scalp," or representative part of the diagnostically determined offending enemy, must be secured for its ritual slaying. Slaying of a scalp is premised on the tenet that body parts and substances from any member of an ethnic group will quell the effect of the death of another member of that group. What is done to the body parts and substances from one member of an ethnic group has the power to influence all other members of the group. Negotiation of this aspect of the principle of synecdoche can be difficult, especially when Navajo people are coping with heartfelt gratitude and a sense of dependency.

In fact, as demonstrated by the next examples, not all Navajo people who have undergone surgery or transplants agree to have Ndáá'. Although his relatives urged him to have a Flint Way as well as an Enemy Way, Tsosie Long, Sr., chose not to undergo the latter after his kidney transplant. As he explained with the help of his nephew Hanson Ashley:

> TL: Enemy Way, I had a conflict with that. . . . Within that ceremony there is a part toward the last day. . . . We believe we shoot at it [the scalp], meaning it is killed. . . . From thereon you are OK; you are free from that. . . . In other words, they kill that spirit, so to speak. . . . But what if I go through that believing that this Mexican boy, the spirit of the Mexican boy, if they shoot at that it might affect my kidney? So that is where I had a conflict. It might do something, but right now it is helping me. It helps me to live, that boy. So in other words, it is the best way for me that I just pray for him.
>
> MS [to HA]: But I thought that you [Navajo people] had to have that Enemy Way because you were cut by the bilagáana doctor.
>
> HA: This is different, but the way he thinks about it is [it] has to be the boy's spirit.
>
> MS: The ethnicity of the donor? Oh, I thought it was the surgeon.
>
> HA: If it is the surgeon, then he can go ahead with it, but the relatives might say it has to be the Mexican skull.
>
> MS: Oh, I haven't heard that before.
>
> HA: So, there is two different viewpoints right now. The relatives keep saying it has to be the Mexican [skull]. That is the one. But he

says, "No. That is what helps me, it helps me to live." But with the surgeon, yes, that is another one, *Bee'sheejí*, the flint metal, the Flint Way. He can go through that ceremony. . . . So the relatives were telling him to go through the Flint Way. (Long, July 13, 2005, translated by Hanson Ashley)

This exchange opened my eyes to alternative Navajo perspectives on notions of contamination. According to Tsosie Long's relatives, he needed an Enemy Way to rectify the negative influences of having the organ of a Mexican donor within his body *and* he needed a Flint Way to offset the effect of having been cut by an allopathic surgeon with metal tools. While Long was more than happy to undergo a Flint Way to rectify problems associated with having been cut by the foreign surgeon's metal instruments, he refused the Enemy Way encouraged by his relatives. He did so because according to the beliefs of Long's family, the Enemy Way would be directed against the organ donor and his ethnicity rather than the surgeon and his metal tools. Understandably, from Long's perspective, that would be potentially very counterproductive because he envisioned the raid on the scalp as possibly harming the donated kidney, upon which he is now dependent.

Long is not alone in opposing having an Enemy Way; Amelda Sandoval Shay was also opposed to having one performed over her. Shay's rationale for not having the ceremony was connected to the principle of synecdoche, despite the fact that she has never had an organ transplant. Instead, a disagreement arose between her and her parents over whether she would have an Enemy Way ceremony performed on herself after being hospitalized for preclampsia that resulted in a stillbirth. In their view, she needed the ceremony because of this treatment as well as having previously had both an appendectomy and a cholecystectomy. She explained:

> ASS: After I was healed, my mom mentioned to my dad that I should have an Enemy Way ceremony, and I look at my mom and says, "No." She says, "Why not? You have been cut over there at the hospital, and this happened before and it hasn't been taken care of." Because my appendix was taken out before I was married and then my gallbladder and then the baby that I lost. I think they

kind of cut me here and there down below. So, "But these are the three things that's been done to you and I think you should have it [the ceremony]." I told my mom, "These doctors helped me to live, so why should we have the Enemy Way done on me?" And I told my mom, "I don't want to do that to my doctor that took care of me. He has family, they have families, no." So my dad told my mom, "Forget it. She won't do it. I know she won't do it."

MS: But what would the ceremony do to the doctors?

AS: Shoot, kill. That is what they do. (Shay, June 15, 2005)

Shay is not alone in having this sentiment—that not all doctors are enemies who should be shot and killed. Frank C. Young made a similar point while noting an enigma involving the Navajo need for Enemy Way: "Today we do not exist with one another the way we did back then [during the time of war with the Ute and the U.S. military]. The same procedure has to be practiced, but . . . it is not a battle-type thing. Still, today most physicians are Europeans or a different nationality that back then were considered enemies so—well, today we don't regard each other that way, and it is probably unnecessary to regard each other that way. But the procedure that was developed is still applied" (F. Young, June 14, 2005, translated by Nora Young). In Frank Young's view, not all bilagáana should necessarily be treated as enemies in the modern world, yet they must be treated as such if they are the 'ana'į, or source of harm, for a healing ceremony such as Enemy Way to be effective. Moreover, Navajo people seem unable to survive without the curing power available only through Enemy Way.

Immediately after a family decides to hold an Enemy Way for one of its members, an agent of the patient's family is sent to procure the scalp. Ideally, an elderly man in the immediate family who has seen bloodshed in combat is available to perform this task. Otherwise, a man from outside the family or clan must be paid to secure it. Formerly, only an actual scalp would do; however, ever since Navajo soldiers returned from World Wars I and II, it has been acceptable to substitute any part of a dead enemy, such as a bit of bone, a lock of hair, or a piece of cloth taken from clothing worn by a member of the appropriate ethnic group (Haile 1938:63).

It was apparent that Julia Mathis felt awkward trying to explain this aspect of the ceremony:

JM: For you to have a Squaw Dance and for it to be effective whatever it is that is ailing you, you have to be specific. . . . See, there are means for each one of them. . . . You can have the Enemy Way ceremony even if it is just surgery because sometimes people have nightmares of the Oriental [Asian] or bilagáana or something that is other than Navajo.

MS: Are the dreams about the doctors?

JM: Uh huh. It can be an Oriental [Asian] doctor, but that covers everything. Anaa' jí ndáá'. It just covers everything. But if it is a Chinese doctor, when they perform the ceremony they would say "Bináá'ádaałts'ózí Dine'é," meaning slant eyes. . . . That is how they would refer to him. Because they say that when a patient is being treated, things of these different races [are needed to serve as a scalp]. It might be one strand of hair, it might be a piece of skull, something specifically from that race or that ethnic community.

MS: So this is something that you are aware of and folks in your community have done after surgery?

JM: Not necessarily, it doesn't have to happen after surgery. It can if a person starts having problems, like medical problems or maybe even their sleep pattern changing—meaning that they are having a lot of nightmares. . . . Just something that has to do with their surgery or their mind. Then they have that Enemy Way ceremony.

MS: So, if complications arise, then they have the Enemy Way?

JM: Right. (Mathis, June 11, 2005)

Requisite scalps are obtained by various means. As Berard Haile noted more than sixty years ago, "Old men in the tribe have been known to have kept trophies of this kind buried in tin cans for just such scalping expeditions. Others remember sites of combat or accident where an enemy has fallen. Still others have visited museums and curio stores to clip a lock of hair, a corner of an enemy's coat or dress from exhibits there. Any of these methods describe 'going on the warpath and bringing home the scalp'" (Haile 1946:8–9). Almost a decade later David McAllester wrote, "When a white man's ghost is bothering a Navaho in the Rimrock area, the trophy is provided by the bones of a certain sheepherder who was murdered by a Mexican and received a shallow burial in an unprotected place some years ago" (1954:8). Mae Ann Bekis shared a similar story:

> MAB: Well, they said there is a bilagáana that way back, that used to be a mail carrier, with a wagon. . . . And he is buried down here somewhere (pointing west with her chin), and they are using him.
>
> MS: So, they are digging up that grave?
>
> MAB: Uh huh. . . . But not a living person. . . . They can't, it is against their religion to pick from a living person because it won't work or something. . . . It has to be a bone, or they use, like [with] Japanese, some of their clothing, or, they pay somebody to pick something from the enemy or something like that. That is how they use it. (Bekis, July 28, 1993)

Anticipating future need, Navajo servicemen collect body parts or other personal items from fallen enemies in combat situations. Men on the reservation are known to have Japanese, German, Korean, and Vietnamese scalps in their possession (Harrison, August 18, 1992; J. Nez, July 3, 1992). Given the number of Navajo men and women in military service, presumably some now have scalps from several other nationalities, including Iraqi. When the need arises, a representative of the patient's family will approach such an individual to purchase an appropriate piece of the requisite enemy.

Puzzlingly to date, a second major component of the Enemy Way—the blackening of the male patient's wife—has been given no more than brief mention in the academic literature; in fact, the total coverage consists of two passages by Berard Haile (1938:73; 1946:34) and a passing mention by David McAllester (1954:12). Haile has noted that an underlying purpose of the rite is to restore the earth's productivity. Within the confines of this interpretation, each element used in the blackening of the male patient's wife—which will be described in detail momentarily—including the sheep fat, yard goods, and blankets with which the woman is covered, represents vegetation (Haile 1938:73, 1946:34). As noted by Nettie Nez in this section's first quotation, as well as by Harry Walters when explaining why Monster Slayer had multiple ceremonies before he fully recovered from slaying the monsters (August 10, 1993), the rite clearly serves other purposes. Indeed, consultants revealed that for male patients of Enemy Way, *the success of the entire ceremony is contingent upon a woman serving as his wife being blackened on the final morning* of the ceremony.

Knowing my wish to witness this portion of an Enemy Way ceremony, Mae Ann Bekis invited me to accompany her to a blackening in July 2000. It was being performed for L.D., a prominent singer in the area, as well as his son, whose wife would be blackened. When we arrived at the site, the family was still throwing candy to those assembled outside the hooghan, as is customarily done at this point in the ceremony. After this distribution, people from the family came out to give special gifts to members of the rattle-stick receiver's family. We went into the cooking shade where I helped Bekis make cornmeal mush in an old pottery bowl. She carefully stirred the mixture as I gradually added pinches of meal to the liquid. She scooped it out into a basket and put it inside the house to cool. We helped make fry bread until Bekis was called inside the house to assist with preparation of the blankets and materials with which the wife would be draped. I continued "helping," but it quickly became clear that I was just in the way, so I excused myself.

At about 11:15, a man in the hooghan signaled that it was time to blacken the patients inside the hooghan and the wife outside. Two of L.D.'s daughters emerged from the house with a huge bundle. The young patient's wife, covered in a shawl, met us outside the cooking shade. Bekis and other female relatives of the patient's were in the lead, carrying the bundle of materials to the shade.

Once there, the wife sat down on a blanket with her legs straight out in front of her. Her mother and an aunt arranged blankets to conceal her, front and back. Another blanket was carefully placed on the ground behind her with the bundle of materials on it. Directly across from her, the young rattle-stick carrier sat facing west. Her legs were also straight out in front of her, and she was clutching a clump of vegetation wrapped in red cloth in her right hand.

One of L.D.'s daughters, covered with a shawl, knelt directly behind the wife. Bekis told me, "When you hear 'Yaa,' you must bow your head because we women aren't supposed to see it" (July 14, 2000). We waited. The call came. We bowed our heads. Rushed footsteps passed the shade house. Soon, a man emerged from the hooghan with a pottery bowl that was handed to Bekis, who handed it to L.D.'s daughter. She reached under the blanket and handed the bowl to the wife. The wife drank from it and then removed a handful of the greenery and rubbed it on her body. The bowl was passed clockwise among all the assembled women. We each took a sip, scooped out some greenery, and applied it to our legs, arms, face, and hair.

Subsequently, the singer's assistant emerged from the hooghan with a small pouch, filled with "dirt from a prairie dog" that was put into the wife's shoes. The assistant then brought another small pouch that was passed to the wife, who put a pinch in her mouth, spit on her hands, and applied the substance to her body before passing it to the young rattle-stick carrier who chewed some and aspirated it onto the vegetation bundle she was holding. Next, the assistant brought out a lump of a black, greasy substance that all present put along our jaw lines from our right ears to our chins and then from our left ears to our chins; this was followed by sheep fat that all present rubbed on any "ailing body parts." Then came a pan of ashes that was passed around and used by all present and a lump of *chiih*, "red ocher," that was applied to the wife and rattle-stick carrier's cheeks before being passed to those assembled for our personal use. Finally, the man emerged with another pouch, the contents of which were used exclusively by the wife and the rattle-stick carrier.

Bekis listened carefully to the singing inside the hooghan. When she heard a certain song, she signaled the woman sitting opposite her to begin draping the wife. They opened the bundle. On top were a deerskin and a sash belt. The woman sitting directly behind the wife wrapped the belt around her in a clockwise direction. The deerskin was put aside. Bekis and her assistant picked up the materials. A corner of each had been tacked into a loop, which was placed over the wife's head. I counted ten blankets and twenty-two twelve- or fourteen-foot-long pieces of satin, velour, and prints. The women carefully extended the full length of each piece out behind the wife, one on top of the other. After being draped, the wife was covered with Pendleton and Pendleton-style blankets and shawls.

Next, a man brought out a wooden talisman called a "crowbill," which was shaped like a crow's bill and had feathers attached. The women removed the covering blankets. The woman behind the wife draped a piece of red material over her shoulders. Next, she draped the deerskin over the wife's right shoulder and handed her the crowbill; the wife clutched it and the end of the deerskin with her right hand. The pointed end of the crowbill was facing up. The woman behind her handed the wife a tied stack of seven blankets to hold in her left hand. She was again covered with blankets.

When the men called out again, we bowed our heads a second time. Soon, rushed footsteps passed the shade, after which we heard gunshots and yells. We kept our heads bowed until the men returned to the hooghan. The women uncovered the wife and told her to stand. Her mother and aunt picked up the layers of material trailing behind her to ease her task. She stood facing east. Women scurried to straighten the materials behind her. She was directed to walk to the east side of her family's cooking shade. The women followed her, maintaining a few feet of distance.

L.D. and his son emerged from the hooghan, walked to the east side of the shade, and stood in front of the wife. Once assembled, they walked to their respective cooking shades—the wife to her family's and L.D. and his son to theirs. Just as Nettie Nez had portended, the blankets and pieces of cloth draped on the wife served to *erase the footprints* of both patients; in every instance of contemporary Enemy Way, as Nez noted, this is so a patient "will get well" and the contamination from contact with an enemy— no matter the source—"will not bother him again" (July 10, 2000).

Next, the patients' families, the wife, Mae Ann Bekis, and the women who had blackened the wife rode in trucks with food for the rattle-stick-receiving family. When they returned, we left for home. We discussed key events of the morning and the entire ceremony (Bekis, July 14, 2000). I thought back to Berard Haile's comments on this ceremonial, which has essentially been ignored by previous generations of scholars:

> In comparison with other Navaho ceremonials, outsiders will not rate Enemy Way much above a minor ceremonial. It features no sand-paintings, no prayer sticks, no masked dancers, but impresses the outsider as a recreational gathering, which at times may include a horse race or a foot race, and primarily serves to bring young people together. . . . Yet *the entire ceremonial seems to be a public and tribal affair*, perhaps more than other ceremonials, many of which are performed for the benefit of an individual and are therefore a private family affair. The reason is that *the ghost of the foreigner is an enemy of the tribe, as well as of the individual*. The feeling in the tribe at large is ordinarily not expressed. (Haile 1938:23, emphasis added)

* * *

Navajo exegeses on acceptance or donation of an organ through transplantation touch on critical issues, including notions of collective identity, kinship obligations, reciprocity, incest, and contamination from death or non-Navajoness. The subjects of organ transplantation and donation also offer the opportunity to explore how Navajo Christians—mainline, Evangelicals, and Catholics—choose to combat the cause of the illness and procure healing.

Two consistent themes run through the illness narratives of mainline and Evangelical Christian Navajo: the power of prayer and the notion of giving it up to the Lord. Giving it up to the Lord is the means by which many surrender their fate to the transcendent deity. Christian healing prayer is believed to have the power to cure all ills. It is therefore a prominent feature of church services, tent revivals, prayer meetings, counseling sessions, and camp meetings. Because the power of prayer is believed to increase proportionate to the number of participants, aid is sought by requesting prayers from congregation members—locally and within multiple states— and through prayer chains.

Non-Evangelical Christian consultants reported use of Catholicism, NAC meetings, herbal remedies, and traditional ceremonies. A critical feature of this group of testimonials is how individuals and families combine religions while crediting each source's contribution to a cure. While consultants reported having had Beauty Way and Evil Way to aid recovery from transplantation, without question the primary ceremony associated with this procedure is the Enemy Way. Indeed, as demonstrated through the cooperation and reciprocity necessary to successfully orchestrate seemingly countless work groups to prepare hooghans, shade houses, and camps in multiple locations; horses and riders; gifts to be exchanged; and vast amounts of food for people in attendance, more than any other traditional ceremony Enemy Way demonstrates how collective identity is reinforced through ritual in the contemporary Navajo world.

CHAPTER EIGHT

Closing Thoughts

It depends on the medical situation. If it's way too critical, we try to get all types of spiritual help. Even if it means going to the [Christian] church and using the Native American [Church] religion and Navajo [traditional]. If it's pretty extreme, we reach out to everything—every spiritual thing that is available out there.

(N. Young, June 14, 2005)

In this ethnographic study of the ways contemporary Navajo people accommodate biomedical technologies such as blood transfusion, cardiopulmonary resuscitation (CPR), surgery, and organ transplantation, I undertook to demonstrate how global forces such as colonial efforts to Christianize Natives and replace traditional healing systems with allopathic medicine are mediated at the local level. Knowing that healing is a central concern and activity for Navajo people past and present, my intent was to gain insight into how Navajo families seeking relief for ailing relatives choose among these various systems; to acquire an appreciation of how the different traditions available to contemporary Navajo people address healing; and to determine to what Navajo patients, donors, recipients, and other consultants attribute moral force within each religious and medical system. To explore the practical mastery by Navajo people such as Nora Young, who, when faced with a serious medical crisis, recognize and deploy connections among the multiple religious and medical options available in their world, this book conflates into a single analytic framework the range of healing specialists and strategies among which people negotiate. This approach allowed documentation of how consultants use bodily experience and moral claims to make sense of their social world, establish their identities within that world, and articulate its contradictions.

While many of the points central to this analysis have not been common knowledge prior to this study, the connections between bodily disorder and global forces are readily apparent in consultants' awareness and conversations. Indeed, as evidenced by the Navajo exegeses throughout this text, testimonies are riddled with links between personal discomfort and global forces as well as patients' and family members' health-seeking behaviors. Close examination of these interrelated topics exposed the need to consider Navajo notions of the body, illness, and curing from every available tradition's perspective. To garner insight into these numerous factors, it was necessary to sort through multiple levels of discourse in an effort to ascertain patterns and discord. Native American Church (NAC) practitioners' testimony, for example, was examined for references attributable to Christian influence, to Navajo tradition, to other indigenous belief systems, as well as to tenets of the NAC as practiced elsewhere in Native North America. The testimony of Navajo Christians was studied for evidence of influences from Navajo traditional religion and other sources. Careful consideration was paid to exactly what was said in regard to the causes of illnesses and the sources of cures. Through these efforts at discernment, followed by triangulation with other consultants, I have attempted to differentiate what can be termed tenets of the Navajo Native American Church, fresh insights into traditional beliefs about the body and life that influence medical decisions today, and what Navajo people are making of Christianity.

The multiple concerns of this project could only be understood within the broader context of two important sources of information—Navajo oral history and documentation of the social, political, and economic changes evident in Navajo life since contact with Europeans. The former is a charter for life, while the latter indexes the introduction of foreign ideologies, which have influenced local identities as well as healing strategies.

Navajo people understand themselves as a chosen people living within a sacred geography created specifically for them and their descendants. As a people, they are linked to those who arose from the womb of Mother Earth at the place of emergence, where First Man and First Woman thought and sang the world into existence. Within this consecrated landscape they were made by Changing Woman, who gave them a set of diné bike'ji as a guide or charter for life. The diné bike'ji constitute the set of beliefs and practices intended to enable Navajo people to keep the world within their sacred mountains in order and to restore it to harmony when the need arises. Importantly, Navajo oral history also provided the Nihookáá Dine'é with a proclivity to seek new forms of supernatural power to solve health problems. With these stories as models, Navajo people can be seen as culturally preconditioned to seek and adopt new sources of healing as they become available. This set the stage for them to appropriate new forms of curing power from every new society with which they came in contact.

Contact with Europeans, which began as a tragedy for individuals and families, became the decisive cultural trauma for the Navajo people. Narratives told by those who survived Kit Carson's onslaught, the forced march to Fort Sumner, and a multiyear confinement expanded over time to become accounts of the loss and disenfranchisement brought on by colonization—loss of language, tradition, and subsistence. These vivid retellings converted this tragedy into a cultural trauma, thereby forming a backdrop against which a collective identity as the Navajo people was forged. The Navajo proclivity to acquire new forms of curing was evidenced at Fort Sumner when prisoners accepted some allopathic treatments as well as entire ceremonies from other Native prisoners who married Navajo women. As a result, religious and medical pluralism is deeply and fully ingrained in the Navajo lived world—on the level of community, family, and married couple.

An overarching emphasis on historical trauma and loss in personal testimonies led me to consider these factors as some of the cultural idioms associated with illness in the contemporary Navajo world and subsequently to consider to what they are attributed. Countless times consultants said, "We never used to have diseases like diabetes, cancer, or heart disease." As has been demonstrated, such claims bear significance because in many narratives, so-called new diseases stand for changes in the Navajo lifestyle—the shift to wage work and women working outside the home, the shift from home-raised crops and livestock to government subsidies, the shift to store-bought canned goods and prepackaged meats or fast food. Consultants directly linked illness in their present world to the breakdown of vital relations between themselves and nature—including such practices as polluting, dumping trash, mining, and engaging in improper burial practices.

Like other Native Americans, Navajo people did not face a single catastrophic period. Instead, since their release from Fort Sumner and the subsequent establishment of a reservation, the Navajo have been constantly dominated and controlled by the larger American society. Colonial assault has been repeatedly demonstrated through repression of Native languages and traditions, threats to Navajo land and resources, and impediments to religious freedom. These concerns, coupled with social and health problems—including economic underdevelopment and chronic unemployment, problems associated with alcohol, and high rates of diabetes and illnesses associated with improperly regulated mining—have resulted in historical trauma. It is within this context of rapid cultural change and fragmentation that Navajo people have searched out new sources of curing powers, including those available from Christianity, the Native American Church, and bio-medical technologies.

Other than fundamentalist Christians, consultants—directly or indirectly—attributed age-old illnesses to contamination resulting from inappropriate contact with death, lightning, or other elements of nature. In marked contrast, however, they attributed illnesses perceived as recent—such as diabetes, cancer, and heart problems—to Nááhwíiłbįįhí, the white-skinned Gambler deity, and his descendants; that is, their colonizers. The ancient story of the Gambler establishes parameters for dealing with outsiders and the dangers of contamination attributed to contact with them. When Gambler lost to Monster Slayer and Born for Water, the Hero Twins had him banished to outer space. The Gambler then pledged to send his offspring to destroy the Navajo people. As promised, the Gambler's descendants returned with a vengeance and wreaked havoc on the Navajo.

In this case, contamination resulted from the Gambler's legendary ability to control the minds of others and make them do as he wishes, or what consultants referred to as the power "to win you over" and take everything from you; this issue has always been at the core of the colonial relationship. Navajo exegeses reveal a sense that descendants of the Gambler have been controlling and continue to control Navajo people by making them live according to the white man's rules. This exposes a fundamental tension between a sense of loss and a resistance to this form of control. As evidenced in consultants' narratives, the more control the Gambler's descendants acquire, the more pollution, fast food, changes in lifestyle, and loss of traditional values and teachings become increasingly prominent on the reservation.

COMPARATIVE VIEWS ON HEALTH AND HEALING

Because Navajo ceremonials were not proving effective against the woes the Navajo faced in the 1940s through the 1960s, Navajo people joined the NAC and Christian sects at record levels. Consideration of this phenomenon provides the opportunity to contemplate what Navajo people are making of Christianity, including the development of an indigenous sect in addition to adoption of mainline denominations. Importantly, Christianity granted converts access to a transcendent god rather than only the immanent form of supernatural power inherent within the traditional religion. Insights into what Navajo people have made of Christianity are gained through the narratives of consultants discussing the experience of Pentecostalism—the fastest-growing religion on the reservation—and that of the Oodláni, a uniquely Navajo form of Christianity.

Many Navajo who first sought relief through the NAC felt helpless because of the Gambler's descendants' seemingly insurmountable power. Today, however, as fewer and fewer young people are taking on the difficult task of learning the ceremonies, the Native American Church has become a sanctuary for retention of traditional Navajo religious practices. This is evidenced by the fact that philosophical tenets, prayers, and other small segments of ceremonials are integrated into NAC meetings.

In addition, this analysis offers new insights into the Navajo version of the NAC. First, it provides the opportunity to fully appreciate the delicate nature of syncretism, such as the role of practitioners in shielding patients from illness in concert with Christian notions of redemptive suffering. Second, an emphasis placed by NAC road men on the need for "one to believe" demonstrates parallels between NAC curing and faith healing. Third, a key tenet of the NAC is religious relativism. This raises the issue of whether the predilection, based on Navajo oral history, to seek out new forms of supernatural power in combination with the NAC tenet of religious relativism has resulted in greater eclecticism among Navajo peyotists than among other Navajo in terms of health-seeking behavior. Among the Navajo consultants, NAC members are the most eclectic in their treatment options, with Navajo Catholics second in diversity of choices selected, followed by traditionalists and fundamentalists, who are the least eclectic in their treatment options.[1]

While differences between Christian and non-Christian perceptions of illness were readily apparent in consultants' narratives—Christians consider illness to be caused by evil—no discernible differences were revealed between Navajo traditionalists and Native American Church understandings of health. Only glimmers of what might be called a singular NAC logic of illness causation were apparent. As illustrated by Johnson Dennison and Thomas Deschene, Jr., NAC practitioners more readily draw on a mixture of beliefs taken from traditional Navajo religion and Christianity in an effort to understand what causes illness.

Dennison retains traditional beliefs about imbalance leading to illness. For Deschene, illness can derive from traditional sources such as monsters or connections to beings like insects and reptiles. His rendition of the restoration episode introduces notions of redemption and sacrifice—concepts frequently discussed by NAC practitioners. In addition, he maintains that a direct correlation exists between the body part affected and the animal offended—if one offends a snake, for example he or she will develop an intestinal ailment. This point contrasts directly with traditional notions of illness in which no direct link is made between cause and symptom. This might be the only strictly Native American Church tenet yet uncovered. Dennison's explanation about how Navajo and biomedical healers are literally speaking past each other can bring us to an understanding of the perceptional gaps between Navajo conceptions of illness and biomedical conceptions of disease and, it is hoped, to an understanding of the types of syncretic bridges being built between the two perspectives.

Mae Ann Bekis's modification of the biomedical model, wherein food choices are considered vital to a diabetic's health, by incorporating lightning to explain *why* the food is dangerous is an ideal example of these bridges. It demonstrates how when Navajo people discuss changes in food,

they are bemoaning a loss of lifestyle and cultural principles rather than
attacking those foods as the fundamental cause of contemporary diseases.
This case illustrates how cause is still attributed to a breach of a taboo,
such as contact with lightning. Importantly, this adjustment to the Indian
Health Service model empowered Bekis to validate traditional Navajo
beliefs about illness causation. Thus, foods are emblematic of colonization,
culture change, and loss; and the underlying message becomes that if Navajo
people return to the old ways, health and harmony will be restored.

MARKING BODILY DIFFERENCES

While in principle biomedical providers insist that all humans are the same,
most Navajo individuals insist that they as a people are distinct. Marking
differences between Navajo and non-Navajo bodies is a means by which
Navajo people assert their collective identity and grant power to their
indigenous religious and medical systems. Contrasts between Navajo and
non-Navajo bodies are marked and maintained to this day as a means by
which to resist colonizers as well as to reinforce collective identity and
tribal solidarity.

While these differences are critical to marking, reinforcing, and maintaining Navajo collective identity, as Navajo exegeses illustrate, no singular
agreed-upon criterion defines the distinctions between Navajo and non-
Navajo in the contemporary Navajo world. Rather, multiple images of
distinction coexist simultaneously based on traditional, Navajo Native
American Church, Navajo Catholic, Navajo Christian, Navajo Pentecostal,
and Evangelical Christian ideologies—although these are yet to be fully
delineated.

Dividing human blood and organs into the categories of Navajo and
non-Navajo distinguishes Diné from outsiders. This, coupled with beliefs
about the problems that will arise from accepting a foreigner's blood or
organs into one's body—the recipient will start having problems elsewhere in his or her body, the person will have horrifying nightmares or
delirium, the presence of the foreign object starts haunting the recipient—
and notions that it is dangerous to allow others to have one's wind in their
bodies, reinforces Navajo collective identity and ensures the need for

ceremonial interventions. The interventions further reinforce tribal solidarity by gathering families and neighbors together in concerted efforts to help Navajo recipients of transfusions or transplants, thereby keeping their traditions and reciprocity alive.

The majority of Navajo consultants do not wish to contaminate themselves with blood or organs from non-Navajo, which they believe will cause harm elsewhere in their bodies, preferring instead to receive blood or organs from Navajo donors. Their first choice is usually for these life-sustaining substances to come from members of their own families—frequently, individuals who fall into incest dyads prohibiting sexual contact, speaking to each other, or, most important, touching. This seemingly imponderable situation is made comprehendible when one considers distinctions between Navajo understandings of genealogical solidarity versus affinal exchange.

I suggest that the cultural fact that motherhood and kinship are synonymous in the Navajo view is the lynchpin for understanding why Navajo people prefer to accept blood or organs from those to whom they are related genealogically. Because of their life-sustaining qualities, blood and organs are shared by kinsmen and kinswomen who routinely seek to support each other's lives by giving or sharing food and other items of subsistence. Furthermore, incest prohibitions focus on controlling or preventing a specific set of direct actions: sexual intercourse, touching, dancing, speaking, and seeing. Exchanging blood or organs in a biomedical context constitutes passive and indirect contact rather than personal action by donors or recipients. Siblings and children do not hand over blood or organs directly; rather, contact is neutralized by intermediary hands and spaces. In the case of blood transfusions and organ transplantation, physicians and other hospital staff serve as intermediaries similar to the one-who-sits-between in ceremonial contexts.

ACCOMMODATING BIOMEDICAL TECHNOLOGY

As John Farella quipped, Navajo people have long been recognized for "altering their technology to maintain their epistemology" (1984:190). As demonstrated by Navajo exegeses throughout this text, biomedical technology is no exception. For countless contemporary Navajo people, age-old diné bike'ji that govern life, the life plan, and care and treatment of the body are used within the context of medical and religious pluralism to mark a clear divide between Navajo people and outsiders. This means Navajo individuals can and do take advantage of biomedical technology, as long as it is couched within some form of spirituality. In other words, intervention—in the form of traditional ceremonies, mainline or indigenous Christian practices, or Navajo Native American Church rites—is necessary for acceptance of allopathic care. In cases where some form of Native ceremony is involved, these rites reinforce nativism and Navajo collective identity through the collaboration and reciprocity required to arrange ceremonies as well as the ties renewed within families and communities.

While Navajo exegeses do provide organized formulas for treatment choice, they do not portray the erasure of local symbolic worlds by an encroaching biomedical hegemony. Instead, surgery and other technologies have been interwoven within the Navajo traditional belief system, the Navajo Native American Church, and Native Christianity. My research indicates that coexistence of these systems is dependent on the biomedical system being integrated into the Navajo world within a set of traditional philosophical tenets governing notions of the body and identity.

Several fundamental tenets of Navajo philosophy influence the way Navajo people respond to new ideas and technologies upon their introduction. The body must not be cut; body integrality must be maintained; one must not permanently mar the body (it can only be painted or otherwise decorated during a ceremony); special care must be taken in disposing of surgically removed body parts; marked differences exist between Navajo and non-Navajo blood, and blood can become contaminated through intimate contact; not all forms of death are dangerous (stillborns and elders who have lived to 102 are considered pure); and every individual has a predetermined life span established before birth.

In a general sense, these tenets govern what is or is not acceptable; yet, as is made clear in consultants' testimonies, the principles are frequently negotiated on a case-by-case basis. Therefore, these Navajo understandings of the body have been maintained while a new medical system has been adopted. That system is appropriated into the Navajo worldview, which means that procedures adopted in are provisional on interventions being needed before, during, or after each procedure.

Previous studies of Navajo adaptation and change by Evon Vogt and Roland Wagner lend insight into this process (Vogt 1961:328; Wagner 1975: 174–175). The same cultural logic is evident in the realm of health care–seeking behaviors, whereby on the basis of religious persuasion individuals select specific treatments, procedures, and interventions (analogous to branch songs noted by Wagner 1975:174–75) from among various biomedical, traditional, Native American Church, and Christian options to devise an acceptable treatment plan (analogous to the underlying skeleton mentioned by Wagner 1975:174–75). This model allows for tremendous variability. For example, while an ach'ą́ą́h sodizin (protection prayer) is strongly recommended before surgery, it need not be performed by a traditional practitioner but instead can consist of a NAC prayer. Furthermore, the patient's biomedical surgery and other treatments are interlaid with NAC meetings or traditional ceremonies such as Life Way, Flint Way, Hóchxǫ'jí, or Enemy Way to encourage healing, purify, or expel evil, as decided by the diagnostician consulted—whether trained in traditional hand trembling, star or crystal gazing, or Native American Church coal or water gazing. By these means, Navajo people once again appropriate technology to maintain their philosophy.

As Vogt noted, Navajo people adapt new technology to fit their indigenous philosophy (1961). Or as John Farella put it, they label the new as old and change in an attempt to stay the same (1984:189). Tracking the way this complicates surgery for a Navajo traditionalist offers insight into the means by which elements of traditional diagnosis and healing are interwoven with allopathic procedures. Consultants describe going to a biomedical clinic followed by a visit to a diagnostician (traditional or NAC), having a Beauty Way or a protection prayer recited for a relative and the surgical team before surgery, holding a NAC meeting for a family member who is in the hospital, being temporarily released from the hospital to go home for a Life Way rite to be performed over the patient, and having ceremonies such as Flint Way, Enemy Way, or Blessing Way performed after surgery. This demonstrates how contemporary Navajo people have incorporated allopathic medicine similarly to the way they incorporated previously appropriated technologies (Vogt 1961; Wagner 1975).

As countless narratives in this text demonstrate, the majority of the Navajo consultants made direct associations between contemporary diseases such as diabetes, heart ailments, and cancer and oppressive social conditions.

They routinely attributed these diseases to loss of traditions, having to live according to the white man's philosophy, eating processed foods, or being exposed to environmental pollutants. Moreover, they articulated their experience of social conflict and distress through local medical discourse, especially discourse that marks clear differences between Navajo and non-Navajo bodies. As illustrated, maintaining these distinctions necessitates the continuance of traditional Navajo and NAC diagnosis, consultations, and ceremonial interventions to correct for contamination caused by contact with non-Navajo blood, breath, organs, and medical personnel. Because they offer insight into the nuanced negotiations of religious and medical pluralism within families and between spouses, these findings offer insight for others conducting research on religious and medical pluralism, as well as for allopathic providers working with indigenous populations across the globe.

Consultants

CONSULTANT	CLASSIFICATION	Traditional	NAC	Oodlání	Baptist
Buella Allen	Biomedical physician	■			
Tso Allen	Public health nurse	■			
Delano Ashley		■			
Eugene Bahe					
Eleanor Begay		■			
Mae Ann Bekis	Traditional Practitioner (Blessing Way), tranditional herbalist	■			
Amelia Benally					
Eugenia Bert					
Kenneth Black		■			
Billie Davis		■	■		
George Davis	Navajo pastor of Christian Church				
Donald Denetdeal	Traditional Practitioner (Blessing Way)	■			
Johnson Dennison	Traditional Practitioner (Wind Way), NAC road man	■	■		
Thomas Deschene, Jr.	NAC road man		■		
Ray Francisco		■			
Sheila Goldtooth	Traditional Practitioner (Blessing Way)	■	■		
Beverlianna Hale		■	■		
Paulla Damon Henderson					■
Sarah Jackson		■			
Leeanne Johnson		■			
Ursula Knoki-Wilson	Nurse-midwife	■	■		
Anna Laughter		■			
Fred Laughter	Traditional diagnostician (crystal gazer)	■			
Hastiin Lonewolf					
Tsosie Long		■	■		
Julia Mathis		■	■		
Don Mose	Traditional diagnostician (hand trembling)	■			
Leroy Nelson	Traditional Practitioner (Blessing Way)	■			
Jonah Nez	NAC road man, traditional herbalist		■		
Donald Sandoval	Traditional Practitioner (Chiricahua Wind Way)	■			
Florence Sandoval	Emergency medical technician	■			
Amelda Sandoval Shay		■			
Ambrose Shepard	NAC road man		■		
Asdzaan Taachiini					
Chee Tapaha		■	■		
Albert Tinhorn			■		
Larry Todachinee	Traditional diagnostician (crystal gazer)	■	■		
Rose Mary Wade		■			
Eloise Watchman		■			
Harrison Watchman					
Josephine Whitegoat	Christian Oodlání			■	
Vivian Yadeesbah		■			
Frank Young	Traditional Practitioner (Ant Way, Snake Way, and Evil Way)	■			
Nora Young		■	■		

AFFILIATION

Catholic	Mormon	Pentecostal	Presbyterian	NOTES
				described Navajo views on surgery, transfusions, CPR, and transplants
				described early efforts to introduce transplants
		■		told story of his wife's conversion to Christianity
■				amputee
■				blood transfusion recipient
■				heart transplant recipient
		■		liver transplant recipient
				has personal experience with autopsy, has donated blood, and has had a transfusion
				amputee
		■		
				director of the office of Navajo healing at Chinle Hospital, Chinle, Arizona
				has cared for blood transfusion and transplant recipients as well as cancer patients
				kidney transplant recipient
				cancer patient
	■			provided a kidney to her brother for a transplant
				blood transfusion recipient
				blood transfusion recipient
■				spoke about Navajo concerns regarding hospitalization and surgery
				elderly tranditionalist
			■	heart transplant recipient
				kidney transplant recipient
■				awaiting a liver transplant
				spoke about how tranditional healing professionals accommodate new technologies
				knows of specific prayers to resolve problems resulting from transfusions
				spoke about influence of CPR
■				recipient of blood transfusion, daughter died of cancer
	■			amputee
		■		awaiting a transplant
				amputee
	■			
■				told story of her brother's struggle with kidney transplants
				husband and daughter underwent kidney transplants
			■	both he and his daughter underwent kidney transplantation
				spoke about Navajo view of being guinea pigs for allophathic providers
				knowledge of early NAC
				amputee and recipient of blood transfusion

Notes

1. Diabetes mellitus is more prevalent among Navajo than within the general U.S. population, with clinical diagnosis rising (Sugarman, Gilbert, and Weiss 1992). As a consequence, the Navajo have the highest lower extremity amputation rates in the world—with an annual rate of 43.9 per 100,000 men (Unwin 1998). American Indians and Alaskan Natives have a prevalence rate of End Stage Renal Disease (ESRD) 3.5 times higher than that of white Americans (Narva 2003). And because of the skyrocketing rate of diabetes mellitus, the Navajo population has an even higher rate of ESRD for which kidney transplantation is the optimal treatment therapy (Eggers 1995).

2. This overview of Navajo origin is incomplete. Over four hundred versions of the Navajo creation story have been transcribed to date; they vary widely in detail—based on the narrator's stage of life, clan affiliations, or specialized knowledge—but an integral core of common elements reflected here permeates all recorded versions.

3. Canonical studies of Asian societies include, but are not limited to, Amarasingham (1980); Kleinman (1980); Leslie (1976); Lock (1980); Nichter (1980); Zimmerman (1978). Analyses from Africa include Comaroff (1980); Feierman and Janzen (1992); Janzen (1978); Young (1976). From the Middle East we have Crapanzano (1973); Early (1988); Good (1976). Contributions from Latin America and the Caribbean include Fabrega and Silver (1973); Laguerre (1987); Littlewood 1993; Sobo (1993).

4. Beginning with the Indian Peace Policy in 1869, the federal government has provided health care to federally recognized tribes such as the Navajo because of the trust relationship established by Article 1, Section 8, Clause 3 of the U.S. Constitution and because the government deemed it a chronic need that, if filled, would help make Native peoples more receptive to acculturation. While army physicians provided limited medical attention to Native peoples in the nineteenth century and religiously based physicians began providing limited assistance in the 1870s, official health care on reservations did not commence until after passage of the Snyder Act in 1921, and comprehensive health care on reservations was not established until the 1950s.

CHAPTER TWO

1. Whether this fact is comfortable to accept or not, the United States in the twenty-first century remains a colonial country. Native Americans—including the Navajo—are still colonized peoples today. Thus, the assumption of medical control over Native American bodies was and is an expression of the power relationship of what some refer to as "internal colonialism" (Kaufert and O'Neil 1993:50). Given changing and emerging federal Indian policies, scholars and politicians suggest use of the term "neocolonialism." The term "post-colonialism" does not apply to the current American situation, however, because the 2.4 million Native Americans living within U.S. boundaries remain a conquered people.

2. At this point, the administrant used a lancet to scratch infected material, referred to as "crusts," from an individual with cowpox (similar to smallpox) under the patient's skin.

3. Tracts of land were annexed to the original reservation at numerous times between 1878 and 1934, and separate tracts of land were subsequently secured for outlying Navajo groups—the Alamo (1946), Canoncito (1949), and Ramah (1956).

4. Ample accounts exist of missionaries in all parts of the world siding with tribal people against governments or those representing commercial interests in direct opposition to colonial goals (Dunch 2002:308; see also Tinker 1993:120).

5. As early as the 1940s, David Aberle heard of different types of peyote meetings referred to as "Pollen Way," "Star Way," and "Eagle Way,"—which he suspected of being syncretic—taking place in the northeastern portion of the reservation. He never had the opportunity to observe one, however (Aberle 1982b). Based on fieldwork conducted on several occasions between 1949 and 1954, Aberle noted, "Road men, whether they are singers or not, claim

that they do not import Navaho ceremonial devices into peyote ceremonies—songs, prayers, or ritual patterns. I have seen two road men who were also singers perform, and they did not deviate in any respect from normal peyotist practice (Aberle 1982b:199). He added, however, that one of these men was in the habit of giving peyote to patients in traditional ceremonies when specifically asked to do so (Aberle 1982b:199).

6. This holds true for men and women but not for *nádlheehé*. Nádlheehé, which literally translates as "one who changes repeatedly," is the term used to refer to male-bodied people who have a capacity for simultaneously filling men's and women's roles. These are not the only three genders recognized in the Navajo worldview.

7. A second reason offered by Pavlik is that each denomination, in its own way, promotes retention of a Navajo identity. The NAC, although it incorporates some Christian elements, maintains a predominantly Indian identity. The LDS church mythology includes Native Americans. Protestant churches have increasing numbers of Navajo pastors (1997:53).

CHAPTER THREE

1. The notion of taking on an adversary "to beat" is similar to the metaphor of "doing battle" with diabetes found by Huttlinger and colleagues (1992) among Navajo diabetics.

2. Spencer notes that this episode connects Hail Way, Water Way, Wind Way, Male Shooting Way, and Feather Way (1957:101). It also appears in Flint Way (Haile 1943:60–76).

3. This does not accord with the perspective attributed to Pentecostals by William Hodge (1969:75), who claimed that in their view, illness is a form of God's punishment for turning away from the gospel and failing to convert others who were also in a state of sin.

CHAPTER FOUR

1. Berard Haile understands this term to derive from *chidí*, "a deprived one." The term for corpse, which literally translates as "he lies there," means the one who is deprived of its life principle, or wind. That which used to stand within him has returned (Haile 1950:ix). The wind does not die; rather, it is understood to return to "its original dispatcher" (Haile 1950:ix).

2. Contemporary Navajo funerals are syncretic events that meld Christian and Navajo beliefs about death and mourning. Mary Shepardson described

Christian funerals for Navajo people after 1970, at which the deceased lay "in state in the church" as relatives and friends of all ages filed past to view the body (1978:389–90). Funeral directors serving Navajo clients told Joyce Griffen they had observed bereaved Navajo attending funerals in funeral homes or in churches on the reservation make eye contact with or touch the body of the deceased (1978:370).

3. Louise Lamphere reported having witnessed Navajo mourners openly shed tears at Christian-style funerals for relatives or friends (April 5, 1999). I do not know if these people limit their expressions of emotion to the time between death and burial.

CHAPTER FIVE

1. Chiih dik'ǫ́ǫ́zh is made with herbs, red ocher, rock salt, various berries, and other substances (Bekis, July 28, 1993; Charley, July 15, 1992; see also Wyman and Bailey 1943:11–12).

2. Some claim that listeners and stargazers are possessed by coyote while performing (Levy, Neutra, and Parker 1987:46).

3. For further information on Navajo methods of diagnosis, see Morgan (1931); Wyman (1936a). For information on the oral histories associated with the origin of each method, see Wyman (1936b).

4. Mico continued, "However, this precept is not fixed too persistently within the perceptual framework, for many prisoners housed temporarily in the local jail will donate blood when time is taken from their sentences for doing so" (1962:16–17).

CHAPTER SIX

1. By way of contrast, at the time Aberle did his research, he noted that many peyotists knew one of several versions of an origin story of peyote and its ritual connected with a woman, or a woman and her child, who while wandering on the Plains discovers and eats peyote and subsequently ascertains the proper ritual for its use (1982b:209).

2. The double-meeting witnessed by Wagner in 1968 is excluded from this analysis because at midnight a clear shift occurred between the NAC meeting and the Navajo ceremonial (Wagner 1975:167–68); therefore, Aberle's point regarding a formulaic versus an idiosyncratic ritual pattern does not apply. It is probably not required that the associated Holy People affiliated with the ceremony be present to use one's knowledge about the herbal medicines associated

with the Snake Way to heal a patient during a peyote meeting (Dennison, June 22, 2005).

3. Indeed, in my study of Navajo women ceremonial practitioners, a man initiated each of the women practitioners with whom I consulted. In contrast, two women maintained that women practitioners can perform initiations (interviews with Agnes Dennison, July 27, 1998; Elizabeth Edison, July 17, 2000), and one—Laura Nix—expressed a desire to do so (July 10, 2000).

4. For further information on this ceremony, see Leland Wyman's detailed description in "The Female Shooting Life Chant" (1936c).

5. For further information on the latter two ceremonies, see Berard Haile's detailed description in *Origin Legend of the Navaho Flintway* (1943).

CHAPTER SEVEN

1. Peritoneal dialysis is a medical treatment for someone with kidney failure. Before the first treatment, a small, soft tube (catheter) is surgically inserted into the abdomen. A sterile mixture of sugar and minerals dissolved in water flows through the catheter into the abdomen by gravity from a bag attached to a pole and positioned higher than the head. By means of osmosis, the high concentration of sugar in the solution draws wastes, chemicals, and extra water from the tiny blood vessels in the peritoneal membrane into the solution. The length of time the solution stays in a person's abdomen can range from one and one-half hours to nine hours or longer. At the completion of the dwell time, the catheter is reconnected to a drain line to drain the fluid from the abdomen. The solution flows from the abdomen into a sterile collection bag, taking the waste products pulled from the tiny blood vessels in the peritoneum with it. Most people require four to six exchanges each day.

2. It was the radical Puritans who, expecting the Holy Spirit to work miracles through them as it had through the first Christians, reinstalled this method of healing (Porterfield 2005:166).

3. For a summary of the story associated with Moth Way, see Levy, Neutra, and Parker 1987:46–47. For further information about the ceremony see Levy, Neutra, and Parker 1987:56.

4. Based on what he learned from consultants, John Ladd maintains that if one engages in incest with a sibling, a parent, or a member of the same clan, he or she "will go crazy and jump like a moth into the fire" (1957:230).

5. For detailed accounts of all events in this important ceremony at different historical periods, see Franciscan Fathers (1910); Haile (1938, 1946); Jacobson (1964); McAllester (1954).

CHAPTER EIGHT

1. This contrasts slightly with Csordas's findings that members of the NAC and Roman Catholics are the most eclectic in their religious choice, with fundamentalists and traditionalists the least eclectic (1999:10).

Glossary

aadi': Euphemism for menstruation

ach'ááh sodizin: Protection prayer

ádistsiin: Stirring sticks

'agiziitsoh: Arthritis

'ałsą' haa'á'éél: Floating out of the abdomen; miscarriage

Anaa' jí ndáá': Enemy Way ceremony

'ana'į: Enemy

as'ah na'adá: Living a healthy life

Asdzą́ą́ Nádleehé: Changing Woman

'Ashįį łikán nish ninil: Are you sugar?

'Ashiih łikán dil biihazlįį: Sugar became present in the blood

'Ashįį łikán 'inilyį́: Sugar killing one

'atá't'ah: The interior recesses, pockets, and folds of the body

'Awéé' ch'ídaadlóóhgó bá na'a'nę́ę́': First Laugh ceremony

'ayeel: Offering

'azee': Medicine

'azee'įįł'ini'na'ałgishigii: Surgeon

'azee'it'ini: Medicine maker

Béeshee ba'ááD'jí, Béeshee bika'jí, Bee'sheejí: Flint Way

'bił hajííjééhigii': Those with whom one came up out of the same womb

bilagáana: European-American, or white person

Bináá'ádaałts'ózí Dine'é: Asian person

biyeel 'áshłééh: Proprietary offerings made to a medicine plant from whose species one needs to collect.

343

ch'įįdii: Disembodied spirit capable of evil
chiih: Red ocher
chiih dik'óózh: Antidote for chooyin
chooyin: Blood shed after second menstrual cycle
chooyin azéé: Arthritis medicine
chooyini: A hunchbacked or stiff-backed person
déest'įį: The crystal gazing or stargazing method of diagnosis
dił: Blood
Dił yiih nakásh: Blood transfusion
Diné: Navajo people
diné: Navajo person
diné ba' hané: Story of the Navajo; Navajo oral history
diné bike'ji: Navajo way(s)
Diné Bikéyah: Navajoland
Dine' hólóníí: The Navajo who live out there
Diyin Dine'é: Holy People; Navajo Supernaturals
haa'eeł: Stillborn(s)
hajiináí: Place of emergence
hataałii: Singer
Hóchxǫ'jí: Evil Way
Hóchxǫ'jí baa nis't'įį': The Evil Way has bothered them, contaminated them
hoł ndaabąąsígíí: Gurney
hooghan: Traditional Navajo earthen-floor home(s)
Hoozhónee: Beauty Way
hózhǫ́ naashá: To walk in beauty
Hózhǫ́ójí: Blessing Way
Hwéeldi: "The place of suffering," commonly known as Fort Sumner, New Mexico
'iinaa' ał'áá 't'éego ndiit'ééh: Life has different endings
Iináá'jí: Life Way
'iists'áá': The listening method of diagnosis
k'é: Compassionate, intense, and enduring solidarity
Kinaaldá: Puberty ceremony
kinaaldá: Person for whom a puberty ceremony is performed; also, the first and second menstrual periods
kinaaldstá: Blood shed during first and second menstruation
lood doo naałdzidi: Polite phrase for cancer
Mą'ii' bizéé'nat'á: Put Bread in Coyote's Mouth ceremony
Nááhwíiłbįįhí: The Gambler; "it will draw you in"
na'iiskáą: "Spent the night again," contamination by means of sexual intercourse
naałdzid: Cancer

Na'at'oyee: Shooting or Lightning Way
Nayéé': Monster
Nayéé' Neezghání: Monster Slayer
Ndáá': Enemy Way
ndishniih: The hand trembling method of diagnosis
né'édił: Nosebleed
Nihookáá Dine'é: Earth Surface People.
niłchi'i: Wind or inner form
ntł'iz: Hard goods
Oodlání: Believers; Navajo indigenous form of Christianity
shik'éí: Relatives connected to me through wombs
Sǫ'tsohjí: Star Chant
t'áá bee bóholnííh: It is up to him or her to decide
t'áadoo ha'cha da: One who died before it cried
tádídíín: Pollen
tádídíín bijish: A pollen pouch
Tiníléí: Gila Monster
tó ał'tahnáschíín: All different kinds of waters come together
tó biyáázh: Child of water
Yé'ii Bicheii: Grandfathers of the Holy People
Yé'iitsoh: Big Monster

Bibliography

PUBLISHED SOURCES

Aberle, David

1961   The Navaho. In *Matrilineal Kinship,* David Schneider and Kathleen Gough, eds., 96–201. Berkeley: University of California Press.

1967   The Navaho Singer's "Fee": Payment or Prestation? In *Studies in Southwestern Ethnolinguistics,* Dell H. Hymes and William E. Bittle, eds., 15–32. Studies in General Anthropology 3. The Hague: Mouton.

1982a   The Future of Navajo Religion. In *Navajo Religion and Culture: Selected Views,* David Brugge and Charlotte Frisbie, eds., 219–31. Museum of New Mexico Papers in Anthropology 17. Santa Fe: Museum of New Mexico Press.

1982b   *The Peyote Religion among the Navaho.* Norman: University of Oklahoma Press.

1993   The Navajo-Hopi Land Dispute and Navajo Relocation. In *Anthropological Approaches to Resettlement: Policy, Practice, and Theory,* Michael Cernea and Scott Guggenheim, eds., 153–200. Boulder, Colo.: Westview.

Aberle, David, and Omer Stewart

1957   *Navaho and Ute Peyotism: A Chronological and Distributional Study.* University of Colorado Studies Series in Anthropology 6. Boulder, Colo.: University of Colorado Press.

Adair, John, Kurt Deuschle, and Clifford Barnett

1988   *The People's Health: Anthropology and Medicine in a Navajo Community.* Albuquerque: University of New Mexico Press.

Adams, David
   1995   *Education for Extinction: American Indians and the Boarding School Experience, 1875–1928.* Lawrence: University Press of Kansas.
Adams, William
   1963   *Shonto: A Study of the Role of the Trader in a Modern Navajo Community.* Bureau of American Ethnology 188. Washington, D.C.: Smithsonian Institution Press.
Alexander, Jeffrey
   2004   Toward a Theory of Cultural Trauma. In *Cultural Trauma and Collective Identity,* Jeffrey Alexander, Ron Eyerman, Bernhard Giesen, Neil Smelser, and Paul Sztompka, eds., 1–30. Berkeley: University of California Press.
Alexander, Jeffrey, Ron Eyerman, Bernhard Giesen, Neil Smelser, and Paul Sztompka, editors
   2004   *Cultural Trauma and Collective Identity.* Berkeley: University of California Press.
Amarasingham, Lorna Rhodes
   1980   Movement among Healers in Sri Lanka. *Culture, Medicine, and Psychiatry* 4:71–92.
Amsden, Charles
   1974[1934]   *Navaho Weaving: Its Technic and History.* Glorieta, N.M.: Rio Grande.
Anderson, Robert
   1979   *The Vision of the Disinherited: The Making of American Pentecostalism.* New York: Oxford University Press.
Andrews, Bridie, and Mary Sutphen
   2003   Introduction. In *Medicine and Colonial Identity,* Mary Sutphen and Bridie Andrews, eds., 1–13. London: Routledge.
Aronilth, Wilson
   1985   Foundations of Navajo Culture. Unpublished manuscript on file at Diné College Library, Tsaile, Ariz.
   1990   Foundation of Navajo Culture. Unpublished manuscript on file at Diné College Library, Tsaile, Ariz.
Baer, Hans
   1995   Medical Pluralism in the United States: A Review. *Medical Anthropology Quarterly* 9(4):493–502.
Bailey, Flora
   1950   *Some Sex Beliefs and Practices in a Navajo Community: With Comparative Material from Other Navaho Areas.* Reports of the Ramah Project. Papers of the Peabody Museum of American Archaeology and Ethnology 40(2). Cambridge, Mass.: Peabody Museum.

Bailey, Garrick, and Roberta Bailey
1982 *Historic Navajo Occupation of the Northern Chaco Plateau.* Navajo Indian Irrigation Project, Contract #NOO C 1420 8136. Tulsa, Okla.: University of Tulsa Faculty of Anthropology.
1986 *A History of the Navajos: The Reservation Years.* Santa Fe, N.M.: School of American Research Press.

Bailey, Lynn
1988[1964] *The Long Walk: A History of the Navajo Wars, 1846–68.* Tucson: Westernlore.

Begay, David, and Nancy Maryboy
2000 The Whole Universe Is My Cathedral: A Contemporary Navajo Spiritual Synthesis. *Medical Anthropology Quarterly* 14(4):498–520.

Berger, Peter
2002 Introduction: The Cultural Dynamics of Globalization. In *Many Globalizations: Cultural Diversity in the Contemporary World,* Peter Berger and Samuel Huntington, eds., 1–16. New York: Oxford University Press.

Berkhofer, Robert
1965 *Salvation and the Savage: An Analysis of Protestant Missions and American Indian Response, 1787–1862.* Westport, Conn.: Greenwood.

Blanchard, Kendall
1977 *The Economics of Sainthood: Religious Change among the Rimrock Navajos.* Cranbury, N.J.: Associated University Press.

Brave Heart, Maria Yellow Horse
1998 The Return of the Sacred Path: Healing the Historical Trauma and Historical Unresolved Grief Response among the Lakota. *Smith College Studies in Social Work* 68(3):287–305.
1999 Oyate Ptayela: Rebuilding the Lakota Nation through Addressing Historical Trauma among Lakota Parents. *Journal of Human Behavior and the Social Environment* 2(1/2):109–126.

Brave Heart, Maria Yellow Horse, and Lemyra DeBruyn
1998 The American Indian Holocaust: Healing Historical Unresolved Grief. *American Indian and Alaska Native Mental Health Research* 8(2):56–78.

Brave Heart–Jordan, Maria, and Lemyra DeBruyn
1995 So She May Walk in Balance: Integrating the Impact of Historical Trauma in the Treatment of Native American Indian Women. In *Racism in the Lives of Women,* J. Adleman and G. Enquidanos, eds., 345–68. New York: Haworth.

Brodwin, Paul
1990 The Power of an "Absent Ethnicity": Social Value and Medical Commodities in Rural Haiti. *Museum Anthropology* 16(3):34–40.

1996   *Medicine and Morality in Haiti: The Contest for Healing Power.*
        New York: Cambridge University Press.

Brooks, James
1997   "This Evil Extends Especially to the Feminine Sex": Captivity and
        Identity in New Mexico, 1700–1846. In *Writing the Range: Race,
        Class, and Culture in the Women's West,* Elizabeth Jameson and Susan
        Armitage, eds., 97–121. Norman: University of Oklahoma Press.
1999   Violence, Justice and State Power in the New Mexican Border-
        lands, 1780–1880. In *Power and Place in the North American West,*
        Richard White and John Findlay, eds., 23–60. Seattle: University of
        Washington Press.

Brugge, David
1978   A Comparative Study of Navajo Mortuary Practices. *American
        Indian Quarterly* 4(4):309–328.
1983   Navajo Prehistory and History to 1850. In *Handbook of North
        American Indians,* vol. 10: *Southwest,* Alfonso Ortiz, ed., 489–501.
        Washington, D.C.: Smithsonian Institution Press.
1985   *Navajos in the Catholic Church Records of New Mexico, 1694–1875.*
        Tsaile, Ariz.: Navajo Community College Press.

Brugge, Doug, Timothy Benally, Phil Harrison, Martha Austin, and Lydia Fasthorse
1997   *Memories Come to Us in the Rain and the Wind: Oral Histories and
        Photographs of Navajo Uranium Miners and Their Families.* Navajo
        Uranium Miners Oral History and Photography Project. Boston:
        Tufts University School of Medicine.

Calabrese, Joseph
1994   Reflexivity and Transformation Symbolism in the Navajo Peyote
        Meeting. *Ethos* 22(4):494–527.

Cambrosio, Alberto, Allan Young, and Margaret Lock
2000   Introduction. In *Living and Working with the New Medical Tech-
        nologies: Intersections of Inquiry,* Margaret Lock, Allan Young,
        and Alberto Cambrosio, eds., 1–16. New York: Cambridge Univer-
        sity Press.

Carrese, Joseph, and Lorna Rhodes
1995   Western Bioethics on the Navajo Reservation: Benefit or Harm.
        Journal of the American Medical Association 274:826–29.
2001   Bridging Cultural Differences in Medical Practice: The Case of
        Discussing Negative Information with Navajo Patients. *Journal of
        General Internal Medicine* 15:92–96.

Carsten, Janet
1995   The Substance of Kinship and the Heat of the Hearth: Feeding, Person-
        hood, and Relatedness among Malays in Pulau Langkawi. *American
        Ethnologist* 22(2):223–41.

2000   Introduction: Cultures of Relatedness. In *Cultures of Relatedness: New Approaches to the Study of Kinship,* Janet Carsten, ed. 1–36. Cambridge: Cambridge University Press.

Chew, Michelle
2000   Hogan in a Hospital: "Medical Co-Existence" on the Navajo Nation; an Analysis of Contemporary Navajo Responses to Western Medicine. M. Phil. thesis, Department of Anthropology and Geography, University of Oxford, Oxford, England.

Chrisman, Noel
1977   The Health-Seeking Process: An Approach to the Natural History of Illness. *Culture, Medicine, and Psychiatry* 1:351–77.

Cirillo, Dexter
1992   *Southwestern Indian Jewelry.* New York: Abbeville.

Cobin, Gina
1998   *The Partnership of Traditional Navajo Medicine and Biomedical Health Care Practices at the Chinle Comprehensive Care Facility.* Cambridge, Mass.: Harvard Project on American Indian Economic Development, Malcolm Wiener Center for Social Policy, John F. Kennedy School of Government.

Comaroff, Jean
1980   Healing and Cultural Order. *American Ethnologist* 7:637–77.
1985   *Body of Power, Spirit of Resistance.* Chicago: University of Chicago Press.

Comaroff, John, and Jean Comaroff
1997   *Of Revelation and Revolution.* Chicago: University of Chicago Press.

Correll, J. Lee
1979   *Through White Men's Eyes: A Contribution to Navajo History,* vols. 1–6. Austin, Tex.: Dissemination and Assessment Center for Bilingual Education.

Coulehan, Jack
1980   Navajo Indian Medicine: Implications for Healing. *Journal of Family Practice* 10(1):55–61.

Craig, David
2000   The King's Law Stops at the Village Gate: Local and Global Pharmacy Regulation in Vietnam. In *Global Health Policy, Local Realities: The Fallacy of the Level Playing Field,* Linda Whiteford and Lenore Manderson, eds., 105–126. Boulder, Colo.: Lynne Rienner.

Crapanzano, Vincent
1973   *The Hamadsha: A Study in Moroccan Ethnopsychiatry.* Berkeley: University of California Press.

Csordas, Thomas
   1989   The Sore That Does Not Heal: Cause and Concept in the Navajo
          Experience of Cancer. *Journal of Anthropological Research* 45(4):
          457–85.
   1999   Ritual Healing and the Politics of Identity in Contemporary Navajo
          Society. *American Ethnologist* 26(1):3–23.
   2000   The Navajo Healing Project. *Medical Anthropology Quarterly* 14(4):
          463–75.
Davies, Wade
   2001   *Healing Ways: Navajo Health Care in the Twentieth Century.* Albu-
          querque: University of New Mexico Press.
Dayton, Donald
   1987   *Theological Roots of Pentecostalism.* Metuchen, N.J.: Scarecrow.
Dolaghan, Thomas, and David Scates
   1978   *The Navajos Are Coming to Jesus.* Pasadena, Calif.: William Carey
          Library.
Dunch, Ryan
   2002   Beyond Cultural Imperialism: Cultural Theory, Christian Missions,
          and Global Modernity. *History and Theory* 41(October):301–325.
Duran, Eduardo, and Bonnie Duran
   1995   *Native American Postcolonial Psychology.* Albany: State University
          of New York Press.
Dyk, Walter
   1951   Notes and Illustrations of Navaho Sex Behavior. In *Psychoanalysis
          and Culture,* George Wilbur and Warner Muensterberger, eds., 108–119.
          New York: International Universities Press.
Early, Evelyn
   1982   The Logic of Well-Being: Therapeutic Narratives in Cairo, Egypt.
          Social Science and Medicine 16(16):1491–97.
   1988   The Baladi Curative System of Cairo, Egypt. *Culture, Medicine,
          and Psychiatry* 12:65–84.
Eggers, Paul
   1995   Racial Differences in Access to Kidney Transplantation. *Health
          Care Financing Review* 17:89–103.
Eichstaedt, Peter
   1994   *If You Poison Us: Uranium and Native Americans.* Santa Fe, N.M.:
          Red Crane Books.
Emerson, Gloria
   1983   Navajo Education. In *Handbook of North American Indians,* vol. 10:
          Southwest, Alfonso Ortiz, ed., 659–71. Washington, D.C.: Smith-
          sonian Institution Press.

Eyerman, Ron
    2004   Cultural Trauma: Slavery and the Formation of African American
            Identity. In *Cultural Trauma and Collective Identity,* Jeffrey Alexander,
            Ron Eyerman, Bernhard Giesen, Neil Smelser, and Paul Sztompka,
            eds., 60–111. Berkeley: University of California Press.
Fabrega, Horacio, Jr., and Daniel Silver
    1973   *Illness and Shamanistic Curing in Zincantan.* Stanford: Stanford
            University Press.
Farella, John
    1984   *The Main Stalk: A Synthesis of Navajo Philosophy.* Tucson: Uni-
            versity of Arizona Press.
Faris, James
    1990   *The Nightway.* Albuquerque: University of New Mexico Press.
Feierman, Steven, and John Janzen, editors
    1992   *The Social Basis of Health and Healing in Africa.* Berkeley: Uni-
            versity of California Press.
Fishler, Stanley
    1953   *In the Beginning: A Navaho Creation Myth.* Anthropological Papers
            13. Salt Lake City: University of Utah Press.
Florio, Maria, and Victoria Mudd
    1986   *Broken Rainbow.* Maria Florio and Victoria Mudd, writers and pro-
            ducers; Martin Sheen, narrator. Los Angeles: Direct Cinema.
Franciscan Fathers
    1910   *An Ethnological Dictionary of the Navaho Language.* Saint Michaels,
            Ariz.: Saint Michaels Press.
Frisbie, Charlotte
    1978   Introduction. *American Indian Quarterly* 4(4):303–308.
    1987   *Navajo Medicine Bundles or Jish.* Albuquerque: University of New
            Mexico Press.
    1992   Temporal Change in Navajo Religion: 1868–1990. *Journal of the
            Southwest* 34(4):457–514.
    1993[1967]   *Kinaaldá: A Study of the Navaho Girl's Puberty Ceremony.*
            Salt Lake City: University of Utah Press.
Frisbie, Charlotte, and David McAllester, editors
    1978   *Navajo Blessingway Singer: The Autobiography of Frank Mitchell
            1881–1967.* Tucson: University of Arizona Press.
Frisbie, Charlotte, and Eddie Tso
    1993   The Navajo Ceremonial Practitioners Registry. *Journal of the South-
            west* 35(1):53–92.
Garrity, John
    2000   Jesus, Peyote, and the Holy People: Alcohol Abuse and the Ethos of
            Power in Navajo Healing. *Medical Anthropology Quarterly* 14(4):521–42.

Gillmor, Frances, and Louisa Wade Wetherill
  1953[1934]   *Traders to the Navajos.* Albuquerque: University of New Mexico Press.
Goddard, Pliny
  1933   Navajo Texts. *Anthropological Papers of the American Museum of Natural History* 34(1):1–180. New York: American Museum of Natural History.
Good, Byron
  1976   The Professionalization of Medicine in a Provincial Iranian Town. In *Transcultural Health Care Issues and Conditions,* Madeline Leniger, ed., 51–65. Philadelphia: F. A. Davis.
Good, Mary-Jo Delvecchio, Byron Good, and Cynthia Schaffer
  1990   American Oncology and the Discourse of Hope. *Culture, Medicine and Psychiatry* 14:59–79.
Griffen, Joyce
  1978   Variations on a Rite of Passage: Some Recent Navajo Funerals. *American Indian Quarterly* 4(4):367–81.
Haile, Father Berard
  1938   *Origin Legends of the Navaho Enemy Way.* Yale University Publications in Anthropology 17. New Haven, Conn.: Yale University Press.
  1943   *Origin Legend of the Navaho Flintway.* Chicago: University of Chicago Press.
  1946   *The Padres Present the Navaho War Dance.* St. Michaels, Ariz: St. Michaels Press.
  1950   *Legend of the Ghostway Ritual in the Male Branch of the Shootingway Suckingway, Its Legend and Practice* (Part 2). Saint Michaels, Ariz.: Saint Michaels Press.
  1979   *Waterway: A Navajo Ceremonial Myth Told by Black Mustache Circle.* American Tribal Religions 5. Flagstaff: Museum of Northern Arizona Press.
  1981   *Women versus Men: A Conflict of Navajo Emergence.* American Tribal Religions 6. Lincoln: University of Nebraska Press.
Hegemann, Elizabeth
  1963   *Navajo Trading Days.* Albuquerque: University of New Mexico Press.
Hodge, Frederick, George Hammond, and Agapito Rey, editors
  1945   *Fray Alonzo de Benavides' Revised Memorial of 1634, with Numerous Supplementary Documents Elaborately Annotated.* Albuquerque: University of New Mexico Press.
Hodge, William
  1969   Navaho Pentecostalism. *Anthropological Quarterly* 37(3):73–93.

Huttlinger, Kathleen, Laura Krefting, Denise Drevdahl, Philip Tree, Elaine Baca,
   and Anita Benally
   1992   "Doing Battle": A Metaphorical Analysis of Diabetes Mellitus among
          Navajo People. *American Journal of Occupational Therapy* 46(8):
          706–712.
Iverson, Peter
   1981   *The Navajo Nation.* Albuquerque: University of New Mexico Press.
   2002   *Diné: A History of the Navajos.* Albuquerque: University of New
          Mexico Press.
Jacobson, Doranne
   1964   Navajo Enemy Way Exchanges. *El Palacio* 71:7–19.
Janzen, John
   1978   *The Quest for Therapy.* Berkeley: University of California Press.
Jilek, Wolfgang
   1981   Anomic Depression, Alcoholism, and a Culture-Congenial Indian
          Response. *Journal of Studies on Alcohol* 9:159–70.
Johnson, Broderick, editor
   1973   *Navajo Stories of the Long Walk Period.* Tsaile, Ariz.: Navajo Com-
          munity College Press.
Kaufert, Patricia A., and John O'Neil
   1993   Analysis of a Dialogue on Risks in Childbirth: Clinicians, Epidemi-
          ologists, and Inuit Women. In *Knowledge, Power and Practice: The
          Anthropology of Medicine and Everyday Life,* Shirley Lindenbaum
          and Margaret Lock, eds., 32–54. Berkeley: University of California
          Press.
Kelley, Klara, and Harris Francis
   1994   *Navajo Sacred Places.* Bloomington: Indiana University Press.
Kent, Kate
   1985   *Navajo Weaving: Three Centuries of Change.* Santa Fe, N.M.:
          School of American Research Press.
Kim, Catherine, and Yeong Kwok
   1998   Navajo Use of Native Healers. *Archives of Internal Medicine* 158(20):
          2245–49.
Kirsch, Thomas
   2004   Restaging the Will to Believe: Religious Pluralism, Anti-Syncretism,
          and the Problem of Belief. *American Anthropologist* 106(4):699–709.
Kleinman, Arthur
   1980   *Patients and Healers in the Context of Culture.* Berkeley: Univer-
          sity of California Press.
Kluckhohn, Clyde
   1944   *Navaho Witchcraft.* Boston: Beacon.

Kluckhohn, Clyde, and Dorothea Leighton
    1974[1946]   *The Navaho.* Cambridge, Mass.: Harvard University Press.
Kluckhohn, Clyde, and Leland Wyman
    1940   *An Introduction to Navaho Chant Practice.* Memoirs of the American
            Anthropological Association 53. Menasha, Wisc.: American Anthro-
            pological Association.
Kopp, Judy
    1986   Crosscultural Contacts: Changes in the Diet and Nutrition of the
            Navajo Indians. *American Indian Culture and Research Journal*
            10(4):1–30.
Kunitz, Stephen
    1983   *Disease Change and the Role of Medicine: The Navajo Experience.*
            Berkeley: University of California Press.
Kunitz, Stephen, and Jerrold Levy
    1994   *Drinking Careers: A Twenty-Five-Year Study of Three Navajo Popu-
            lations.* New Haven, Conn.: Yale University Press.
Ladd, John
    1957   *The Structure of a Moral Code.* Cambridge, Mass.: Harvard Univer-
            sity Press.
Laguerre, Michel
    1987   *Afro-Caribbean Folk Medicine.* South Hadley, Mass.: Bergin and
            Garvey.
Lamphere, Louise
    1977   *To Run after Them: Cultural and Social Bases of Cooperation in a
            Navajo Community.* Tucson: University of Arizona Press.
    2001   Whatever Happened to Kinship Studies? Reflections of a Feminist
            Anthropologist. In *New Directions in Anthropological Kinship,* Linda
            Stone, ed., 21–47. Boston: Rowman & Littlefield.
Lang, Gretchen Chesley
    1989   "Making Sense" about Diabetes: Dakota Narratives of Illness. *Medi-
            cal Anthropology* 11:305–327.
Leighton, Alexander, and Dorothea Leighton
    1944   *The Navaho Door: An Introduction to Navaho Life.* Cambridge, Mass.:
            Harvard University Press.
Leighton, Dorothea, and Clyde Kluckhohn
    1947   *Children of the People: The Navaho Individual and His Development.*
            Cambridge, Mass.: Harvard University Press.
Leslie, Charles
    1976   *Asian Medical Systems.* Berkeley: University of California Press.
    1978   Medical Pluralism in World Perspective. *Social Science and Medi-
            cine* 14B:191–95.

Levi-Strauss, Claude
1969[1949]   *The Elementary Structures of Kinship.* Boston: Beacon.
Levy, Jerrold, and Stephen Kunitz
1974   *Indian Drinking: Navajo Practices and Anglo-American Theories.*
        New York: John Wiley & Sons.
Levy, Jerrold, and Stephen Kunitz, with K. Ruben Gabriel, Eric Henderson,
        Joanne McCloskey, Gilbert Quintero, and Scott Russell
2000   *Drinking, Conduct Disorder, and Social Change: Navajo Experiences.*
        New York: Oxford University Press.
Levy, Jerrold, Raymond Neutra, and Dennis Parker
1987   *Hand Trembling, Frenzy Witchcraft, and Moth Madness.* Tucson:
        University of Arizona Press.
Lewton, Elizabeth
1997   Living Harmony: The Transformation of Self in Three Navajo Reli-
        gious Healing Traditions. Doctoral thesis, Department of Anthro-
        pology, Case Western Reserve University, Cleveland, Ohio.
Lewton, Elizabeth, and Victoria Bydone
2000   Identity and Healing in Three Navajo Religious Traditions: Sa'ah
        Naagháí Bik'eh Hózho. *Medical Anthropology Quarterly* 14(4):
        476–97.
Lincoln, Louise
1982   *Southwest Indian Silver from the Doneghy Collection.* Austin: Uni-
        versity of Texas Press.
Linthicum, Leslie
2005   The Long Walk. *The Albuquerque Journal,* B-1, May 8.
Littlewood, Roland
1993   *Pathology and Identity.* Cambridge: Cambridge University Press.
Lock, Margaret
1980   *East Asian Medicine in Urban Japan.* Berkeley: University of Cali-
        fornia Press.
Manderson, Lenore, and Linda Whiteford
2000   Introduction: Health, Globalization, and the Fallacy of the Level
        Playing Field. In *Global Health Policy, Local Realities: The Fal-
        lacy of the Level Playing Field,* Linda Whiteford and Lenore Man-
        derson, eds., 1–19. Boulder, Colo.: Lynne Rienner.
Matthews, Washington
1902   *The Night Chant: A Navaho Ceremony.* Memoirs of the American
        Museum of Natural History 6. New York: American Museum of
        Natural History.
1994[1897]   *Navaho Legends.* Salt Lake City: University of Utah
        Press.

Mauss, Marcel
    1972[1902]   *A General Theory of Magic.* Robert Brain, trans. New York:
        W. W. Norton.
McAllester, David
    1954   *Enemy Way Music.* Papers of the Peabody Museum of Archaeology
        and Ethnology, Harvard University 41(3). Cambridge, Mass.: Pea-
        body Museum.
McNally, Michael
    2000   The Practice of Native American Christianity. *Church History* 69(4):
        834–59.
McNeley, James
    1981   *Holy Wind in Navajo Philosophy.* Tucson: University of Arizona
        Press.
McNitt, Frank
    1962   *The Indian Traders.* Norman: University of Oklahoma Press.
    1972   *Navajo Wars: Military Campaigns, Slave Raids, and Reprisals.*
        Albuquerque: University of New Mexico Press.
Meigs, Anna, and Kathleen Barlow
    2002   Beyond the Taboo: Imagining Incest. *American Anthropologist*
        104(1):38–49.
Mico, Paul
    1962   Navajo Perception of Anglo Medicine. Navajo Health Education
        Project. Mimeographed report. Tuba City, Ariz.: P.H.S. Indian Hos-
        pital.
Milne, Derek, and Wilson Howard
    2000   Rethinking the Role of Diagnosis in Navajo Religious Healing.
        Medical Anthropology Quarterly 14(4):543–70.
Moon, Samuel
    1992   *Tall Sheep: Harry Goulding, Monument Valley Trader.* Norman:
        University of Oklahoma Press.
Moore, Sally Falk
    2004   Combined Reviews. *American Anthropologist* 106(4):744–46.
Morgan, William
    1931   Navaho Treatment of Sickness: Diagnosticians. *American Anthro-
        pologist* (new series) 33:390–402.
    1932   Navaho Dreams. *American Anthropologist* (new series) 34(3):390–405.
Morris, Rosalind
    1995   All Made Up. *Annual Review of Anthropology* 24:567–92.
Mustache, Curly
    1970   Unpublished transcription of Mr. Mustache's interview with Jones
        Van Winkle, Tsaile, Ariz. Manuscript in author's possession.

Narva, Andrew
    2003   Pathophysiology and Etiology of Chronic Renal Disease. *Kidney International* 63, supplement 83:53–57.
Nichter, Mark
    1980   The Layperson's Perception of Medicine as Perspective into the Utilization of Multiple Therapy Systems in the Indian Context. *Social Science and Medicine* 14B:225–33.
Niezen, Ronald
    2003   *The Origins of Indigenism: Human Rights and the Politics of Identity.* Berkeley: University of California Press.
O'Bryan, Aileen
    1956   *The Diné: Origin Myths of the Navaho Indians.* Bureau of American Ethnology, Bulletin 163. Washington, D.C.: Government Printing Office.
O'Nell, Theresa
    1996   *Disciplined Hearts: History, Identity, and Depression in an American Indian Community.* Berkeley: University of California Press.
Parezo, Nancy
    1991[1983]   *Navajo Sandpainting: From Religious Act to Commercial Art.* Tucson: University of Arizona Press.
Parker, Andrew, and Eve Kosofsky Sedgwick
    1995   Introduction: Performativity and Performance. In *Performativity and Performance,* Andrew Parker and Eve Kosofsky Sedgwick, eds., 1–18. New York: Routledge.
Pavlik, Steve
    1997   Navajo Christianity: Historical Origins and Modern Trends. *Wicazo Sa Review* 12(2):43–58.
Peletz, Michael
    1995   Kinship Studies in Late Twentieth-Century Anthropology. *Annual Review of Anthropology* 24:343–72.
Pinxten, Rik, and Claire Farrer
    1990   On Learning a Comparative View. *Cultural Dynamics* 3(3):233–51.
Polletta, Francesca, and James Jasper
    2001   Collective Identity and Social Movements. *Annual Review of Sociology* 27:283–305.
Porterfield, Amanda
    2005   *Healing in the History of Christianity.* New York: Oxford University Press.
Porvaznik, John
    1967   Traditional Navajo Medicine. *General Practice* 36(4):179–82.

Powers, Willow
    2001   *Navajo Trading: The End of an Era.* Albuquerque: University of New Mexico Press.

Quintero, Gilbert
    1995   Gender, Discord, and Illness: Navajo Philosophy and Healing in the Native American Church. *Journal of Anthropological Research* 51:69–89.

Rapoport, Robert
    1954   *Changing Navaho Religious Values: A Study of Christian Missions to the Rimrock Navahos.* Papers of the Peabody Museum of Archaeology and Ethnology, Harvard University 41(2). Cambridge, Mass.: Peabody Museum.

Reichard, Gladys
    1928   *Social Life of the Navaho Indians.* New York: Columbia University Press.
    1944   *The Story of the Navajo Hail Chant.* New York: Barnard College, Columbia University Press.
    1949   The Navaho and Christianity. *American Anthropologist* 51(1):66–71.
    1950   *Navaho Religion: A Study of Symbolism.* New York: Pantheon.

Roessel, Robert
    1980   *Pictorial History of the Navajo from 1860 to 1910.* Rough Rock, Ariz.: Navajo Curriculum Center.

Rubel, Arthur, editor
    1979   Parallel Medical Systems: Papers from a Workshop on "The Healing Process." *Social Science and Medicine* 13B(1):1–84.

Russell, Scott
    1985   The Navajo and the 1918 Influenza Pandemic. In *Health and Disease in the Prehistoric Southwest,* Charles Merbs and Robert Miller, eds., 380–90. Arizona State University Anthropological Research Papers 34. Tempe: Arizona State University, Department of Anthropology. More information is available at www.shesc.asu.edu/node/246.

Said, Edward
    1979   *Orientalism.* New York: Vintage.

Schneider, David
    1968   *American Kinship: A Cultural Account,* 2nd ed. Chicago: University of Chicago Press.
    1984   *A Critique of the Study of Kinship.* Ann Arbor: University of Michigan Press.

Schneider, David, as told to Richard Handler
    1995   *Schneider on Schneider: The Conversion of the Jews and Other Anthropological Stories,* Richard Handler, ed. Durham, N.C.: Duke University Press.

Schultes, Richard
  1938 The Appeal of Peyote (*Lophophora Williamsii*) as a Medicine. *American Anthropologist* (new series) 40(4):698–715.
Schwarz, Maureen Trudelle
  1995 The Explanatory and Predictive Powers of History: Coping with the "Mystery Illness," 1993. *Ethnohistory* 42(3):375–401.
  1997 *Molded in the Image of Changing Woman: Navajo Views on the Human Body and Personhood.* Tucson: University of Arizona Press.
  2001 *Navajo Lifeways: Contemporary Issues, Ancient Knowledge.* Norman: University of Oklahoma Press.
  2003 *Blood and Voice: The Life-Courses of Navajo Women Ceremonial Practitioners.* Tucson: University of Arizona Press.
  2008 "Lightning Followed Me": Contemporary Navajo Cancer Therapeutic Strategies. In *Pathways for Renewal: Religion and Healing in Native America,* Suzanne Crawford, volume ed., Linda Barnes and Susan Sered, series eds., 68–109. Connecticut: Praeger.
Shaw, Rosalind, and Charles Stewart
  1994 Introduction: Problematizing Syncretism. In *Syncretism/Anti-syncretism: The Politics of Religious Synthesis,* Charles Stewart and Rosalind Shaw, eds., 1–26. New York: Routledge.
Shepardson, Mary
  1978 Changes in Navajo Mortuary Practices and Beliefs. *American Indian Quarterly* 4(4):383–95.
  1995 The Gender Status of Navajo Women. In *Women and Power in Native North America,* Laura Klein and Lillian Ackerman, eds., 159–76. Norman: University of Oklahoma Press.
Shufeldt, Robert W.
  1891 Mortuary Customs of the Navajo Indians. *The American Naturalist* 25:303–306.
Sobo, Elisa
  1993 *One Blood.* Albany: State University of New York Press.
Spencer, Katherine
  1957 *Mythology and Values, an Analysis of Navaho Chantway Myths.* Memoirs of the American Folklore Society 48. Philadelphia: American Folklore Society.
Spicer, Edward
  1961 Types of Contact and Processes of Change. In *Perspectives in American Indian Culture Change,* Edward Spicer, ed., 517–44. Chicago: University of Chicago Press.
Spieldoch, Rachel
  1996 Uranium Is in My Body. *American Indian Culture and Research Journal* 20(2):173–85.

Steggerda, M., and R. B. Eckhardt
  1941 Navajo Foods and Their Preparation. *Journal of the American Dietetics Association* 17:217–25.
Stephen, Alexander
  1930 Navajo Origin Legend. *Journal of American Folk-Lore* 43(167): 88–104.
Stewart, Omer
  1987 *Peyote Religion: A History.* Norman: University of Oklahoma Press.
Stewart, Omer, and David Aberle
  1957 *Navaho and Ute Peyotism: A Chronological and Distributional Study.* University of Colorado Studies Series in Anthropology 6. Boulder: University of Colorado Press.
  1984 *Peyotism in the West.* University of Utah Anthropological Papers 108. Salt Lake City: University of Utah Press.
Stone, Linda
  2001 Introduction: Theoretical Implications of New Directions in Anthropological Kinship. In *New Directions in Anthropological Kinship,* Linda Stone, ed., 1–20. Boston: Rowman & Littlefield.
Storck, Michael, Thomas Csordas, and Milton Strauss
  2000 Depressive Illness and Navajo Healing. *Medical Anthropology Quarterly* 14(4):571–97.
Sugarman, J. R., T. J. Gilbert, and N. S. Weiss
  1992 Prevalence of Diabetes and Impaired Glucose Tolerance among Navajo Indians. *Diabetes Care* 15(1):114–20.
Tinker, George
  1993 *Missionary Conquest: The Gospel and Native American Cultural Genocide.* Minneapolis: Fortress.
Tom-Orme, Lillian
  1988 Diabetes in a Navajo Community: A Qualitative Study of Health/Illness Beliefs and Practices. PhD dissertation, College of Nursing, University of Utah, Salt Lake City.
Townsley, H. C., and George Goldstein
  1977 One View of the Etiology of Depression in American Indian Youth. *Public Health Reports* 92:458–61.
Trawick, Margaret
  1992 An Ayurvedic Theory of Cancer. In *Anthropological Approaches to the Study of Ethnomedicine,* Mark Nichter, ed., 207–22. Langhorne, Pa.: Gordon and Breach.
Trennert, Robert
  1998 *White Man's Medicine: Government Doctors and the Navajo, 1863–1955.* Albuquerque: University of New Mexico Press.

Unwin, Nigel
  1998   Epidemiology of Lower Extremity Amputation in Centers in Europe,
         North America and East Asia. *British Journal of Surgery* 87(3):
         328–37.
Vogt, Evon
  1961   The Navaho. In *Perspectives in American Indian Culture Change,*
         Edward Spicer, ed., 278–336. Chicago: University of Chicago Press.
Wagner, Roland
  1975   Pattern and Process in Ritual Syncretism: The Case of Peyotism
         among the Navajo. *Journal of Anthropological Research* 31(2):162–81.
Warner, Michael
  1970   Protestant Missionary Activity among the Navaho, 1890–1912.
         New Mexico Historical Review 45(3):209–32.
  1973   The Fertile Ground: The Beginnings of Protestant Missionary Work
         with the Navajos, 1852–1890. In *The Changing Ways of Southwestern
         Indians,* Albert H. Schroeder, ed., 189–203. Glorieta, N.M.: Rio
         Grande.
Weber, Max
  1968   *Economy and Society.* Berkeley: University of California Press.
Weston, Kath
  2001   Kinship, Controversy, and the Sharing of Substance: The Race/Class
         Politics of Blood Transfusion. In *Relative Values: Reconfiguring
         Kinship Studies,* Sarah Franklin and Susan McKinnon, eds., 147–74.
         Durham, N.C.: Duke University Press.
Wheat, Joe
  2003   *Blanket Weaving in the Southwest,* Ann Hedlund, ed. Tucson: Uni-
         versity of Arizona Press.
Wheelwright, Mary
  1946   *Hail Chant and Water Chant.* Navajo Religion Series, vol. 2. Boston:
         Museum of Navaho Ceremonial Art.
Wheelwright, Mary, and David McAllester
  1956   *The Myth and Prayers of the Great Star Chant and the Myth of the
         Coyote Chant.* Navajo Religion Series, vol. 4. Santa Fe, N.M.: Museum
         of Navajo Ceremonial Art.
Whitbeck, Les, Gary Adams, Dan Hoyt, and Xiaojin Chen
  2004   Conceptualizing and Measuring Historical Trauma among American
         Indian People. *American Journal of Community Psychology* 33(3/4):
         119–30.
Whiteford, Linda
  2000   Local Identity, Globalization, and Health in Cuba and the Dominican
         Republic. In *Global Health Policy, Local Realities: The Fallacy of*

the Level Playing Field, Linda Whiteford and Lenore Manderson, eds., 57–78. Boulder, Colo.: Lynne Rienner.

Witherspoon, Gary
1975   *Navajo Kinship and Marriage.* Chicago: University of Chicago Press.
1977   *Language and Art in the Navajo Universe.* Ann Arbor: University of Michigan Press.
1987   *Navajo Weaving: Art in Its Cultural Context.* Flagstaff: Museum of Northern Arizona.

Wolfe, Wendy
1994   Dietary Change among the Navajo: Implications for Diabetes. In *Diabetes as a Disease of Civilization: The Impact of Culture Change on Indigenous Peoples,* Jennie Joe and Robert Young, eds., 435–49. New York: Mouton de Gruyter.

Wood, John
1982   Western Navajo Religious Affiliations. In *Navajo Religion and Culture: Selected Views,* David Brugge and Charlotte Frisbie, eds., 176–86. Museum of New Mexico Papers in Anthropology 17. Santa Fe: Museum of New Mexico Press.

Wood, John, and Walter Vannette
1979   *A Preliminary Assessment of the Significance of Navajo Sacred Places in the Vicinity of Big Mountain, Arizona.* U.S. Department of the Interior, Bureau of Indian Affairs, Navajo Area Office, Window Rock, Ariz.

Wyman, Leland
1936a Navaho Diagnosticians. *American Anthropologist* (new series) 38:236–46.
1936b Origin Legends of Navaho Divinatory Rites. *Journal of American Folklore* 49:134–42.
1936c The Female Shooting Life Chant. *American Anthropologist* 38:634–53.
1965   *The Red Antway of the Navajo.* Navajo Religion Series, vol. 5. Santa Fe, N.M.: Museum of Navaho Ceremonial Art (Wheelwright Museum of the American Indian).
1970   *Blessingway.* Tucson: University of Arizona Press.

Wyman, Leland, and Flora Bailey
1943   Navaho Girl's Puberty Rite. *New Mexico Anthropologist* 15(1):3–12.

Wyman, Leland, and Stuart Harris
1941   Navajo Indian Medical Ethnobotany. *University of New Mexico Bulletin* 3(5):1–76.

Wyman, Leland, W. W. Hill, and Iva Osanai
1942   Navajo Eschatology. *University of New Mexico Bulletin* 4(1):1–47.

Wyman, Leland, and Clyde Kluckhohn
1938   *Navaho Classification of Their Song Ceremonials.* Memoirs of the American Anthropological Association Memoirs 50. Menasha, Wisc.: American Anthropological Association.

Yazzie, Ethelou
1971   *Navajo History,* vol. 1. Navajo Curriculum Center. Rough Rock, Ariz.: Rough Rock Demonstration School.

Young, Allan
1976   Internalizing and Externalizing Medical Belief Systems. *Social Science and Medicine* 10:147–56.

Young, James Clay, and Linda Garro
1981   *Medical Choice in a Mexican Village.* New Brunswick, N.J.: Rutgers University Press.

Zimmerman, Francis
1978   From Classic Texts to Learned Practice. *Social Science and Medicine* 12:97–103.

Zolbrod, Paul
1984 *Diné Bahane': The Navajo Creation Story.* Albuquerque: University of New Mexico Press.

INTERVIEWS

Allen, Buella
2005   Interview by author, Tsaile, Arizona, June 10.

Allen, Tso
2005   Interview by author, Fort Defiance, Arizona, July 15.

Anonymous Elder
2005   Interview by author, Kayenta, Arizona, June 8.

Ashley, Delano
2005   Interview by author, north of Tsegi, Arizona, June 16.

Ashley, Hanson
1993   Interview by author, Tsaile, Arizona, July 27.

Bahe, Eugene
2004   Interview by author, Nazlini, Arizona, July 22.

Begay, Eleanor
2005   Interview by author, June 10.

Begay, Traci Michelle
1991   Interview by author, July 26.

Bekis, Mae Ann
1992   Interview by author, Tó'tsoh, Arizona, August 5.

1993 Interview by author, Tó'tsoh, Arizona, July 28.
1995 Interview by author, Tó'tsoh, Arizona, March 22.
1998 Interviews by author, Tó'tsoh, Arizona, July 23, 28, 31.
2000 Personal communication with author, Upper Greasewood, Arizona, July 14.
2004 Interviews by author, Tó'tsoh, Arizona, July 15, 22.
2005 Personal communications with author, Tó'tsoh, Arizona, March 22, August 5.
2006 Personal communications with author, Tó'tsoh, Arizona, March 9, April 4.

Benally, Amelia
2004 Interview by author, Klagetoh, Arizona, July 13.

Benally, La Naya
2004 Interview by author, Klagetoh, Arizona, July 13.

Bert, Eugenia
2004 Interview by author, Nazlini, Arizona, July 22.

Billie, Sadie
1992 Personal conversation with author, Tsaile, Arizona, July 23.
1992 Interview by author, Tsaile, Arizona, August 24.

Black, Kenneth, Jr.
2005 Interview by author, Kayenta, Arizona, June 16.

Charley, Mae
1992 Interview by author, North of Rock Point, Arizona, July 15.

Chavez, Madalin
2000 Interview by author, Coolridge, New Mexico, June 29.

Dahozy, Louva
1992 Interview by author, Fort Defiance, Arizona, August 19.

Davis, Billie
2005 Interview by author, Lukachukai, Arizona, June 11.

Davis, George S.
2005 Interview by author, Lukachukai, Arizona, July 18.

Denetdeal, Donald
2004 Interview by author, St. Michaels, Arizona, July 11.

Dennison, Agnes
1998 Interview by author, Round Rock, Arizona, July 27.

Dennison, Alfred
1998 Interview by author, Round Rock, Arizona, July 27.

Dennison, Johnson
2005 Interview by author, Chinle, Arizona, June 22.

Denny, Avery
1993 Interviews by author, Chinle, Arizona, August 11; Tsaile, Arizona, October 8.

Denny, Gladys
    2000   Interview by author, Polacca, Arizona, July 17.
Deschene, Thomas, Jr.
    2005   Interview by author, Kayenta, Arizona, June 15.
Dooley, Sunny
    1992   Interviews by author, Gallup, New Mexico, August 19, 21.
Edison, Elizabeth
    2000   Interview by author, Bear Spring, Arizona, July 17.
Francisco, Ray
    2005   Interview by author, Vanderwagen, New Mexico, July 7.
Goldtooth, Sheila
    2005   Interview by author, Round Rock, Arizona, July 18.
Hale, Beverlianna
    2005   Interview by author, Tsaile, Arizona, June 15.
Harrison, David
    1992   Interview by author, Wheatfields, Arizona, August 18.
Henderson, Paulla Damon
    2005   Interview by author, St. Michaels, Arizona, July 14.
Jackson, Sarah
    2004   Interview by author, Fort Defiance, Arizona, July 20.
Johnson, Leeanne
    2005   Interview by author, Vanderwagen, New Mexico, July 3.
Kee, Irene
    1992   Interview by author, Crystal, New Mexico, August 3.
Knoki-Wilson, Ursula
    1992   Interview by author, Chinle, Arizona, August 10.
    1993   Interview by author, Chinle, Arizona, July 29.
    2005   Interview by author, Chinle, Arizona, July 5.
Lamphere, Louise
    1999   Personal correspondence with author, April 5.
Laughter, Anna
    2005   Interview by author, north of Tsegi, Arizona, June 16.
Laughter, Fred
    2005   Interview by author, north of Tsegi, Arizona, June 16.
Lonewolf, Hastiin
    2005   Interview by author, north of Del Muerto, Arizona, June 10.
Long, Tsosie, Sr.
    2005   Interview by author, Shonto, Arizona, July 13.
Mace, Juanita
    1998   Interview by author, Torreon, New Mexico, July 23.
Mariano, Jean
    2000   Interview by author, Mariano Lake, New Mexico, June 29.

Mathis, Julia
   2005   Interview by author, Chinle, Arizona, June 11.
Mose, Don, Jr.
   2005   Interview by author, Kayenta, Arizona, June 13.
Nelson, Leroy
   2004   Interviews by author, Window Rock, Arizona, July 19, 20.
   2005   Interview by author, Window Rock, Arizona, July 20.
Nez, Jonah
   1992   Personal conversation with author, Lukachukai, Arizona, July 3.
   2005   Interview by author, Lukachukai, Arizona, June 12.
Nez, Nettie
   2000   Interview by author, Saltwater, Arizona, July 10.
Nix, Laura
   2000   Interview by author, Tuba City, Arizona, July 10.
Sandoval, Florence
   2005   Interview by author, Valley Store, Arizona, June 25.
Sandoval, Ronald
   2005   Interview by author, Valley Store, Arizona, June 25.
Shay, Amelda Sandoval
   2005   Interviews by author, Lukachukai, Arizona, June 6, 15.
Shepard, Ambrose
   2005   Interview by author, Ganado, Arizona, June 3.
Shorthair, Gaye
   2000   Interview by author, Piñon, Arizona, July 11.
Taachiini, Asdzaan
   2005   Interview by author, Vanderwagen, New Mexico, June 7.
Tapaha, Chee
   2005   Interview by author, Klagetoh, Arizona, June 2.
Tinhorn, Albert
   2005   Interview by author, Kayenta, Arizona, June 14.
Todachinee, Larry
   2005   Interview by author, Chinle, Arizona, June 28.
Tso, Oscar
   1991   Interview by author, White Valley, Arizona, July 14.
   1992   Interview by author, Many Farms, Arizona, July 18.
Wade, Rose Mary
   2005   Interview by author, Pine Springs, Arizona, June 17.
Walters, Harry
   1992   Interviews by author, Tsaile, Arizona, August 18, 20.
   1993   Interviews by author, Tsaile, Arizona, August 10, 12.
Watchman, Eloise
   2005   Interview by author, St. Michaels, Arizona, June 21.

Watchman, Harrison
    2005   Interview by author, St. Michaels, Arizona, June 21.

Whitegoat, Josephine
    2005   Interview by author, Lukachukai, Arizona, July 17.

Yadeesbah, Vivian
    2005   Interview by author, Lukachukai, Arizona, July 5.

Yazzie, Pearly
    1998   Interview by author, Rim Range near Newlands, Arizona, July 30.

Young, Frank C.
    2005   Interview by author, Kayenta, Arizona, June 14.

Young, Nora
    2005   Interview by author, Kayenta, Arizona, June 14.

Index